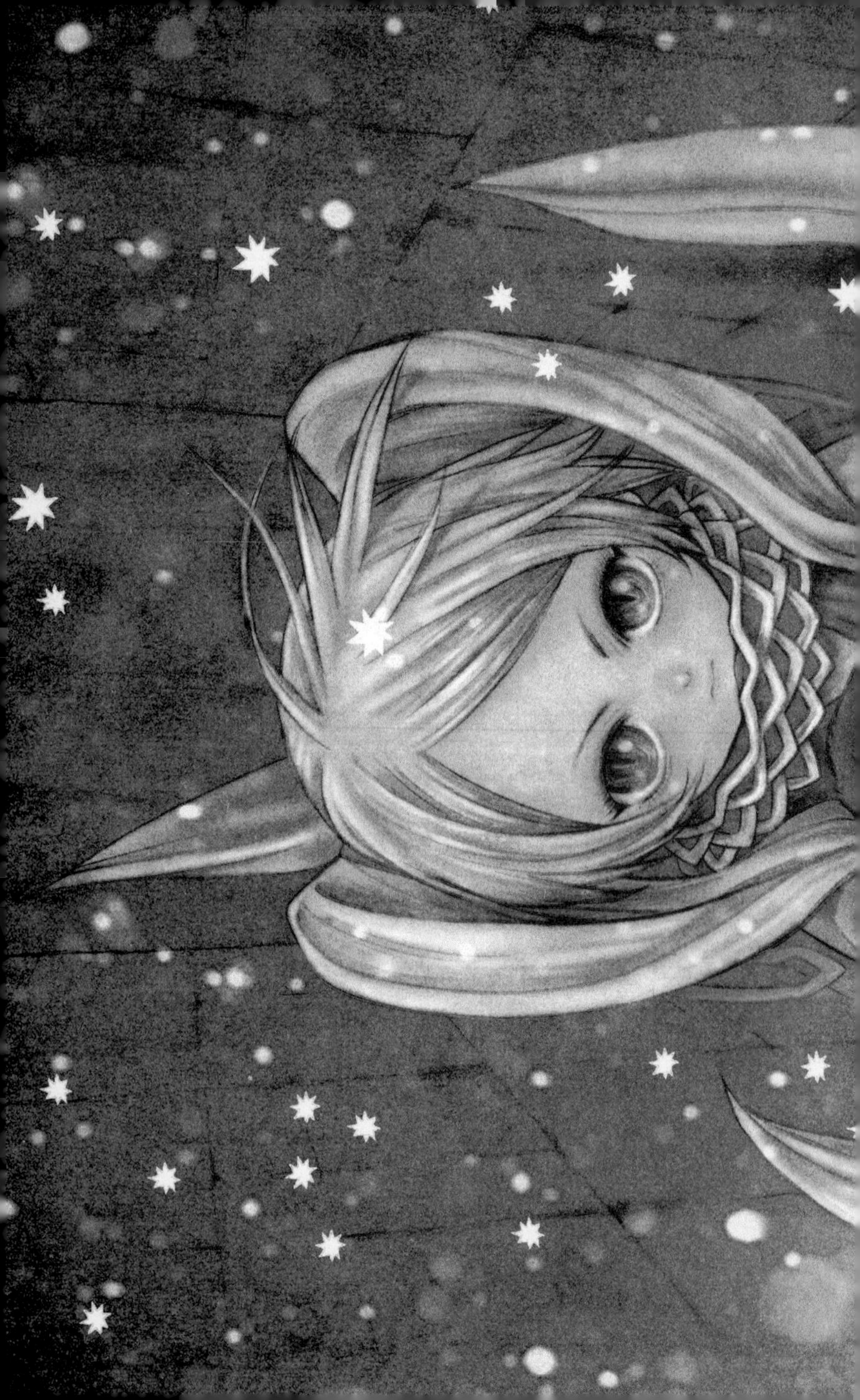

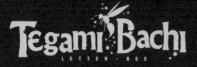

Tegami Bachi
LETTER · BEE

Volume 5

SHONEN JUMP Manga Edition

Story and Art by Hiroyuki Asada

English Adaptation/Rich Amtower
Translation/JN Productions
Touch-up & Lettering/Annaliese Christman
Design/Frances O. Liddell, Amy Martin
Editor/Daniel Gillespie

TEGAMIBACHI © 2006 by Hiroyuki Asada. All rights reserved.
First published in Japan in 2006 by SHUEISHA Inc., Tokyo. English
translation rights arranged by SHUEISHA Inc.

The rights of the author(s) of the work(s) in this publication to be so
identified have been asserted in accordance with the Copyright, Designs
and Patents Act 1988. A CIP catalogue record for this book is available
from the British Library.

The stories, characters and incidents mentioned in this publication are
entirely fictional.

No portion of this book may be reproduced or transmitted in any form or
by any means without written permission from the copyright holders.

Printed in the U.S.A.

Published by VIZ Media, LLC
P.O. Box 77010
San Francisco, CA 94107

10 9 8 7 6 5 4 3 2 1
First printing, May 2011

PARENTAL ADVISORY
RATED T FOR TEEN
TEGAMI BACHI is rated T for Teen
and is recommended for ages
13 and up. This volume contains
fantasy violence and tobacco use.
ratings.viz.com

www.viz.com

THE WORLD'S
MOST POPULAR MANGA

SHONEN JUMP
www.shonenjump.com

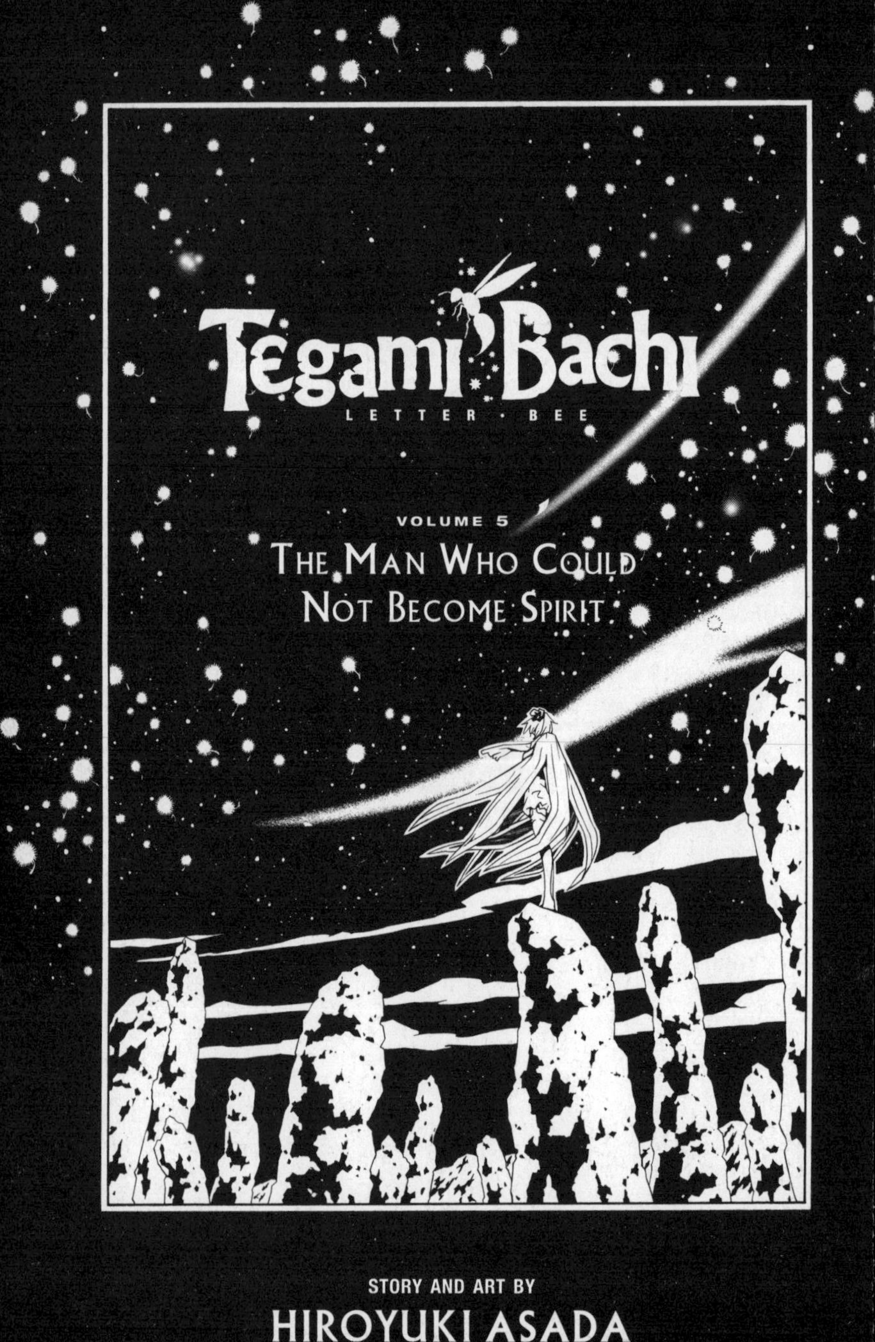
Tegami Bachi
LETTER · BEE
VOLUME 5
THE MAN WHO COULD
NOT BECOME SPIRIT

STORY AND ART BY

HIROYUKI ASADA

This is a country known as Amberground, where night never ends.

Its capital, Akatsuki, is illuminated by a man-made sun. The farther one goes from the capital, the more its light wanes. An ephemeral light shines over the lands surrounding Akatsuki, casting twilight across the Yuusari region and shining like pale moonlight in the Yodaka region.

Letter Bee Gauche Suede and young Lag Seeing meet in the Yodaka region—a postal worker and the "letter" he must deliver. In their short time together, they form a fast friendship, but when the journey ends, each departs down his own path. Gauche longs to become Head Bee, while Lag himself wants to be a Letter Bee, like Gauche.

Five years later, Lag leaves for Yuusari to interview for the post of Letter Bee. On his way, he meets Niche, a legendary Child of Maka who decides to join Lag as his "dingo."

After his interview, Lag learns from Zazie, the observer for his test, that Gauche is no longer a Letter Bee. Lag seeks out Sylvette, Gauche's sister, to discover that Gauche had been dismissed from his post and had vanished after losing his *heart*.

Now working as a Letter Bee, Lag is heading for Honey Waters, a town in northwest Yuusari. But his one hope of finding Gauche, the Man Who Could Not Become Spirit, turns out to be a fake. On top of that, the town is under attack by a Gaichuu! Lag and his friends do their best to battle the beast...

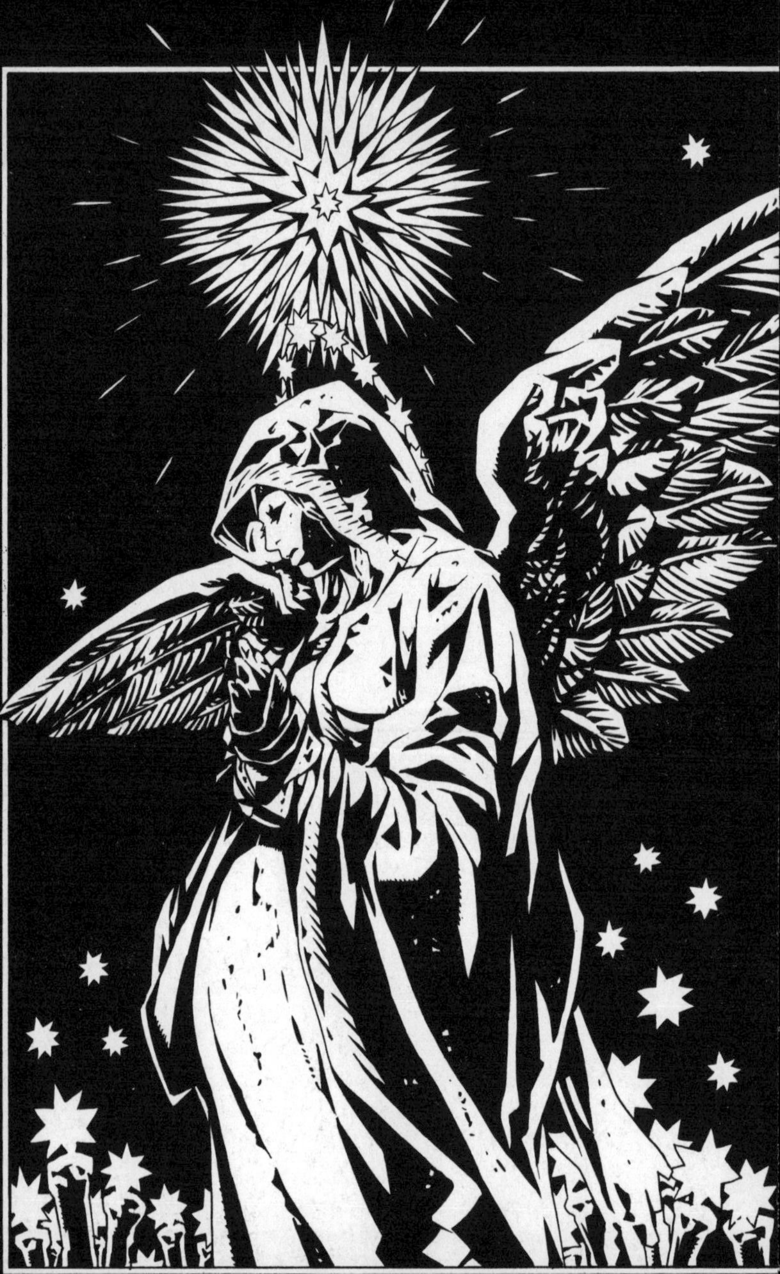

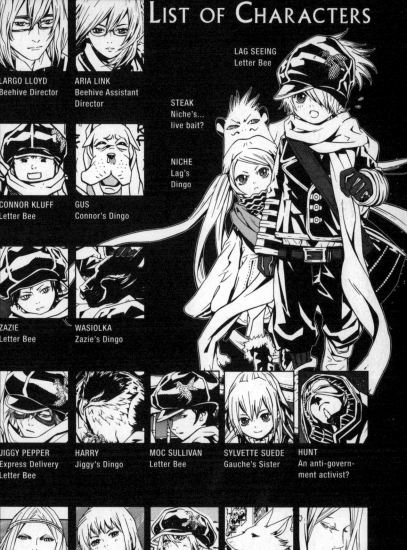

LIST OF CHARACTERS

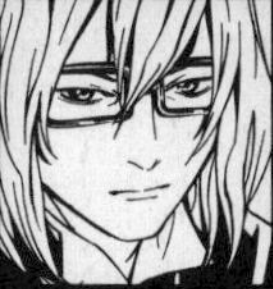
LARGO LLOYD
Beehive Director

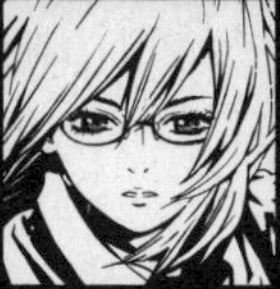
ARIA LINK
Beehive Assistant Director

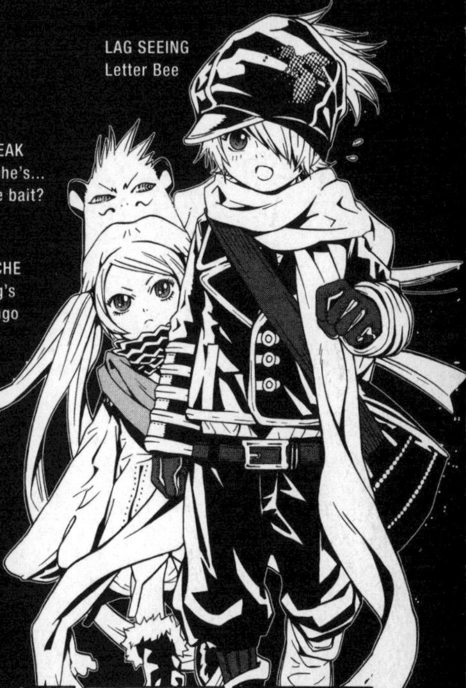
LAG SEEING
Letter Bee

STEAK
Niche's... live bait?

NICHE
Lag's Dingo

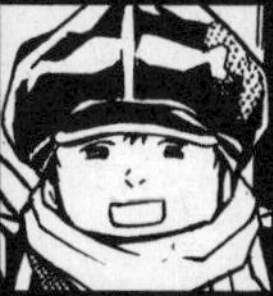
CONNOR KLUFF
Letter Bee

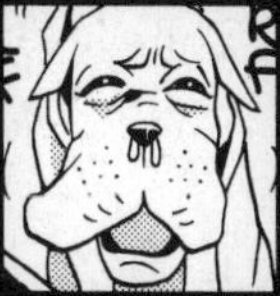
GUS
Connor's Dingo

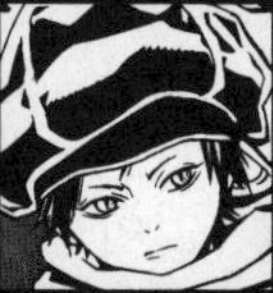
ZAZIE
Letter Bee

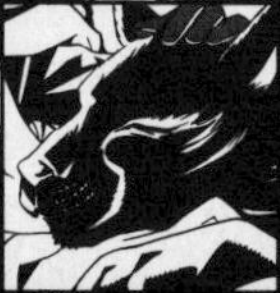
WASIOLKA
Zazie's Dingo

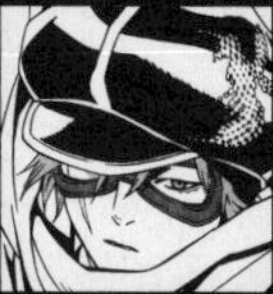
JIGGY PEPPER
Express Delivery Letter Bee

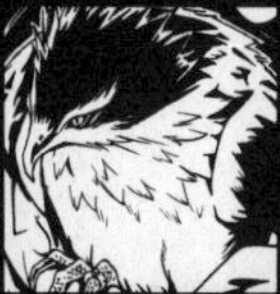
HARRY
Jiggy's Dingo

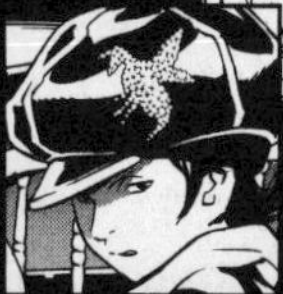
MOC SULLIVAN
Letter Bee

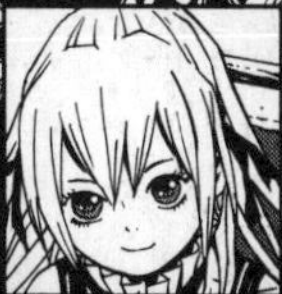
SYLVETTE SUEDE
Gauche's Sister

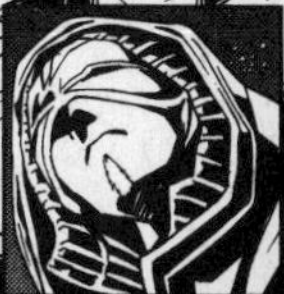
HUNT
An anti-government activist?

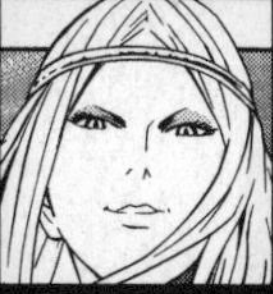
SARA
An anti-government activst?

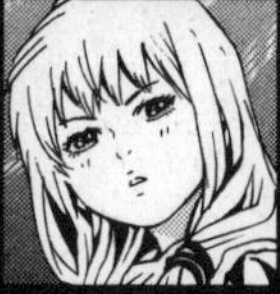
ANNE
A resident of Honey Waters

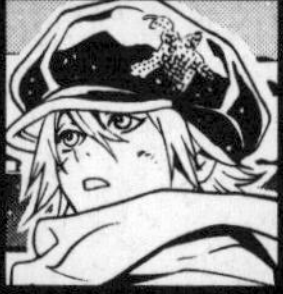
GAUCHE SUEDE
Ex–Letter Bee
(Missing)

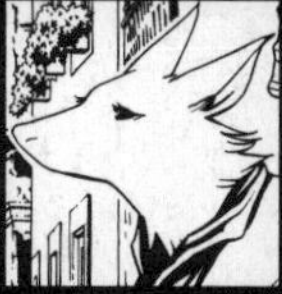
RODA
Gauche's Dingo
(Missing)

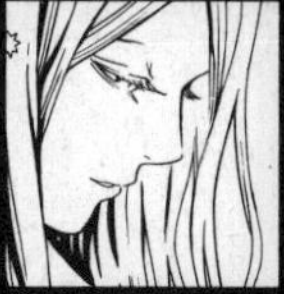
ANNE SEEING
Lag's Mother
(Missing)

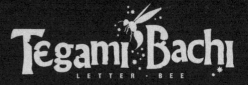

VOLUME 5
THE MAN WHO COULD NOT BECOME SPIRIT

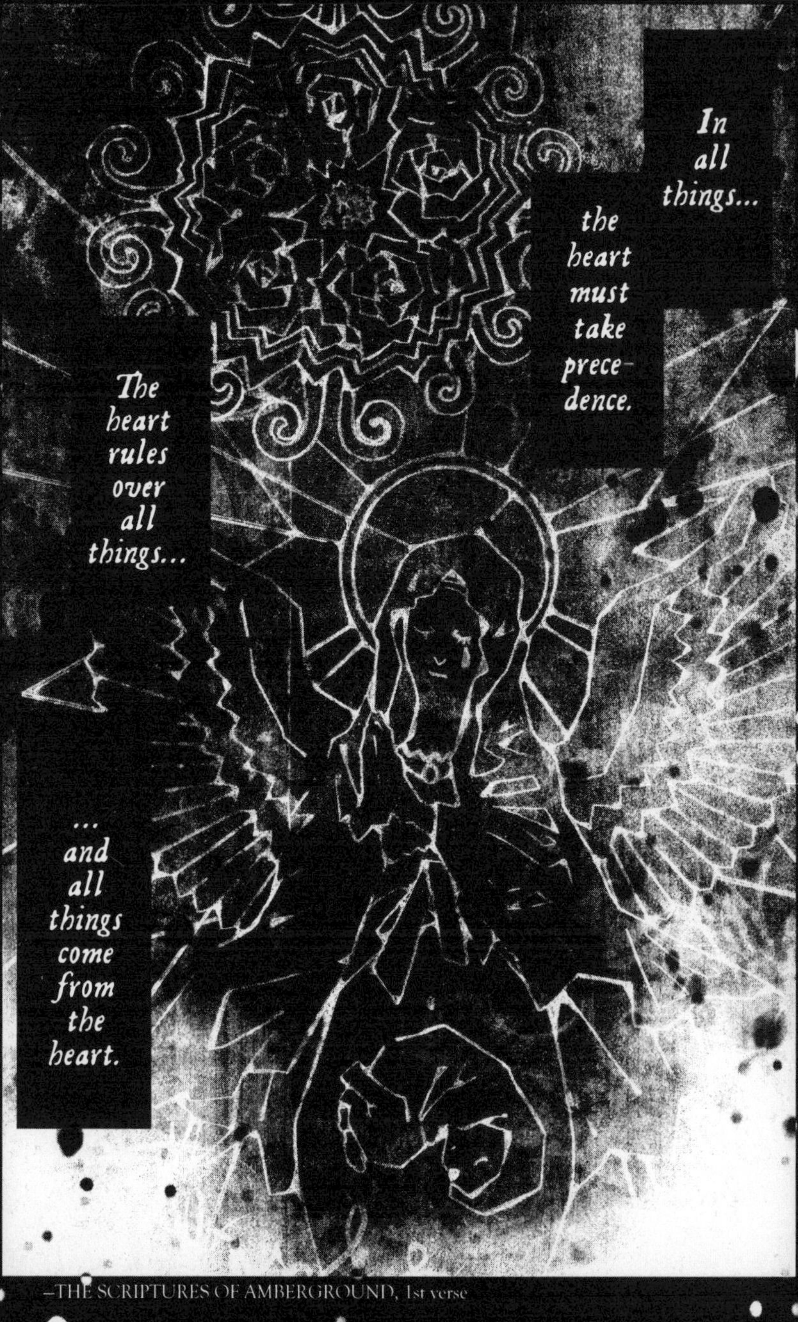
In all things...
the heart must take precedence.
The heart rules over all things...
... and all things come from the heart.

–THE SCRIPTURES OF AMBERGROUND, 1st verse

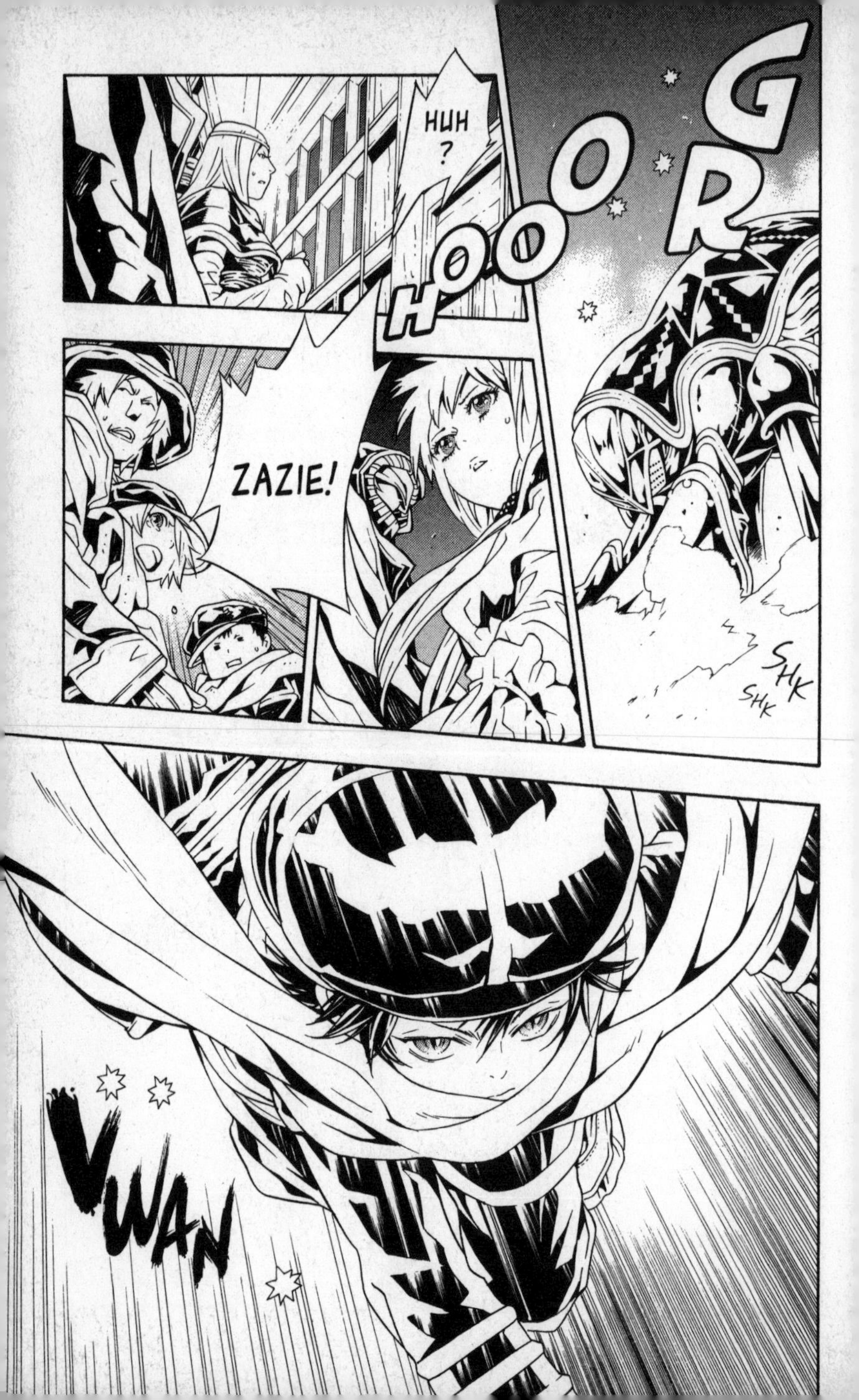
GROOOOH
SHK
SHK
HUH ?
ZAZIE!
VWAN

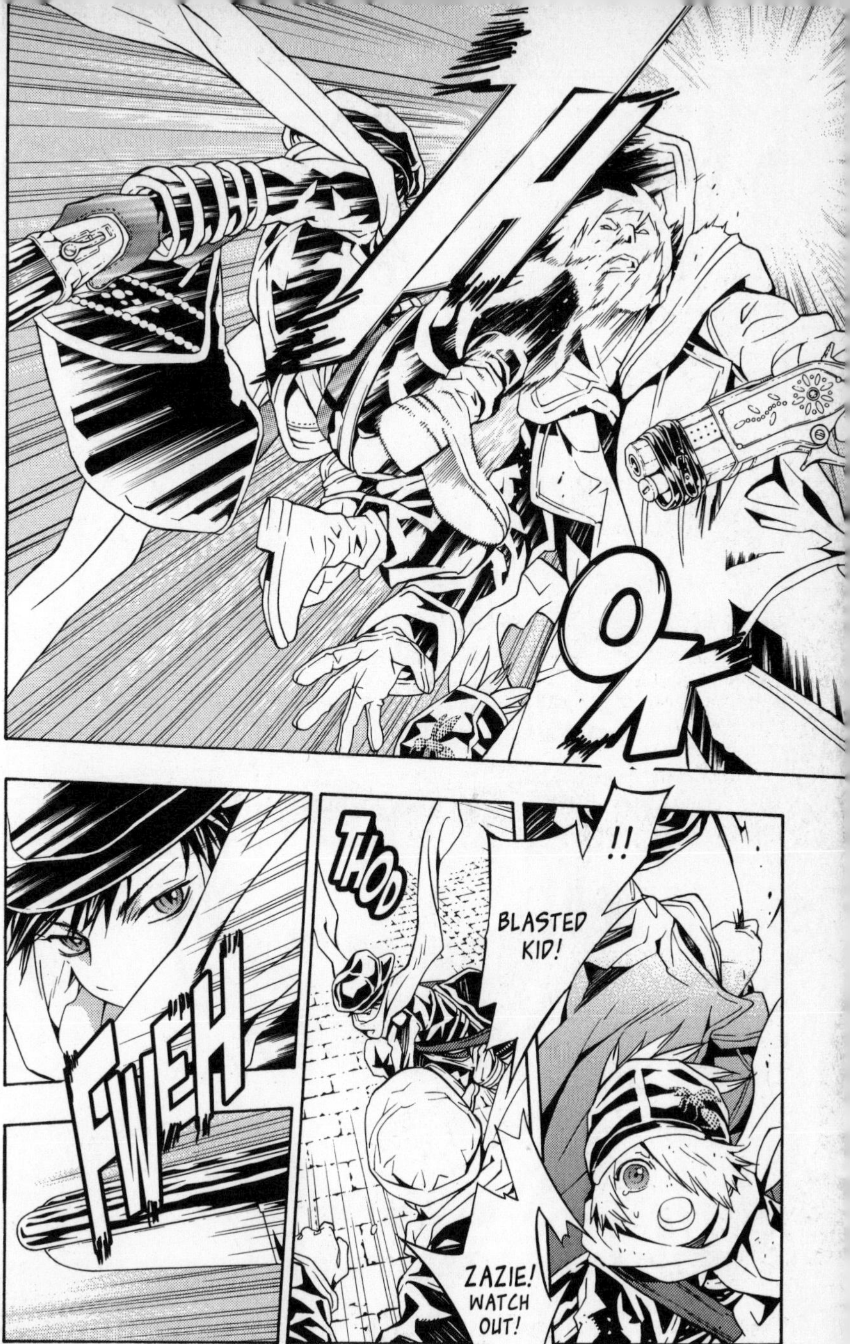
THOD
!!
BLASTED KID!
ZAZIE! WATCH OUT!
FWEH

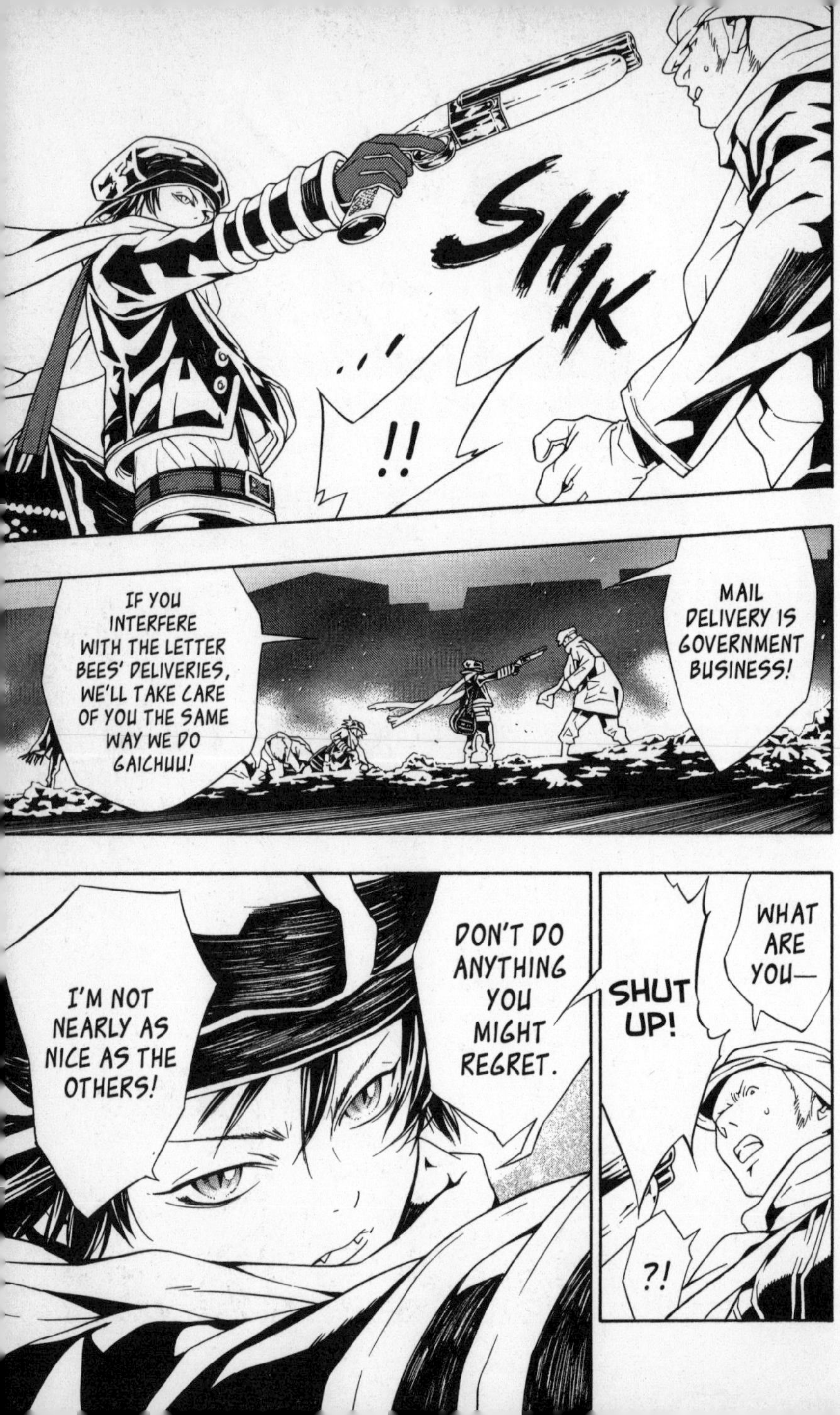

SHK
...
!!
MAIL DELIVERY IS GOVERNMENT BUSINESS!
IF YOU INTERFERE WITH THE LETTER BEES' DELIVERIES, WE'LL TAKE CARE OF YOU THE SAME WAY WE DO GAICHUU!
WHAT ARE YOU—
SHUT UP!
?!
DON'T DO ANYTHING YOU MIGHT REGRET.
I'M NOT NEARLY AS NICE AS THE OTHERS!

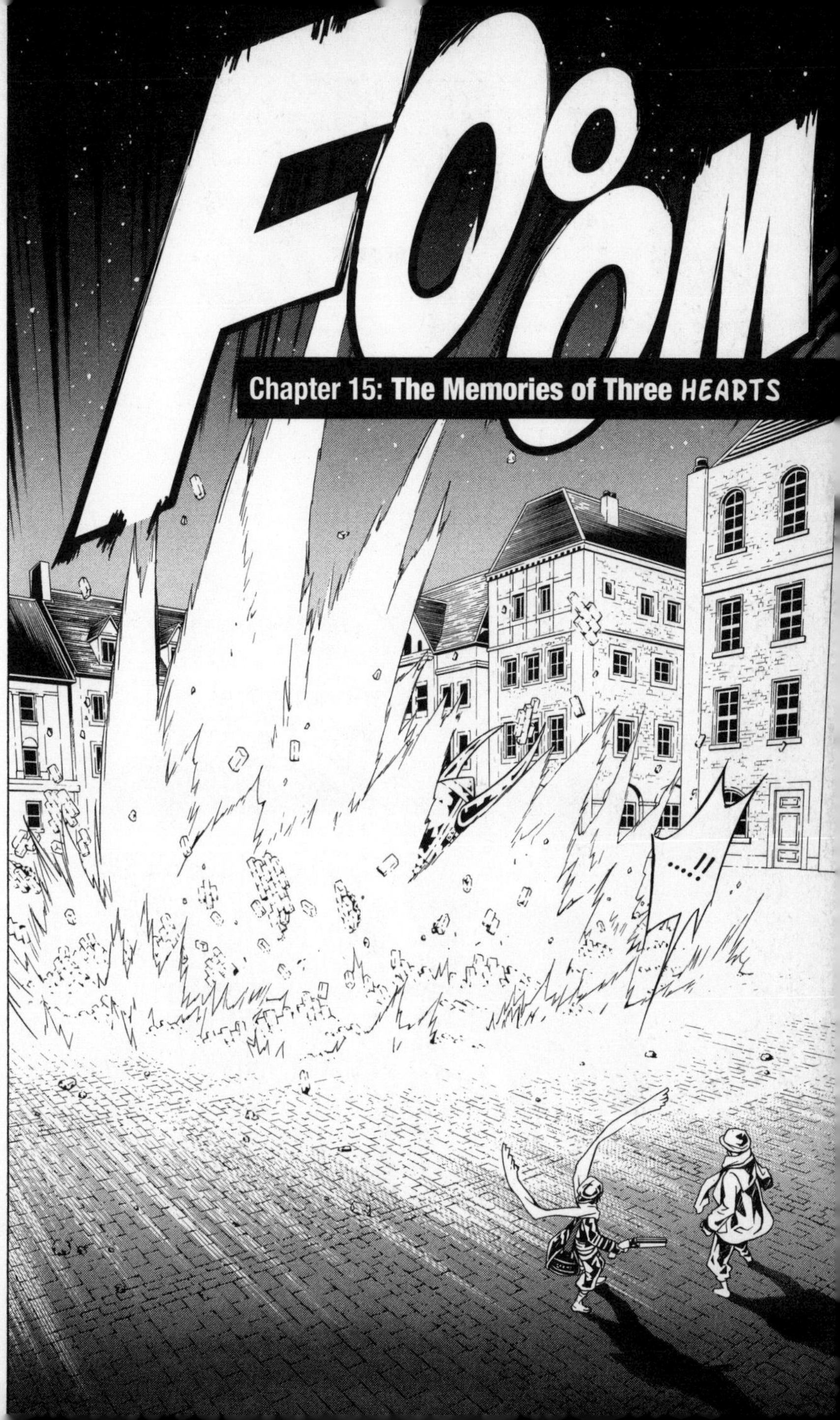
FOOM
Chapter 15: The Memories of Three HEARTS
....!!

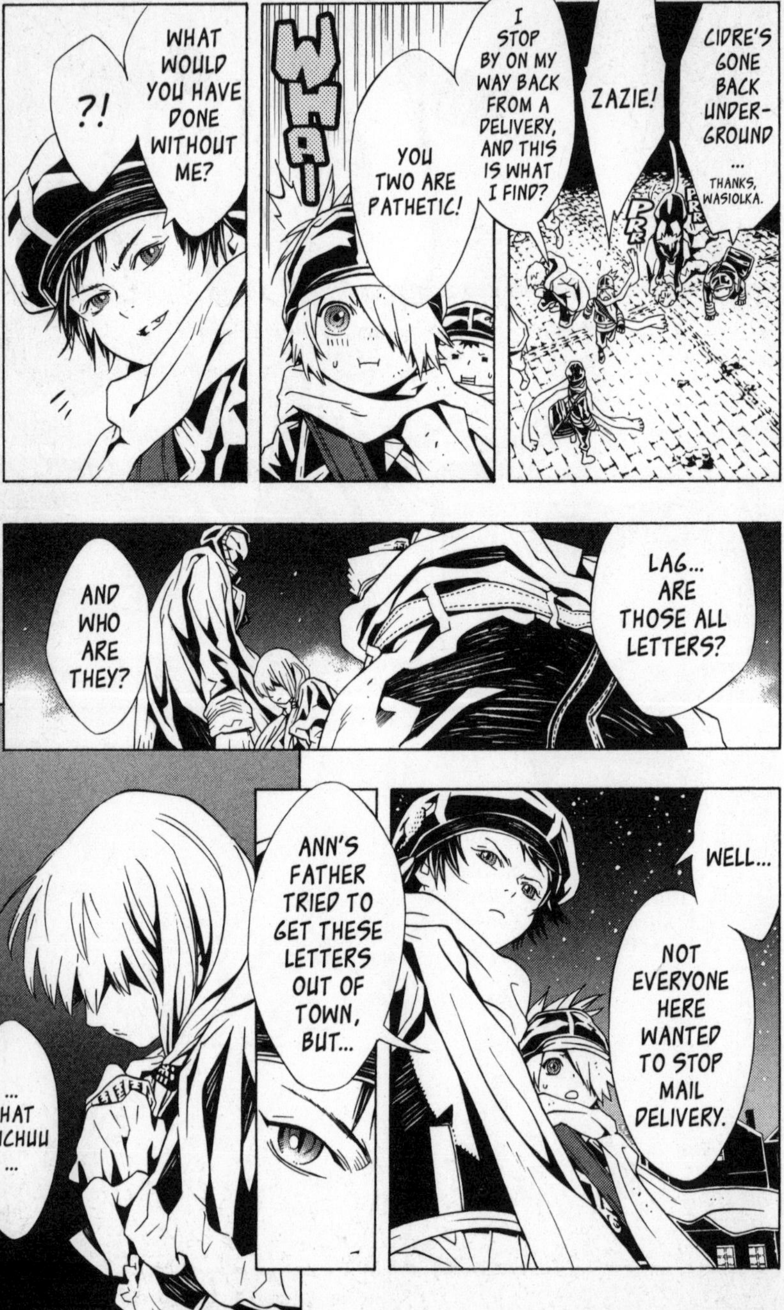
CIDRE'S GONE BACK UNDER-GROUND ...
THANKS, WASIOLKA.
ZAZIE!
PRR
PRR
I STOP BY ON MY WAY BACK FROM A DELIVERY, AND THIS IS WHAT I FIND?
YOU TWO ARE PATHETIC!
WHAT
WHAT WOULD YOU HAVE DONE WITHOUT ME?
?!
LAG... ARE THOSE ALL LETTERS?
AND WHO ARE THEY?
WELL...
NOT EVERYONE HERE WANTED TO STOP MAIL DELIVERY.
ANN'S FATHER TRIED TO GET THESE LETTERS OUT OF TOWN, BUT...
... THAT GAICHUU ...

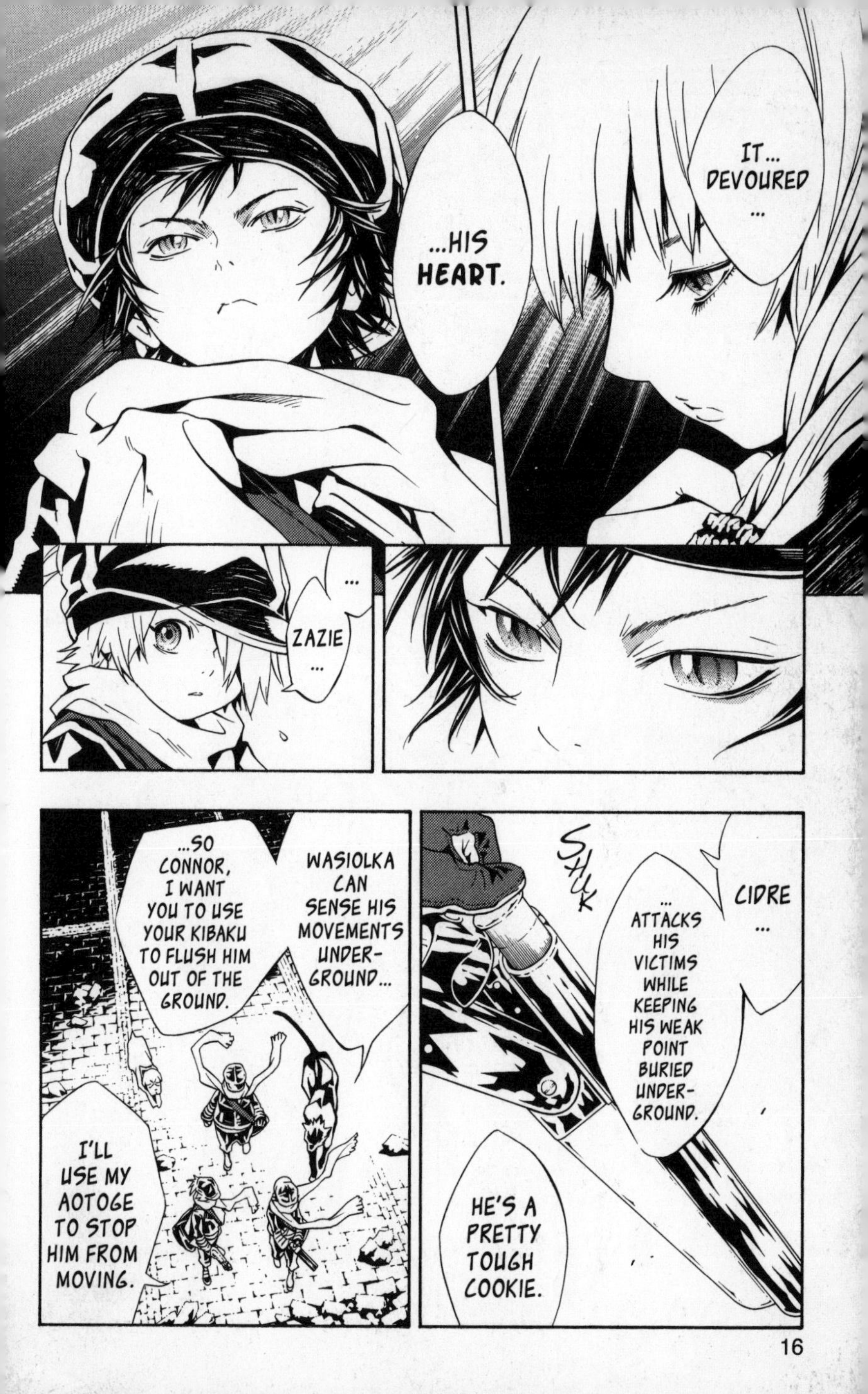
IT... DEVOURED ...
...HIS HEART.
...
ZAZIE ...
CIDRE ...
SHUK
... ATTACKS HIS VICTIMS WHILE KEEPING HIS WEAK POINT BURIED UNDER-GROUND.
HE'S A PRETTY TOUGH COOKIE.
WASIOLKA CAN SENSE HIS MOVEMENTS UNDER-GROUND...
...SO CONNOR, I WANT YOU TO USE YOUR KIBAKU TO FLUSH HIM OUT OF THE GROUND.
I'LL USE MY AOTOGE TO STOP HIM FROM MOVING.

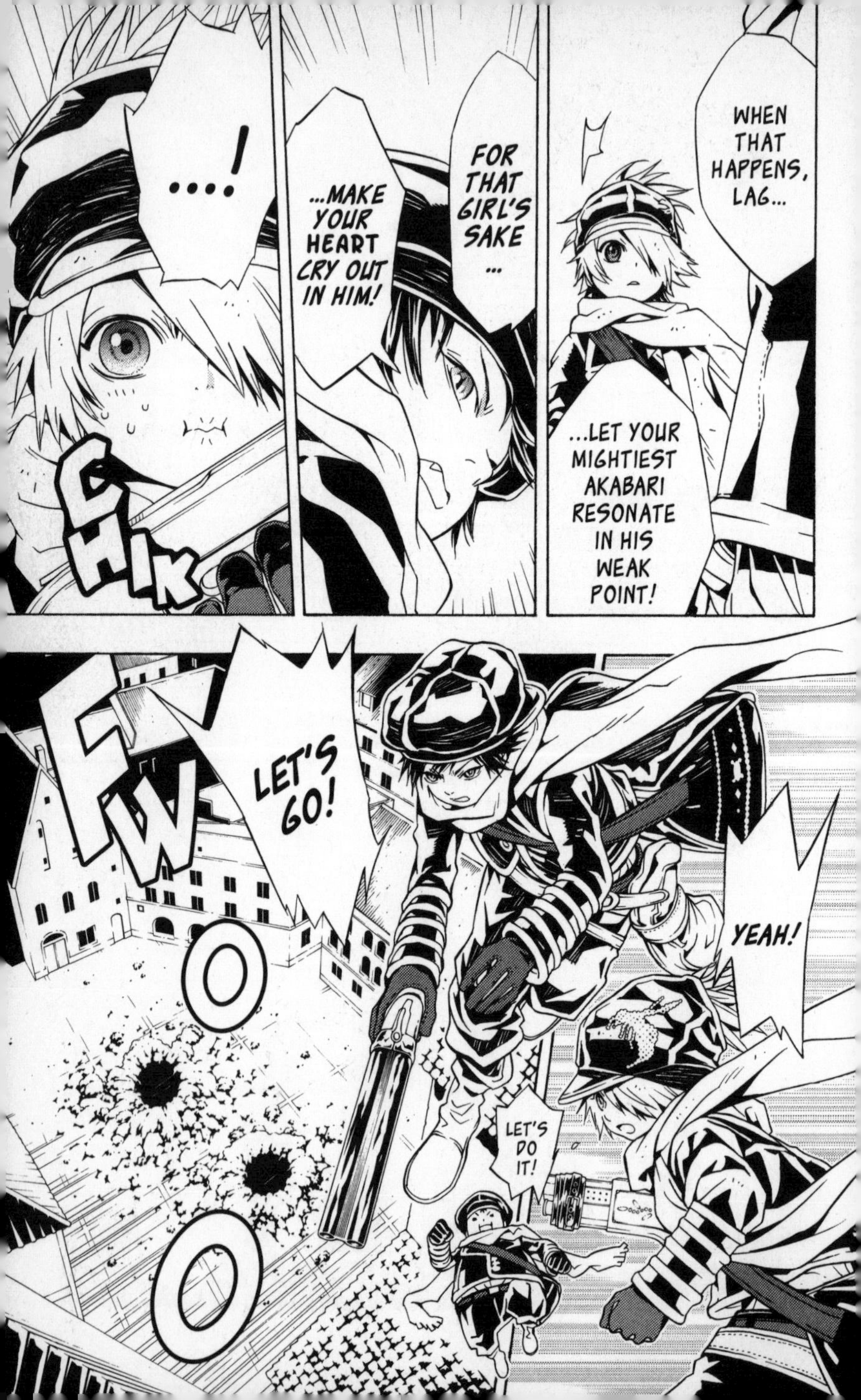
WHEN THAT HAPPENS, LAG...
...LET YOUR MIGHTIEST AKABARI RESONATE IN HIS WEAK POINT!
!
FOR THAT GIRL'S SAKE ...
...MAKE YOUR HEART CRY OUT IN HIM!
...!
CHIK
LET'S GO!
YEAH!
FWOOO
LET'S DO IT!

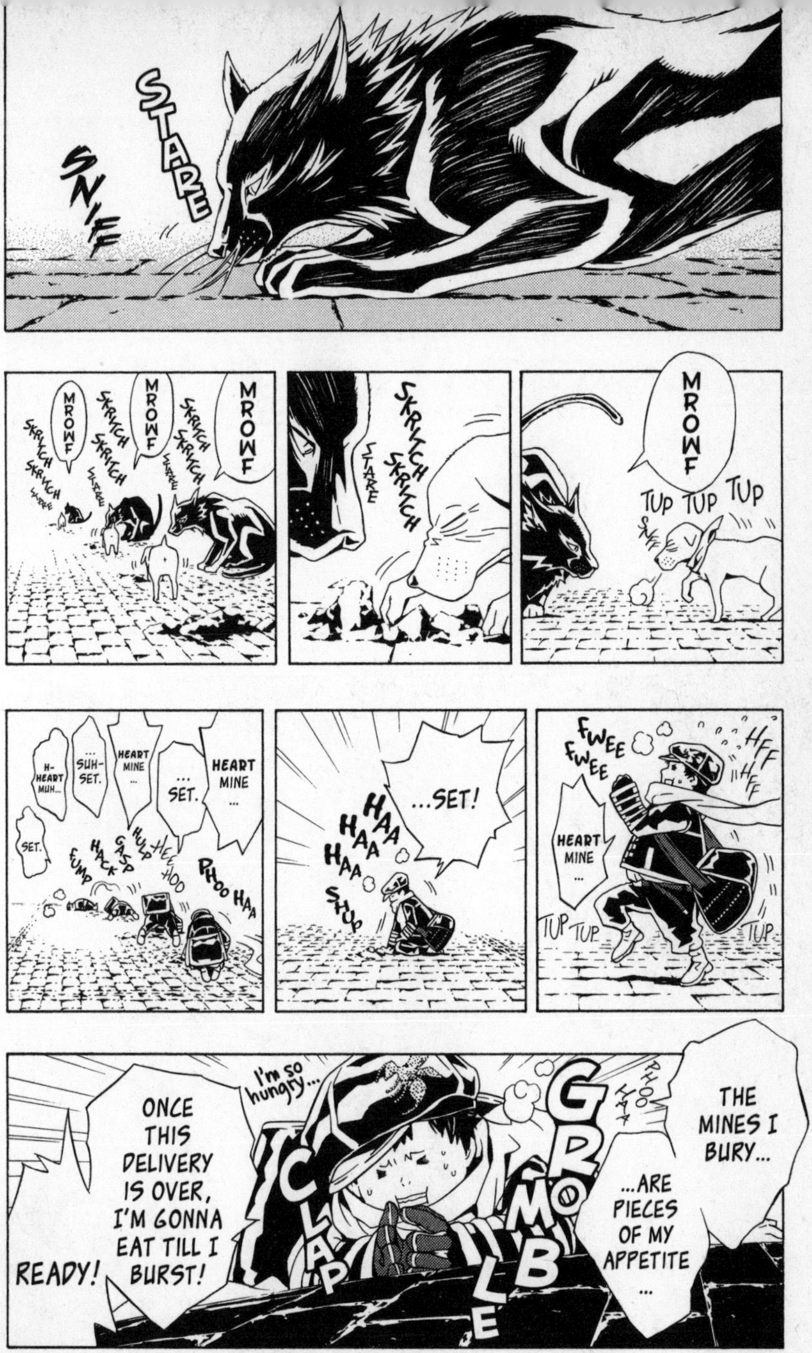
STARE
SNIFF
MROWF
TUP TUP TUP
SNIFF
SKRITCH SKRITCH
STARE
MROWF
SKRITCH SKRITCH
STARE
MROWF
SKRITCH SKRITCH
STARE
MROWF
SKRITCH SKRITCH
STARE
FWEE FWEE
HFF HFF
HEART MINE ...
TUP TUP TUP
...SET!
HAA HAA HAA
SHUP
HEART MINE ...
... SET.
HEART MINE ...
... SUH-SET.
H-HEART MUH...
SET.
PHOO HAA
HEE HOO
HULP
GASP
HACK
FUMP
THE MINES I BURY...
...ARE PIECES OF MY APPETITE ...
PHOO
GROMBLE
I'm so hungry...
ONCE THIS DELIVERY IS OVER, I'M GONNA EAT TILL I BURST!
CLAP
READY!

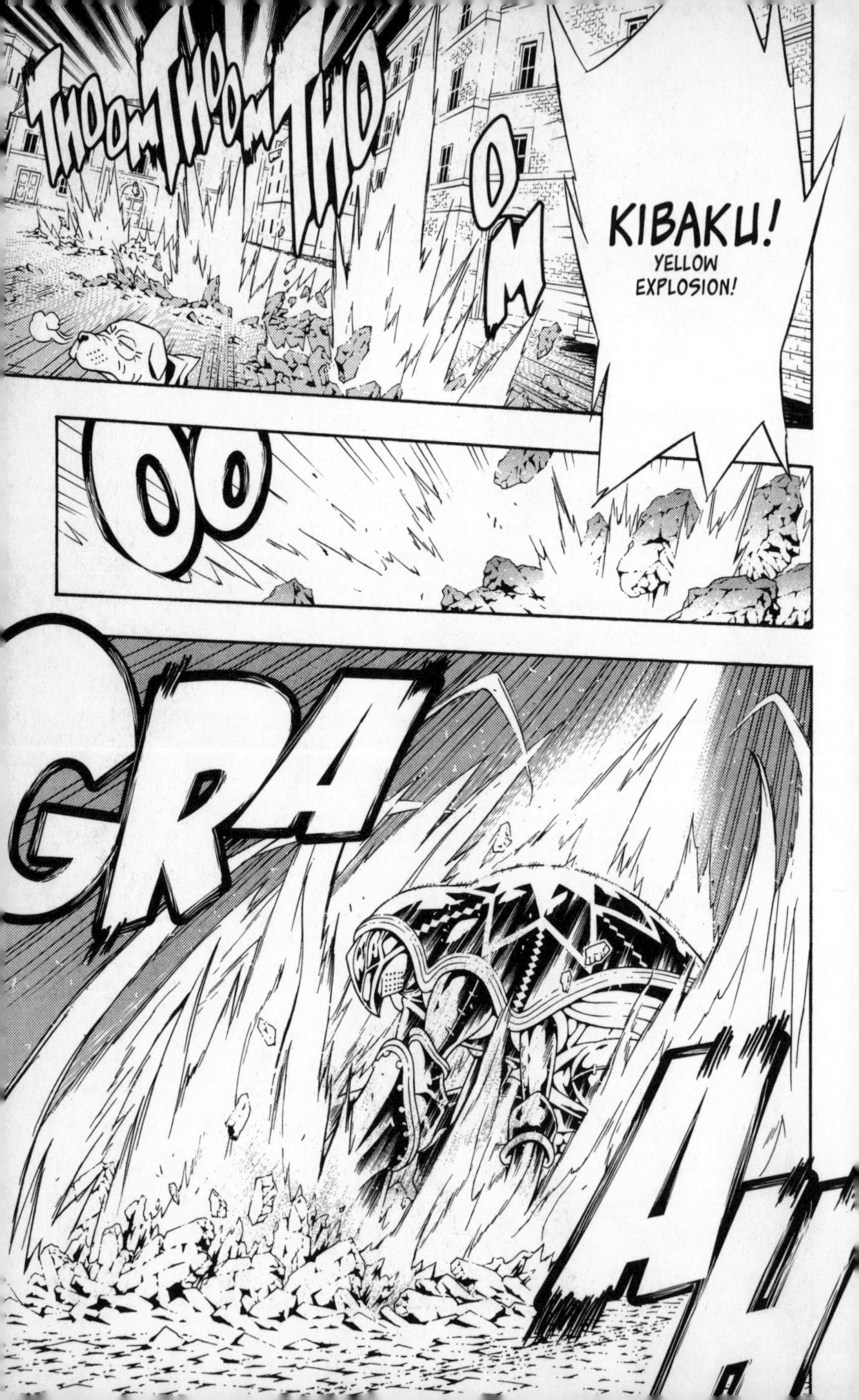
KIBAKU!
YELLOW EXPLOSION!
THOOM THOOM THOOOM
OO
GRA
AH

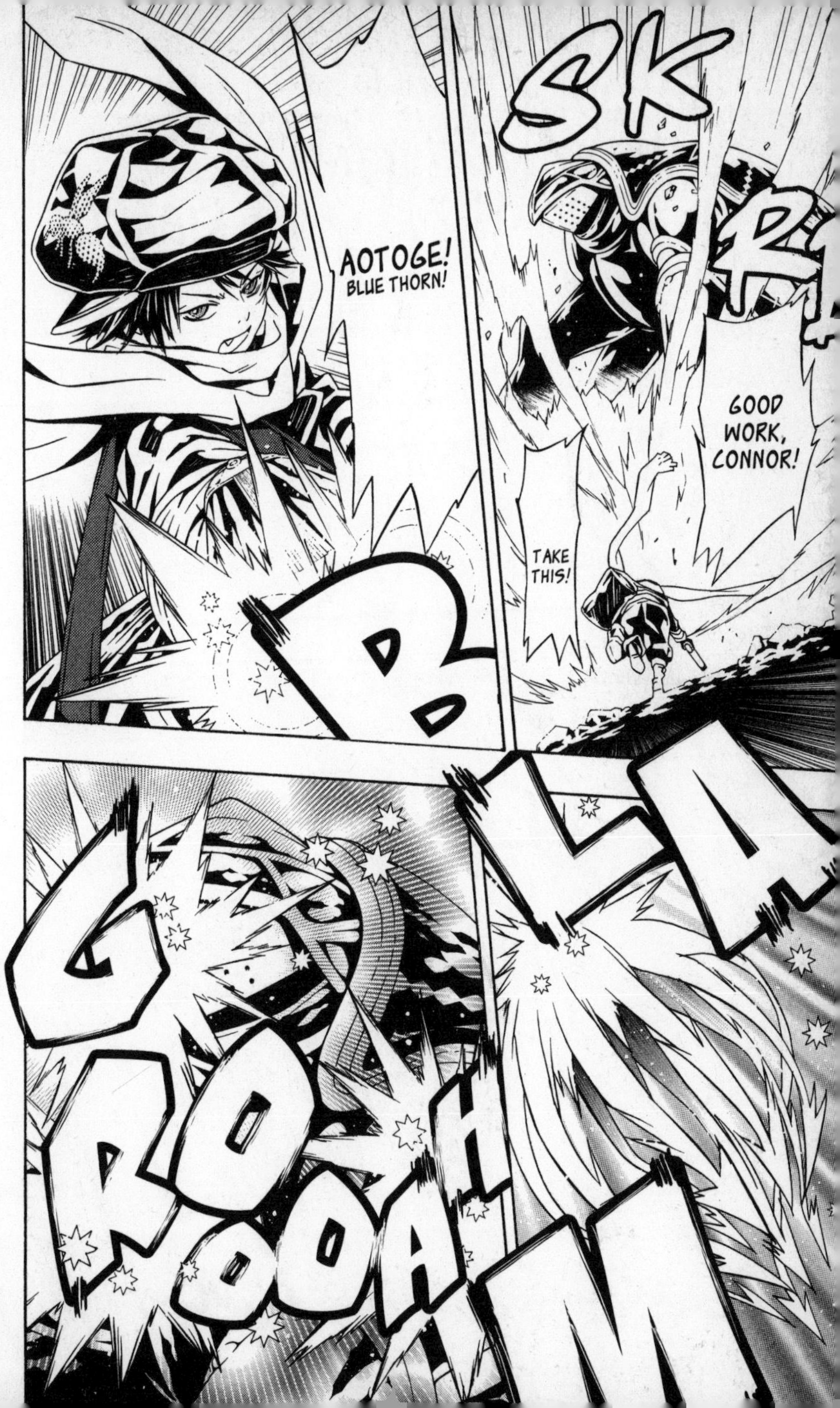
SK
GOOD WORK, CONNOR!
TAKE THIS!
AOTOGE!
BLUE THORN!

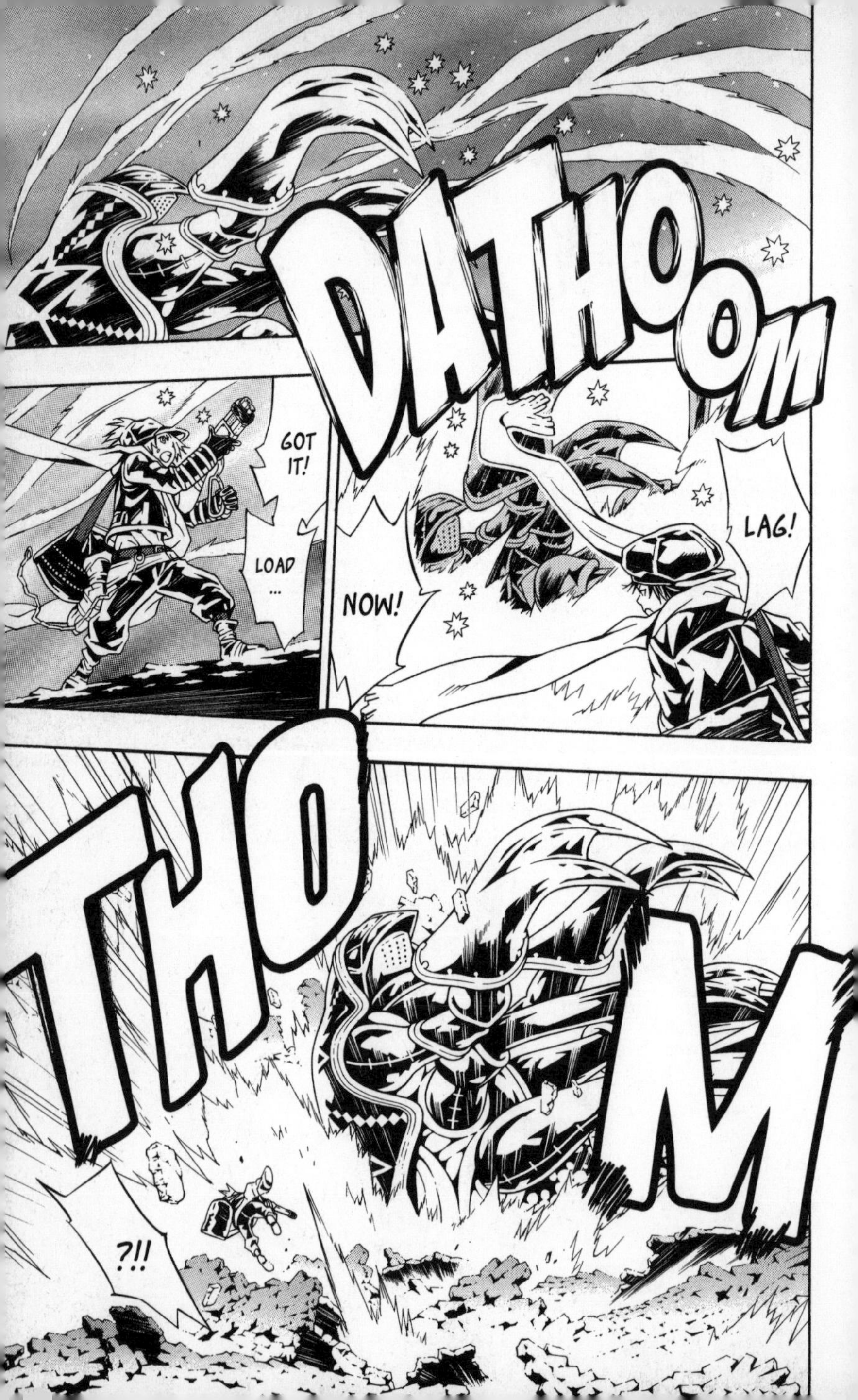
DATHOOM
LAG!
NOW!
GOT IT!
LOAD ...
THO
M
?!!

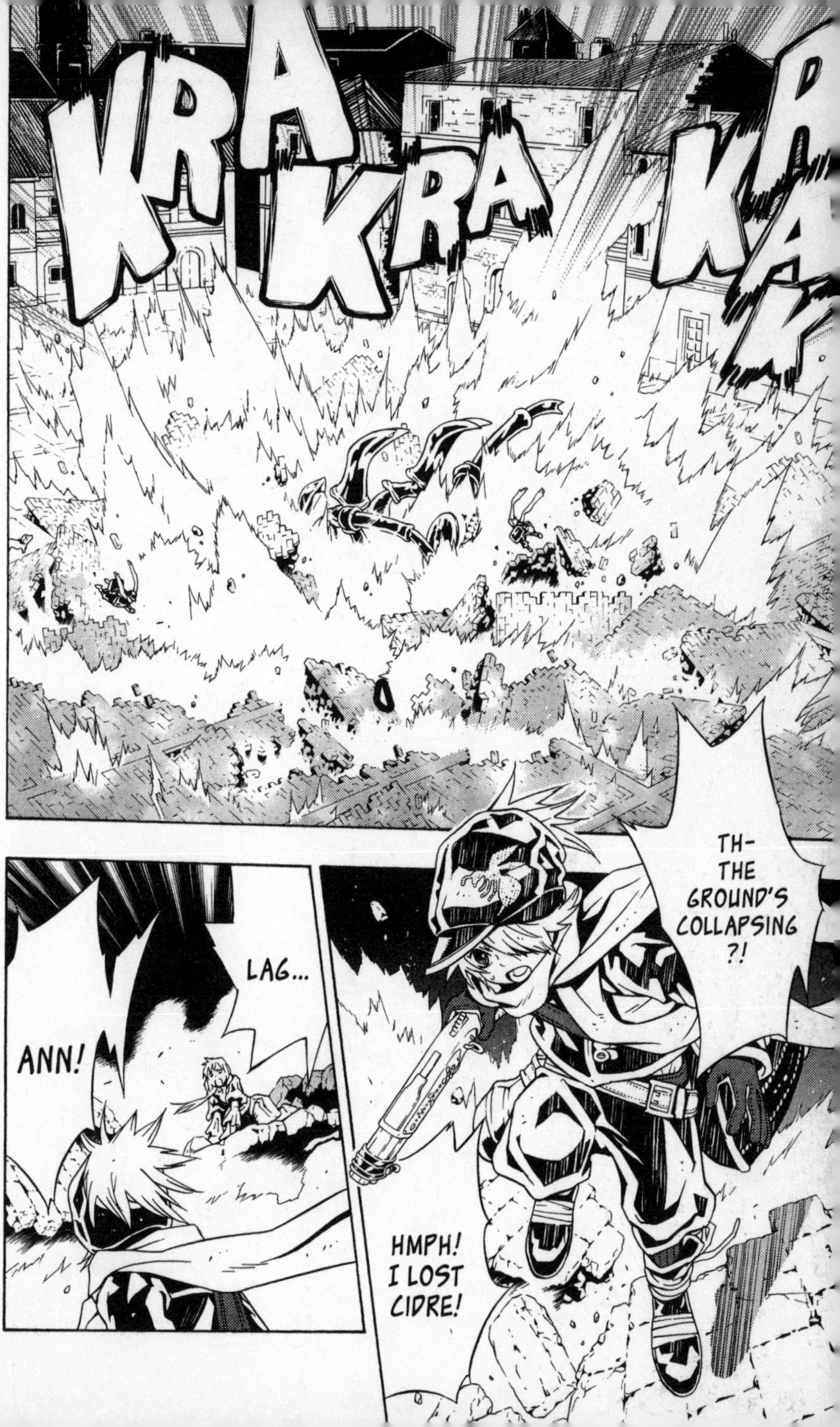
KRA
TH- THE GROUND'S COLLAPSING?!
HMPH! I LOST CIDRE!
LAG...
ANN!

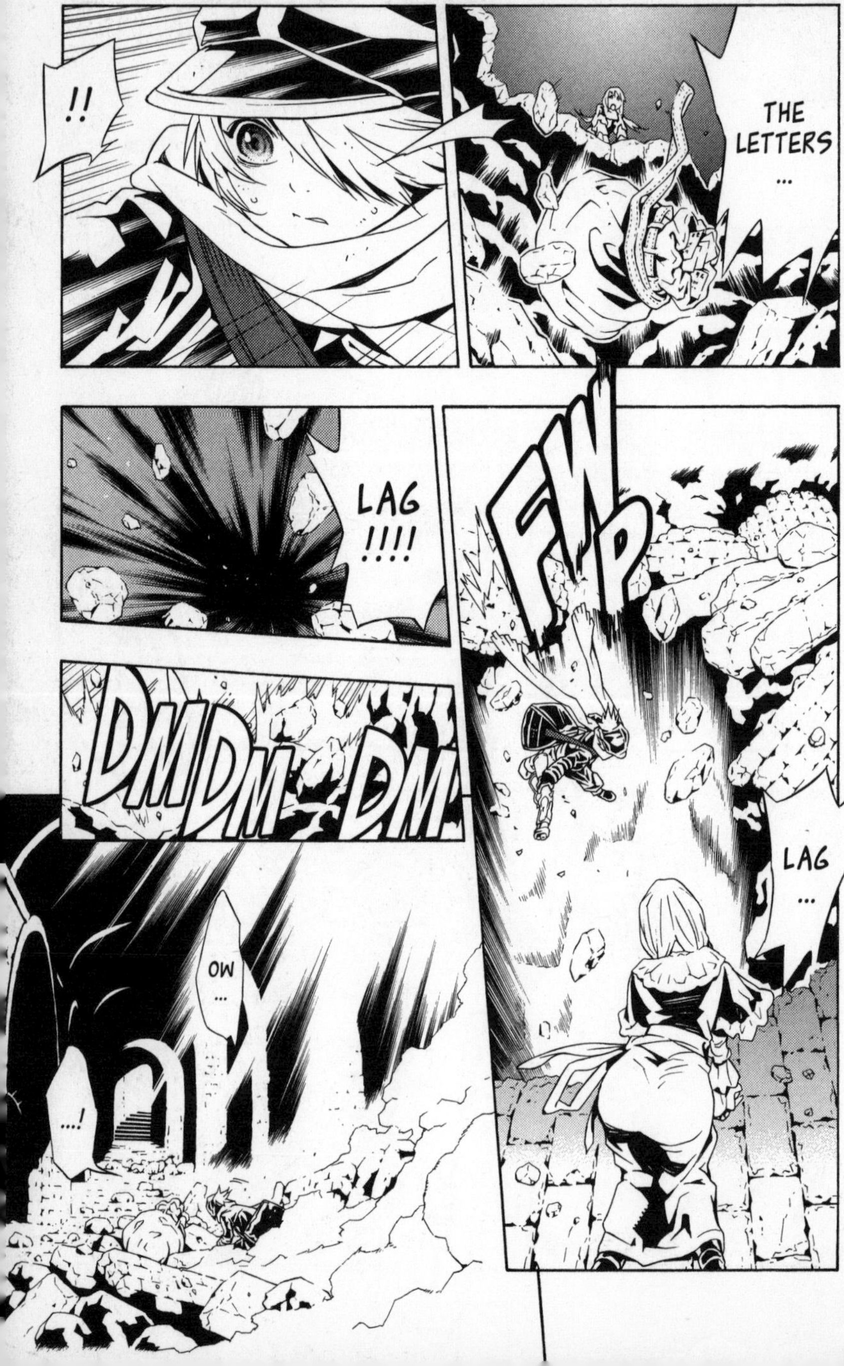
THE LETTERS ...
!!
FWP
LAG ...
LAG !!!!
DMDM-DM
OW ...
...!

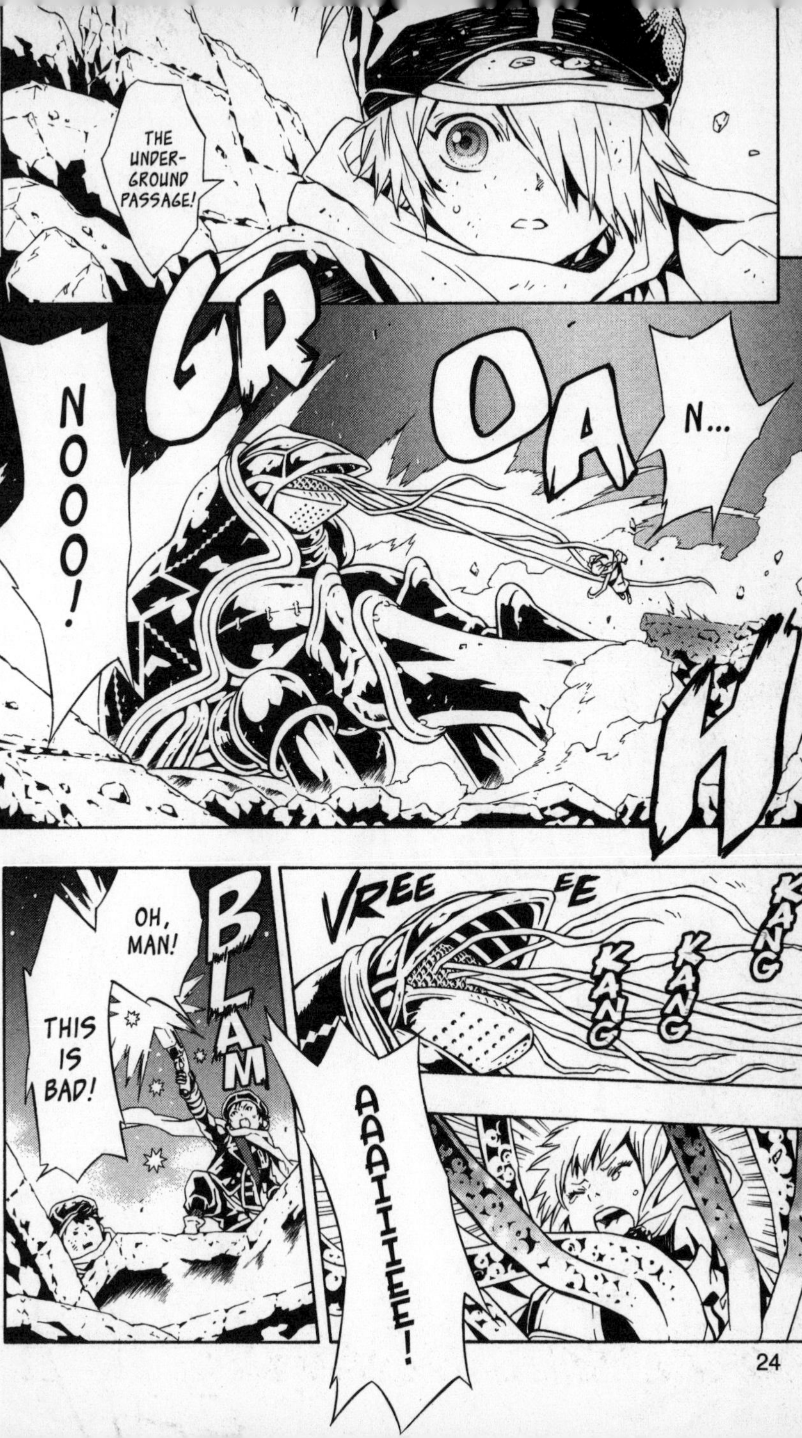
THE UNDER-GROUND PASSAGE!
GROAN...
NOOOO!
VREEEE
KANG
KANG
KANG
AAAIIIEEE!
OH, MAN!
THIS IS BAD!
BLAM

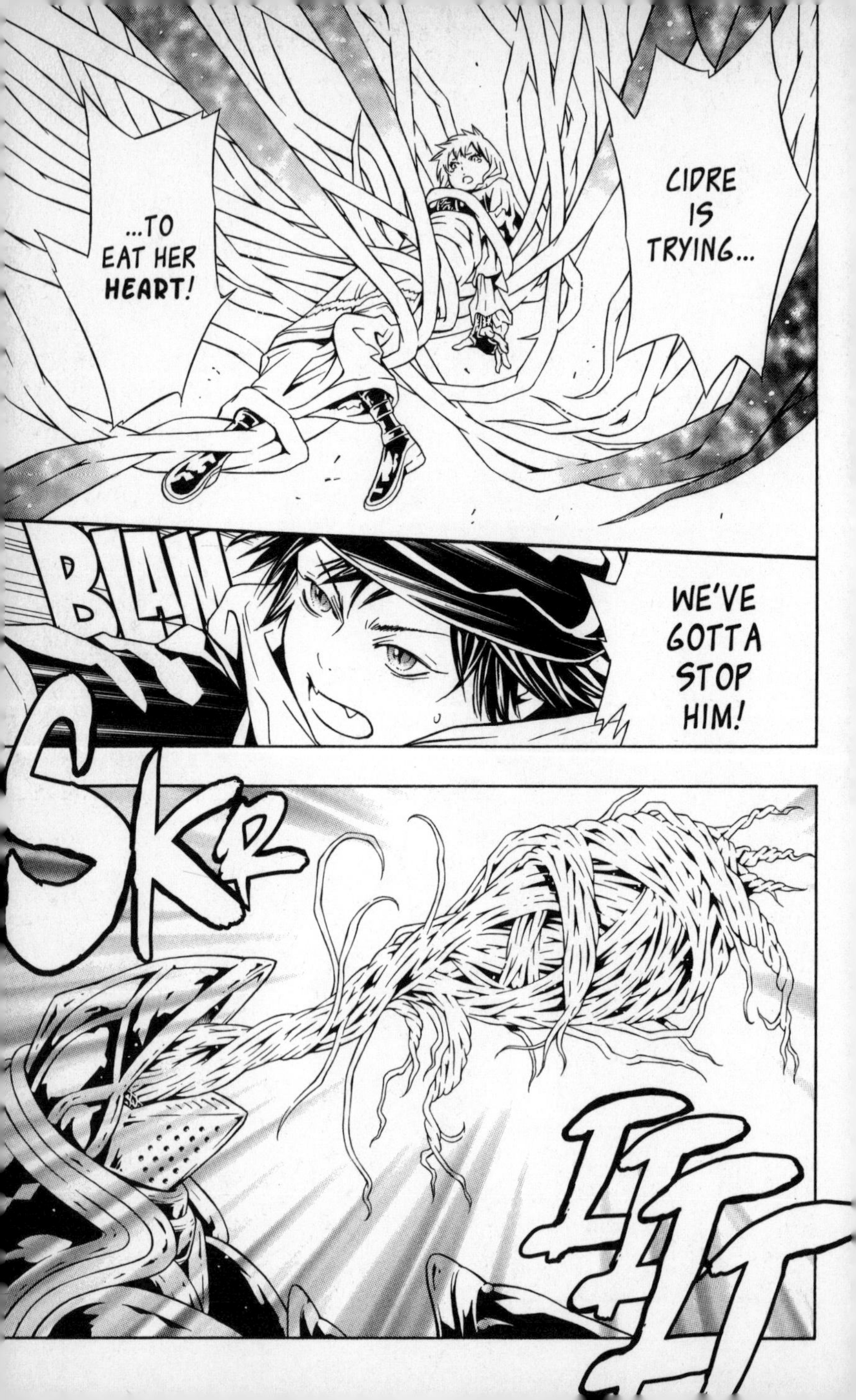
CIDRE IS TRYING...
...TO EAT HER HEART!
WE'VE GOTTA STOP HIM!
BLAM
SKR
IIT

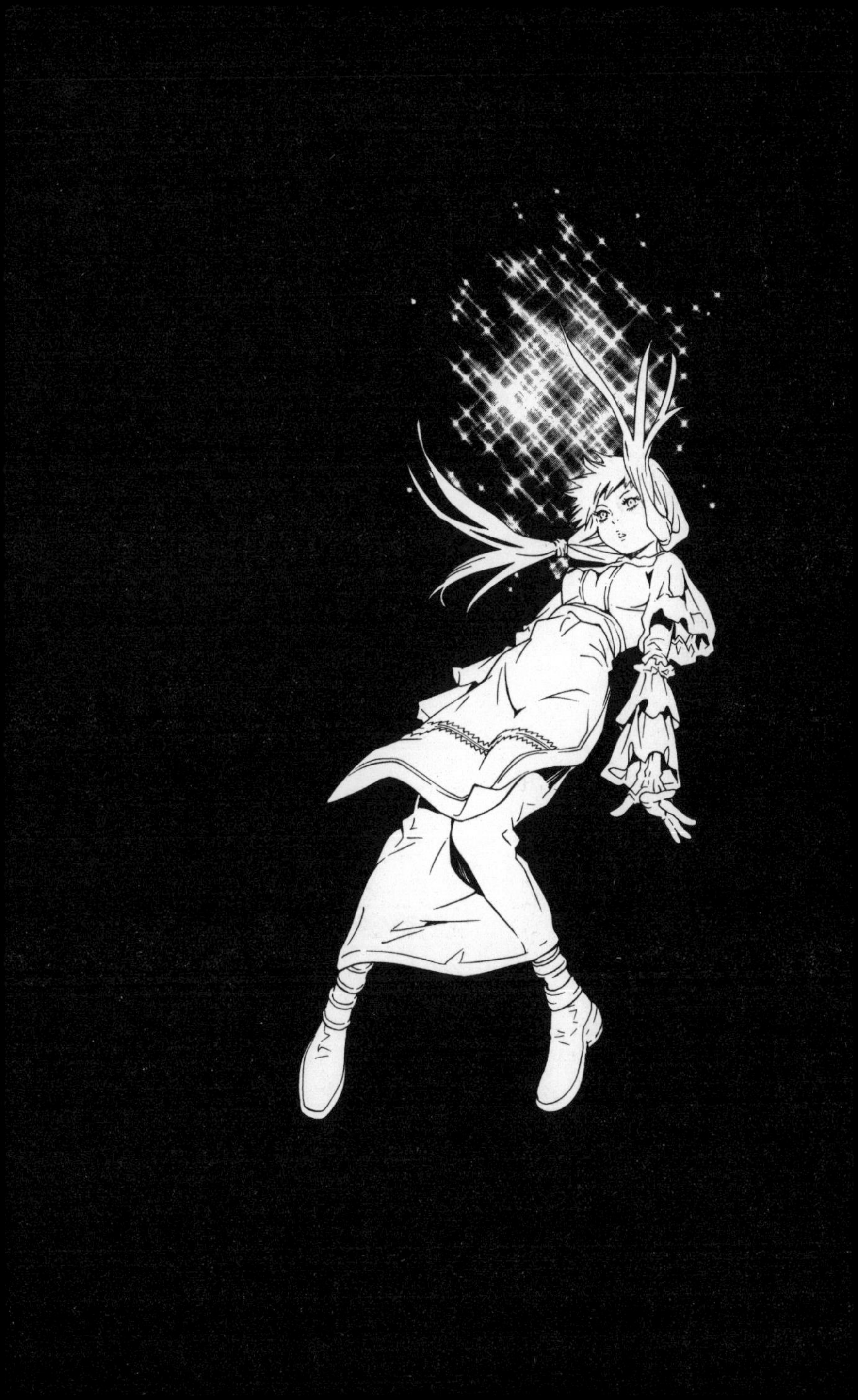

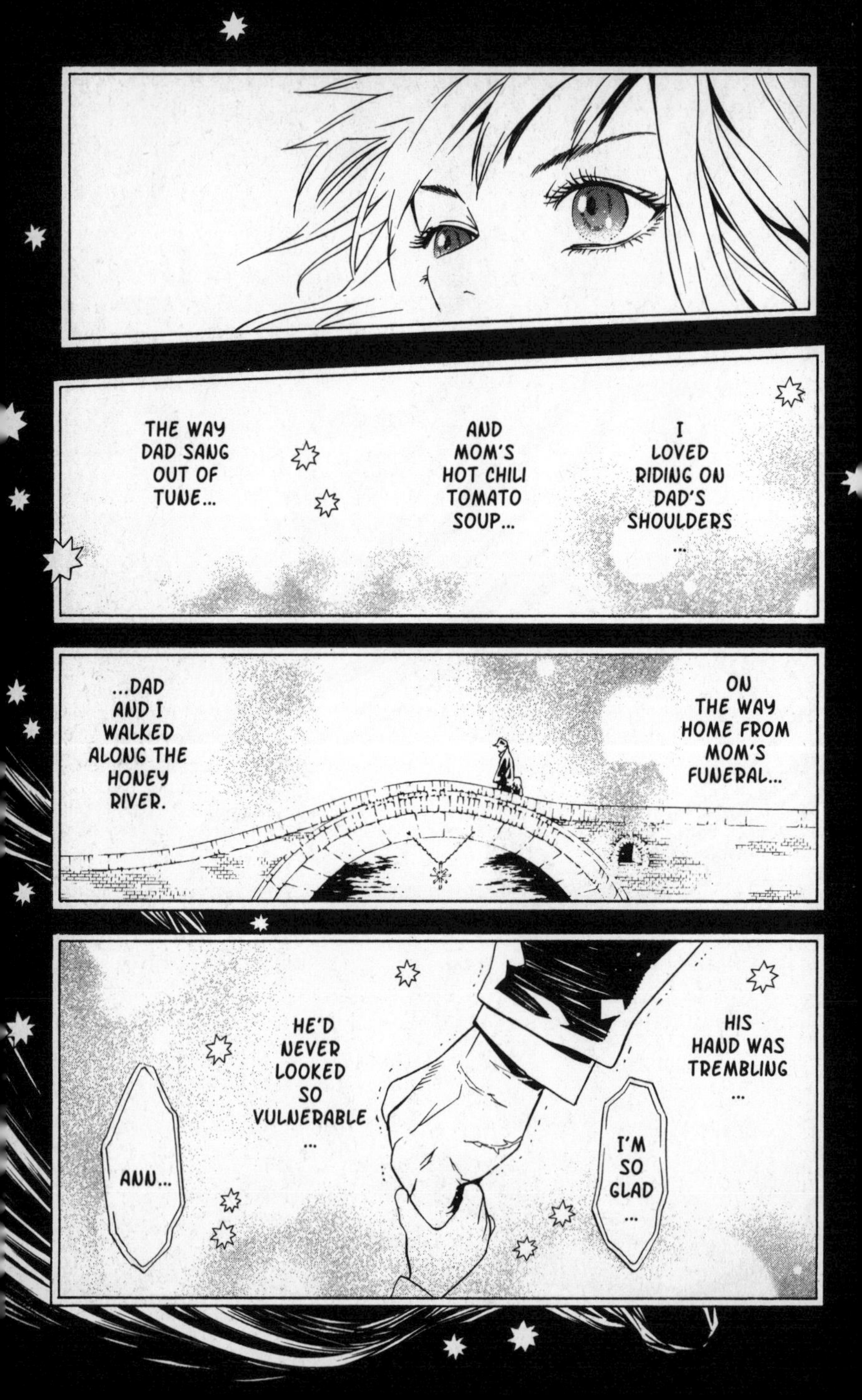
I LOVED RIDING ON DAD'S SHOULDERS ...
AND MOM'S HOT CHILI TOMATO SOUP...
THE WAY DAD SANG OUT OF TUNE...
ON THE WAY HOME FROM MOM'S FUNERAL...
...DAD AND I WALKED ALONG THE HONEY RIVER.
HIS HAND WAS TREMBLING ...
I'M SO GLAD ...
HE'D NEVER LOOKED SO VULNERABLE ...
ANN...

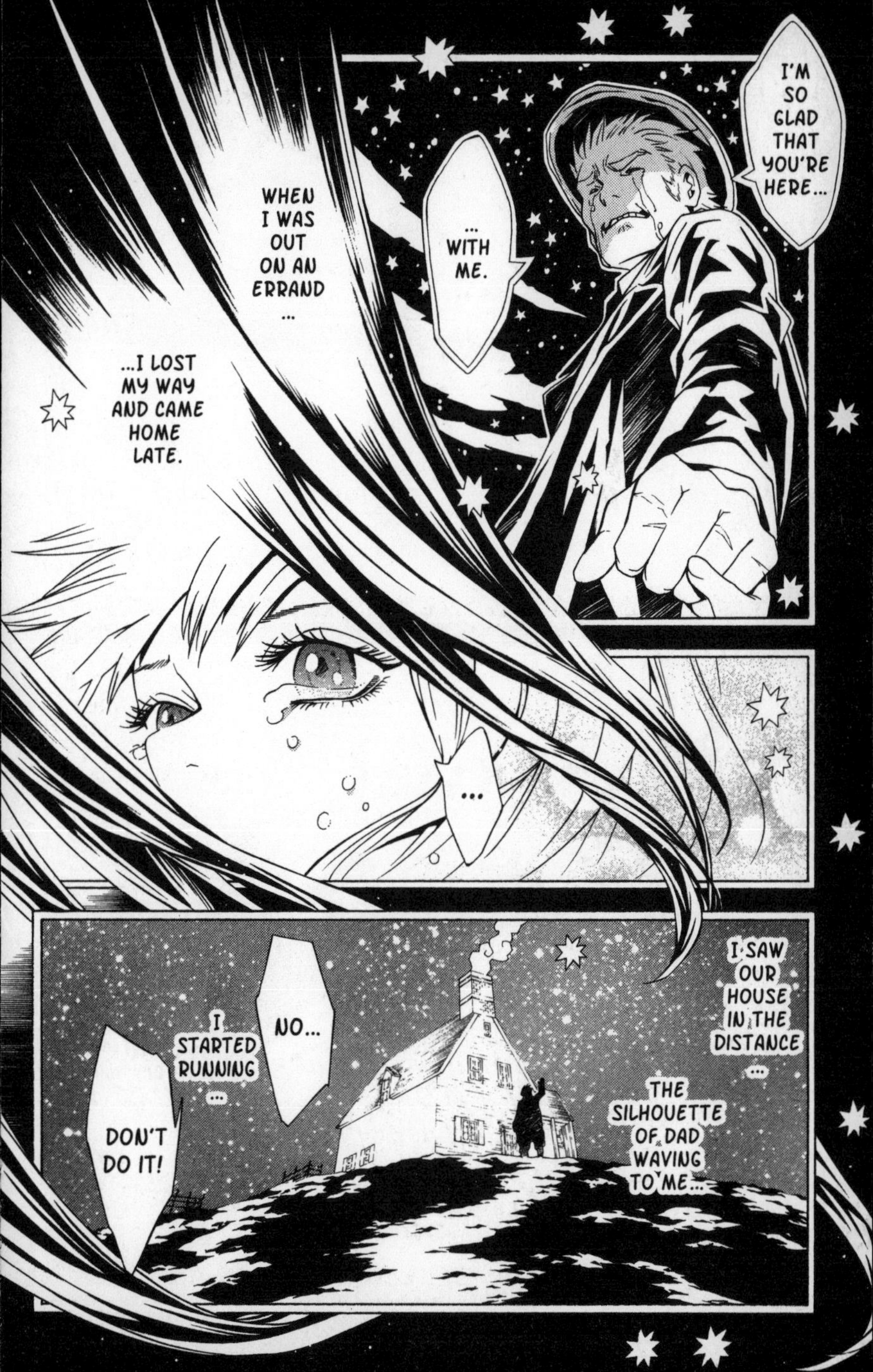
I'M SO GLAD THAT YOU'RE HERE...
... WITH ME.
WHEN I WAS OUT ON AN ERRAND ...
...I LOST MY WAY AND CAME HOME LATE.
...
I SAW OUR HOUSE IN THE DISTANCE ...
THE SILHOUETTE OF DAD WAVING TO ME...
NO...
I STARTED RUNNING ...
DON'T DO IT!

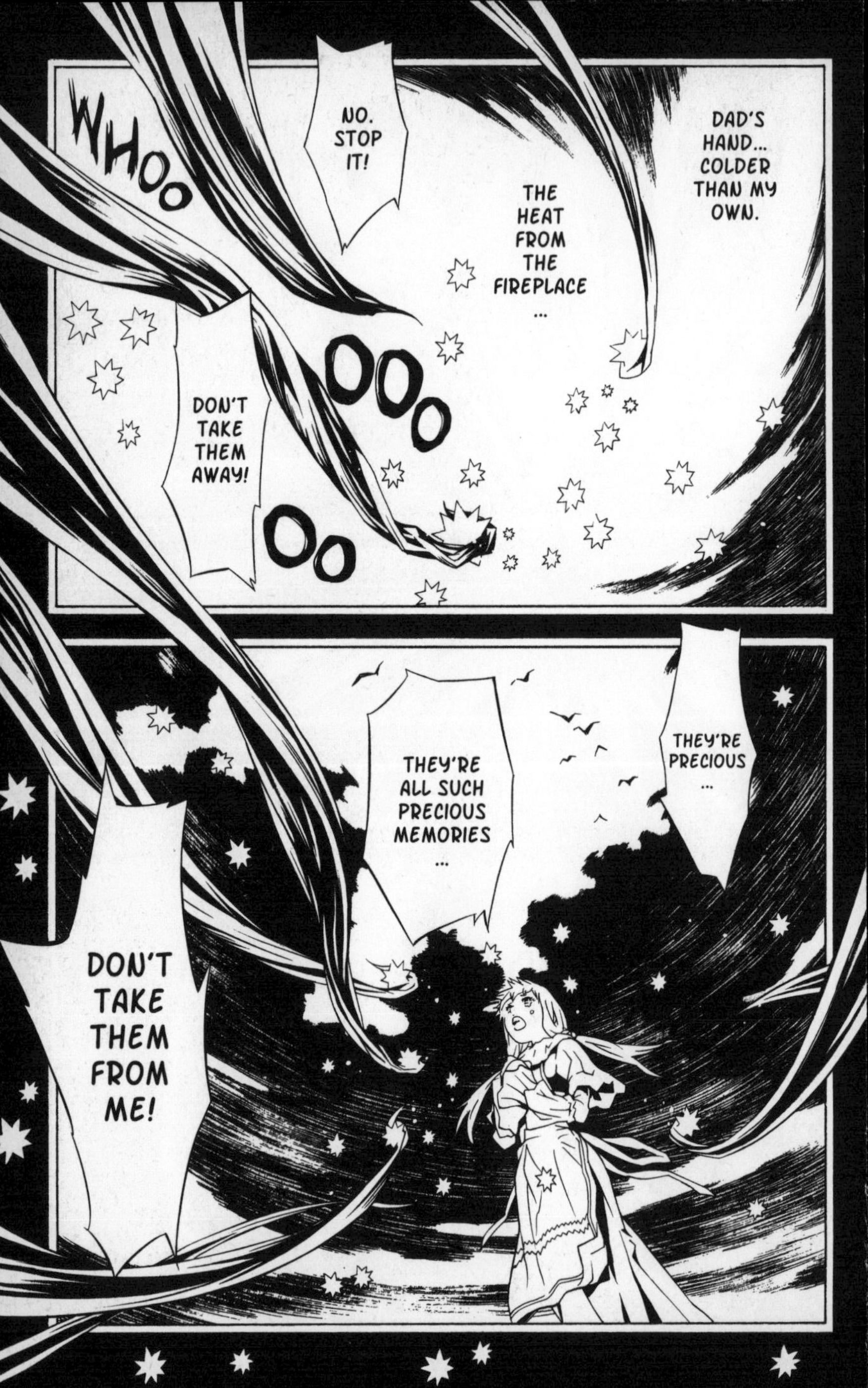
DAD'S HAND... COLDER THAN MY OWN.
THE HEAT FROM THE FIREPLACE ...
NO. STOP IT!
WHOO
OOOO
OO
DON'T TAKE THEM AWAY!
THEY'RE PRECIOUS ...
THEY'RE ALL SUCH PRECIOUS MEMORIES ...
DON'T TAKE THEM FROM ME!

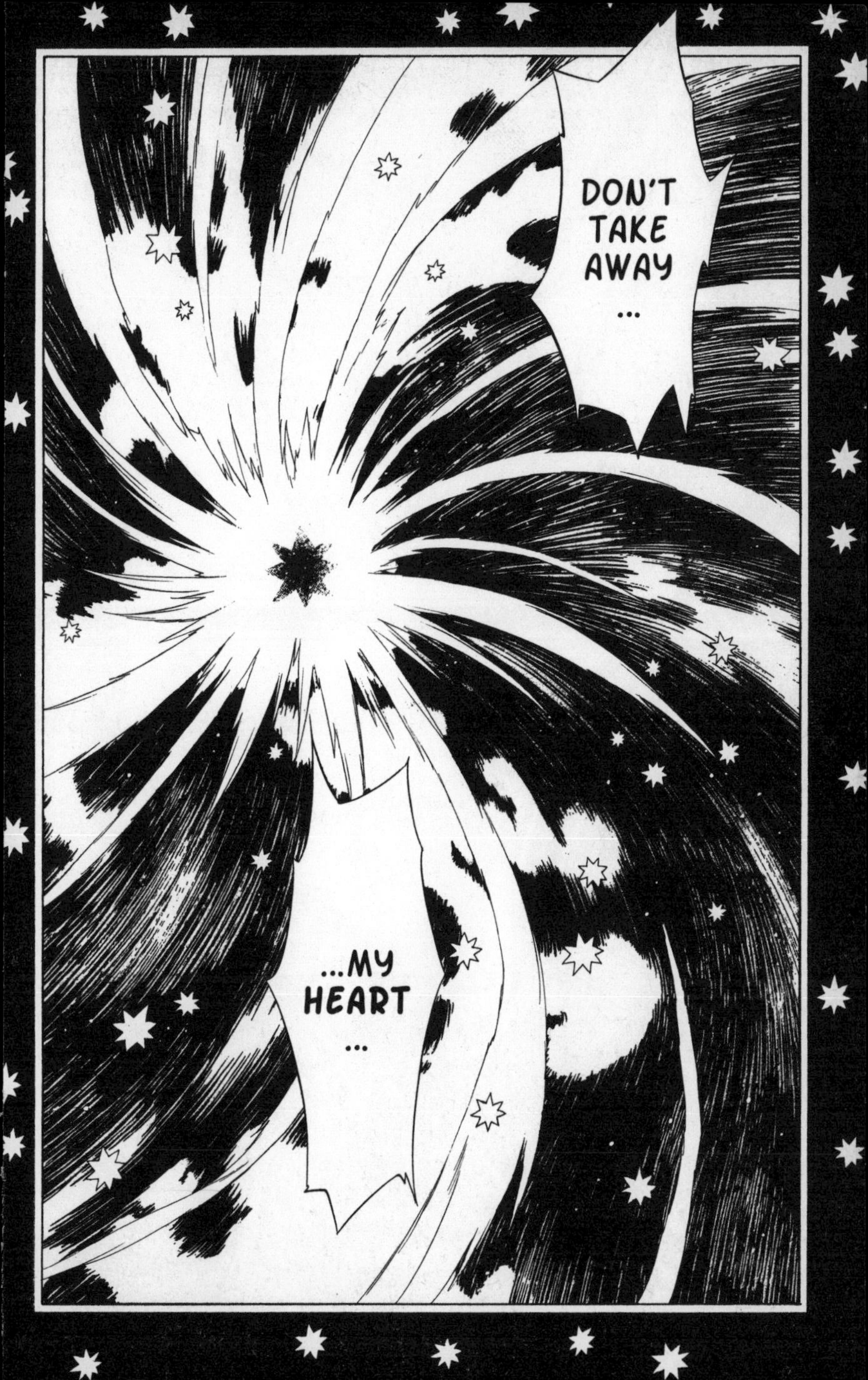
DON'T TAKE AWAY ...
...MY HEART ...

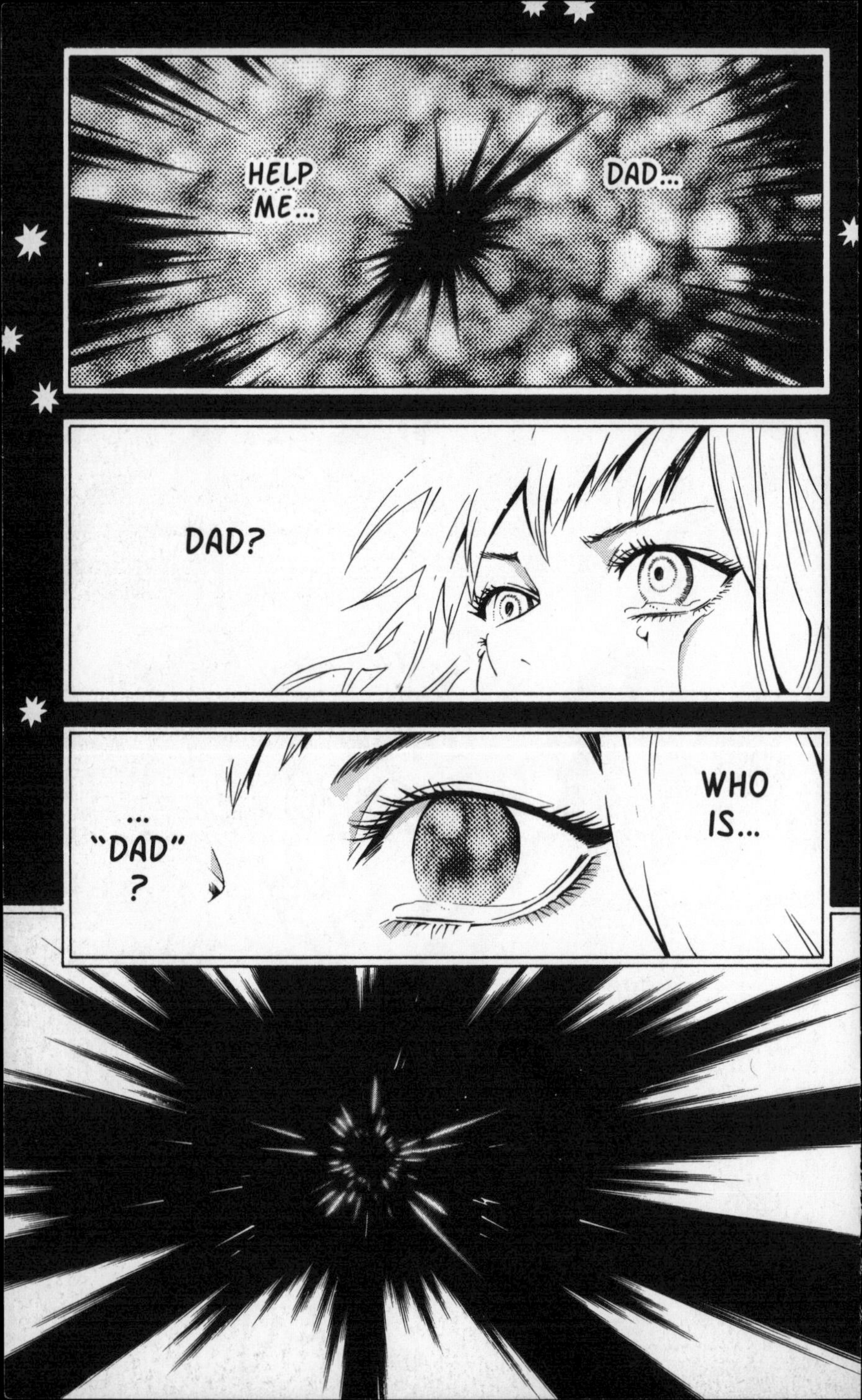
DAD...
HELP ME...
DAD?
WHO IS...
... "DAD" ?

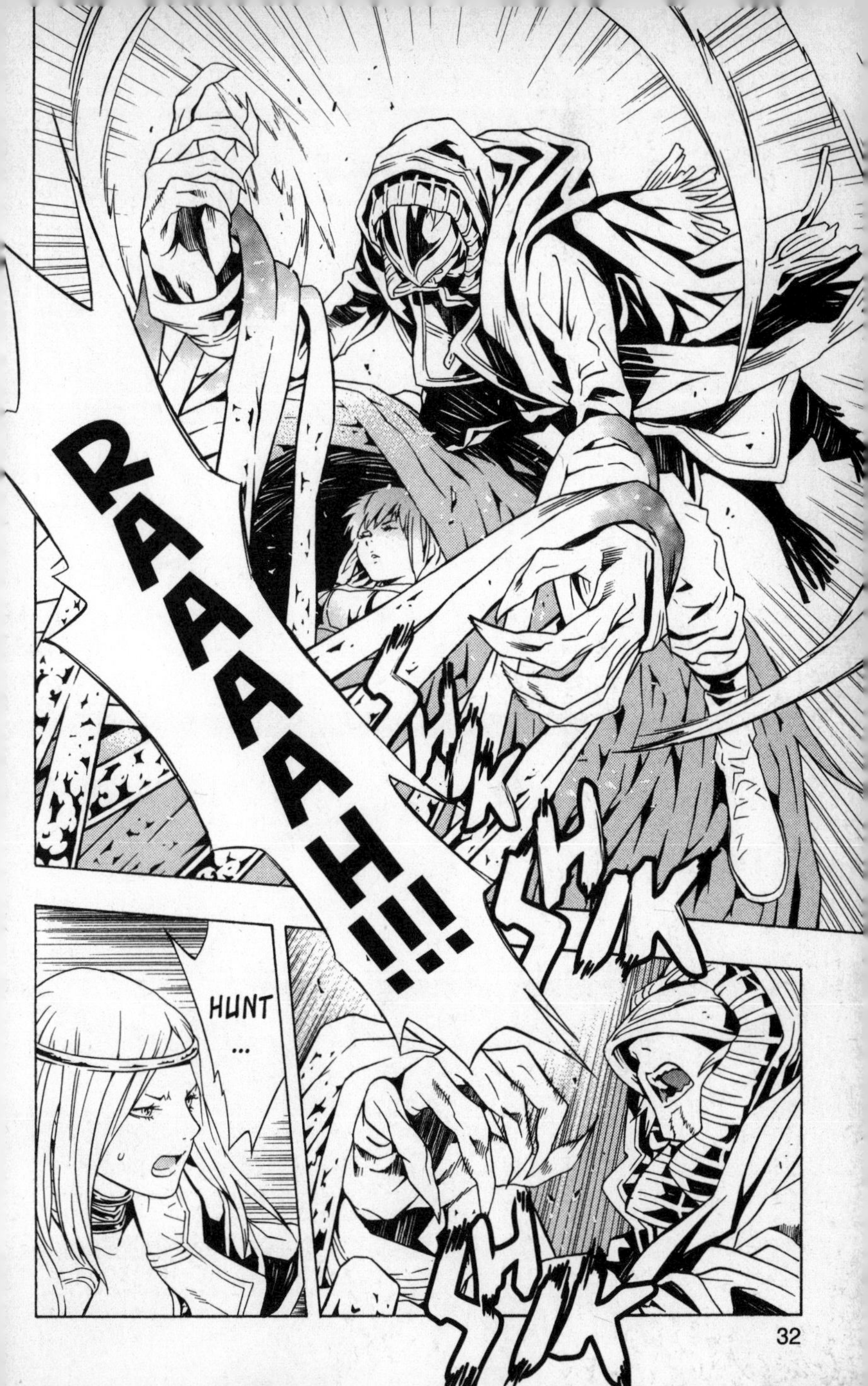
RAAAAH!!!
SHK
SHK
HUNT
...
SHK

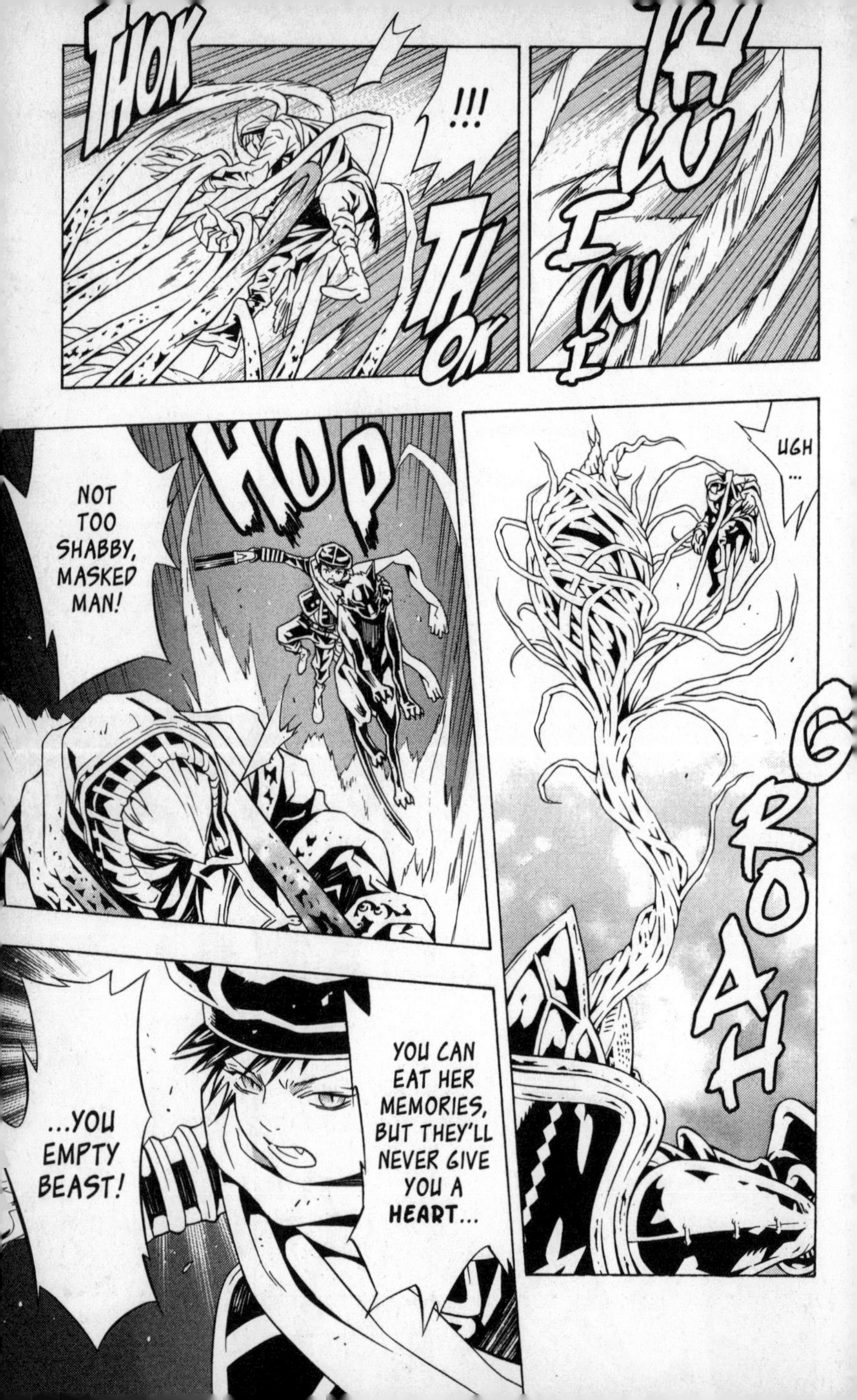
THWIWI
THOK
!!!
...
THOK
UGH ...
GROAH
HOP
NOT TOO SHABBY, MASKED MAN!
YOU CAN EAT HER MEMORIES, BUT THEY'LL NEVER GIVE YOU A HEART...
...YOU EMPTY BEAST!

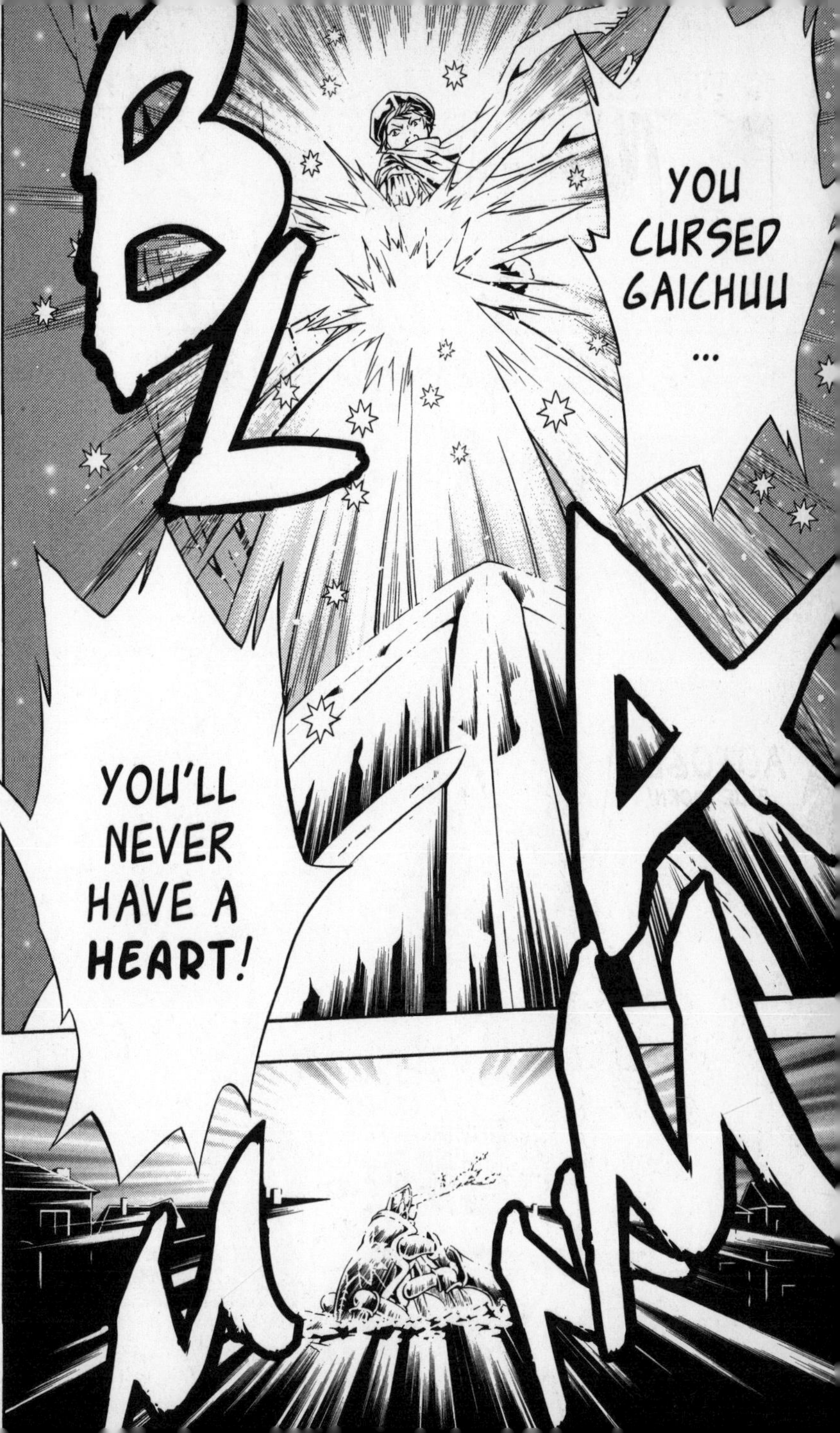
YOU CURSED GAICHUU ...
YOU'LL NEVER HAVE A HEART!

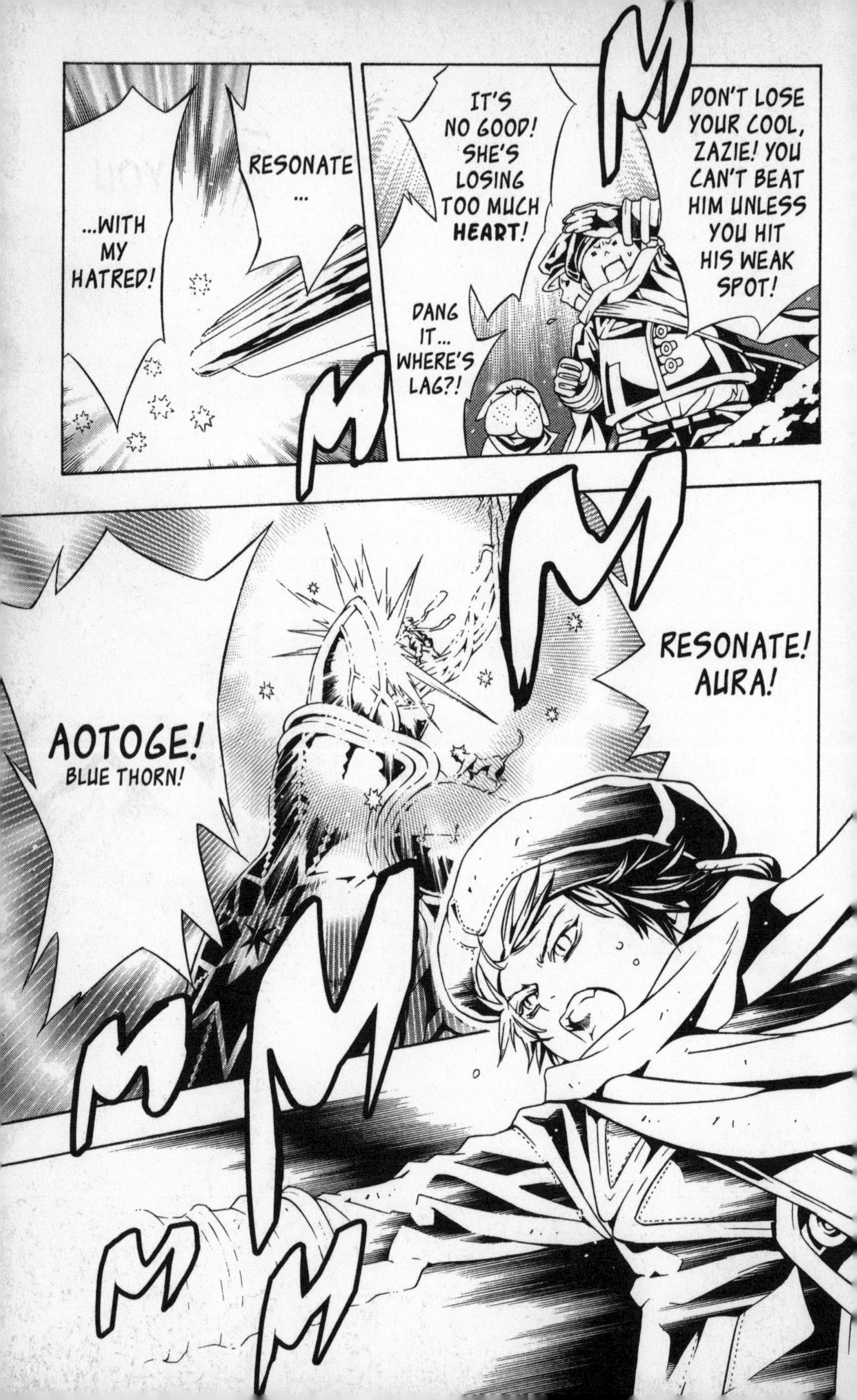
DON'T LOSE YOUR COOL, ZAZIE! YOU CAN'T BEAT HIM UNLESS YOU HIT HIS WEAK SPOT!
IT'S NO GOOD! SHE'S LOSING TOO MUCH **HEART**!
DANG IT... WHERE'S LAG?!
RESONATE ...
...WITH MY HATRED!
RESONATE! AURA!
AOTOGE!
BLUE THORN!

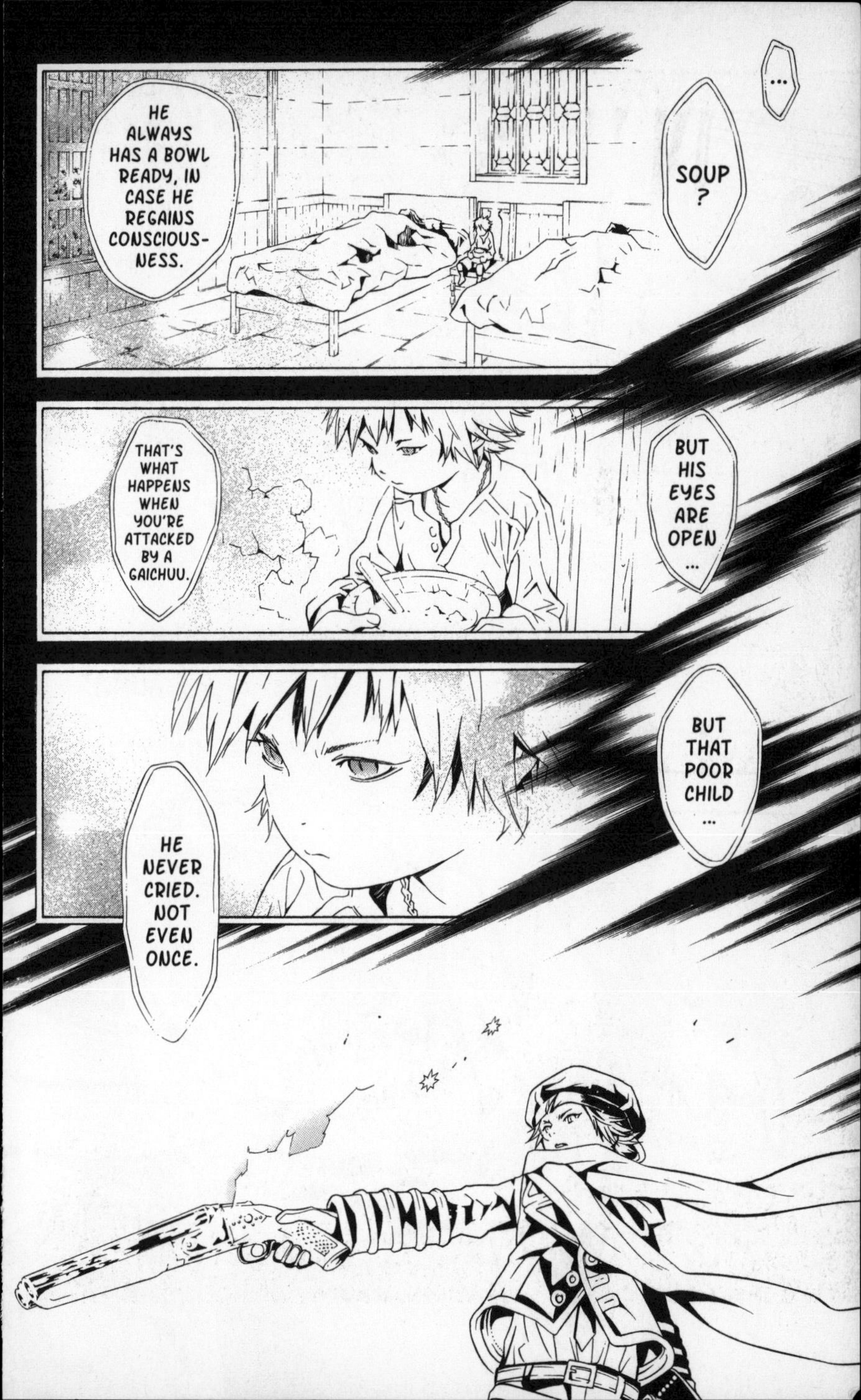
...
SOUP?
HE ALWAYS HAS A BOWL READY, IN CASE HE REGAINS CONSCIOUSNESS.
BUT HIS EYES ARE OPEN...
THAT'S WHAT HAPPENS WHEN YOU'RE ATTACKED BY A GAICHUU.
BUT THAT POOR CHILD...
HE NEVER CRIED. NOT EVEN ONCE.

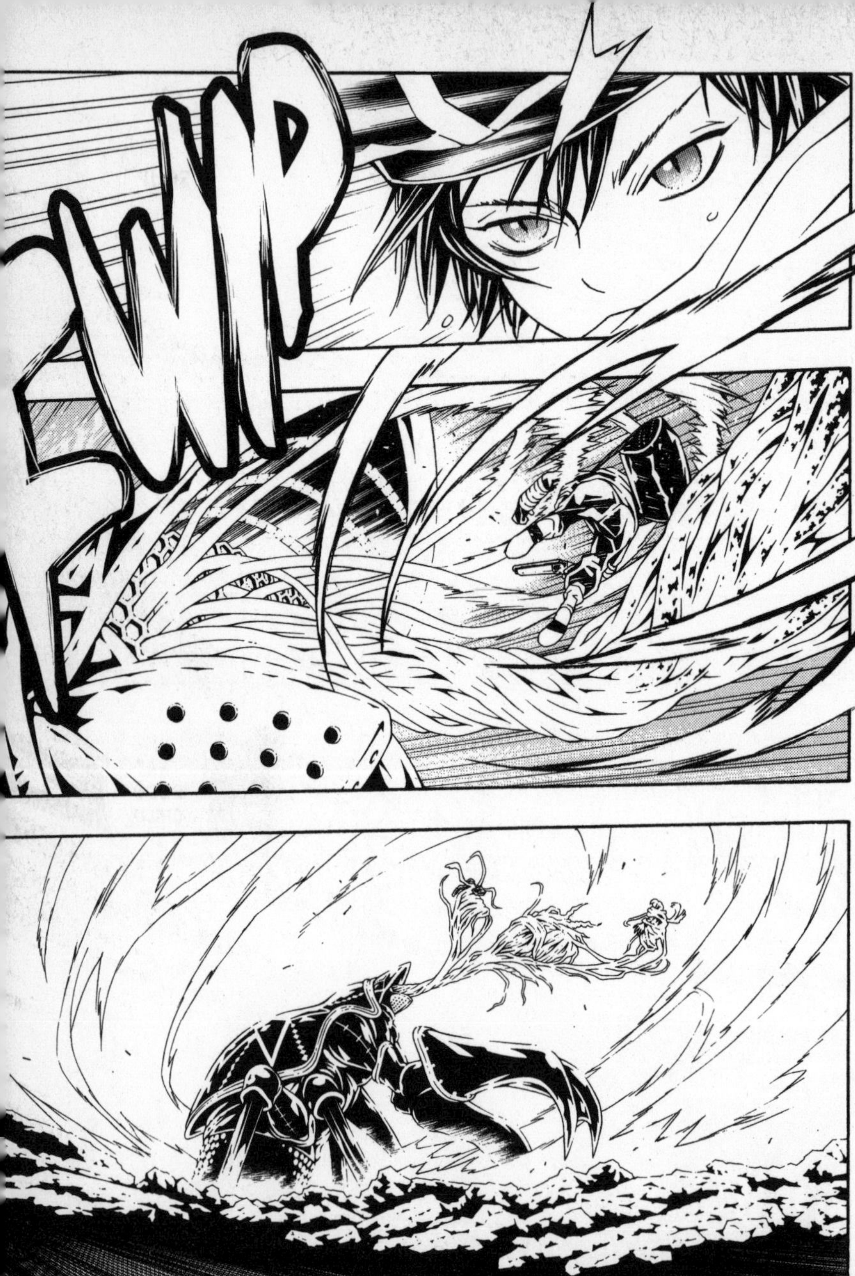
SWIP

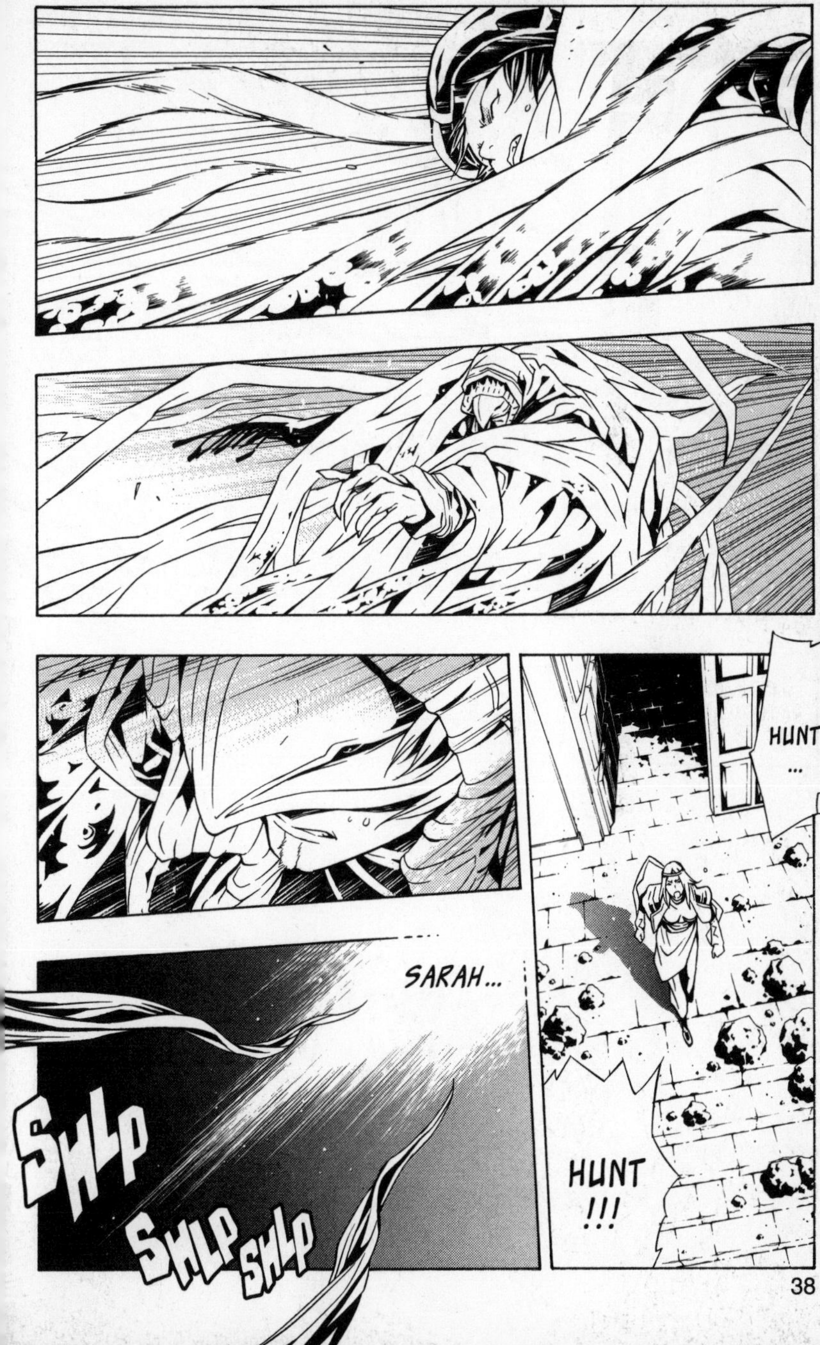
HUNT ...
SARAH...
HUNT !!!
SHLP
SHLP SHLP

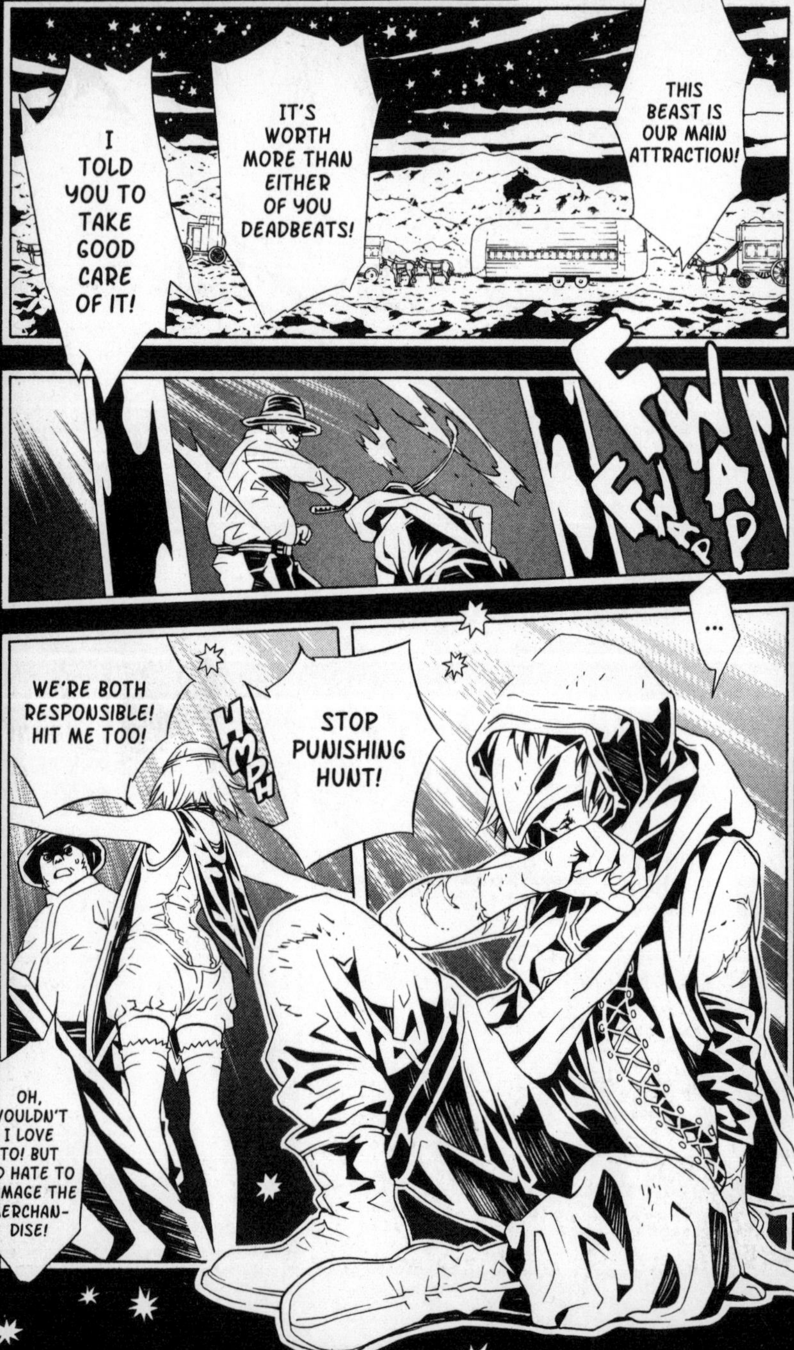
THIS BEAST IS OUR MAIN ATTRACTION!
IT'S WORTH MORE THAN EITHER OF YOU DEADBEATS!
I TOLD YOU TO TAKE GOOD CARE OF IT!
FWAP
FWAP
...
STOP PUNISHING HUNT!
HMPH
WE'RE BOTH RESPONSIBLE! HIT ME TOO!
OH, WOULDN'T I LOVE TO! BUT I'D HATE TO DAMAGE THE MERCHAN-DISE!

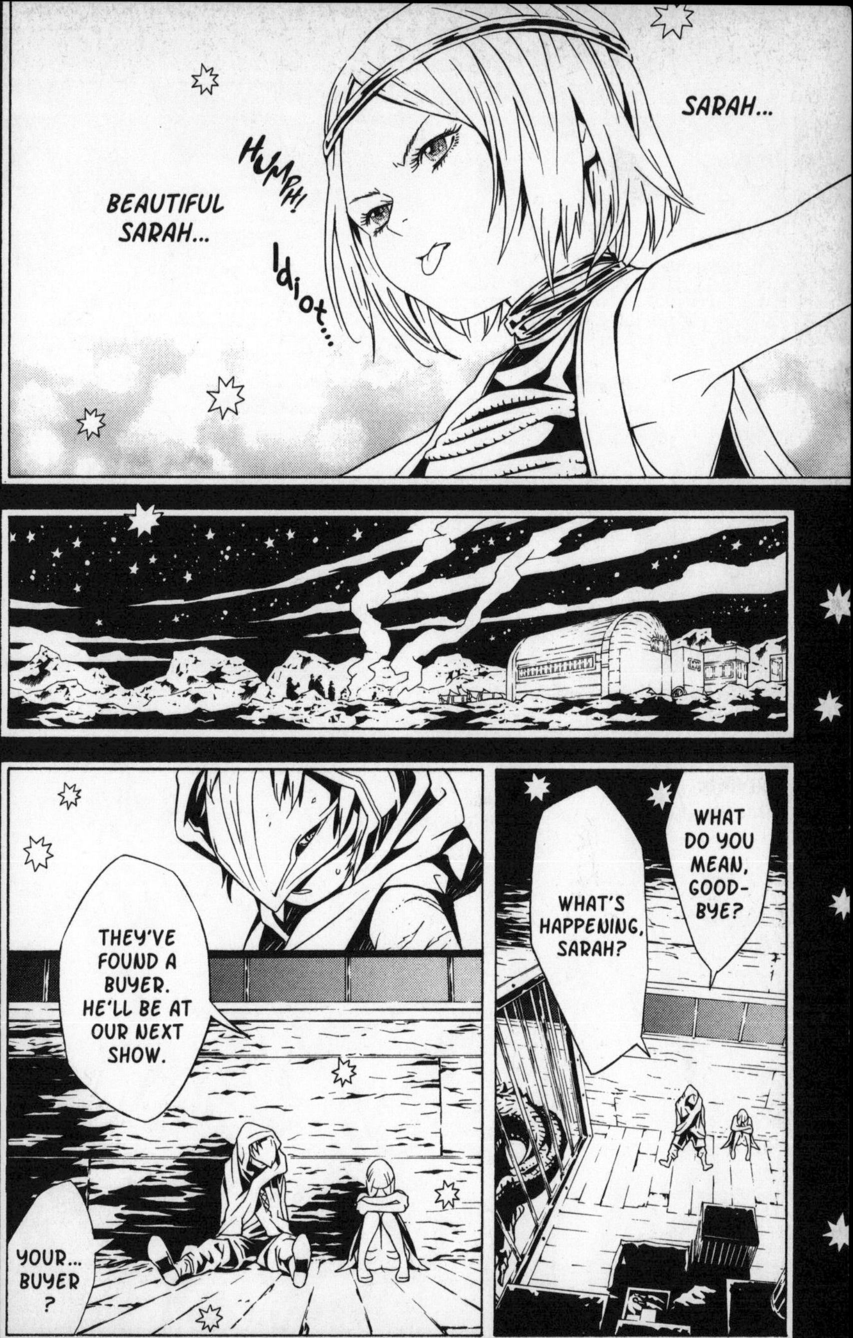
SARAH...
HUMPH!
BEAUTIFUL SARAH...
Idiot...
WHAT DO YOU MEAN, GOOD-BYE?
WHAT'S HAPPENING, SARAH?
THEY'VE FOUND A BUYER. HE'LL BE AT OUR NEXT SHOW.
YOUR... BUYER ?

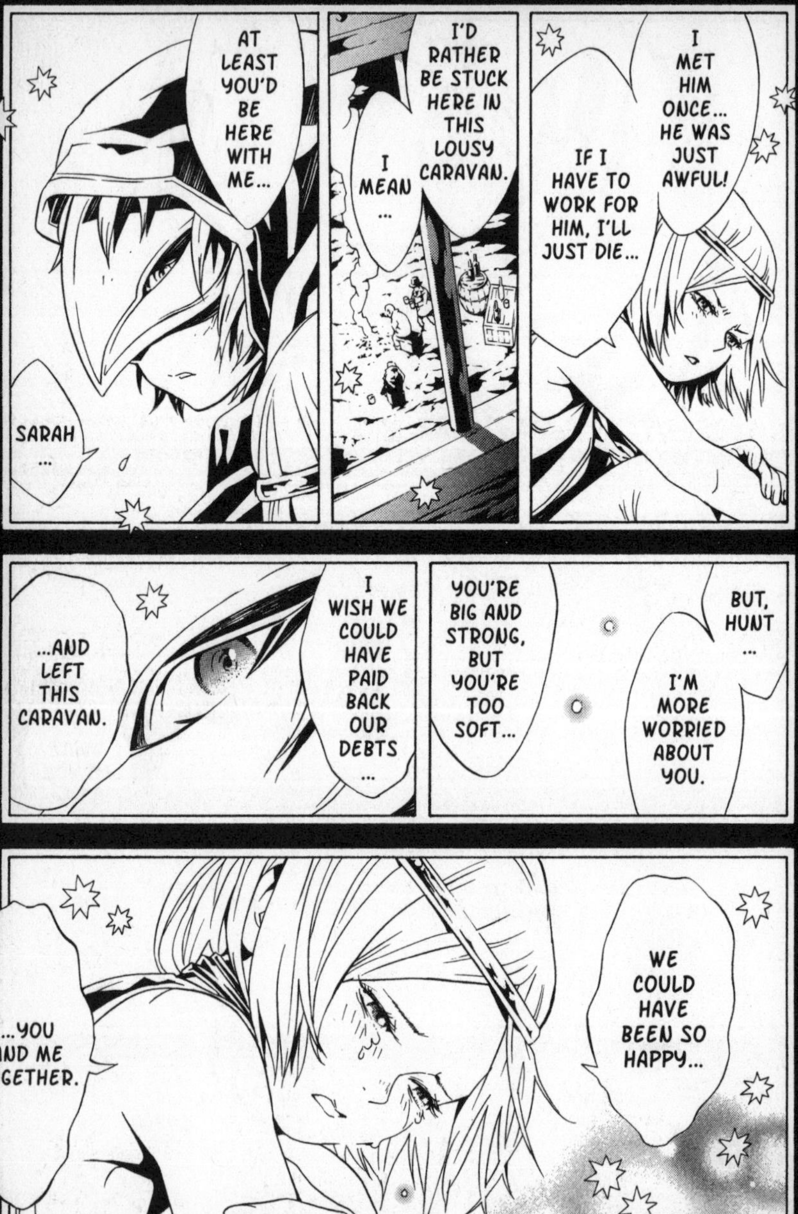
I MET HIM ONCE... HE WAS JUST AWFUL!
IF I HAVE TO WORK FOR HIM, I'LL JUST DIE...
I'D RATHER BE STUCK HERE IN THIS LOUSY CARAVAN.
I MEAN ...
AT LEAST YOU'D BE HERE WITH ME...
SARAH ...
BUT, HUNT ...
I'M MORE WORRIED ABOUT YOU.
YOU'RE BIG AND STRONG, BUT YOU'RE TOO SOFT...
I WISH WE COULD HAVE PAID BACK OUR DEBTS ...
...AND LEFT THIS CARAVAN.
WE COULD HAVE BEEN SO HAPPY...
...YOU AND ME TOGETHER.

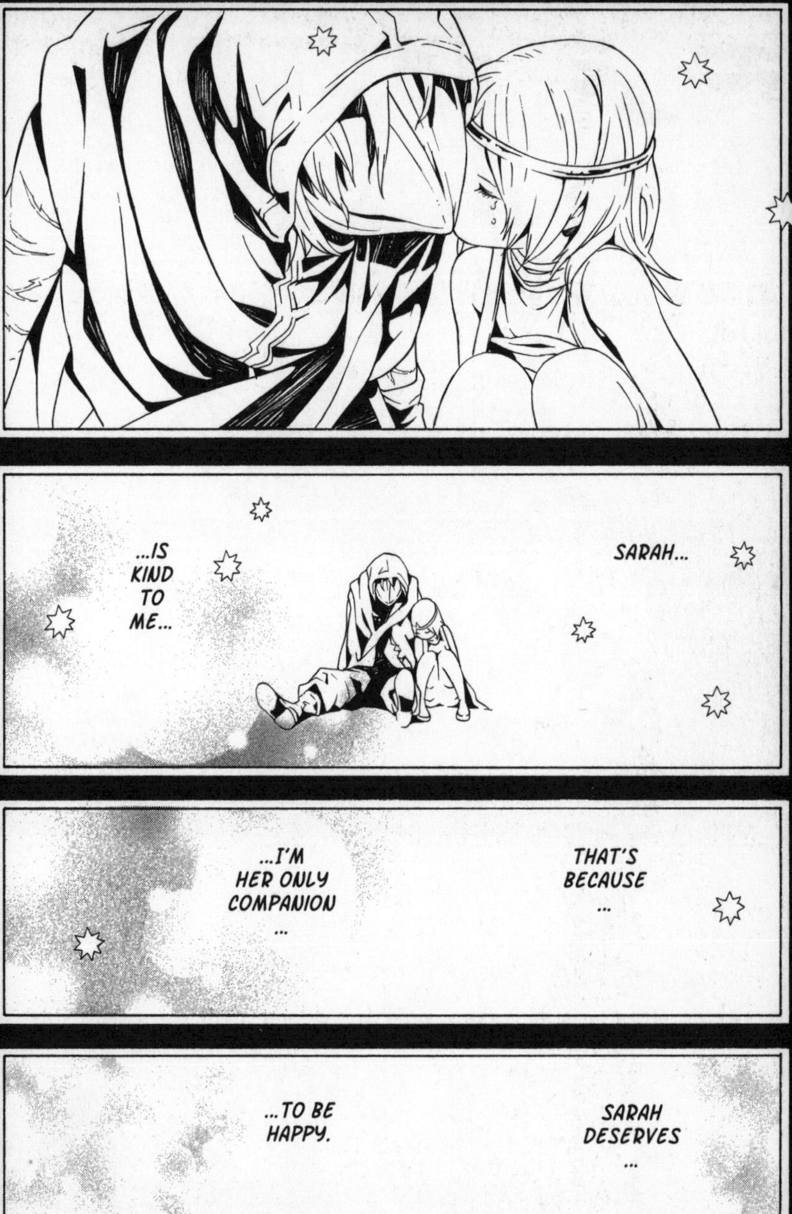
SARAH...
...IS KIND TO ME...
THAT'S BECAUSE ...
...I'M HER ONLY COMPANION ...
SARAH DESERVES ...
...TO BE HAPPY.

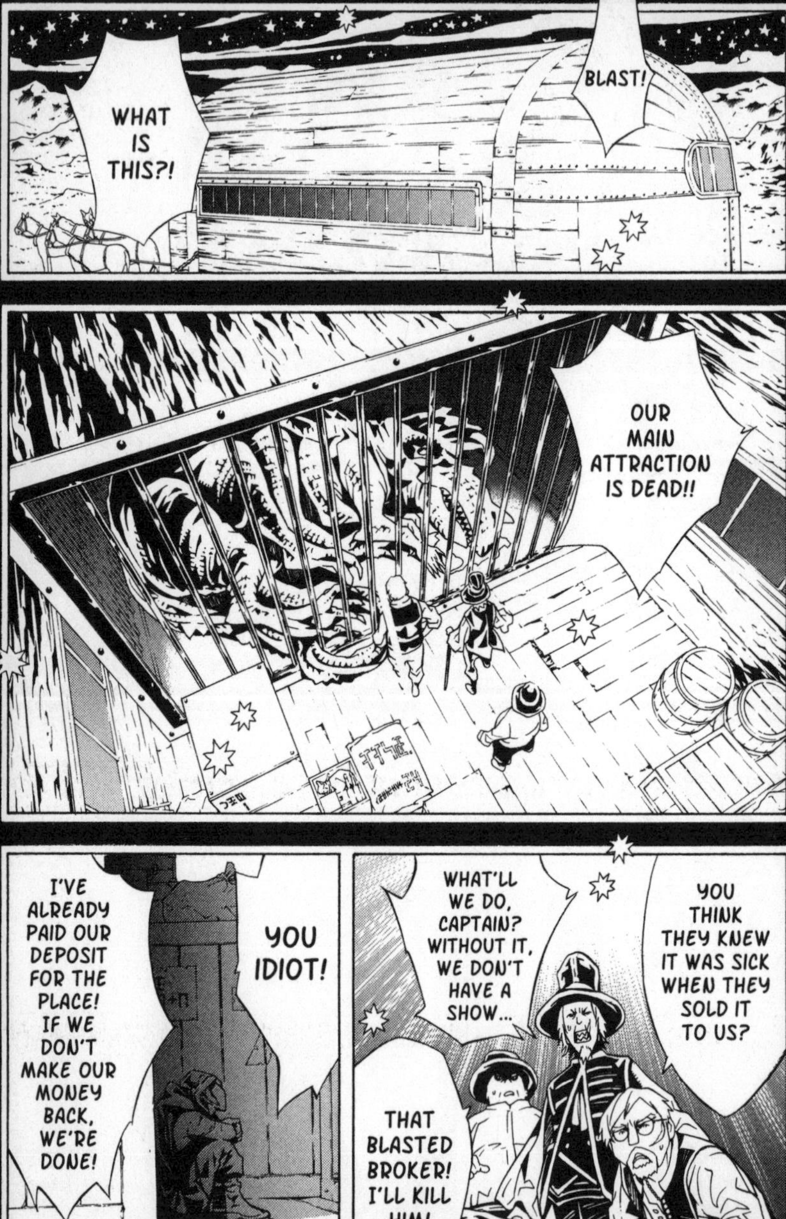
BLAST!
WHAT IS THIS?!
OUR MAIN ATTRACTION IS DEAD!!
YOU THINK THEY KNEW IT WAS SICK WHEN THEY SOLD IT TO US?
WHAT'LL WE DO, CAPTAIN? WITHOUT IT, WE DON'T HAVE A SHOW...
THAT BLASTED BROKER! I'LL KILL HIM!
YOU IDIOT!
I'VE ALREADY PAID OUR DEPOSIT FOR THE PLACE! IF WE DON'T MAKE OUR MONEY BACK, WE'RE DONE!

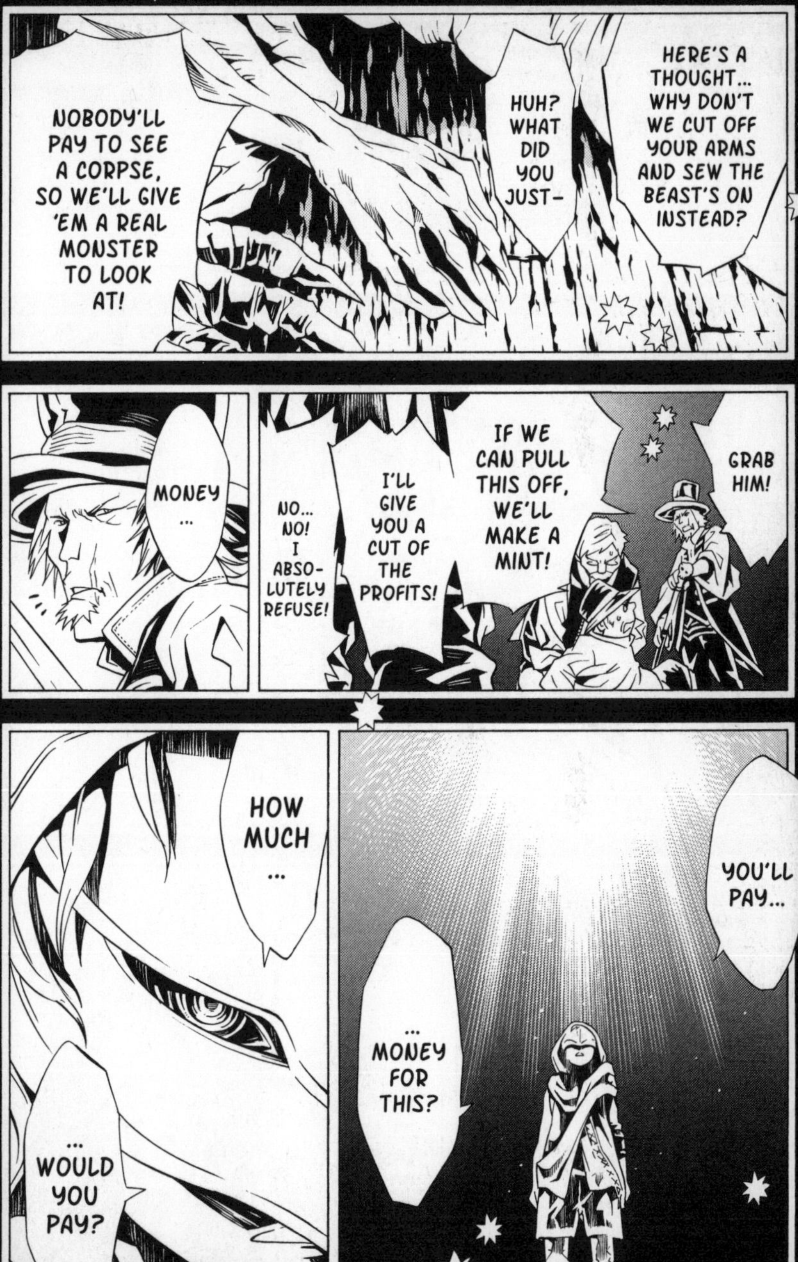
HERE'S A THOUGHT... WHY DON'T WE CUT OFF YOUR ARMS AND SEW THE BEAST'S ON INSTEAD?
HUH? WHAT DID YOU JUST-
NOBODY'LL PAY TO SEE A CORPSE, SO WE'LL GIVE 'EM A REAL MONSTER TO LOOK AT!
GRAB HIM!
IF WE CAN PULL THIS OFF, WE'LL MAKE A MINT!
I'LL GIVE YOU A CUT OF THE PROFITS!
NO... NO! I ABSOLUTELY REFUSE!
MONEY ...
YOU'LL PAY...
... MONEY FOR THIS?
HOW MUCH ...
... WOULD YOU PAY?

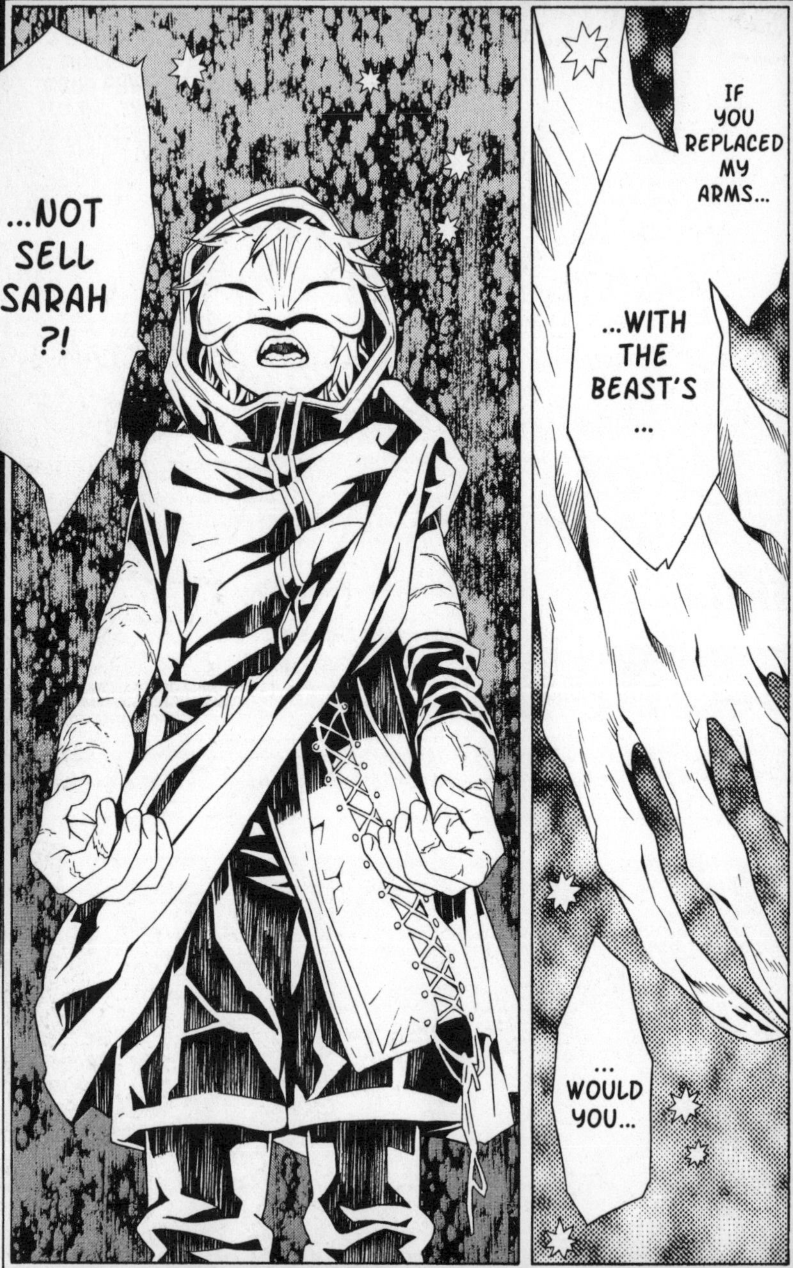
IF YOU REPLACED MY ARMS...
...WITH THE BEAST'S ...
... WOULD YOU...
...NOT SELL SARAH ?!

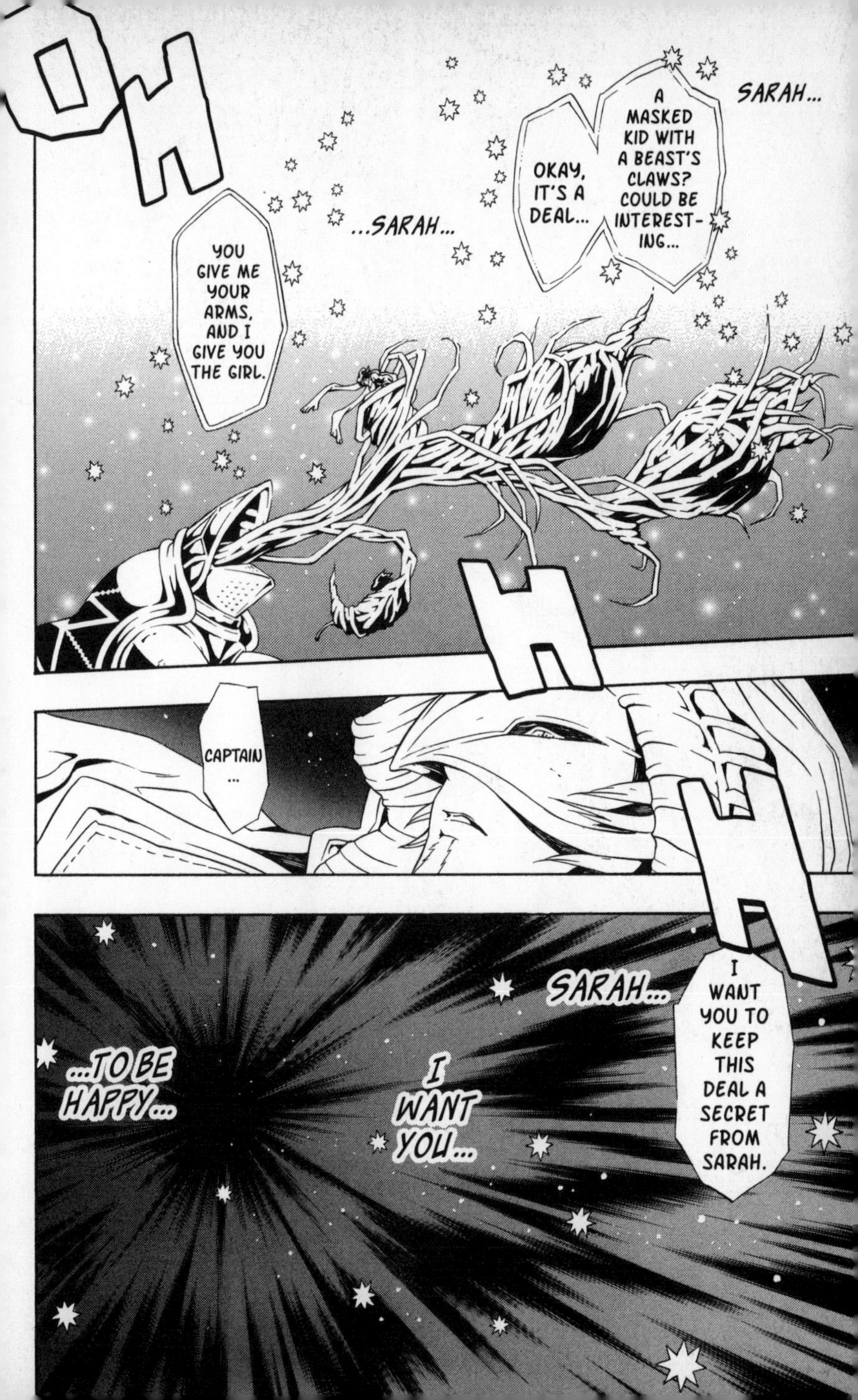
OHHH
SARAH...
A MASKED KID WITH A BEAST'S CLAWS? COULD BE INTEREST-ING...
OKAY, IT'S A DEAL...
...SARAH...
YOU GIVE ME YOUR ARMS, AND I GIVE YOU THE GIRL.
CAPTAIN ...
I WANT YOU TO KEEP THIS DEAL A SECRET FROM SARAH.
SARAH...
I WANT YOU...
...TO BE HAPPY...

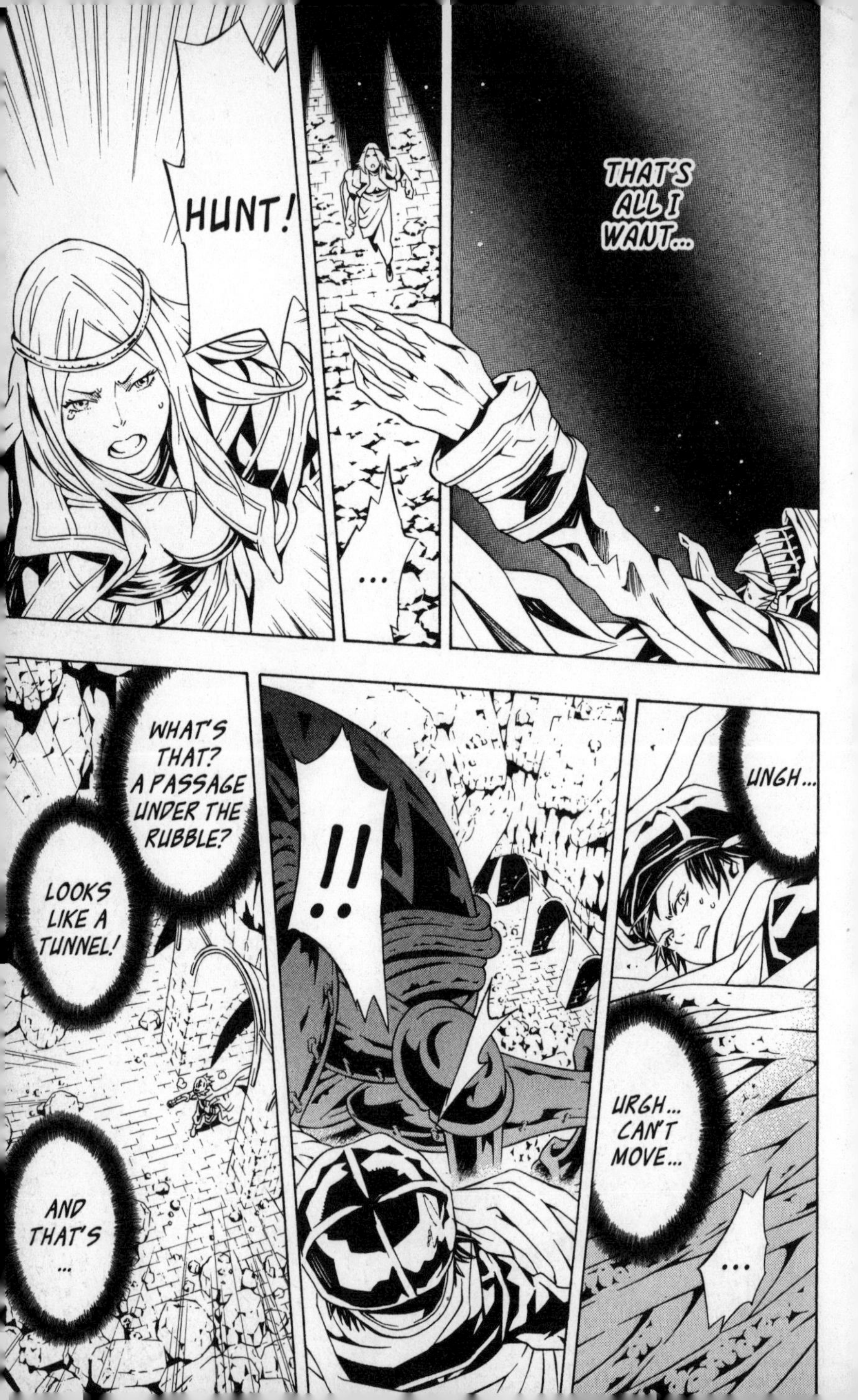
THAT'S ALL I WANT...
...
HUNT!
UNGH...
URGH... CAN'T MOVE...
...
!!
WHAT'S THAT? A PASSAGE UNDER THE RUBBLE?
LOOKS LIKE A TUNNEL!
AND THAT'S ...

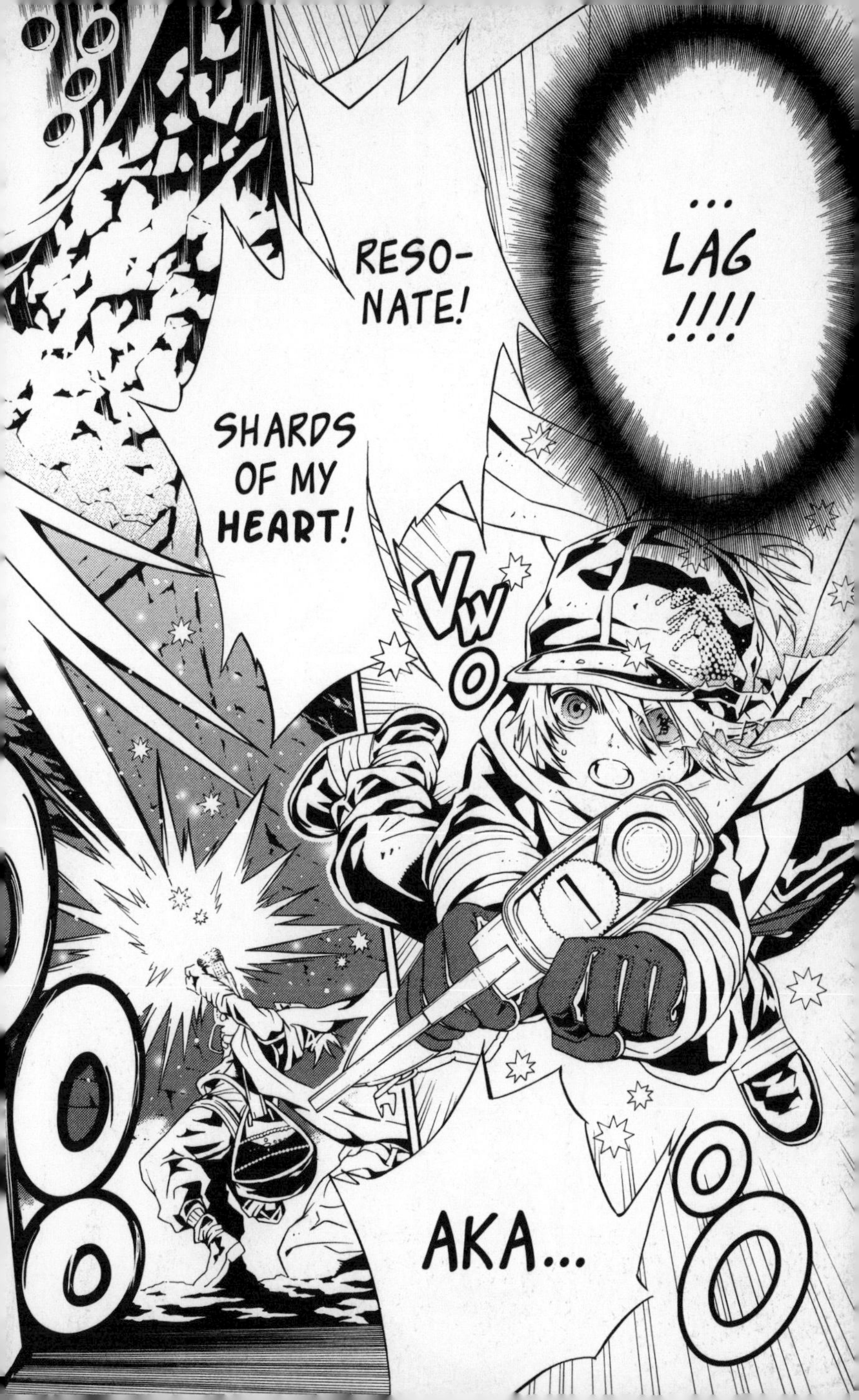
... LAG !!!!
RESO-NATE!
SHARDS OF MY HEART!
VWO
AKA...

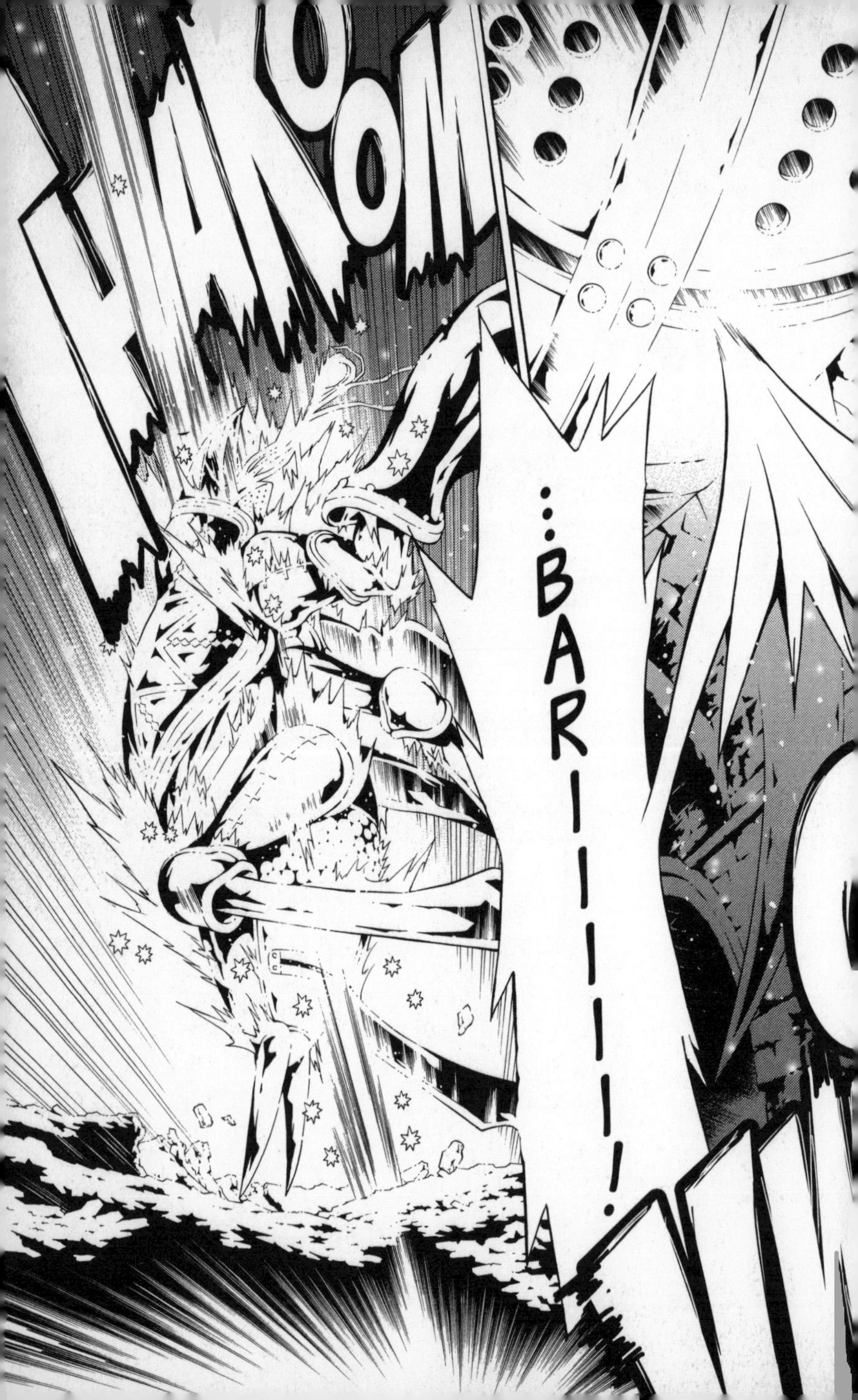
...BAR---------!

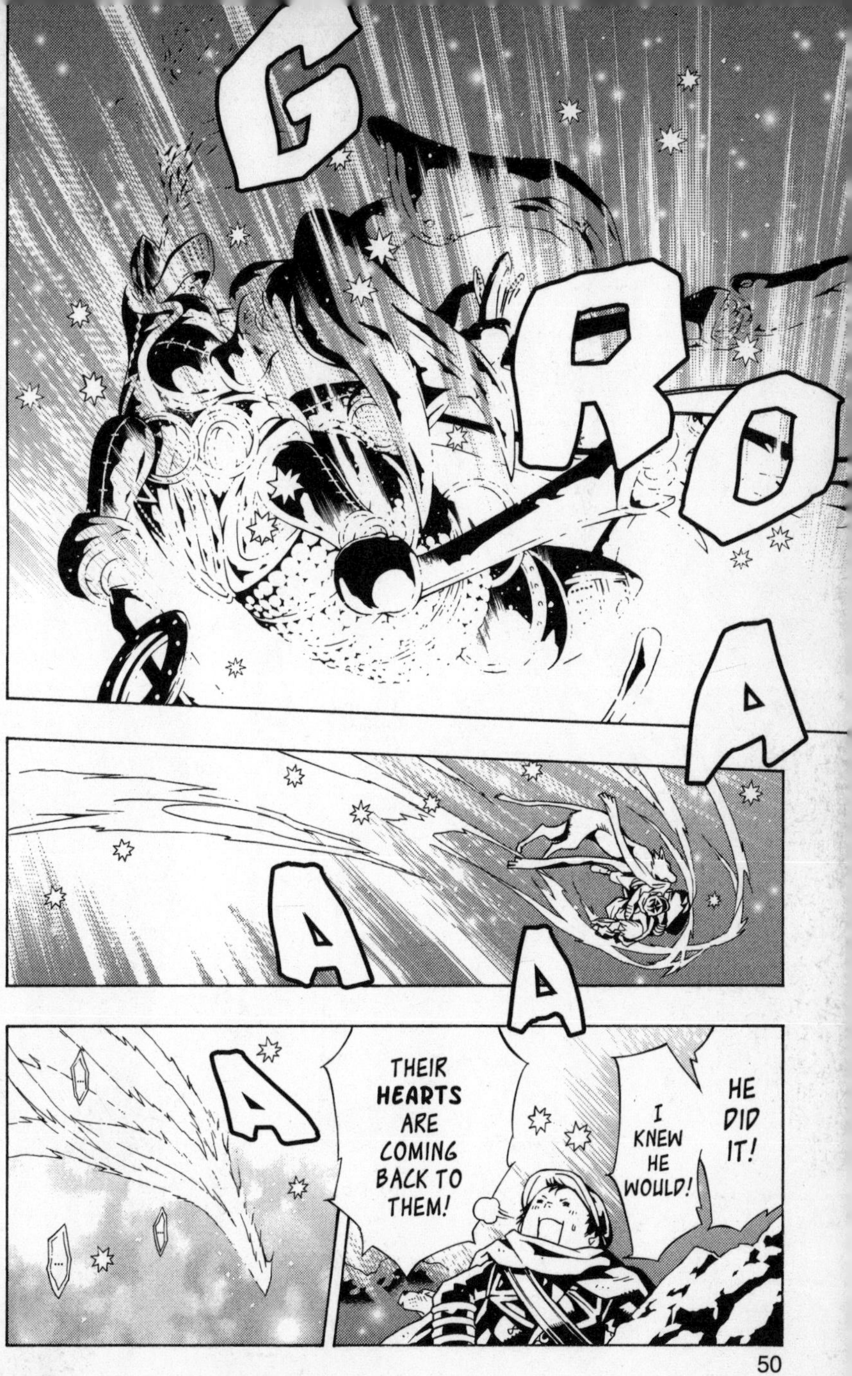
GROAAAA
HE DID IT!
I KNEW HE WOULD!
THEIR HEARTS ARE COMING BACK TO THEM!

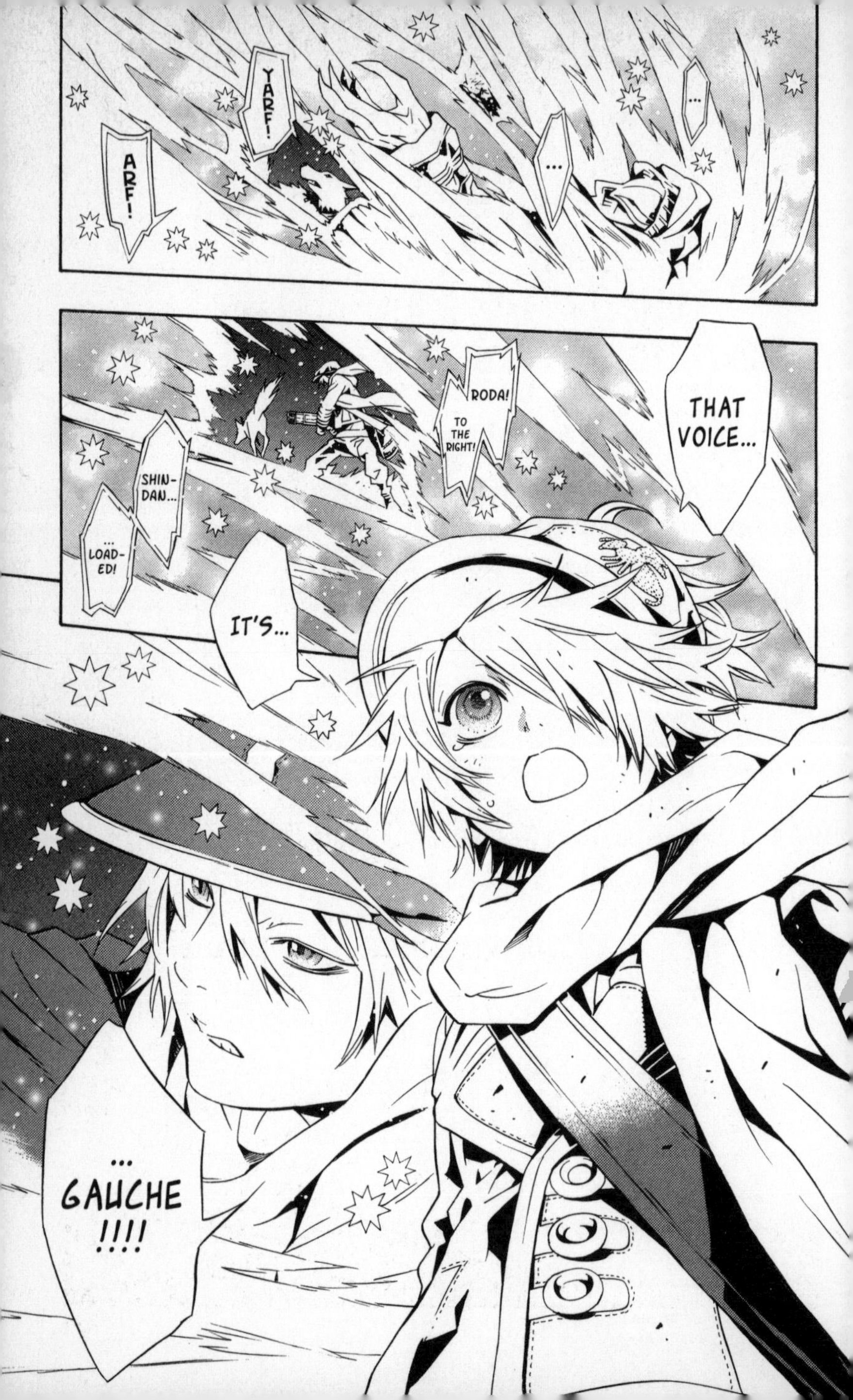
...
...
YARF!
ARF!
THAT VOICE...
RODA! TO THE RIGHT!
SHIN-DAN...
... LOADED!
IT'S...
... GAUCHE !!!!

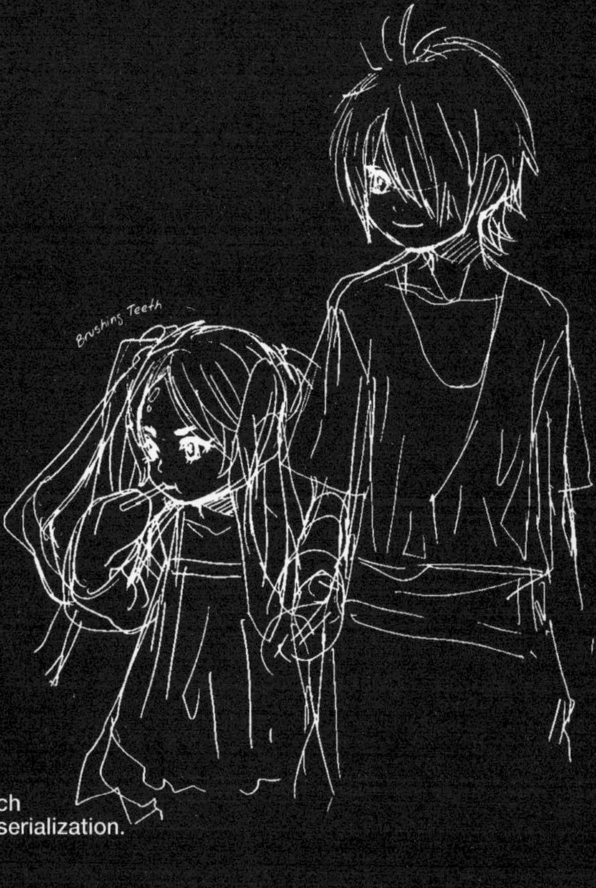
Brushing Teeth

A rough sketch
done before serialization.

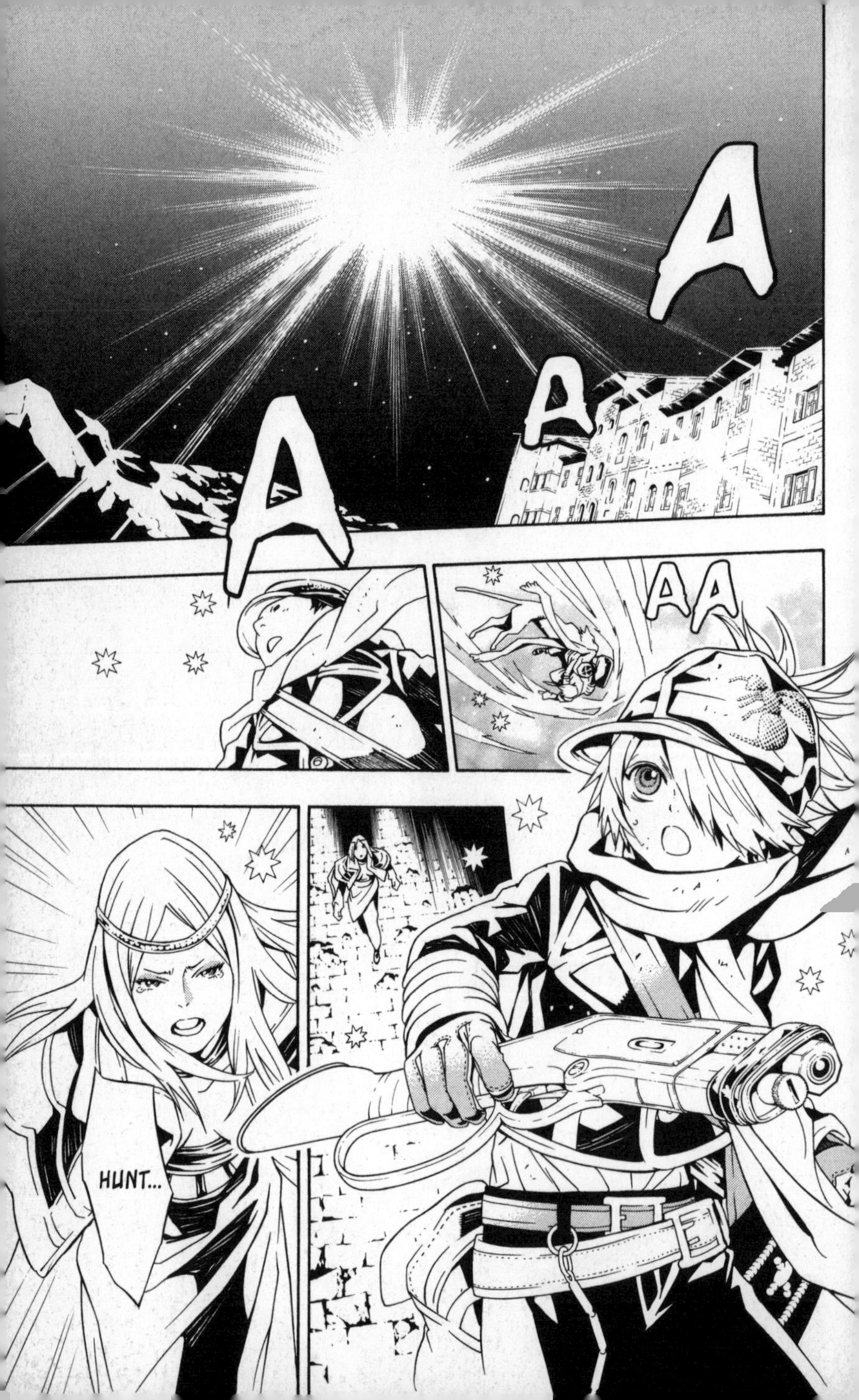
A
A
A
A
AA
HUNT...

Chapter 16: The Man Who Could Not Become Spirit

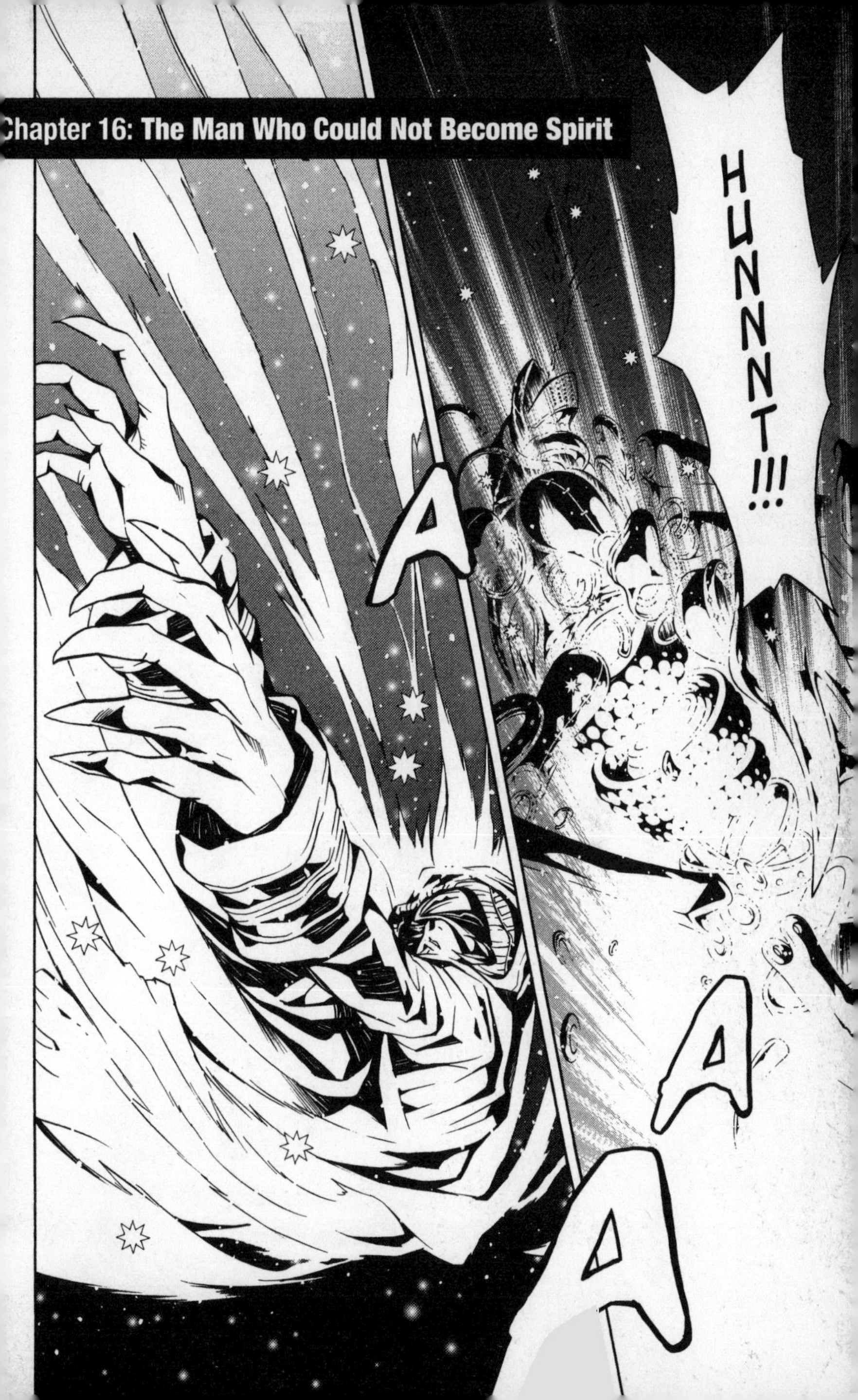
HUNNNT!!!
AAA

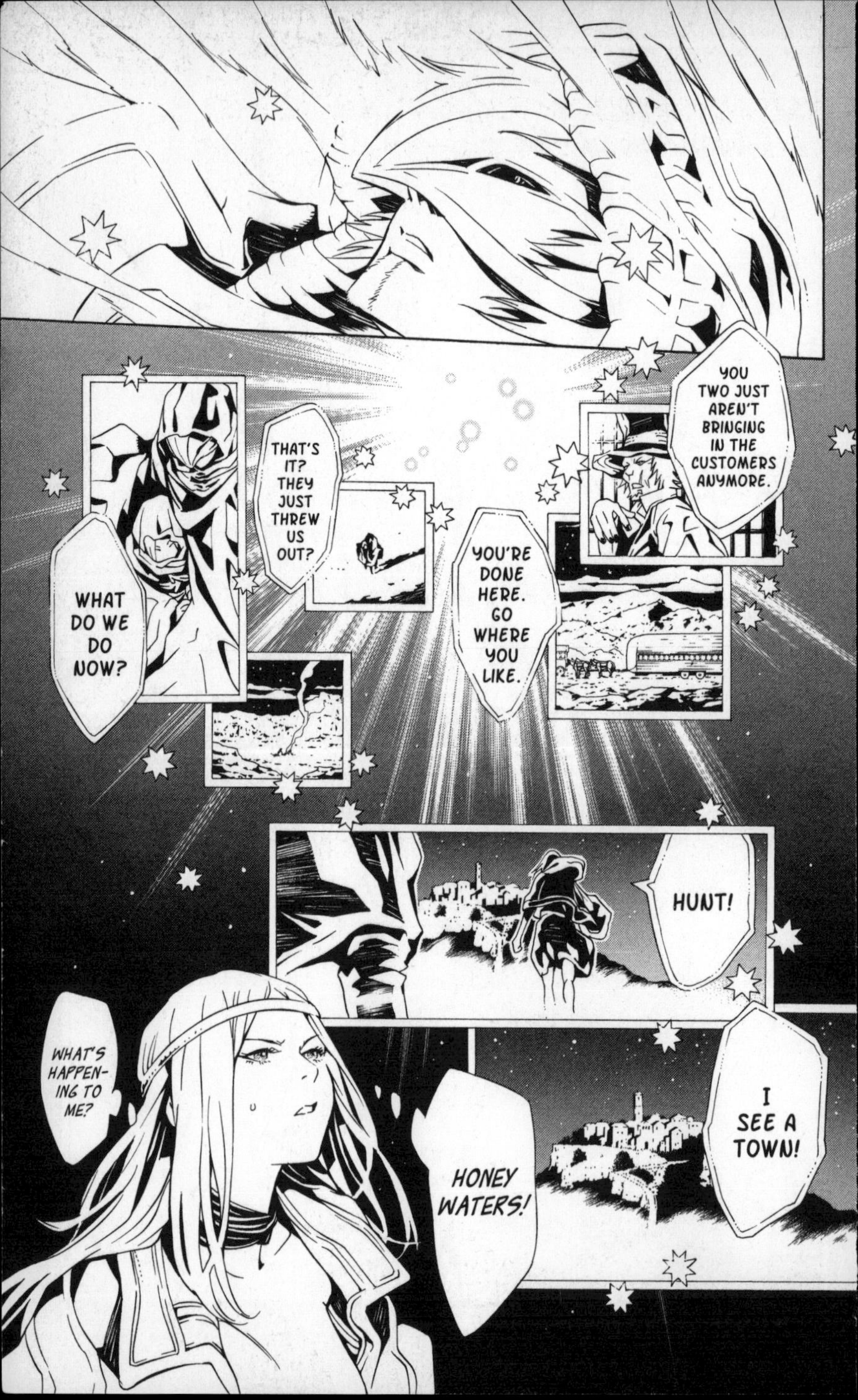
YOU TWO JUST AREN'T BRINGING IN THE CUSTOMERS ANYMORE.
YOU'RE DONE HERE. GO WHERE YOU LIKE.
THAT'S IT? THEY JUST THREW US OUT?
WHAT DO WE DO NOW?
HUNT!
I SEE A TOWN!
HONEY WATERS!
WHAT'S HAPPEN-ING TO ME?

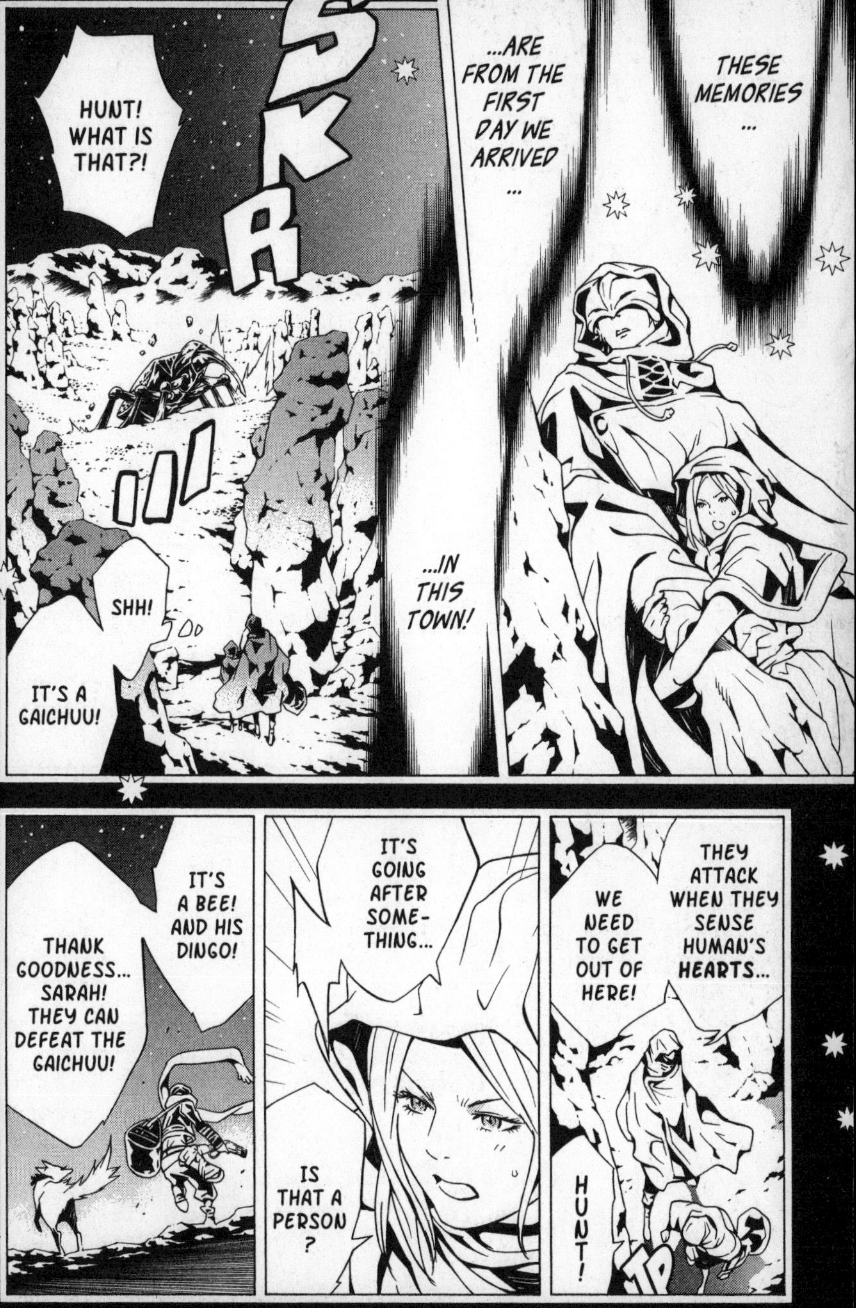
THESE MEMORIES ...
...ARE FROM THE FIRST DAY WE ARRIVED ...
...IN THIS TOWN!
HUNT! WHAT IS THAT?!
SKR
SHH!
IT'S A GAICHUU!
THEY ATTACK WHEN THEY SENSE HUMAN'S HEARTS...
WE NEED TO GET OUT OF HERE!
HUNT!
IT'S GOING AFTER SOME-THING...
IS THAT A PERSON?
IT'S A BEE! AND HIS DINGO!
THANK GOODNESS... SARAH! THEY CAN DEFEAT THE GAICHUU!

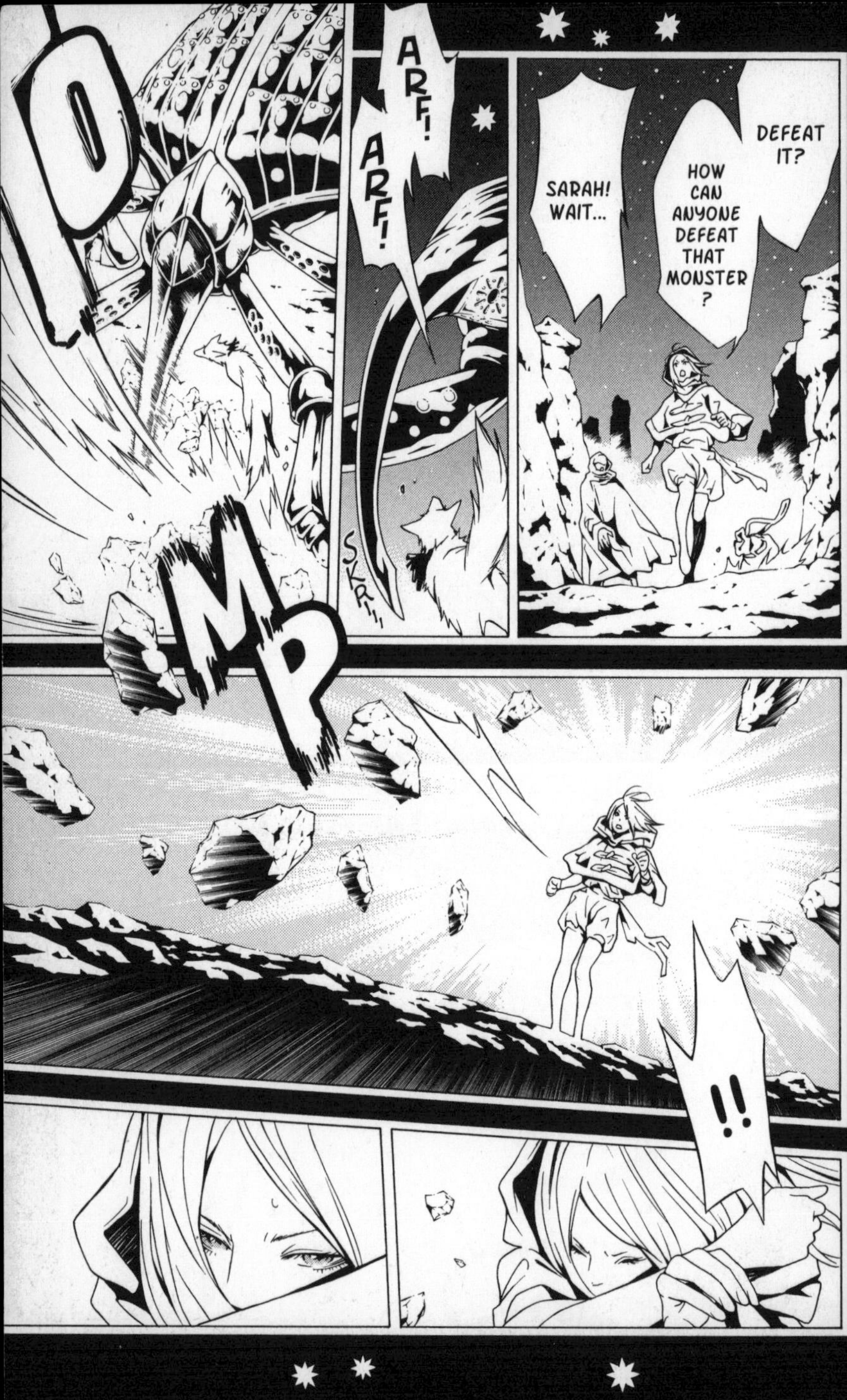
DEFEAT IT?
HOW CAN ANYONE DEFEAT THAT MONSTER?
SARAH! WAIT...
ARF!
ARF!
SKR
!!

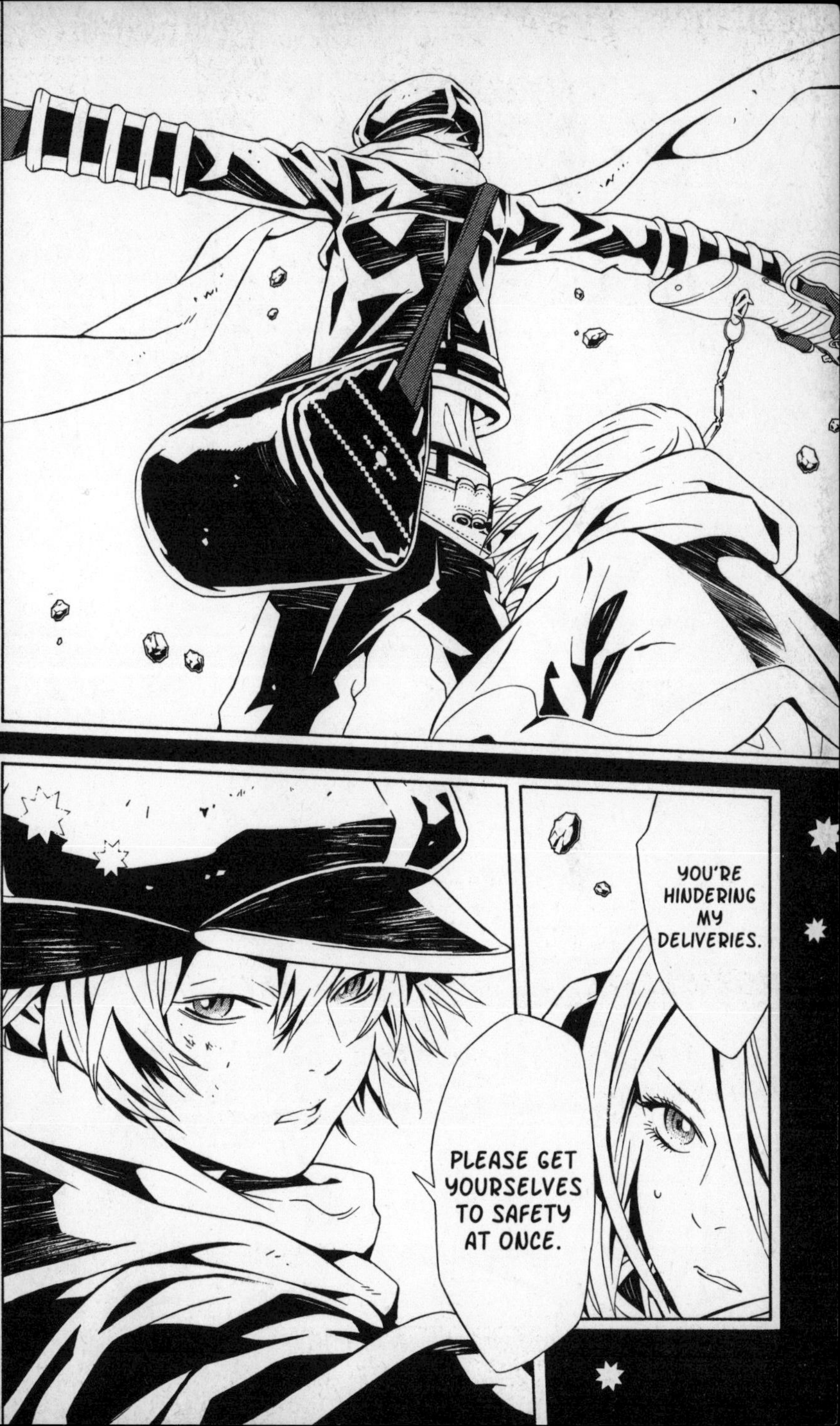
YOU'RE HINDERING MY DELIVERIES.
PLEASE GET YOURSELVES TO SAFETY AT ONCE.

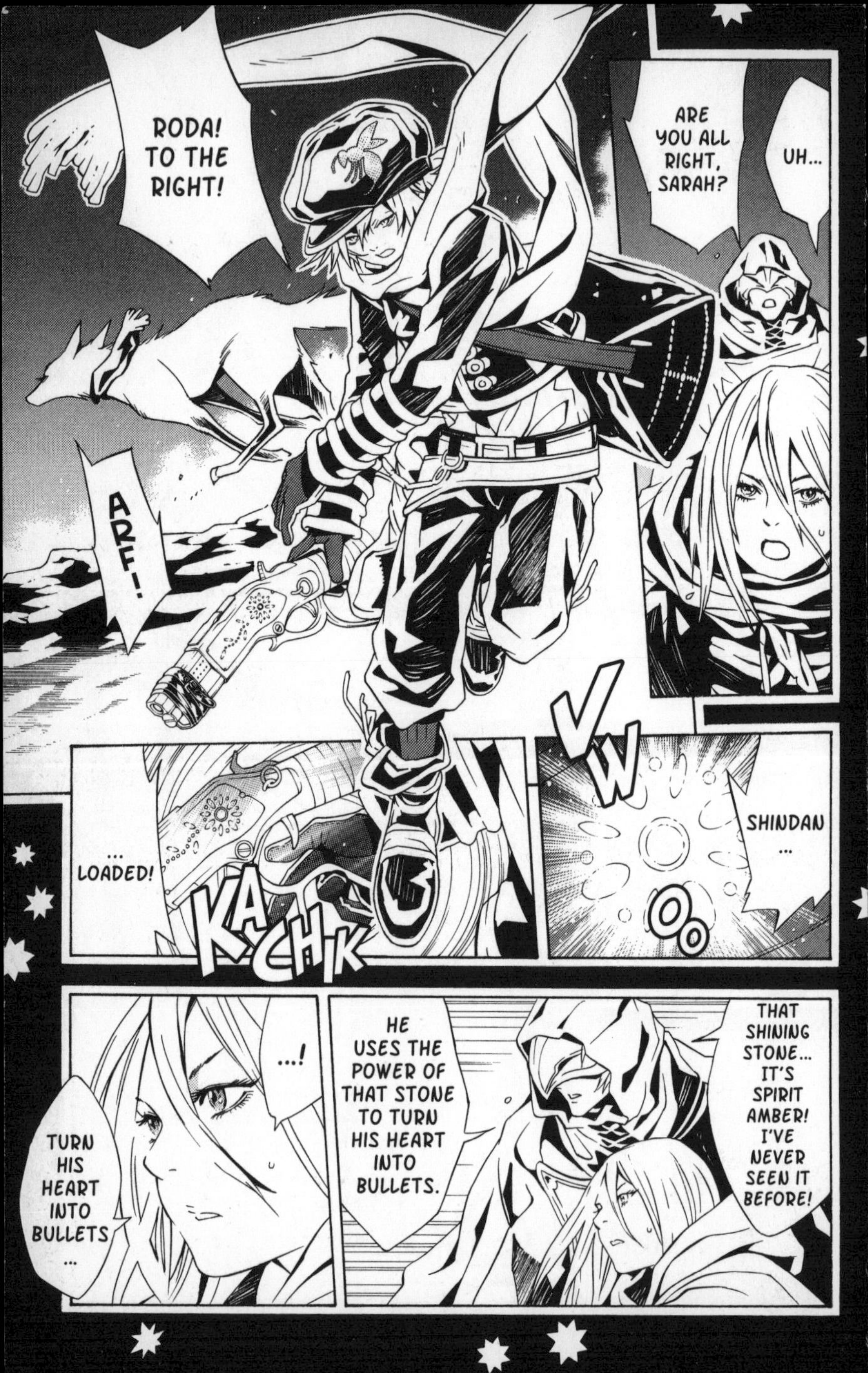
ARE YOU ALL RIGHT, SARAH?
UH...
RODA! TO THE RIGHT!
ARF!
VWOO
SHINDAN ...
... LOADED!
KACHIK
THAT SHINING STONE... IT'S SPIRIT AMBER! I'VE NEVER SEEN IT BEFORE!
HE USES THE POWER OF THAT STONE TO TURN HIS HEART INTO BULLETS.
...!
TURN HIS HEART INTO BULLETS ...

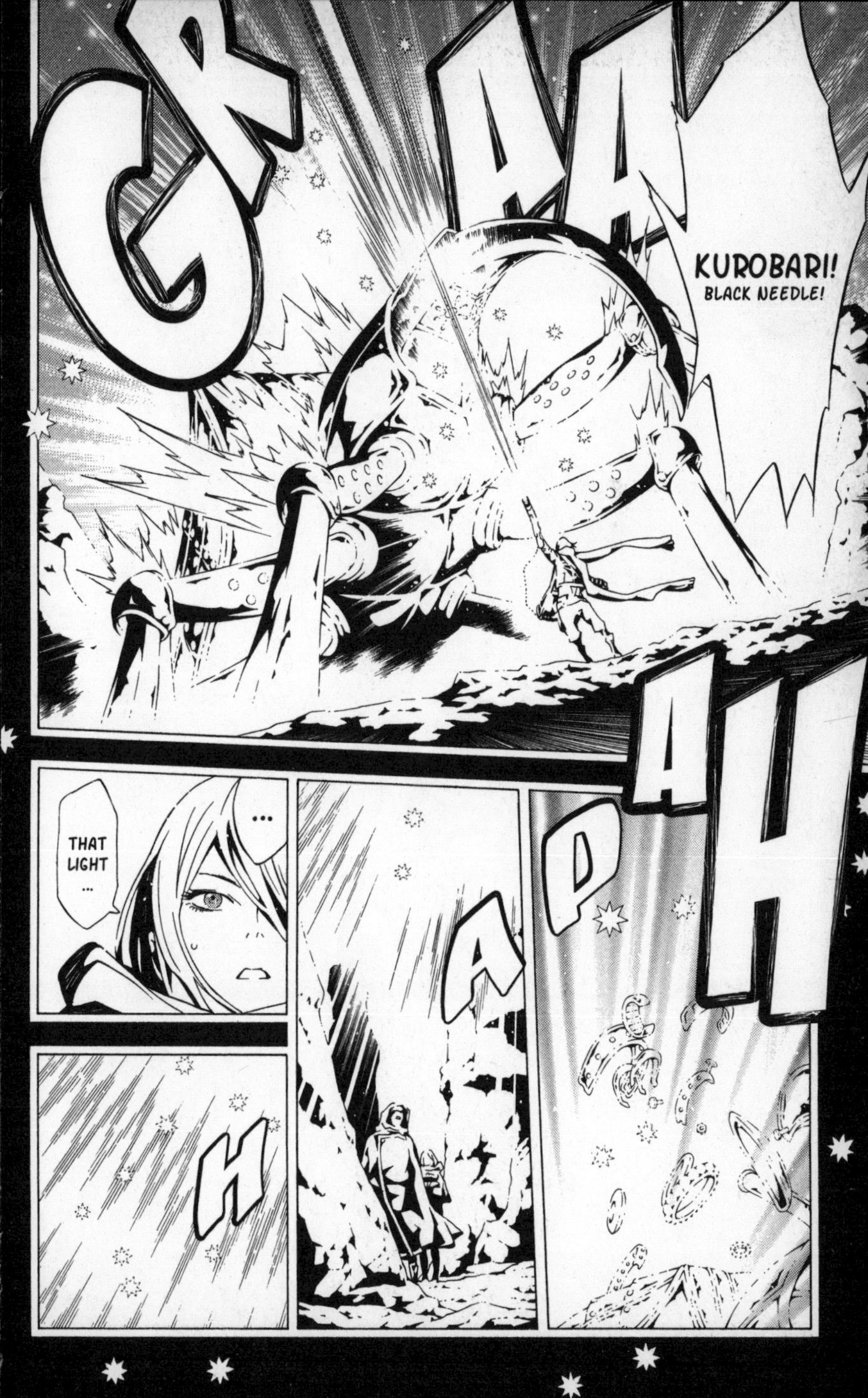
CRAAASH
KUROBARI!
BLACK NEEDLE!
...
THAT LIGHT ...
APAH

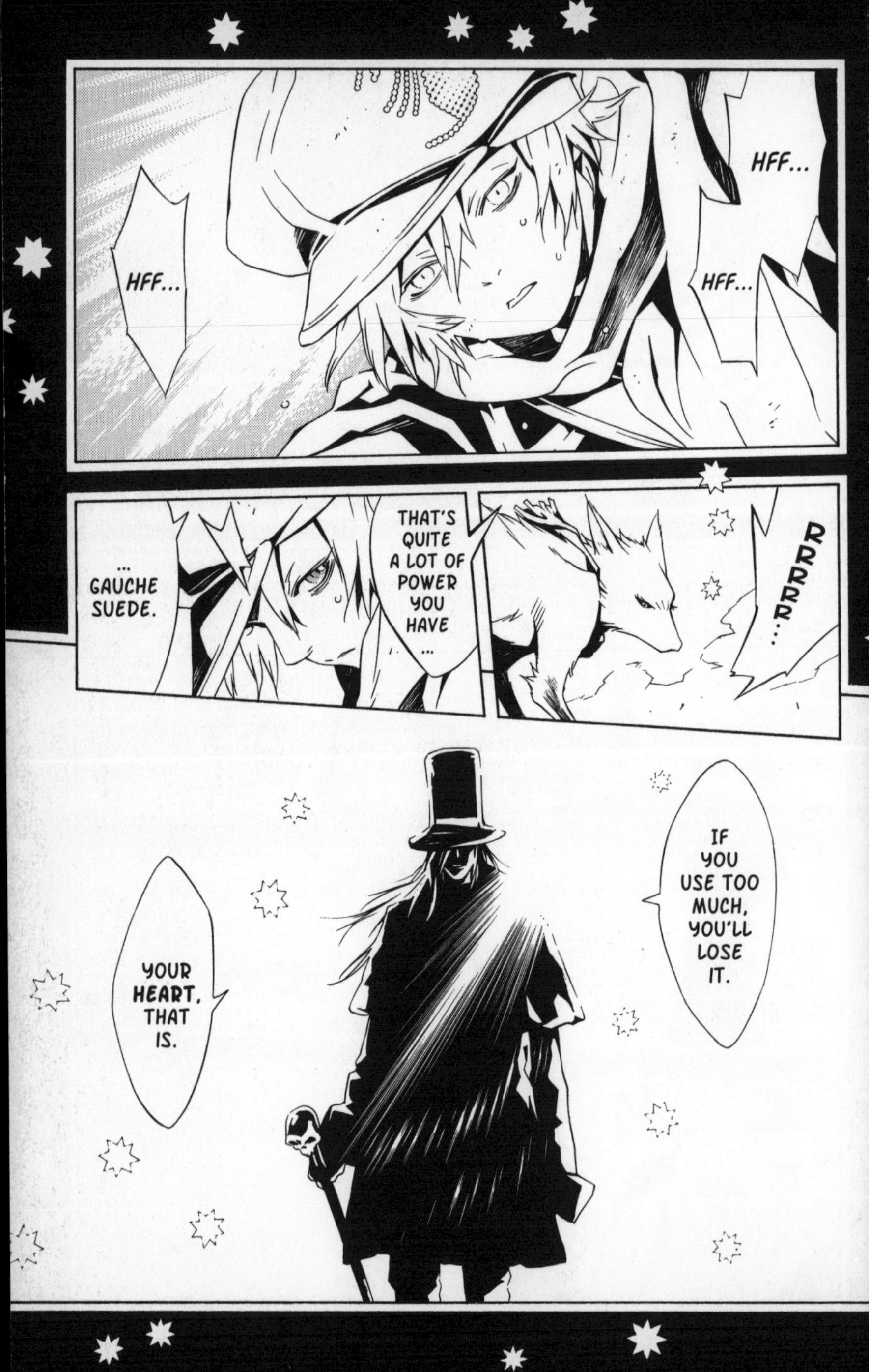
HFF...
HFF...
HFF...
RRRRR...
THAT'S QUITE A LOT OF POWER YOU HAVE ...
... GAUCHE SUEDE.
IF YOU USE TOO MUCH, YOU'LL LOSE IT.
YOUR HEART, THAT IS.

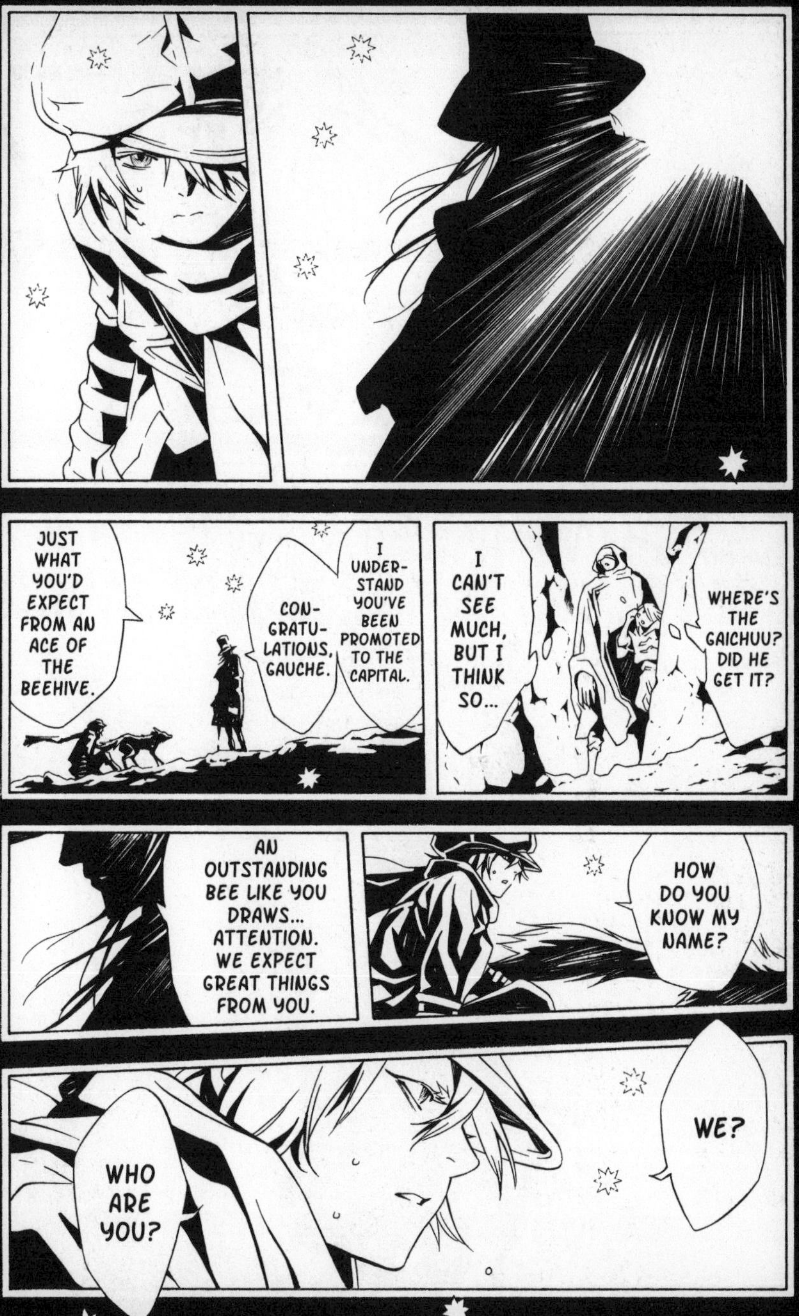
WHERE'S THE GAICHUU? DID HE GET IT?
I CAN'T SEE MUCH, BUT I THINK SO...
I UNDER-STAND YOU'VE BEEN PROMOTED TO THE CAPITAL.
CON-GRATU-LATIONS, GAUCHE.
JUST WHAT YOU'D EXPECT FROM AN ACE OF THE BEEHIVE.
HOW DO YOU KNOW MY NAME?
AN OUTSTANDING BEE LIKE YOU DRAWS... ATTENTION. WE EXPECT GREAT THINGS FROM YOU.
WE?
WHO ARE YOU?

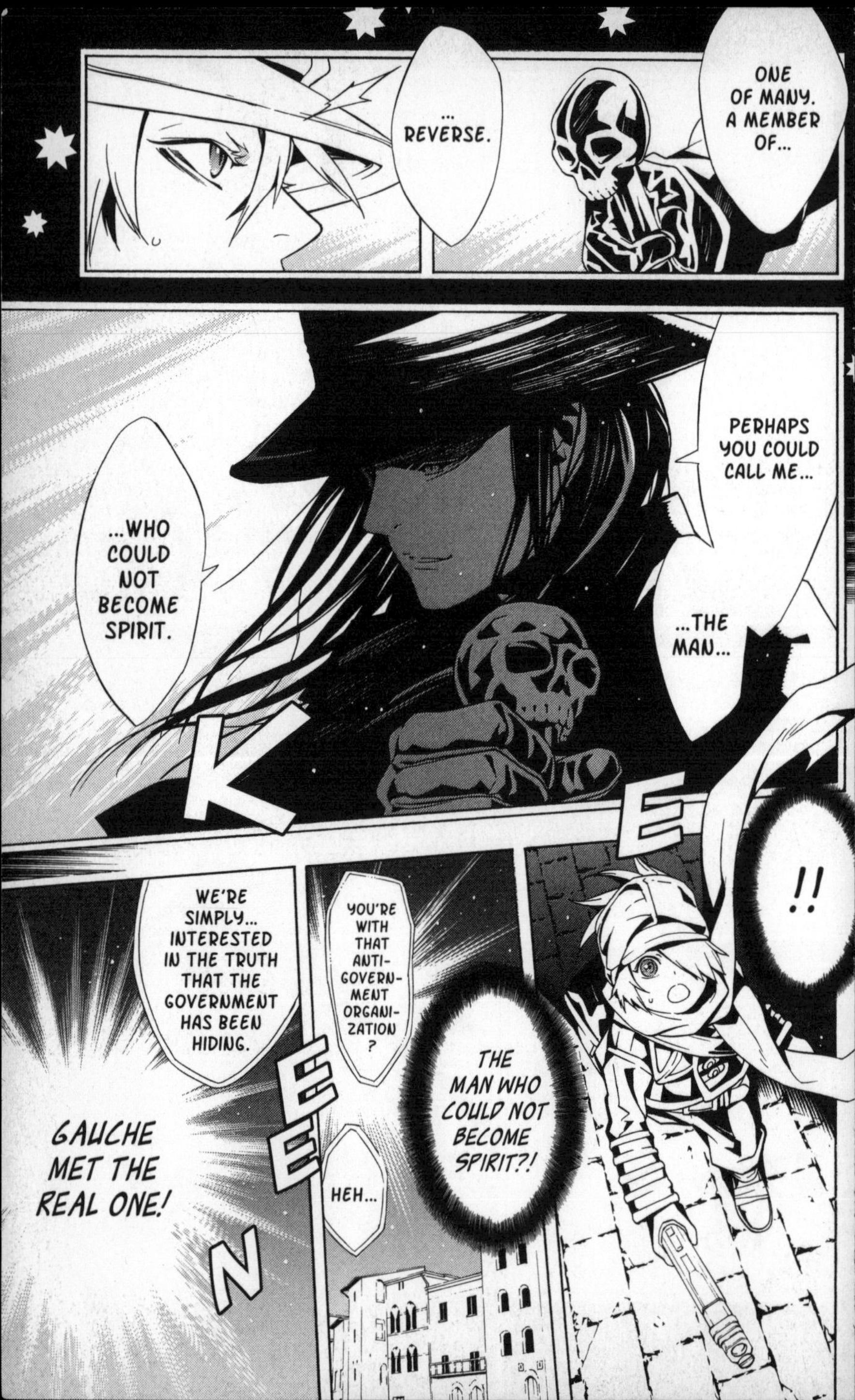
ONE OF MANY. A MEMBER OF...
... REVERSE.
PERHAPS YOU COULD CALL ME...
...THE MAN...
...WHO COULD NOT BECOME SPIRIT.
KEEEN
!!
THE MAN WHO COULD NOT BECOME SPIRIT?!
YOU'RE WITH THAT ANTI-GOVERNMENT ORGANIZATION?
HEH...
WE'RE SIMPLY... INTERESTED IN THE TRUTH THAT THE GOVERNMENT HAS BEEN HIDING.
GAUCHE MET THE REAL ONE!

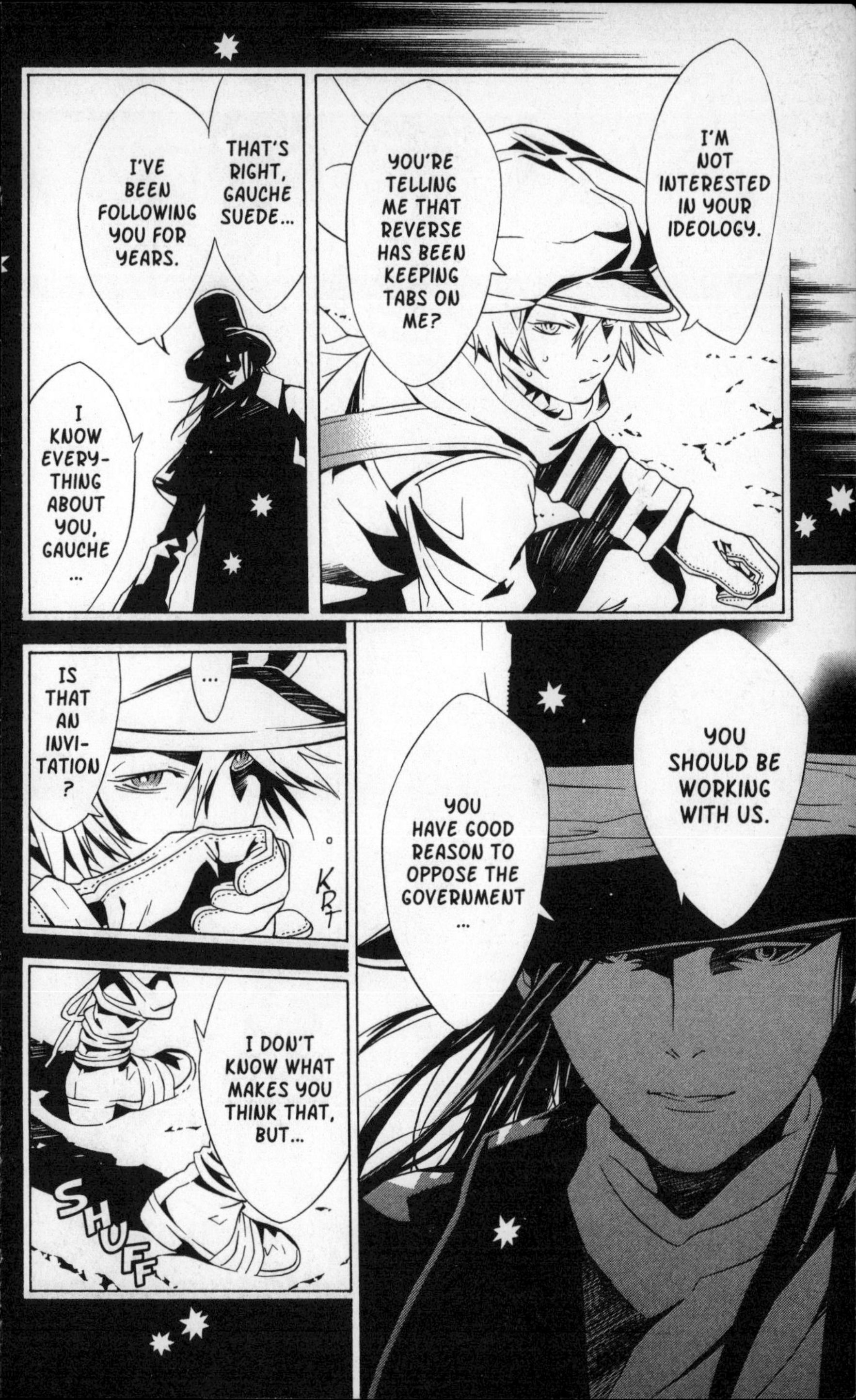
I'M NOT INTERESTED IN YOUR IDEOLOGY.
YOU'RE TELLING ME THAT REVERSE HAS BEEN KEEPING TABS ON ME?
THAT'S RIGHT, GAUCHE SUEDE...
I'VE BEEN FOLLOWING YOU FOR YEARS.
I KNOW EVERYTHING ABOUT YOU, GAUCHE...
YOU SHOULD BE WORKING WITH US.
YOU HAVE GOOD REASON TO OPPOSE THE GOVERNMENT...
...
IS THAT AN INVITATION?
KRT
I DON'T KNOW WHAT MAKES YOU THINK THAT, BUT...
SHUFF

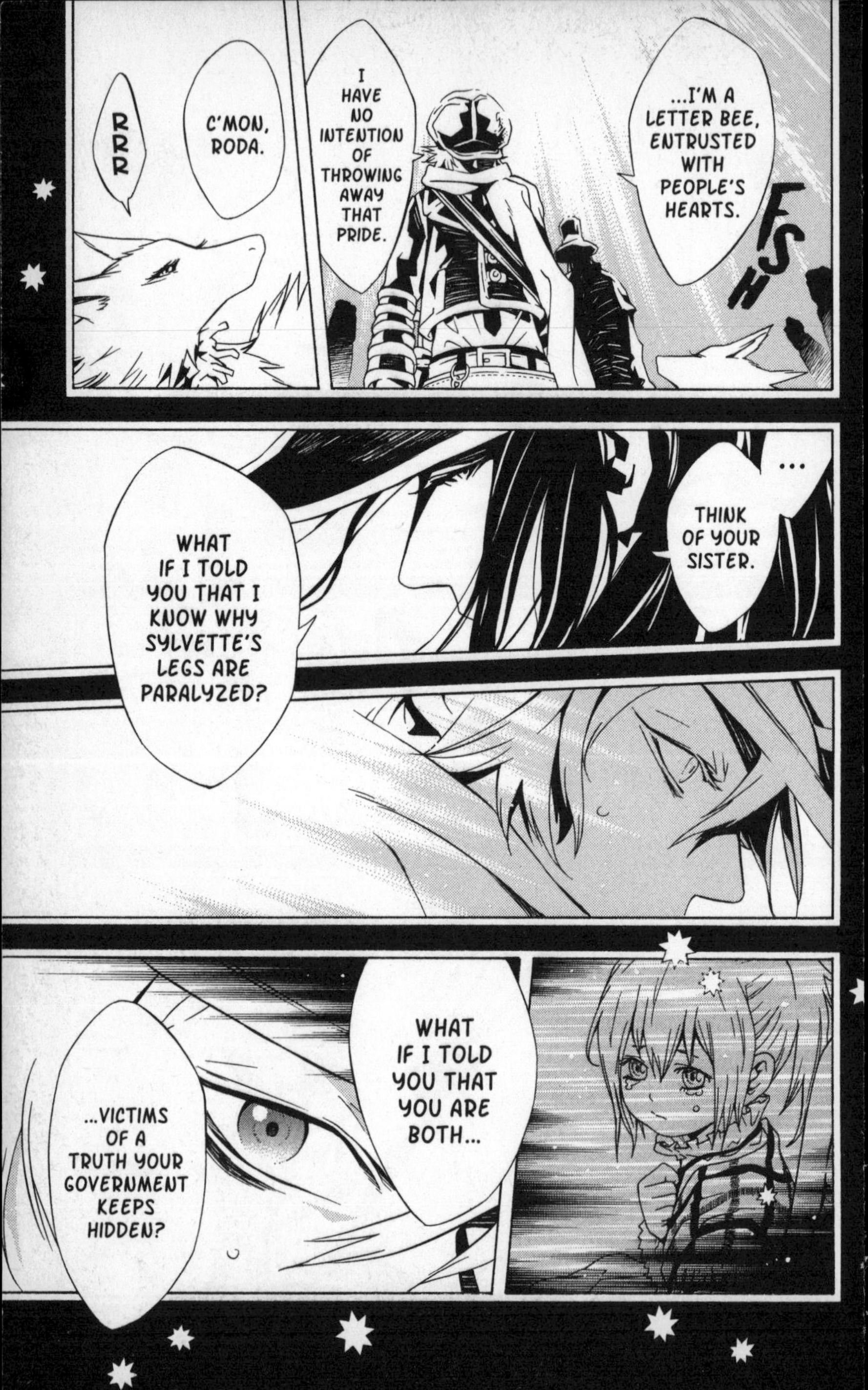
...I'M A LETTER BEE, ENTRUSTED WITH PEOPLE'S HEARTS.
FSH
I HAVE NO INTENTION OF THROWING AWAY THAT PRIDE.
C'MON, RODA.
RRR
...
THINK OF YOUR SISTER.
WHAT IF I TOLD YOU THAT I KNOW WHY SYLVETTE'S LEGS ARE PARALYZED?
WHAT IF I TOLD YOU THAT YOU ARE BOTH...
...VICTIMS OF A TRUTH YOUR GOVERNMENT KEEPS HIDDEN?

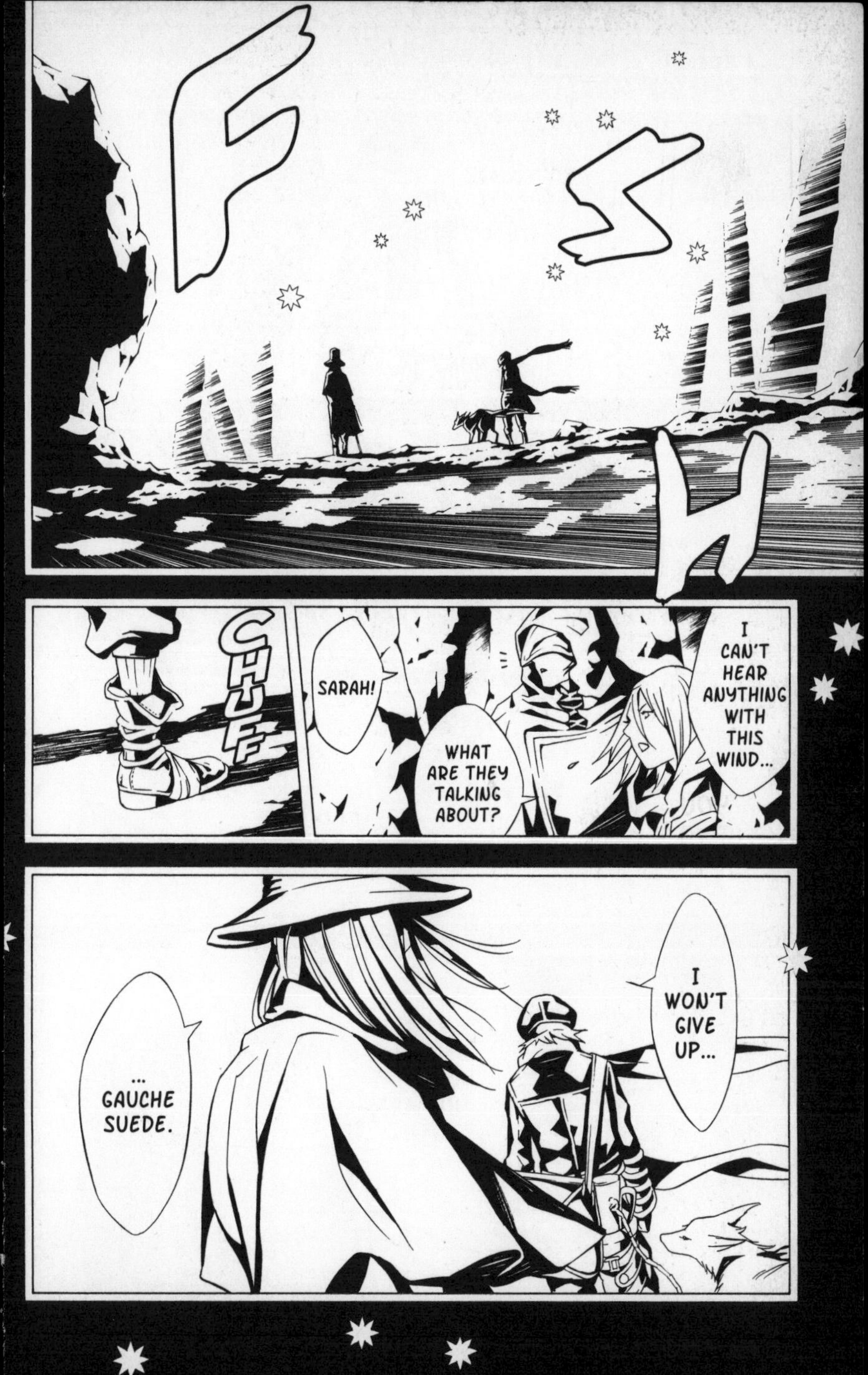
FSSH
SARAH!
WHAT ARE THEY TALKING ABOUT?
I CAN'T HEAR ANYTHING WITH THIS WIND...
CHUFF
I WON'T GIVE UP...
... GAUCHE SUEDE.

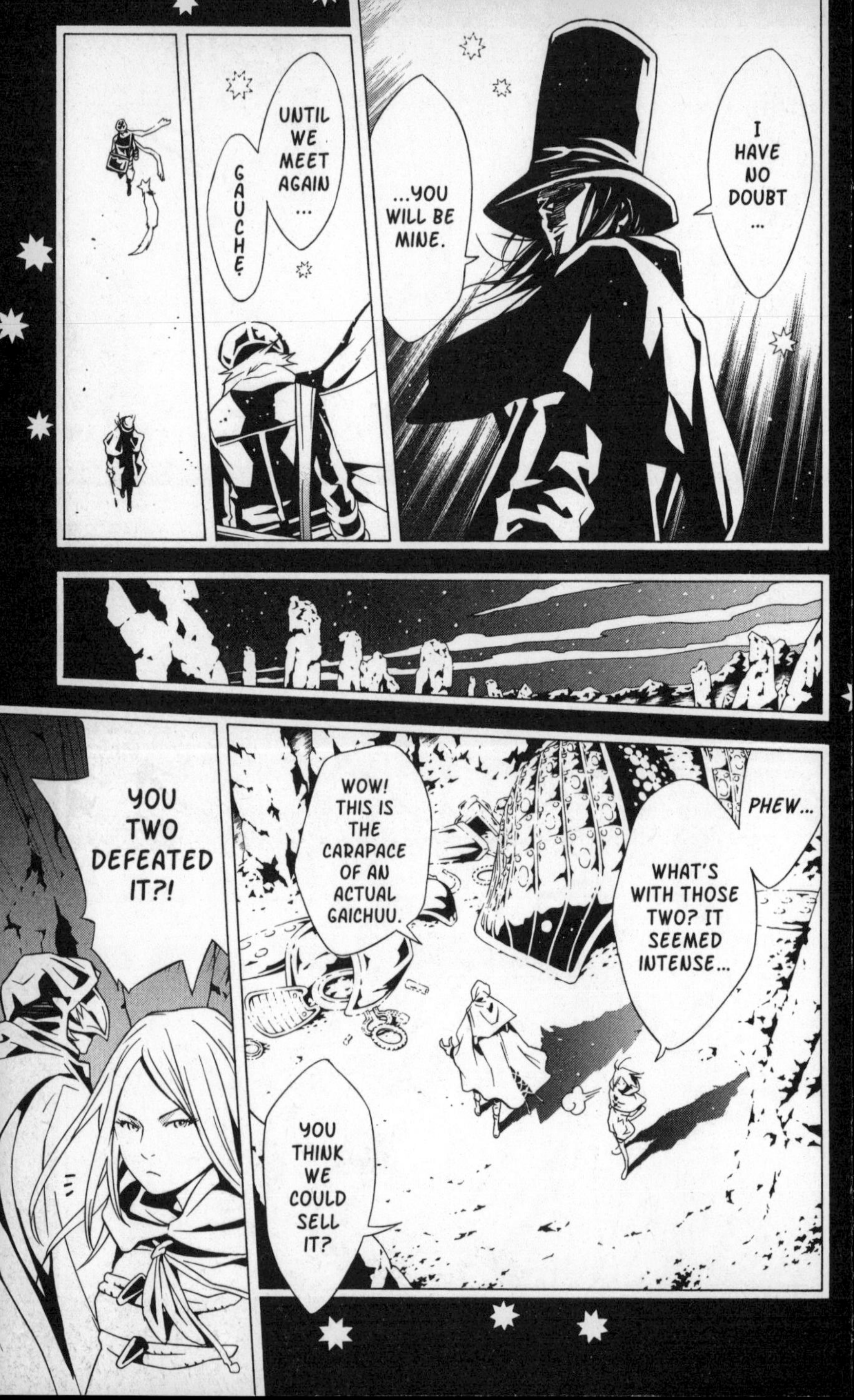
I HAVE NO DOUBT...
...YOU WILL BE MINE.
UNTIL WE MEET AGAIN...
GAUCHE.
PHEW...
WHAT'S WITH THOSE TWO? IT SEEMED INTENSE...
WOW! THIS IS THE CARAPACE OF AN ACTUAL GAICHUU.
YOU THINK WE COULD SELL IT?
YOU TWO DEFEATED IT?!

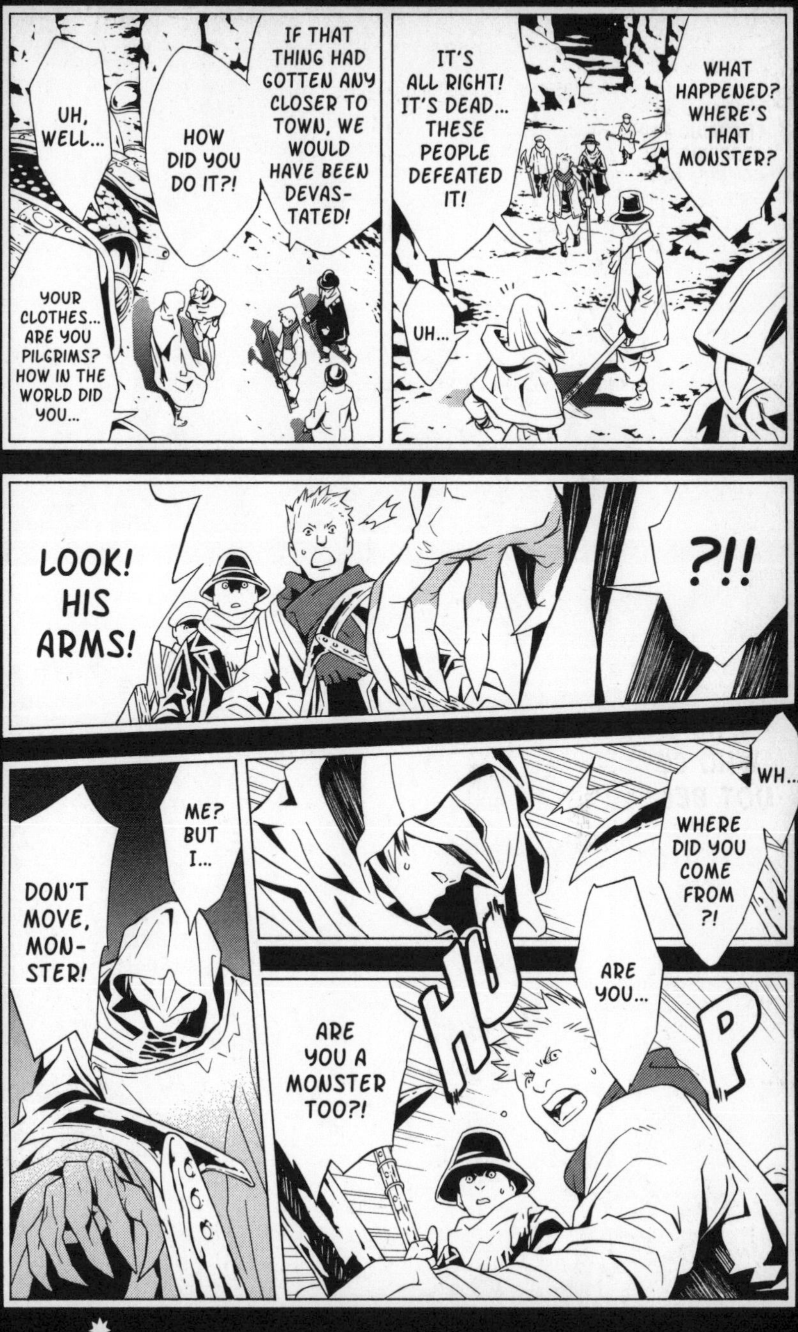
WHAT HAPPENED? WHERE'S THAT MONSTER?
IT'S ALL RIGHT! IT'S DEAD... THESE PEOPLE DEFEATED IT!
UH...
IF THAT THING HAD GOTTEN ANY CLOSER TO TOWN, WE WOULD HAVE BEEN DEVASTATED!
HOW DID YOU DO IT?!
UH, WELL...
YOUR CLOTHES... ARE YOU PILGRIMS? HOW IN THE WORLD DID YOU...
?!!
LOOK! HIS ARMS!
WH... WHERE DID YOU COME FROM ?!
ARE YOU...
HUP
ARE YOU A MONSTER TOO?!
ME? BUT I...
DON'T MOVE, MONSTER!

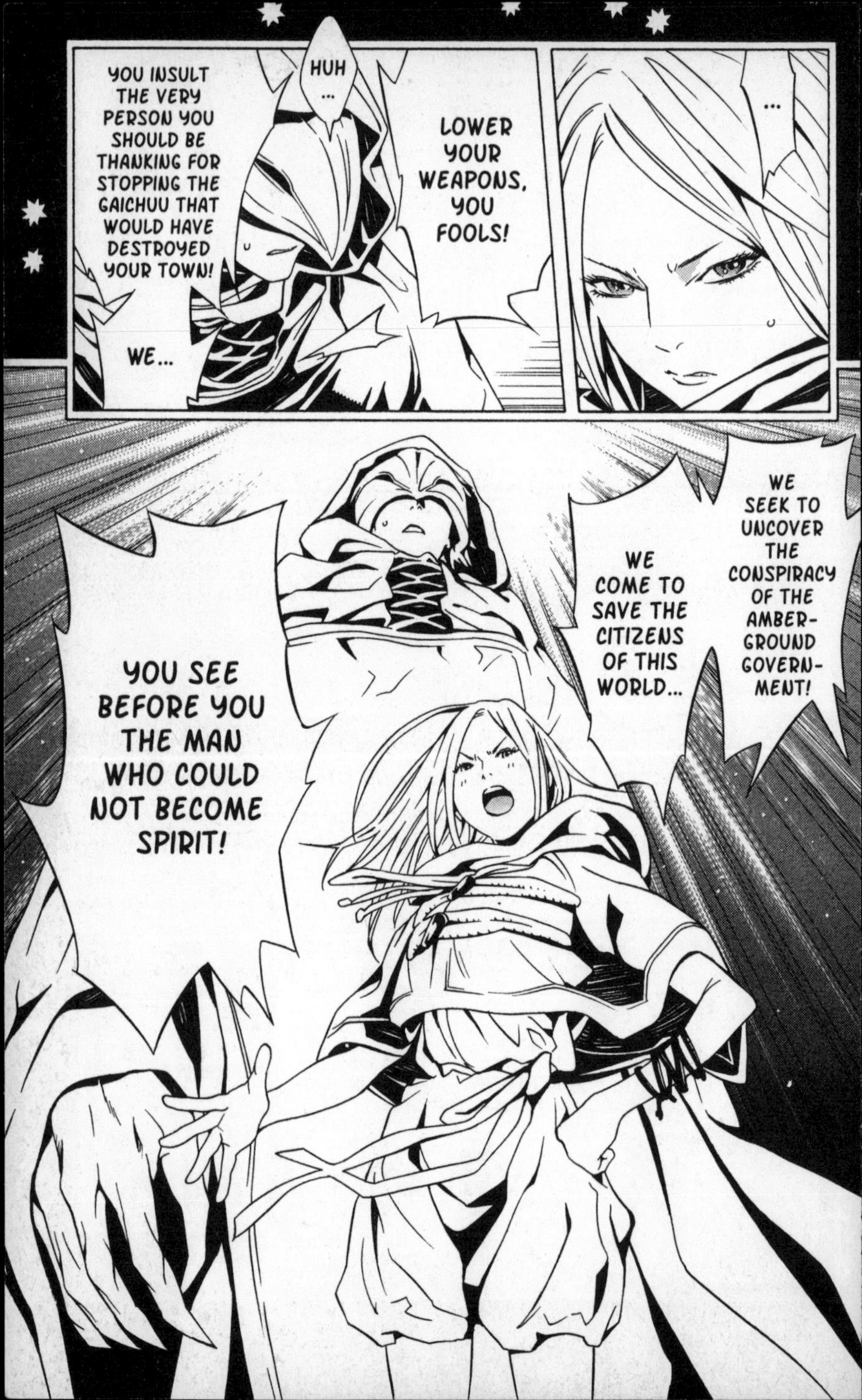
...
LOWER YOUR WEAPONS, YOU FOOLS!
HUH ...
YOU INSULT THE VERY PERSON YOU SHOULD BE THANKING FOR STOPPING THE GAICHUU THAT WOULD HAVE DESTROYED YOUR TOWN!
WE...
WE SEEK TO UNCOVER THE CONSPIRACY OF THE AMBER-GROUND GOVERN-MENT!
WE COME TO SAVE THE CITIZENS OF THIS WORLD...
YOU SEE BEFORE YOU THE MAN WHO COULD NOT BECOME SPIRIT!

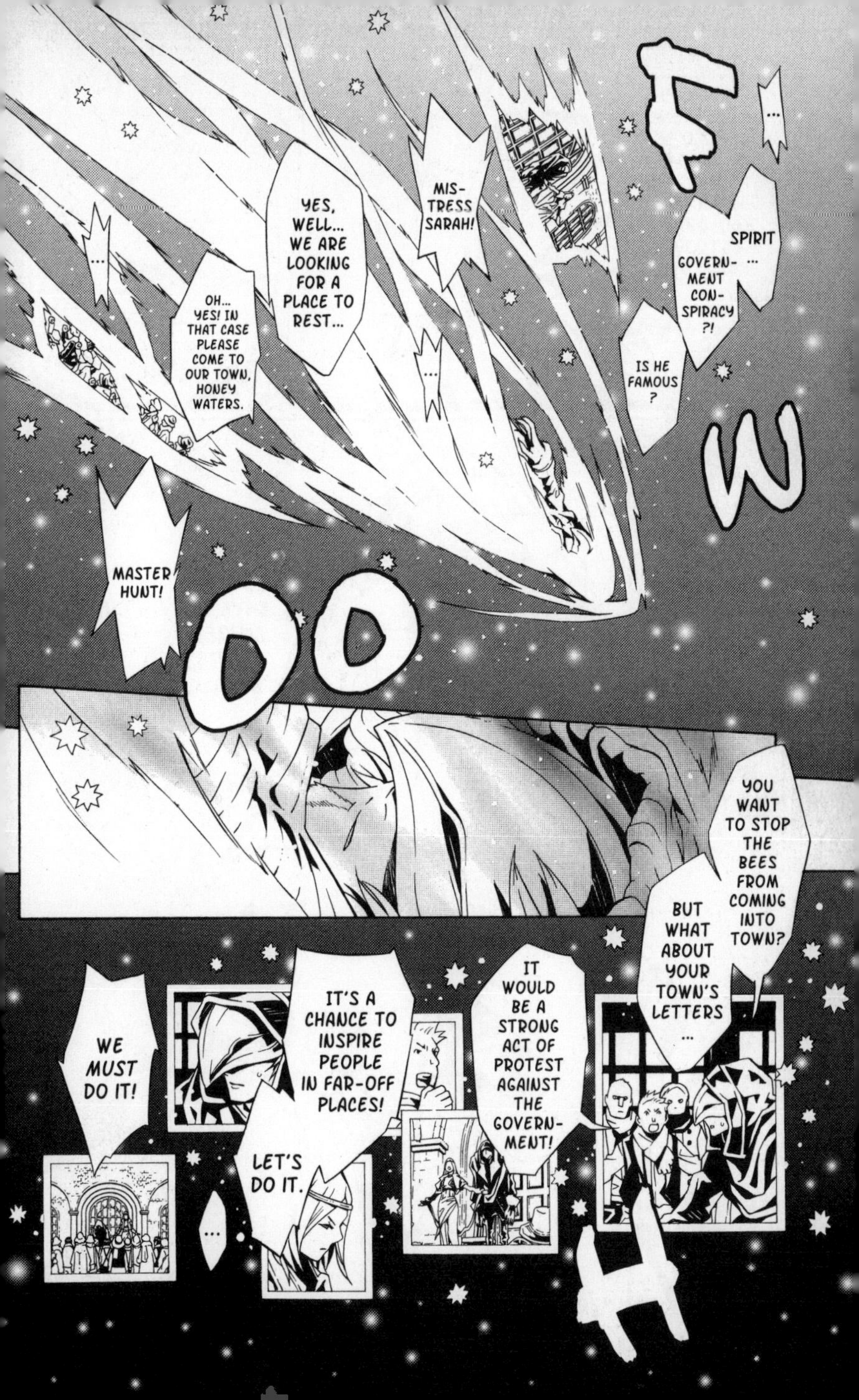
F
...
SPIRIT ...
GOVERNMENT CONSPIRACY ?!
IS HE FAMOUS ?
W
MISTRESS SARAH!
YES, WELL... WE ARE LOOKING FOR A PLACE TO REST...
...
OH... YES! IN THAT CASE PLEASE COME TO OUR TOWN, HONEY WATERS.
...
MASTER HUNT!
OO
YOU WANT TO STOP THE BEES FROM COMING INTO TOWN?
BUT WHAT ABOUT YOUR TOWN'S LETTERS ...
IT WOULD BE A STRONG ACT OF PROTEST AGAINST THE GOVERNMENT!
IT'S A CHANCE TO INSPIRE PEOPLE IN FAR-OFF PLACES!
LET'S DO IT.
WE MUST DO IT!
...
H

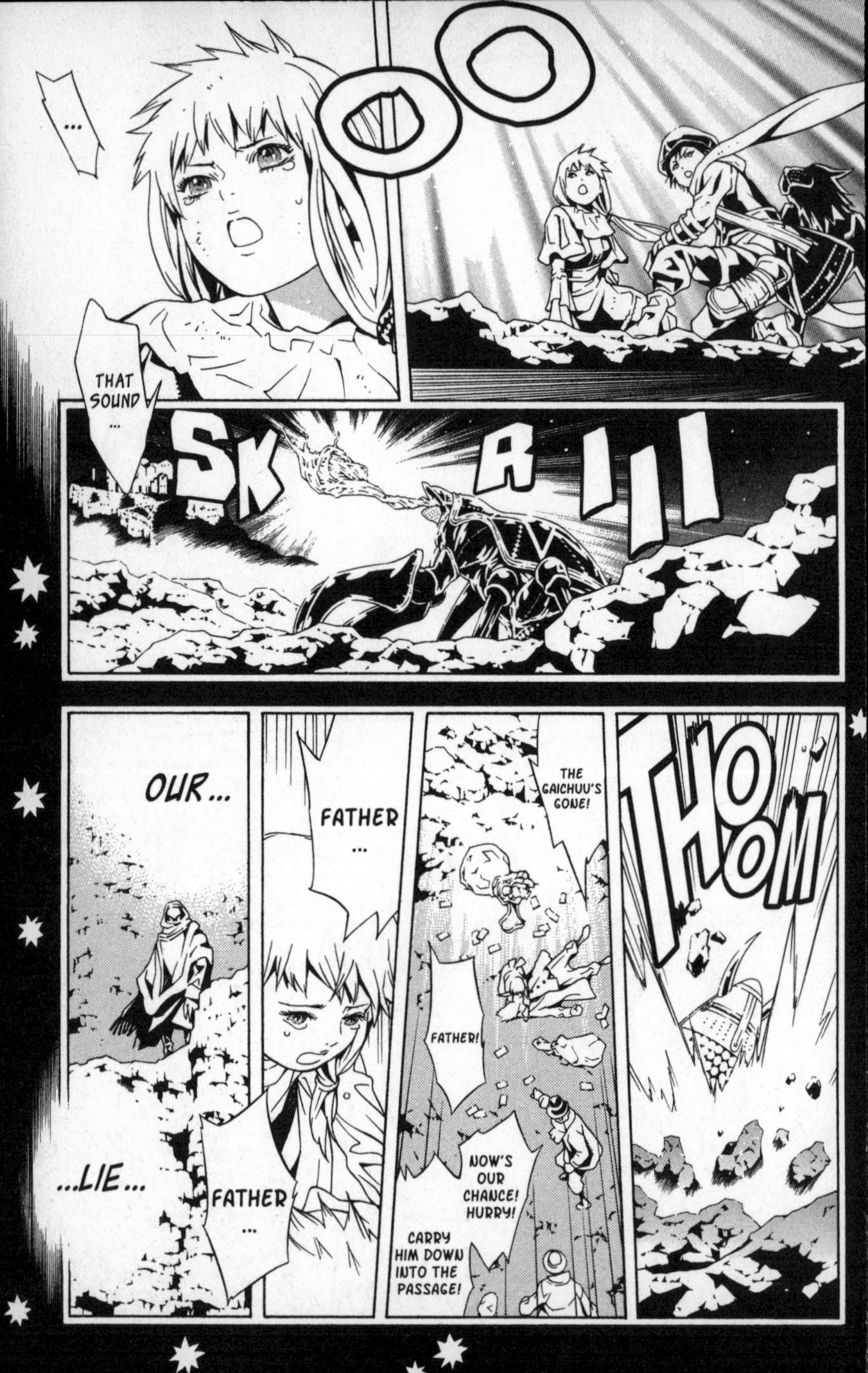
...
THAT SOUND ...
SKRIII
THOOM
THE GAICHUU'S GONE!
FATHER!
NOW'S OUR CHANCE! HURRY!
CARRY HIM DOWN INTO THE PASSAGE!
FATHER ...
FATHER ...
OUR...
...LIE...

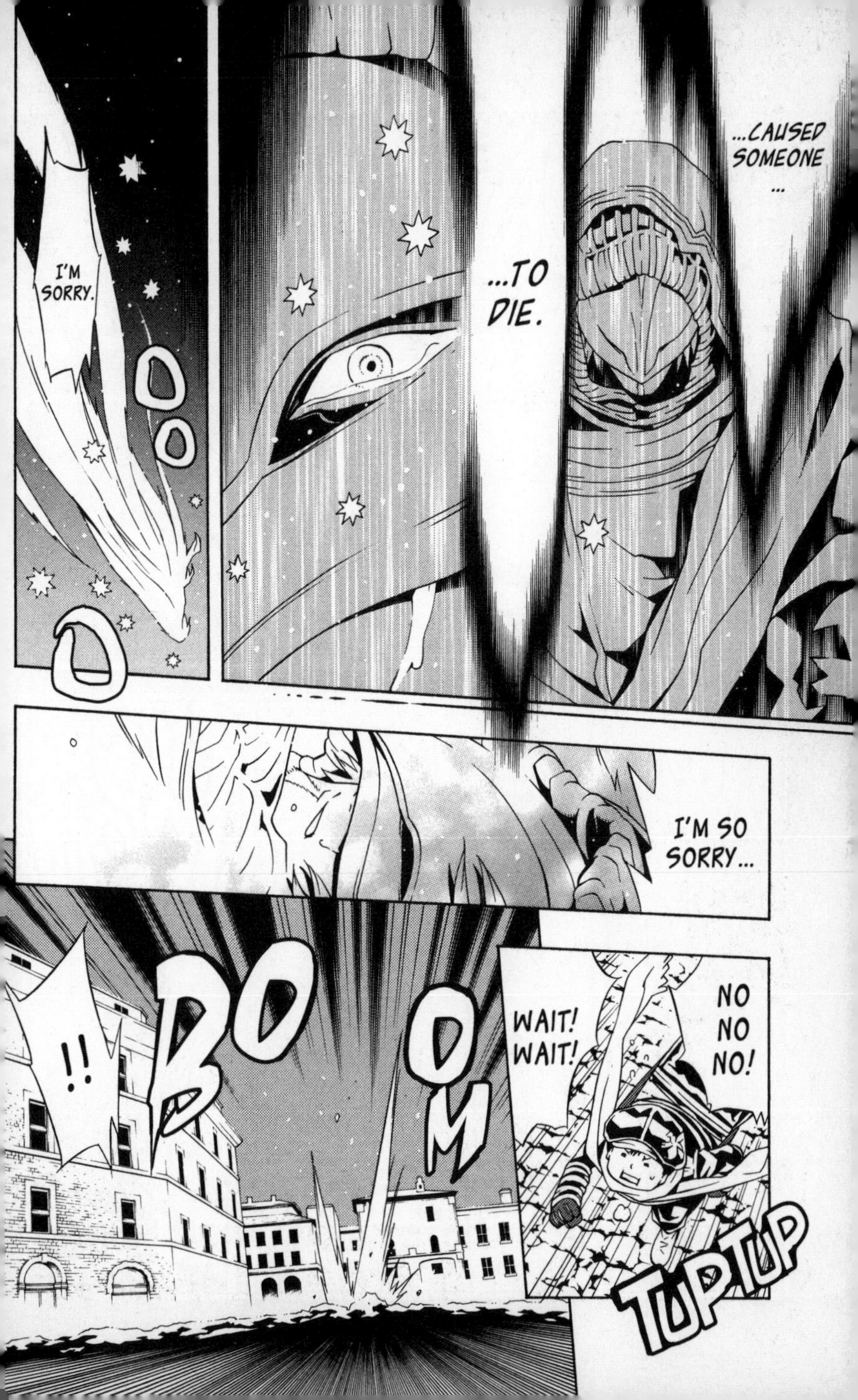
...CAUSED SOMEONE ...
...TO DIE.
I'M SORRY.
OOO
I'M SO SORRY...
NO NO NO!
WAIT! WAIT!
TUPTUP
BOOM
!!

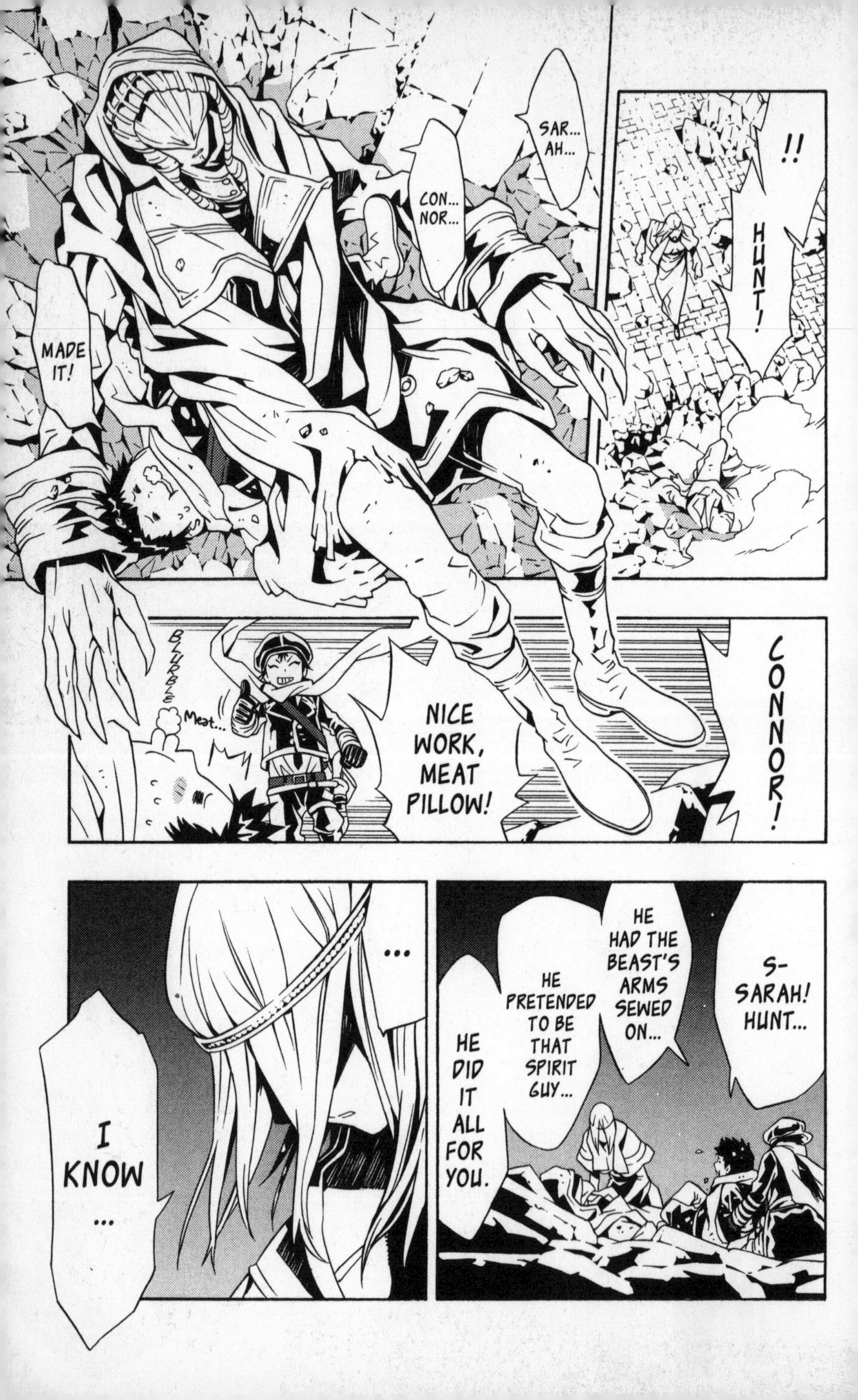
!!
HUNT!
SAR... AH...
CON... NOR...
MADE IT!
CONNOR!
NICE WORK, MEAT PILLOW!
BLURBLE
Meat...
S-SARAH! HUNT...
HE HAD THE BEAST'S ARMS SEWED ON...
HE PRETENDED TO BE THAT SPIRIT GUY...
HE DID IT ALL FOR YOU.
...
I KNOW ...

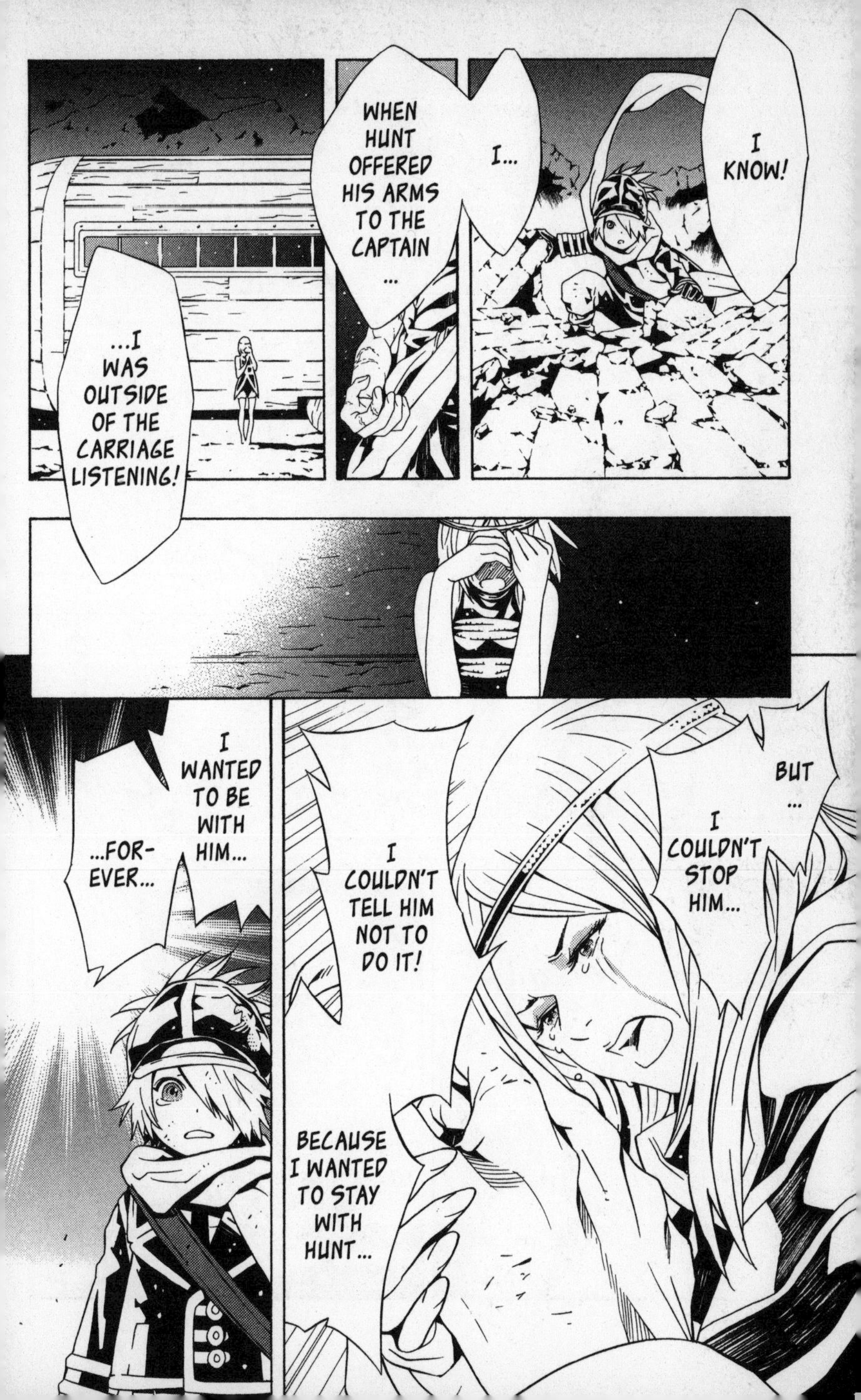
I KNOW!
I...
WHEN HUNT OFFERED HIS ARMS TO THE CAPTAIN ...
...I WAS OUTSIDE OF THE CARRIAGE LISTENING!
BUT ...
I COULDN'T STOP HIM...
I COULDN'T TELL HIM NOT TO DO IT!
BECAUSE I WANTED TO STAY WITH HUNT...
I WANTED TO BE WITH HIM...
...FOR-EVER...

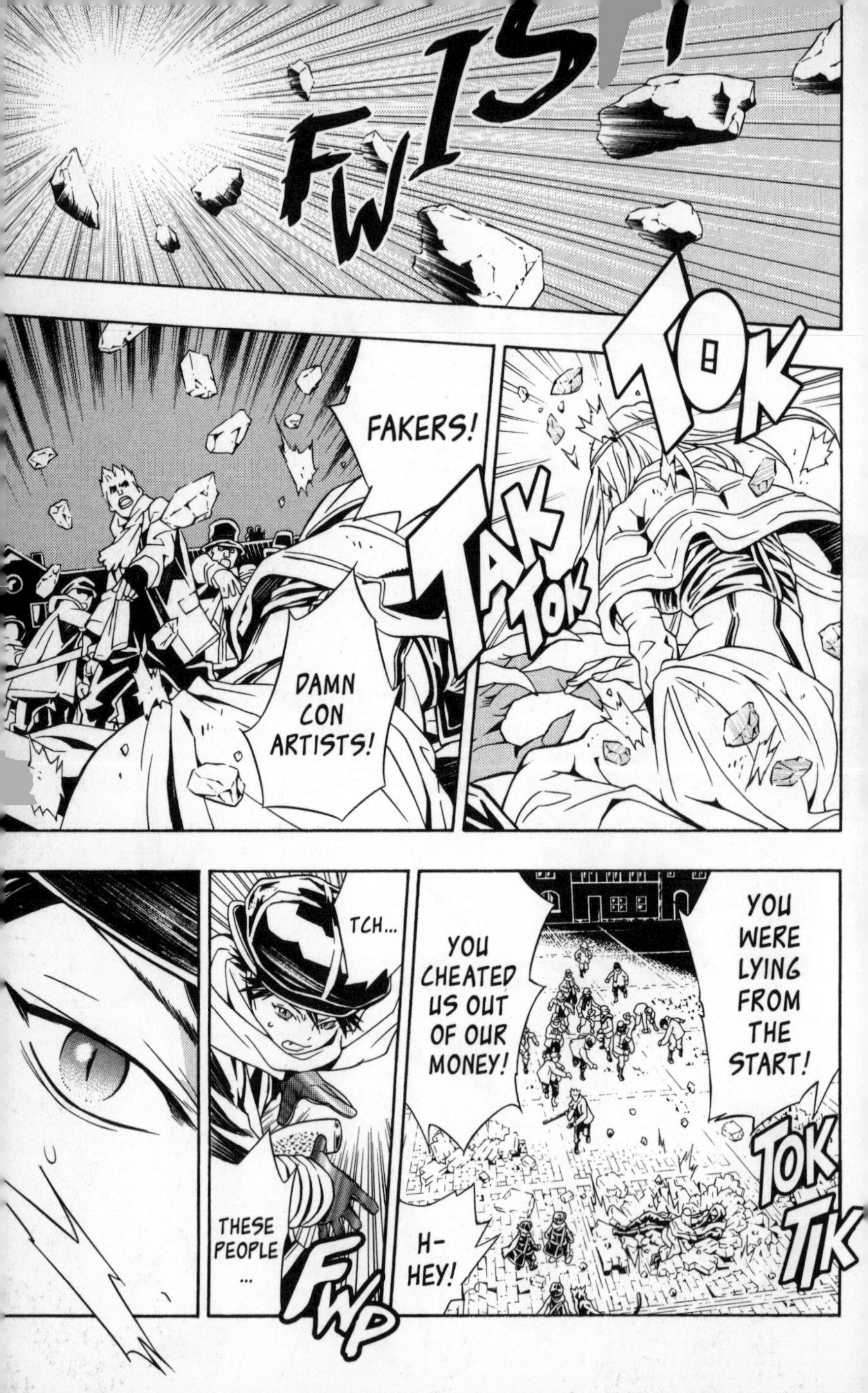
FWIS!
TOK
TAK
TOK
FAKERS!
DAMN CON ARTISTS!
YOU WERE LYING FROM THE START!
YOU CHEATED US OUT OF OUR MONEY!
TOK
TIK
H-HEY!
TCH...
THESE PEOPLE ...
FWP

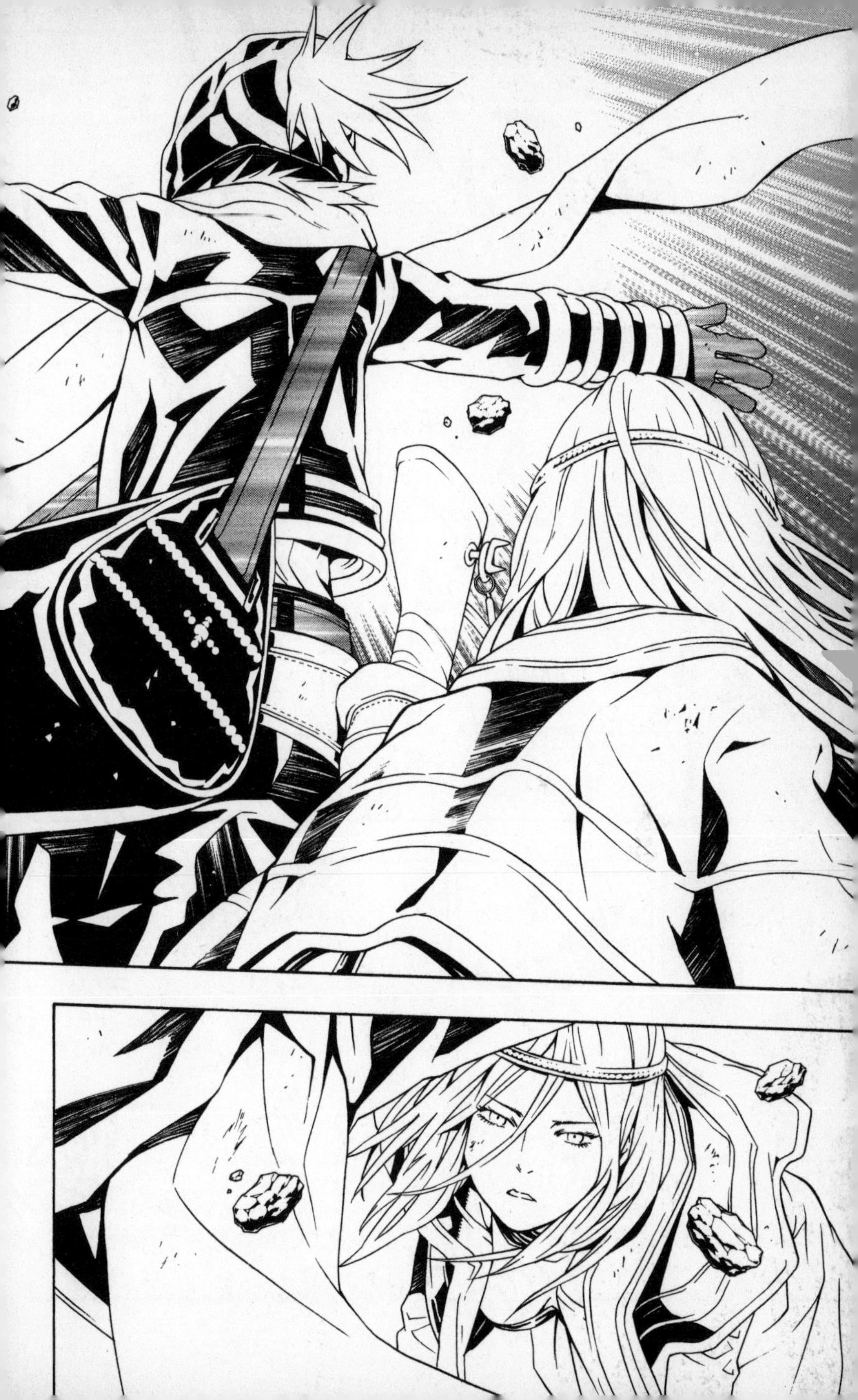

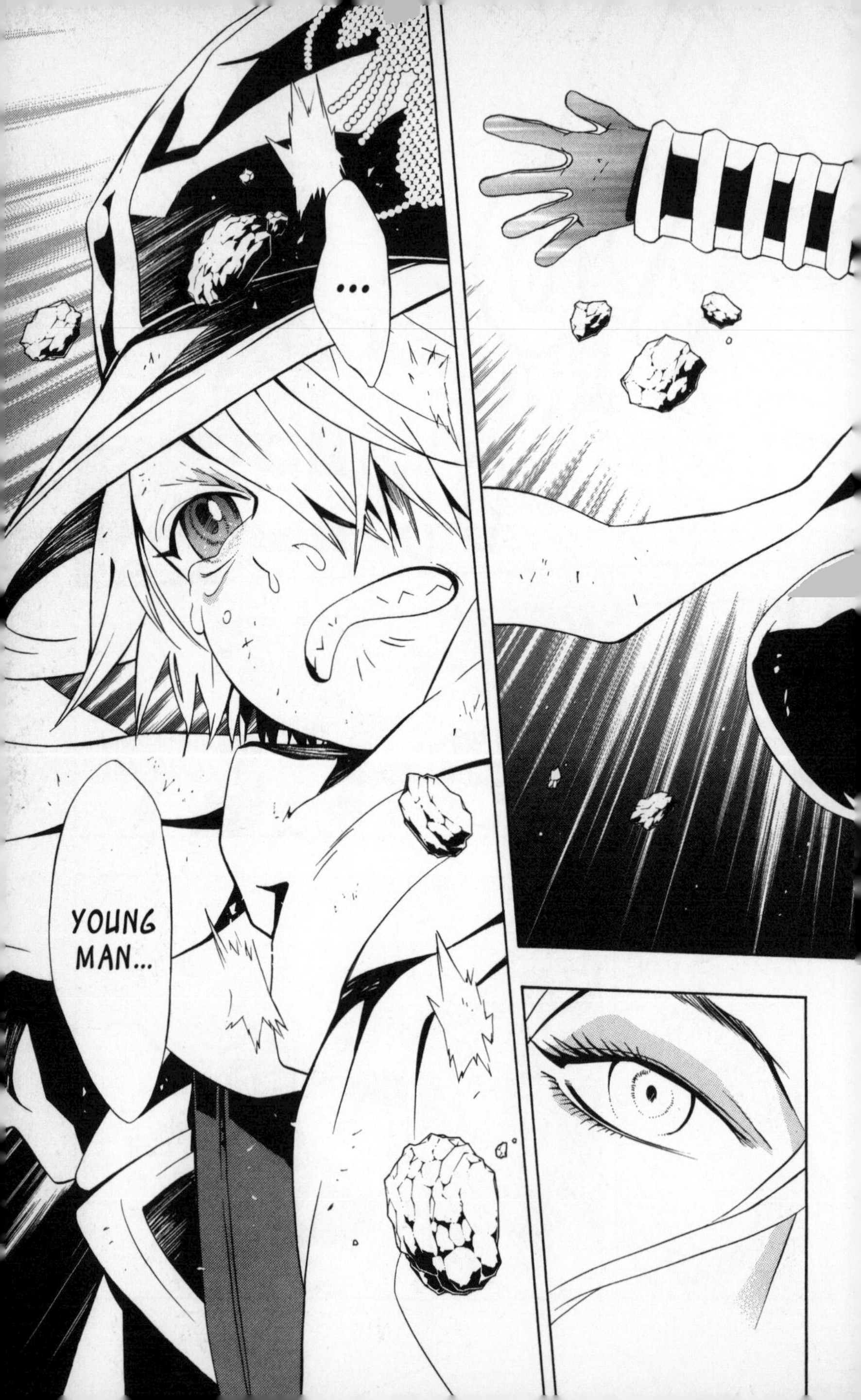
...
YOUNG MAN...

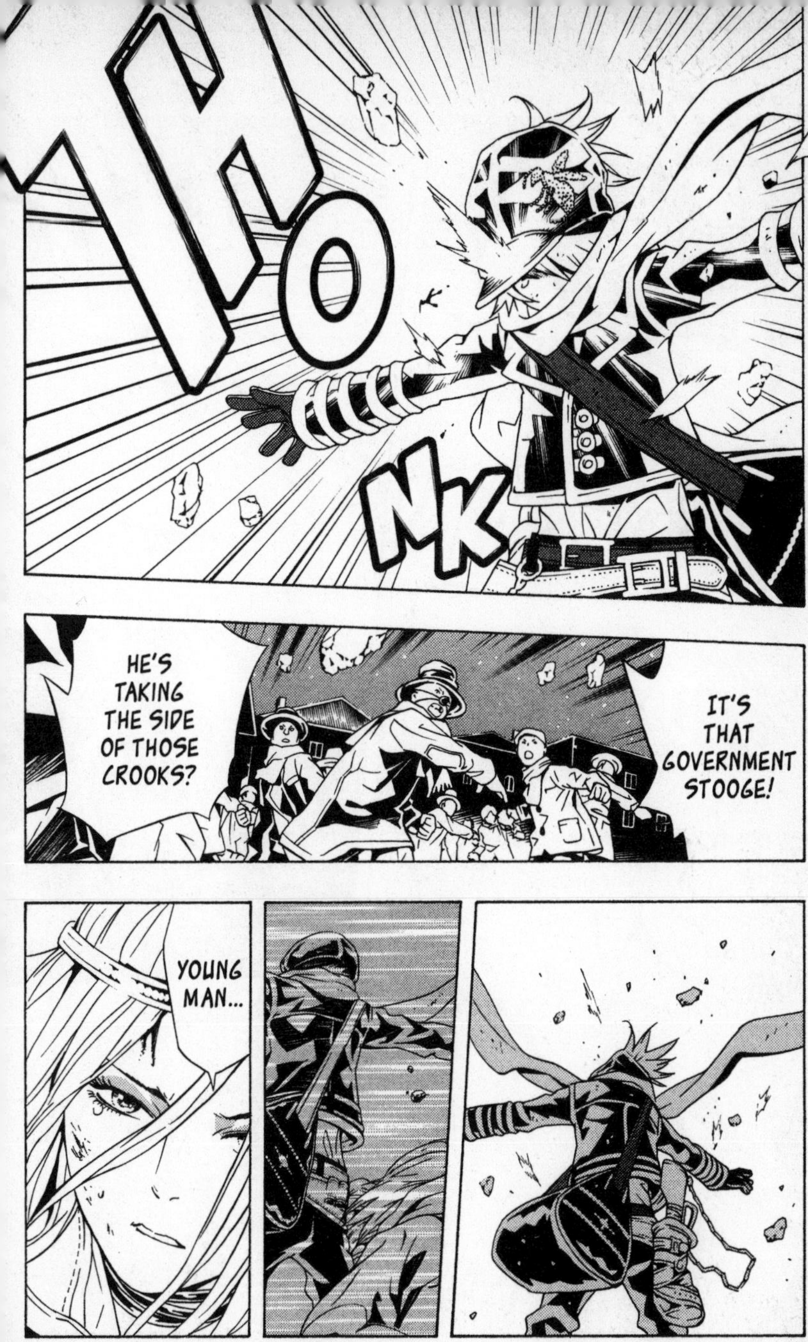
HONK
IT'S THAT GOVERNMENT STOOGE!
HE'S TAKING THE SIDE OF THOSE CROOKS?
YOUNG MAN...

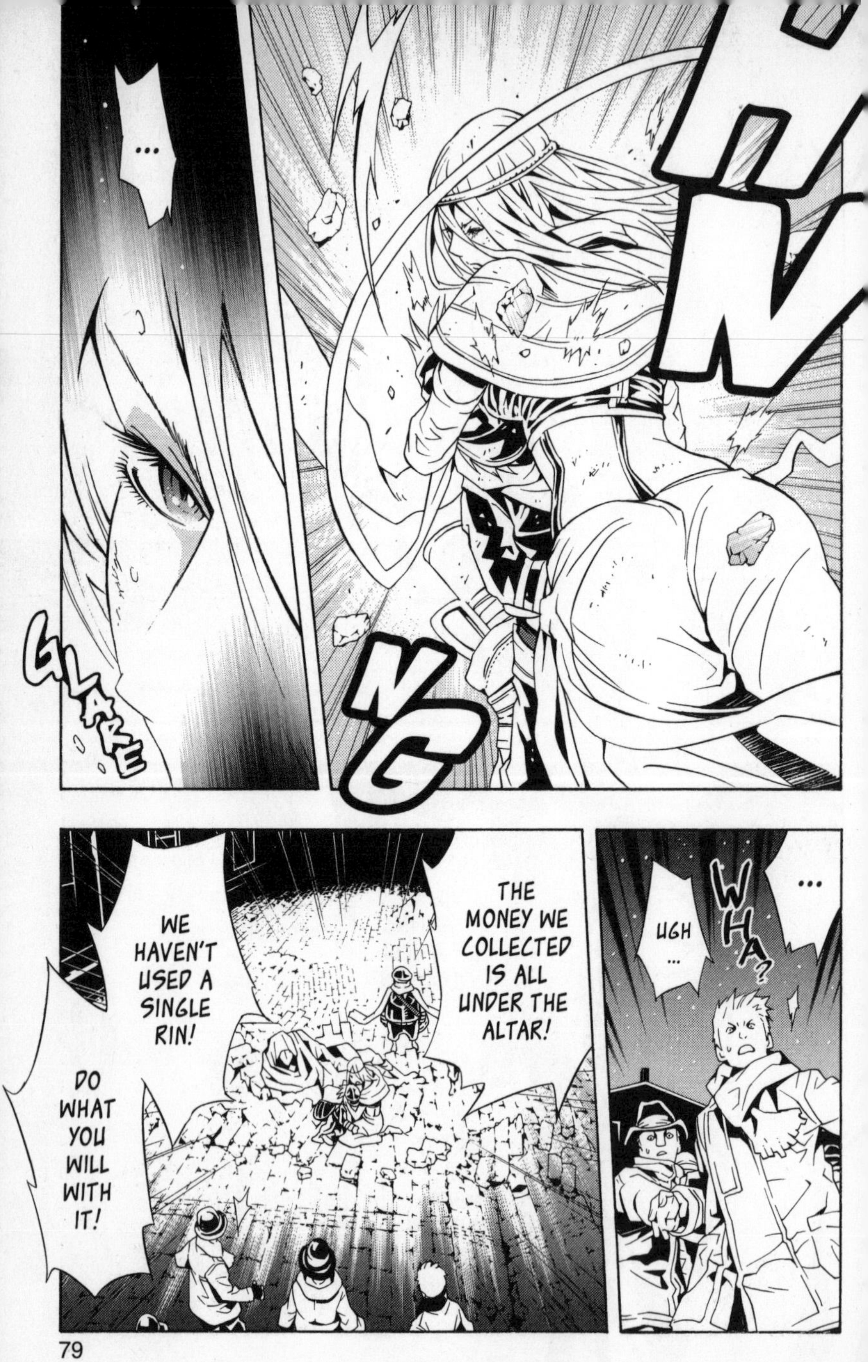

...
GLARE
NG
THE MONEY WE COLLECTED IS ALL UNDER THE ALTAR!
WE HAVEN'T USED A SINGLE RIN!
DO WHAT YOU WILL WITH IT!
...
WHA?
UGH ...

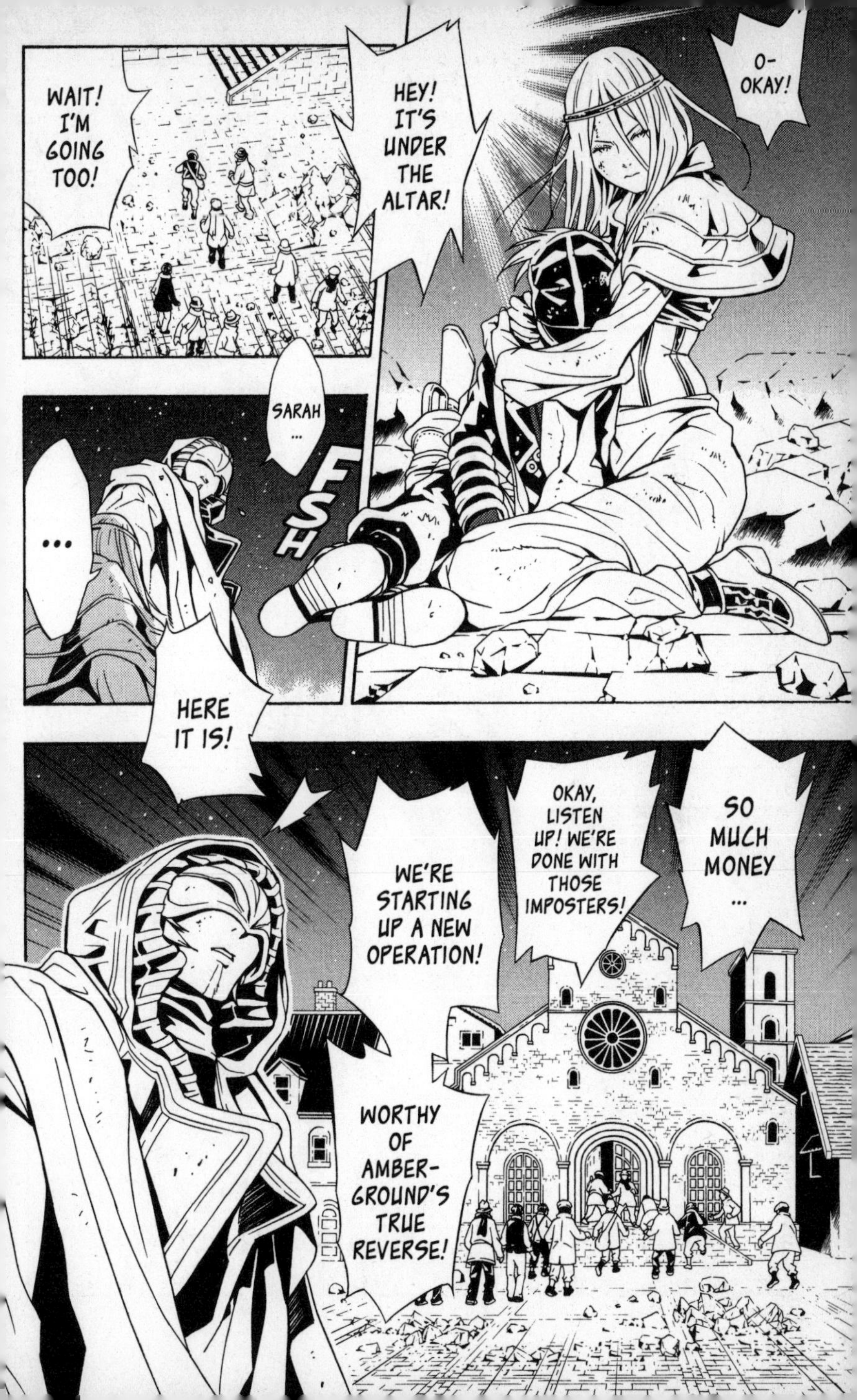
O-OKAY!
HEY! IT'S UNDER THE ALTAR!
WAIT! I'M GOING TOO!
SARAH...
FSH
...
HERE IT IS!
SO MUCH MONEY...
OKAY, LISTEN UP! WE'RE DONE WITH THOSE IMPOSTERS!
WE'RE STARTING UP A NEW OPERATION!
WORTHY OF AMBER-GROUND'S TRUE REVERSE!

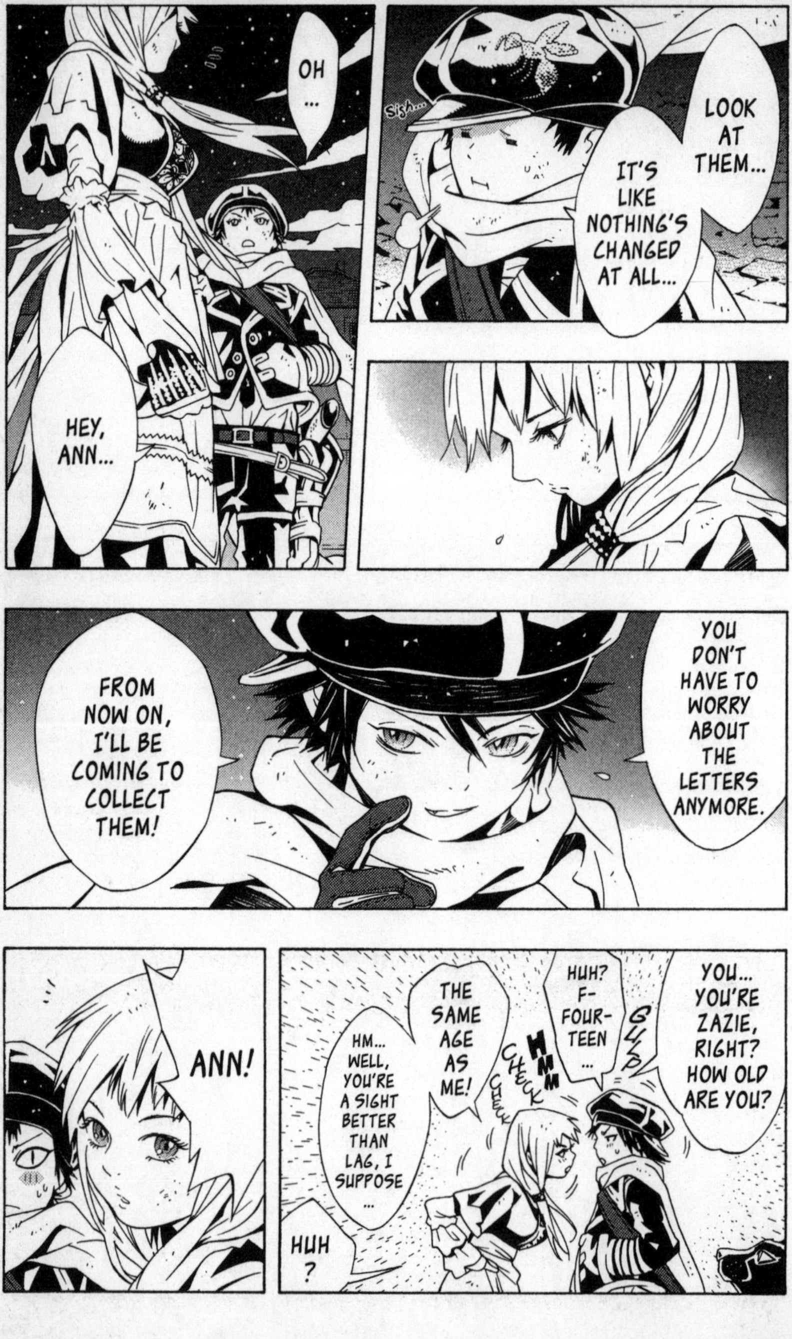
LOOK AT THEM...
IT'S LIKE NOTHING'S CHANGED AT ALL...
Sigh...
OH ...
HEY, ANN...
YOU DON'T HAVE TO WORRY ABOUT THE LETTERS ANYMORE.
FROM NOW ON, I'LL BE COMING TO COLLECT THEM!
YOU... YOU'RE ZAZIE, RIGHT? HOW OLD ARE YOU?
GULP
HUH? F-FOUR-TEEN ...
HMM
CHECK CHECK
THE SAME AGE AS ME!
HM... WELL, YOU'RE A SIGHT BETTER THAN LAG, I SUPPOSE ...
HUH ?
ANN!

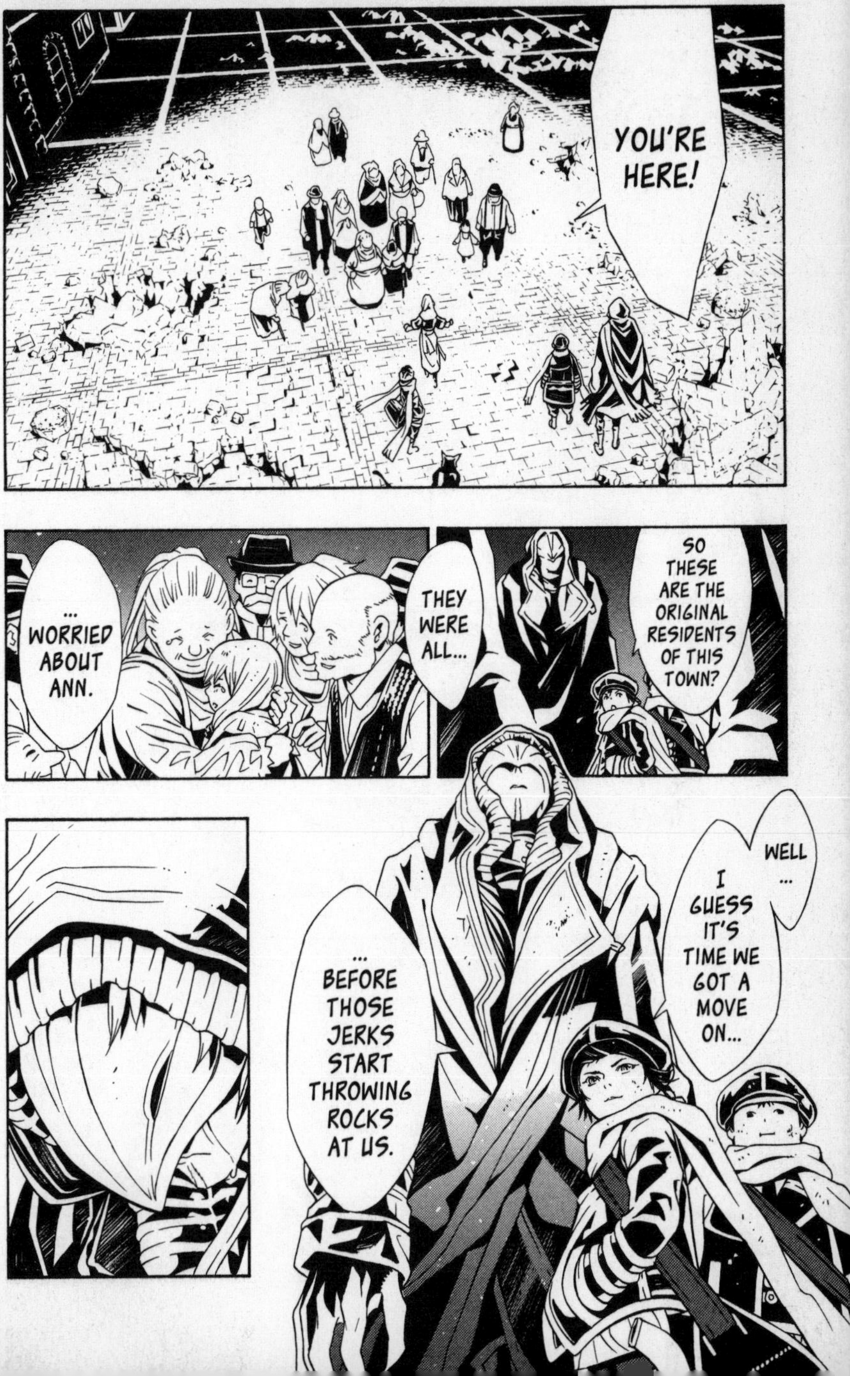
YOU'RE HERE!
SO THESE ARE THE ORIGINAL RESIDENTS OF THIS TOWN?
THEY WERE ALL...
... WORRIED ABOUT ANN.
WELL ...
I GUESS IT'S TIME WE GOT A MOVE ON...
... BEFORE THOSE JERKS START THROWING ROCKS AT US.

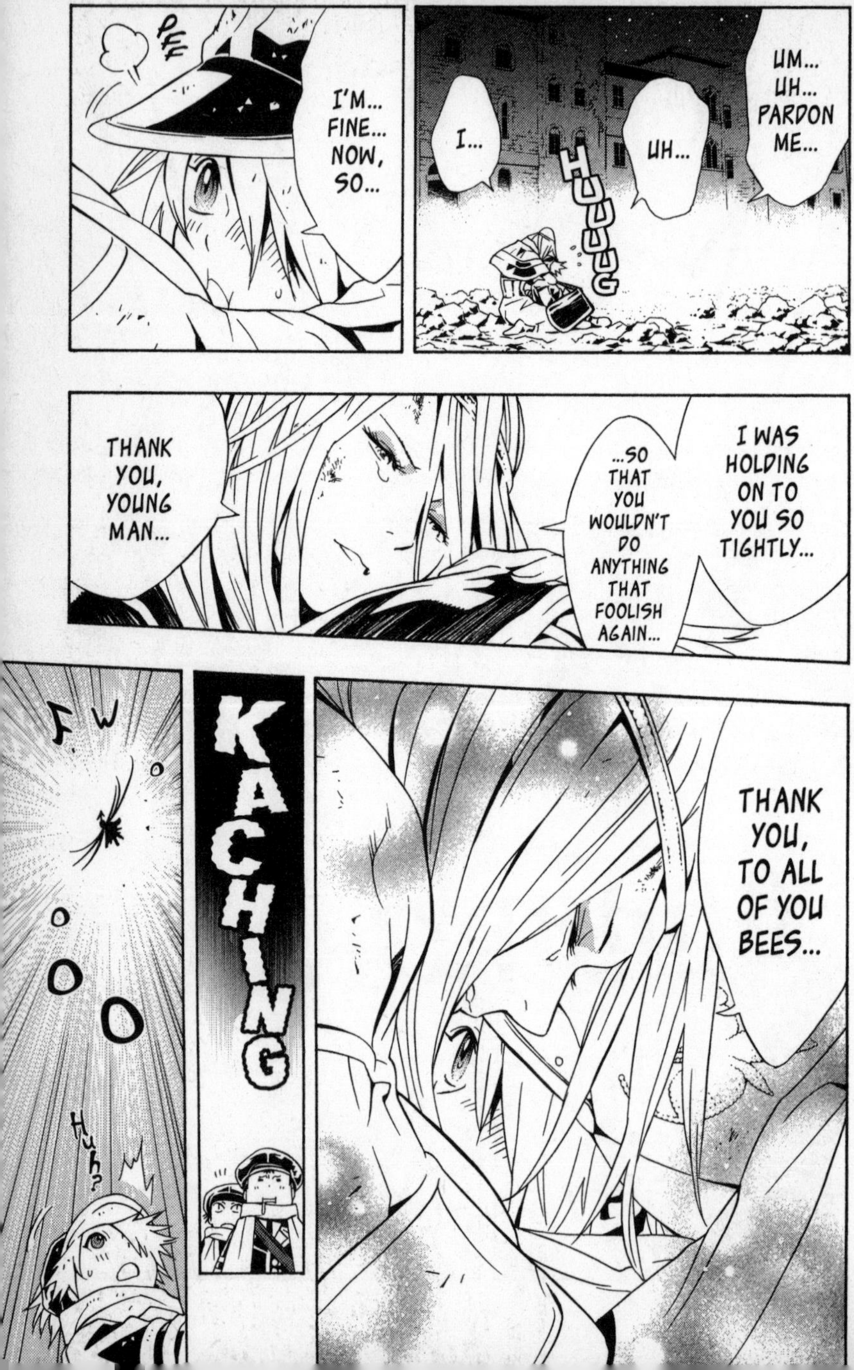
UM... UH... PARDON ME...
UH...
I...
HUUUUG
I'M... FINE... NOW, SO...
I WAS HOLDING ON TO YOU SO TIGHTLY...
...SO THAT YOU WOULDN'T DO ANYTHING THAT FOOLISH AGAIN...
THANK YOU, YOUNG MAN...
THANK YOU, TO ALL OF YOU BEES...
KACHING
FWOOO
Huh?

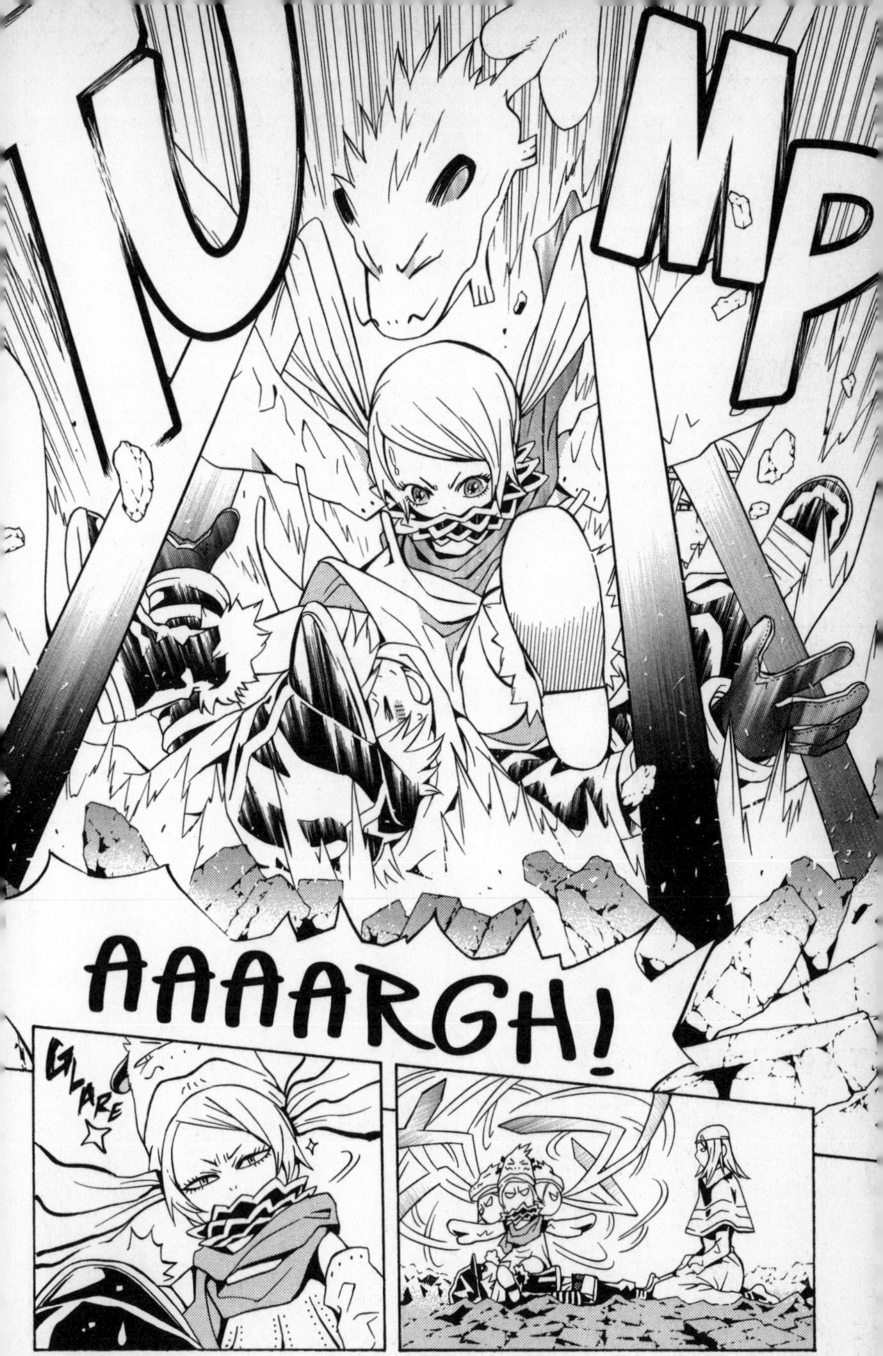
THUMP
AAAARGH!
GLARE

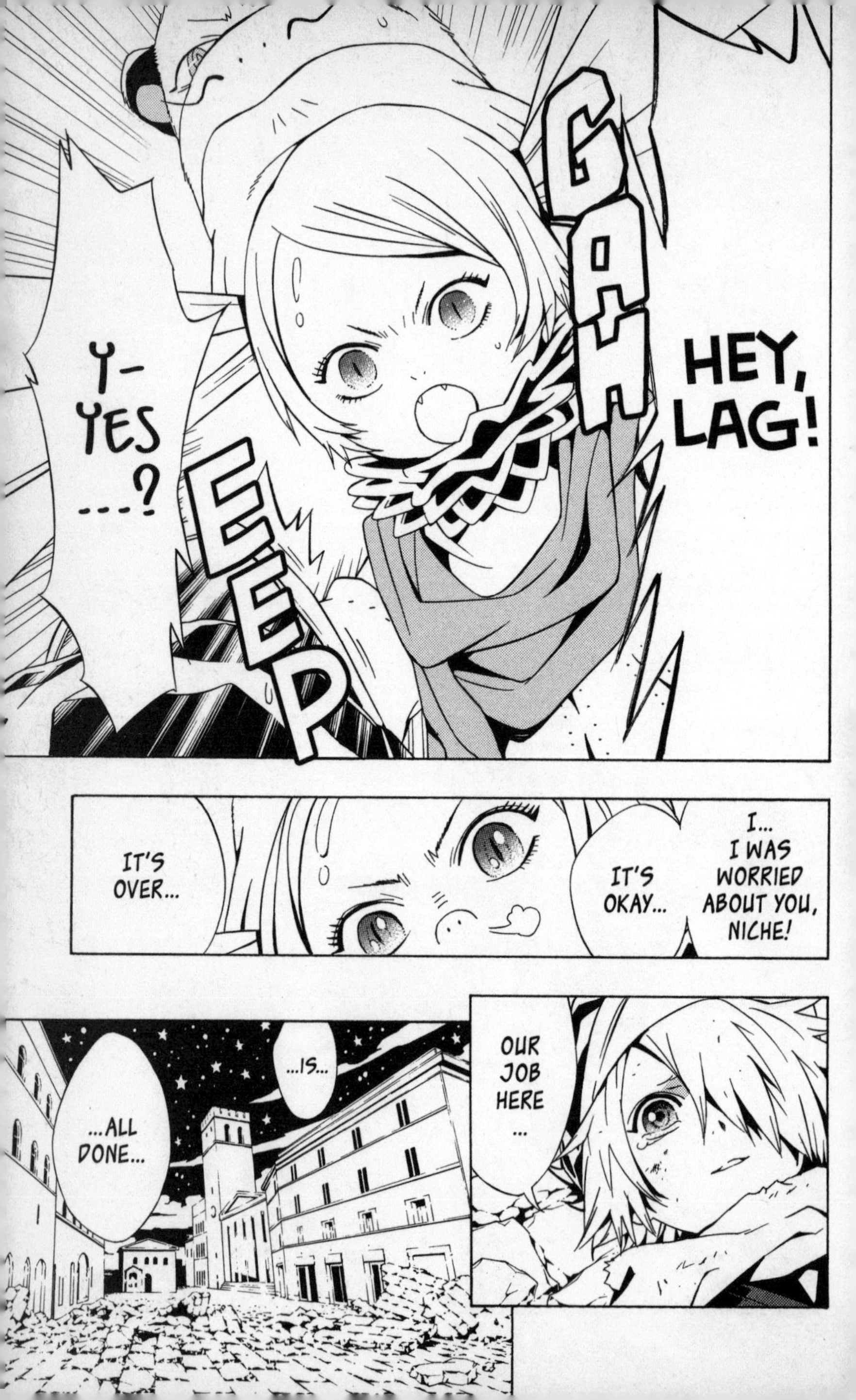
HEY, LAG!
GAH
EEP
Y-YES...?
I... I WAS WORRIED ABOUT YOU, NICHE!
IT'S OKAY...
IT'S OVER...
OUR JOB HERE ...
...IS...
...ALL DONE...

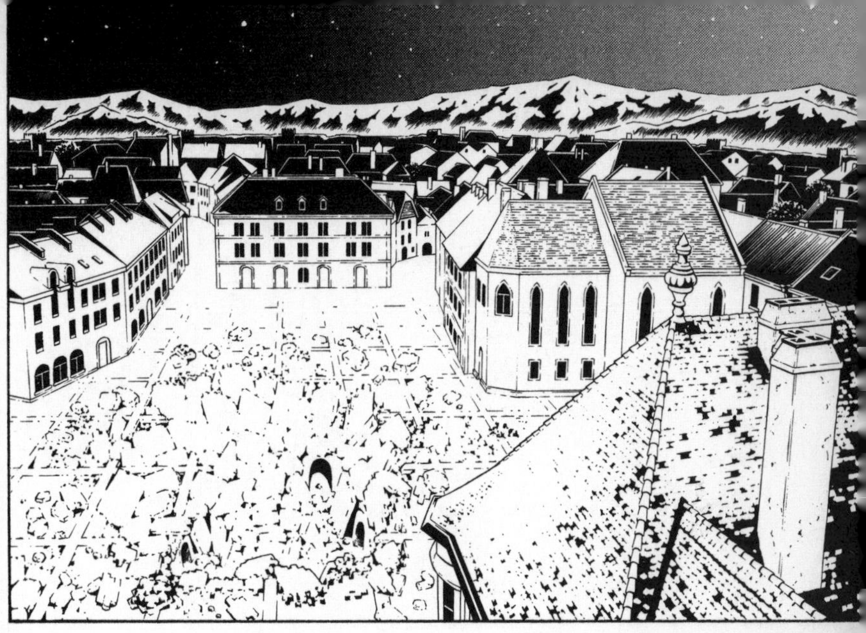

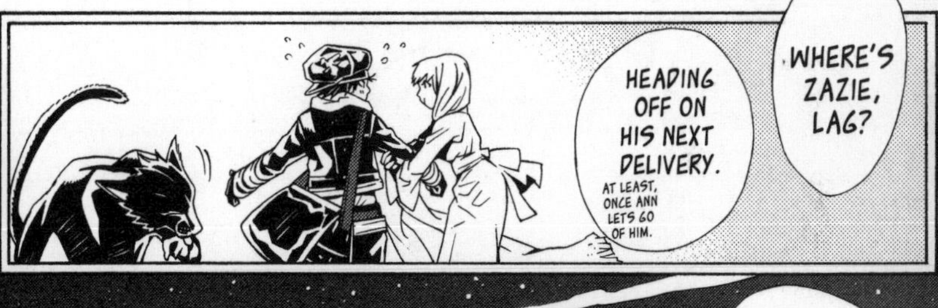
WHERE'S ZAZIE, LAG?
HEADING OFF ON HIS NEXT DELIVERY.
AT LEAST, ONCE ANN LETS GO OF HIM.

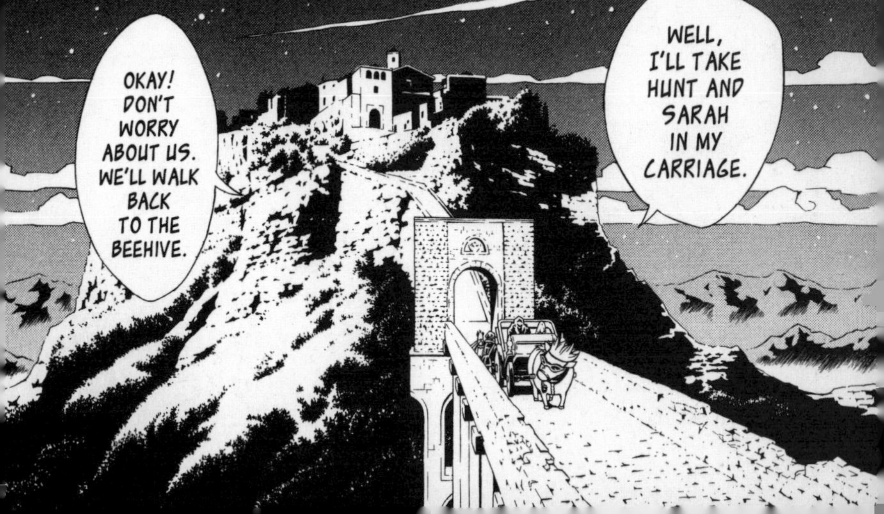
WELL, I'LL TAKE HUNT AND SARAH IN MY CARRIAGE.
OKAY! DON'T WORRY ABOUT US. WE'LL WALK BACK TO THE BEEHIVE.

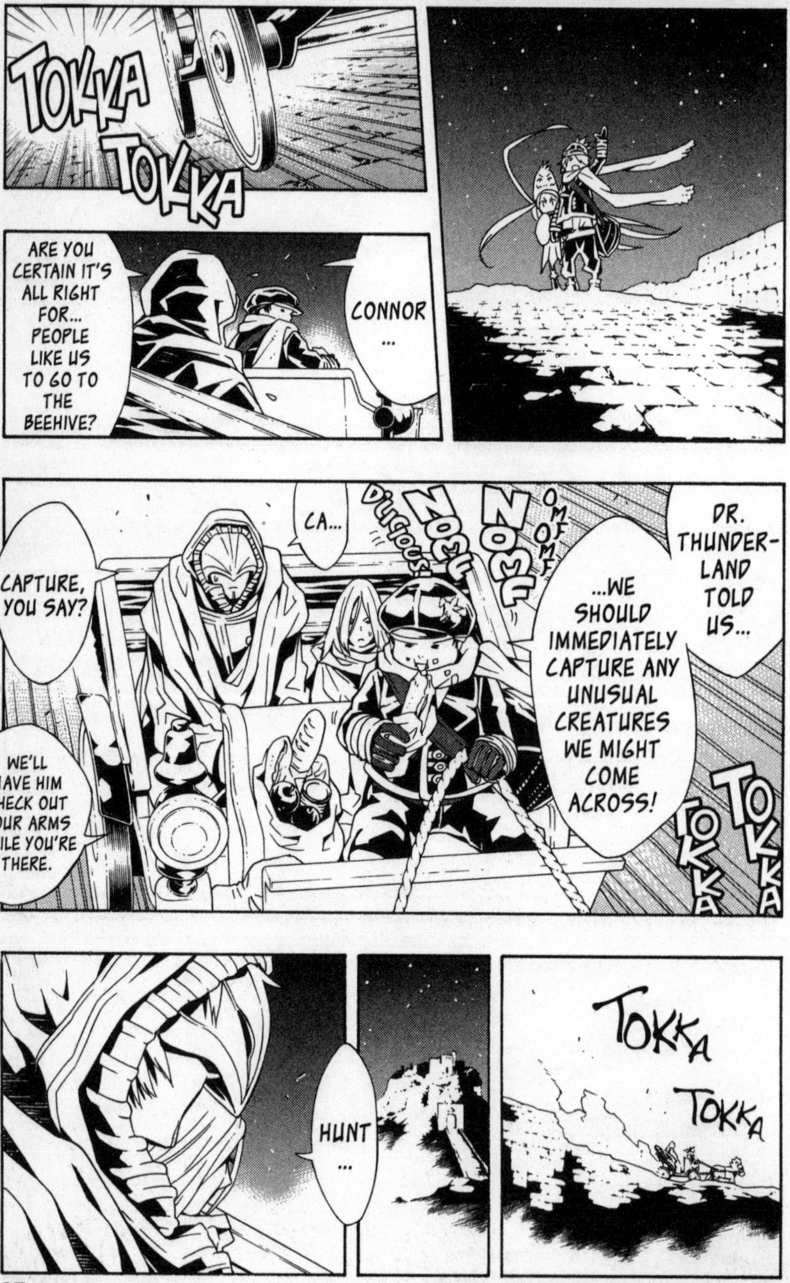
TOKKA TOKKA
CONNOR ...
ARE YOU CERTAIN IT'S ALL RIGHT FOR... PEOPLE LIKE US TO GO TO THE BEEHIVE?
DR. THUNDER-LAND TOLD US...
...WE SHOULD IMMEDIATELY CAPTURE ANY UNUSUAL CREATURES WE MIGHT COME ACROSS!
TOKKA TOKKA
NOMF NOMF OMF OMF
D'LICIOUS
CA...
CAPTURE, YOU SAY?
WE'LL HAVE HIM CHECK OUT YOUR ARMS WHILE YOU'RE THERE.
TOKKA TOKKA
HUNT ...

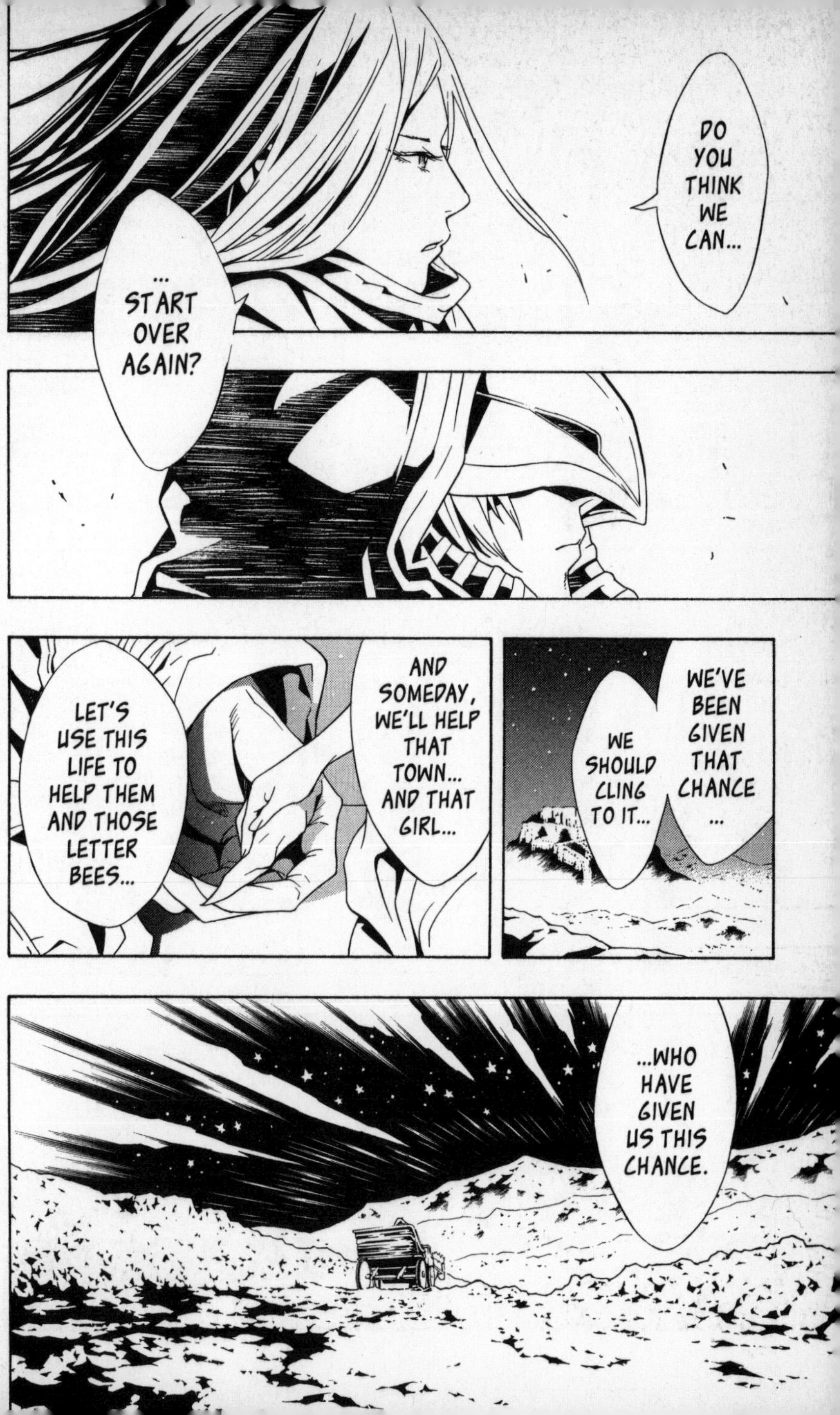
DO YOU THINK WE CAN...
... START OVER AGAIN?
WE'VE BEEN GIVEN THAT CHANCE ...
WE SHOULD CLING TO IT...
AND SOMEDAY, WE'LL HELP THAT TOWN... AND THAT GIRL...
LET'S USE THIS LIFE TO HELP THEM AND THOSE LETTER BEES...
...WHO HAVE GIVEN US THIS CHANCE.

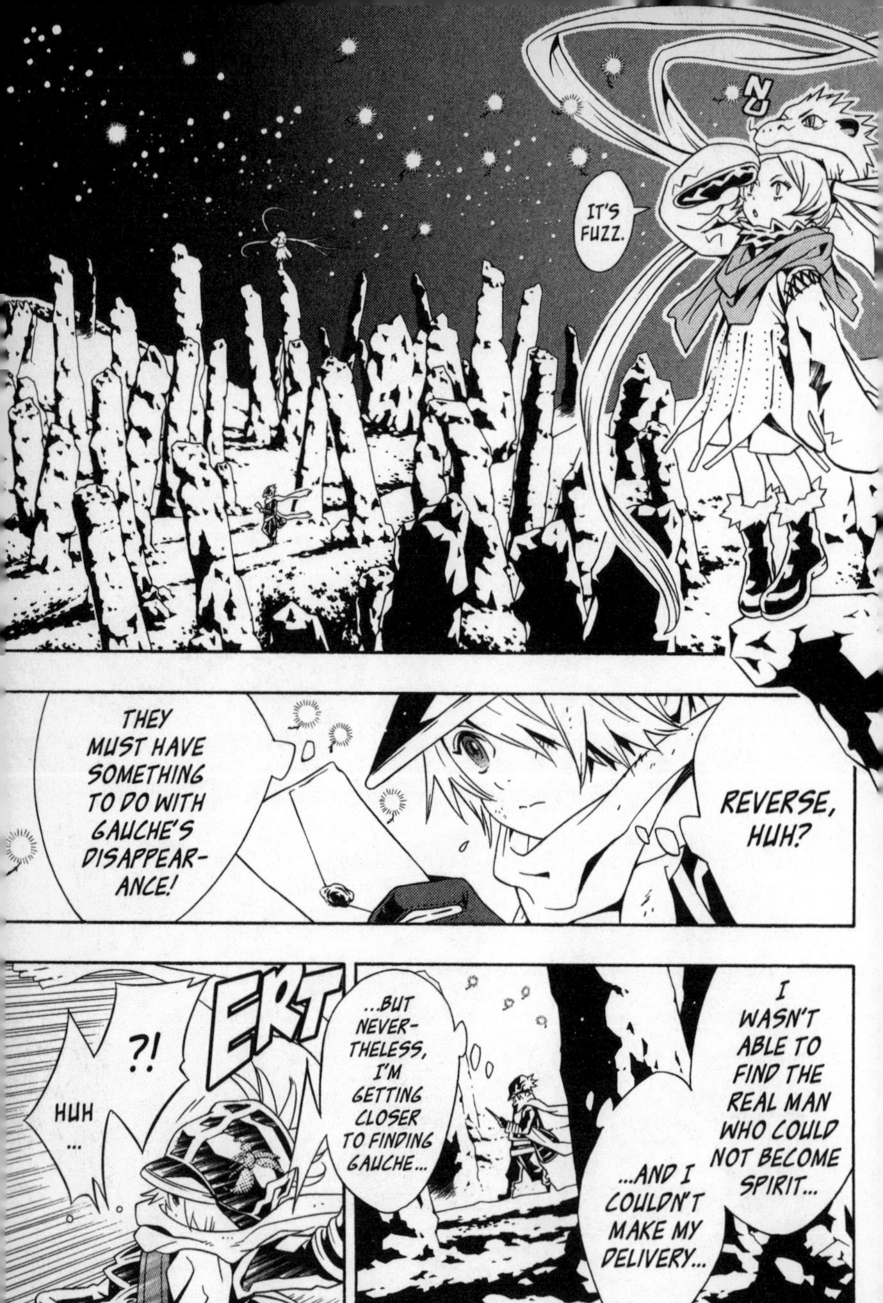
NU
IT'S FUZZ.
REVERSE, HUH?
THEY MUST HAVE SOMETHING TO DO WITH GAUCHE'S DISAPPEARANCE!
I WASN'T ABLE TO FIND THE REAL MAN WHO COULD NOT BECOME SPIRIT...
...AND I COULDN'T MAKE MY DELIVERY...
...BUT NEVERTHELESS, I'M GETTING CLOSER TO FINDING GAUCHE...
ERT
?!
HUH ...

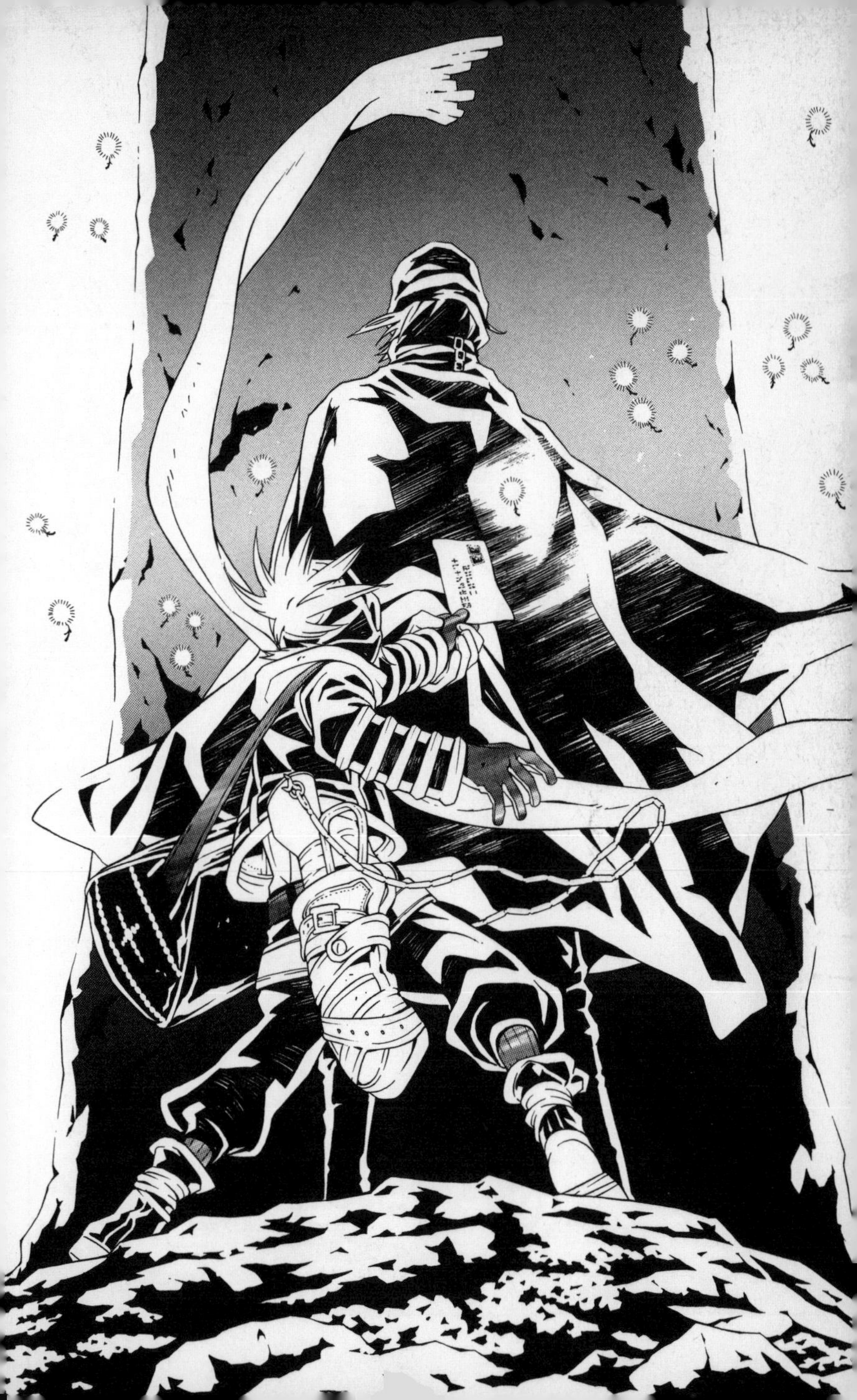

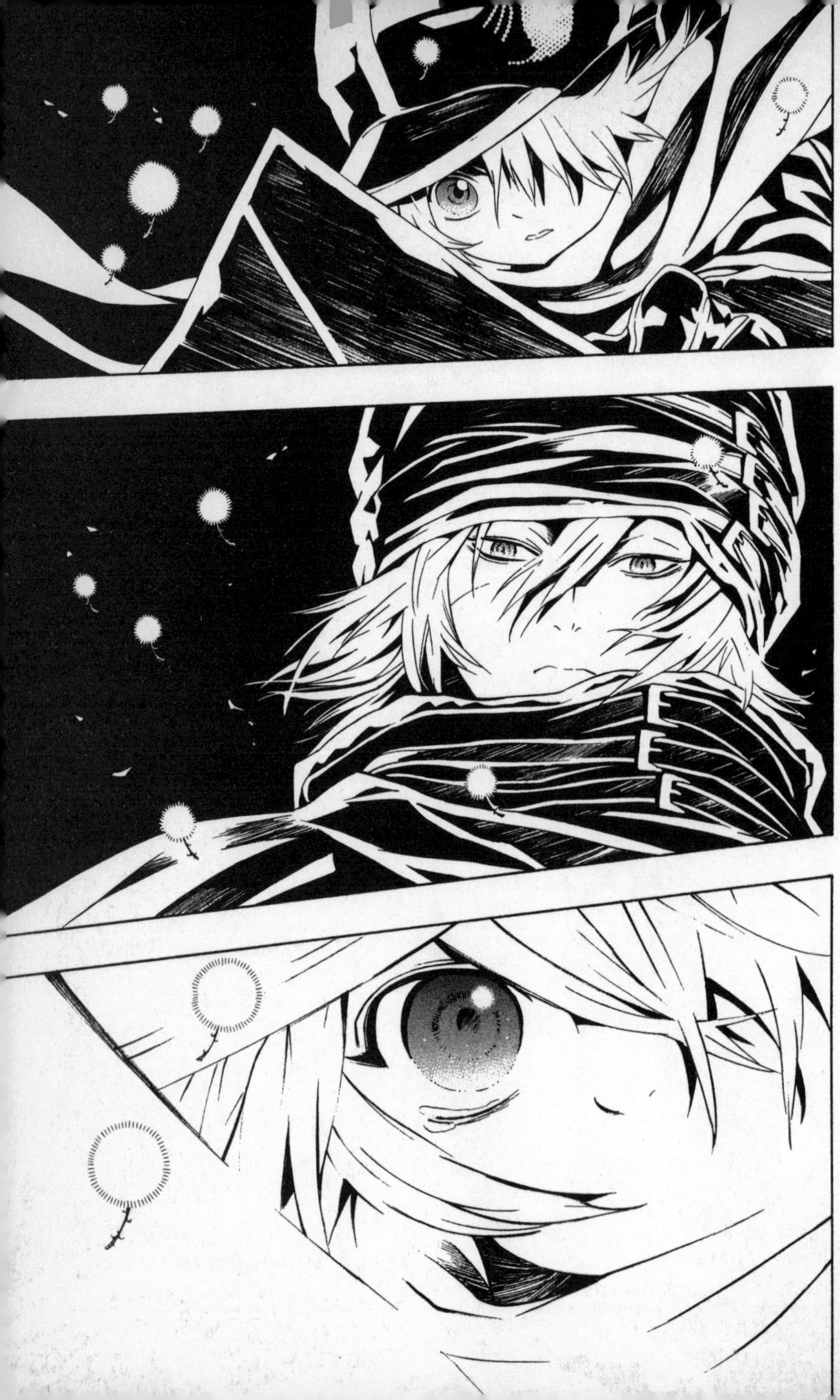

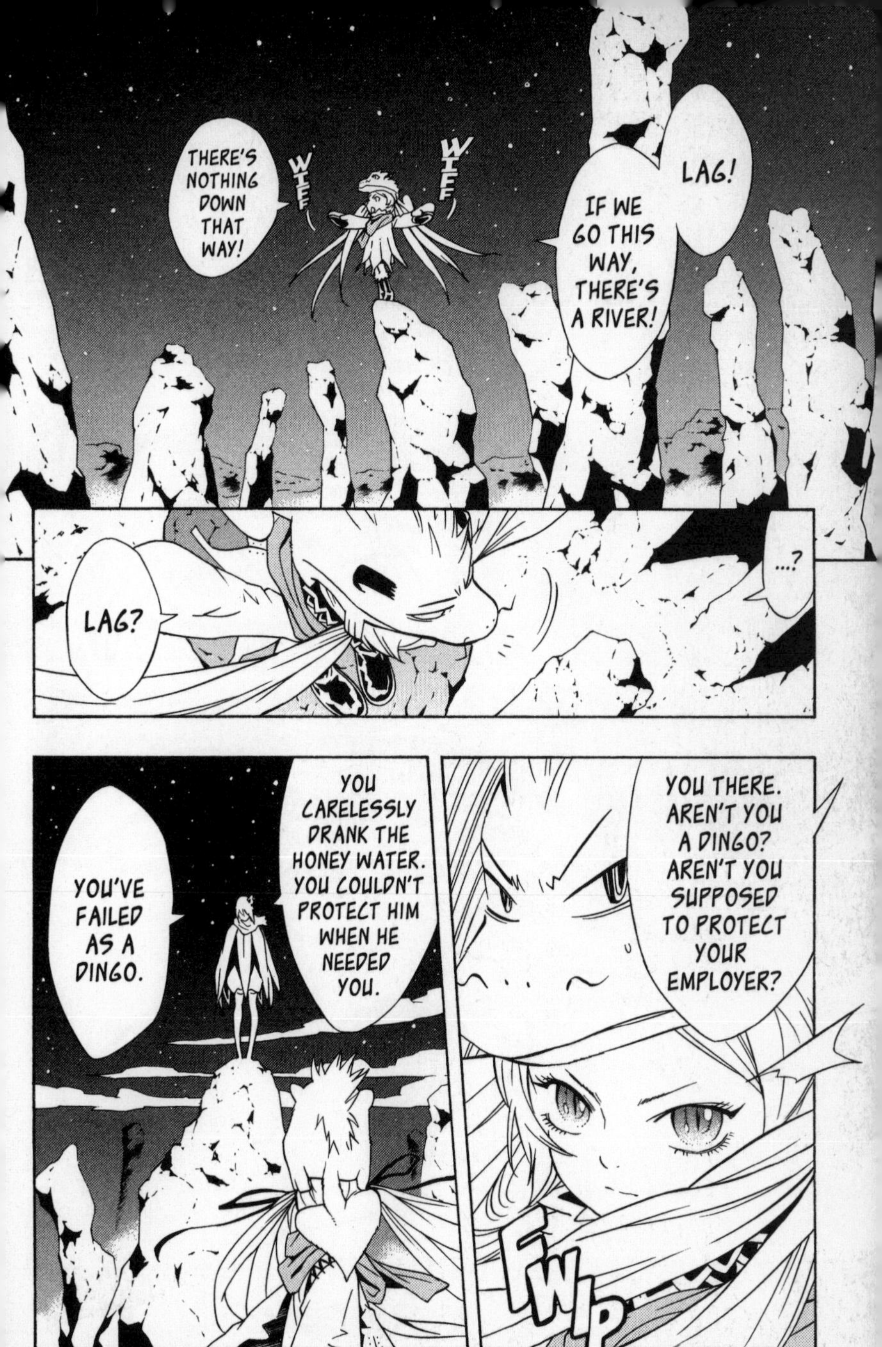
LAG!
IF WE GO THIS WAY, THERE'S A RIVER!
WIFF
WIFF
THERE'S NOTHING DOWN THAT WAY!
...?
LAG?
YOU THERE. AREN'T YOU A DINGO? AREN'T YOU SUPPOSED TO PROTECT YOUR EMPLOYER?
FWIP
YOU CARELESSLY DRANK THE HONEY WATER. YOU COULDN'T PROTECT HIM WHEN HE NEEDED YOU.
YOU'VE FAILED AS A DINGO.

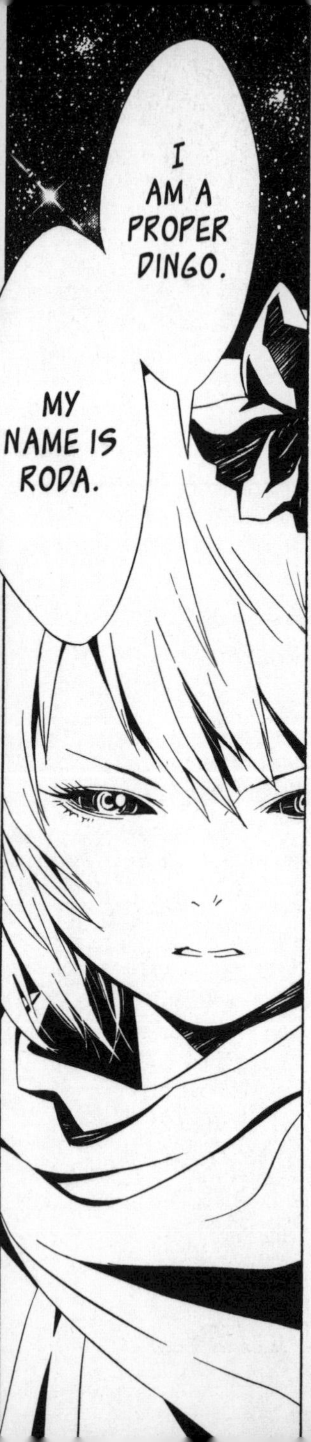
I AM A PROPER DINGO.
MY NAME IS RODA.
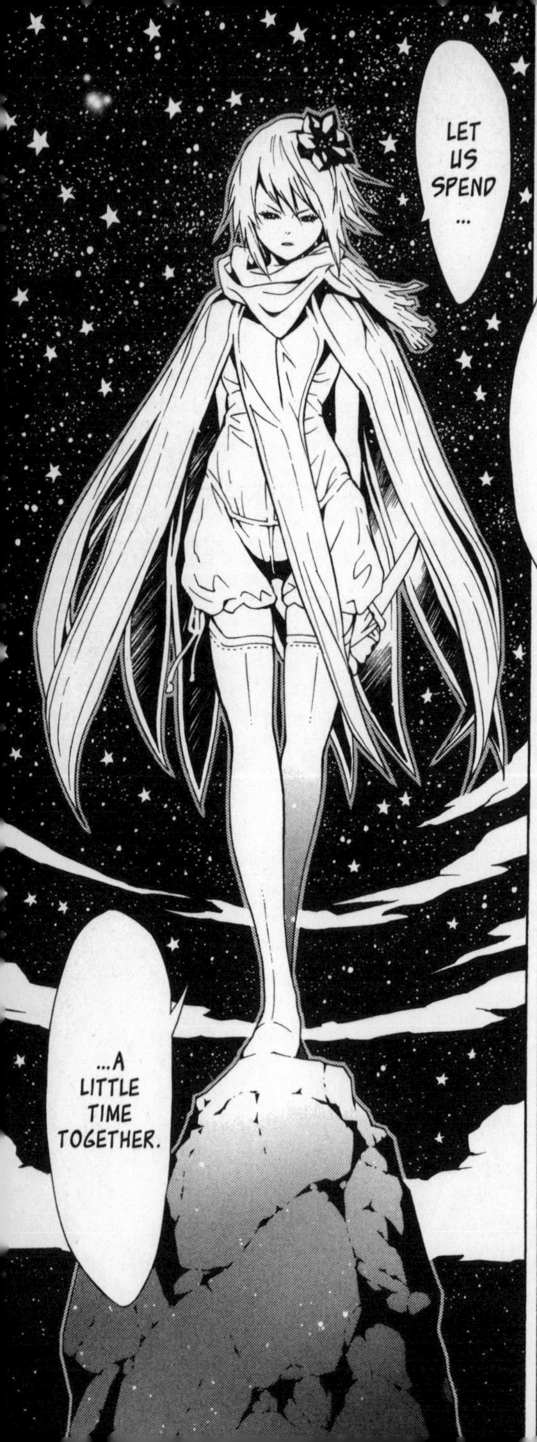
LET US SPEND ...
...A LITTLE TIME TOGETHER.

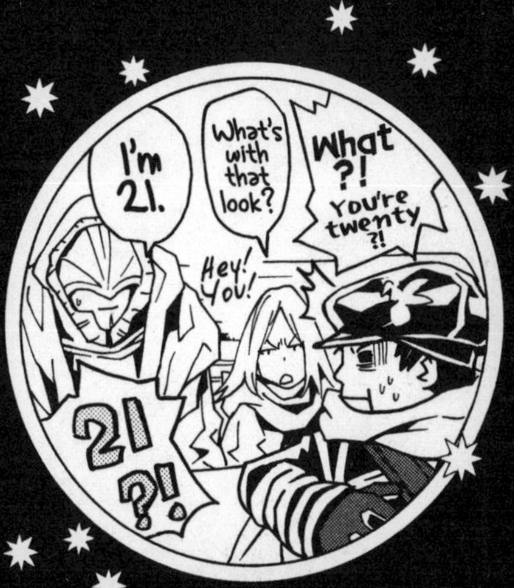
What?!
You're twenty?!
What's with that look?
I'm 21.
Hey! You!
21?!

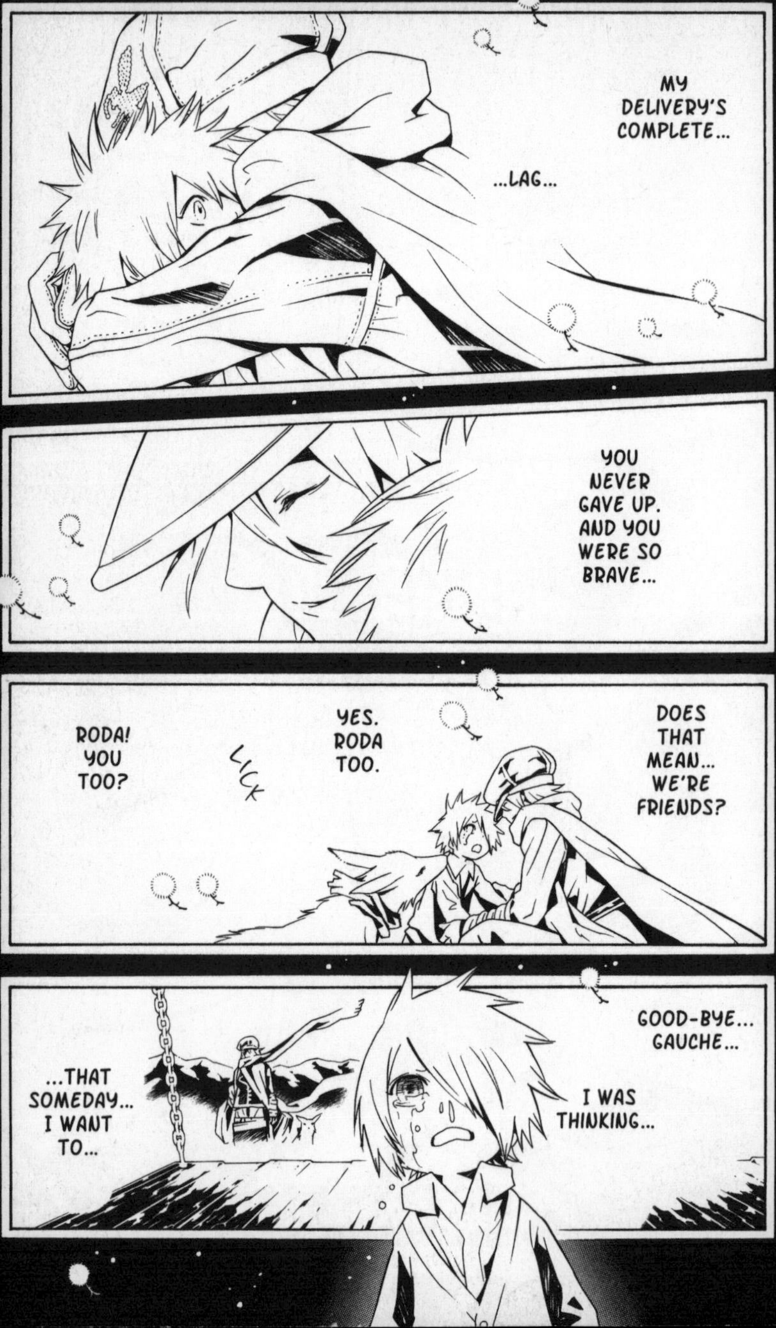
MY DELIVERY'S COMPLETE...
...LAG...
YOU NEVER GAVE UP. AND YOU WERE SO BRAVE...
DOES THAT MEAN... WE'RE FRIENDS?
YES. RODA TOO.
LICK
RODA! YOU TOO?
GOOD-BYE... GAUCHE...
I WAS THINKING...
...THAT SOMEDAY... I WANT TO...

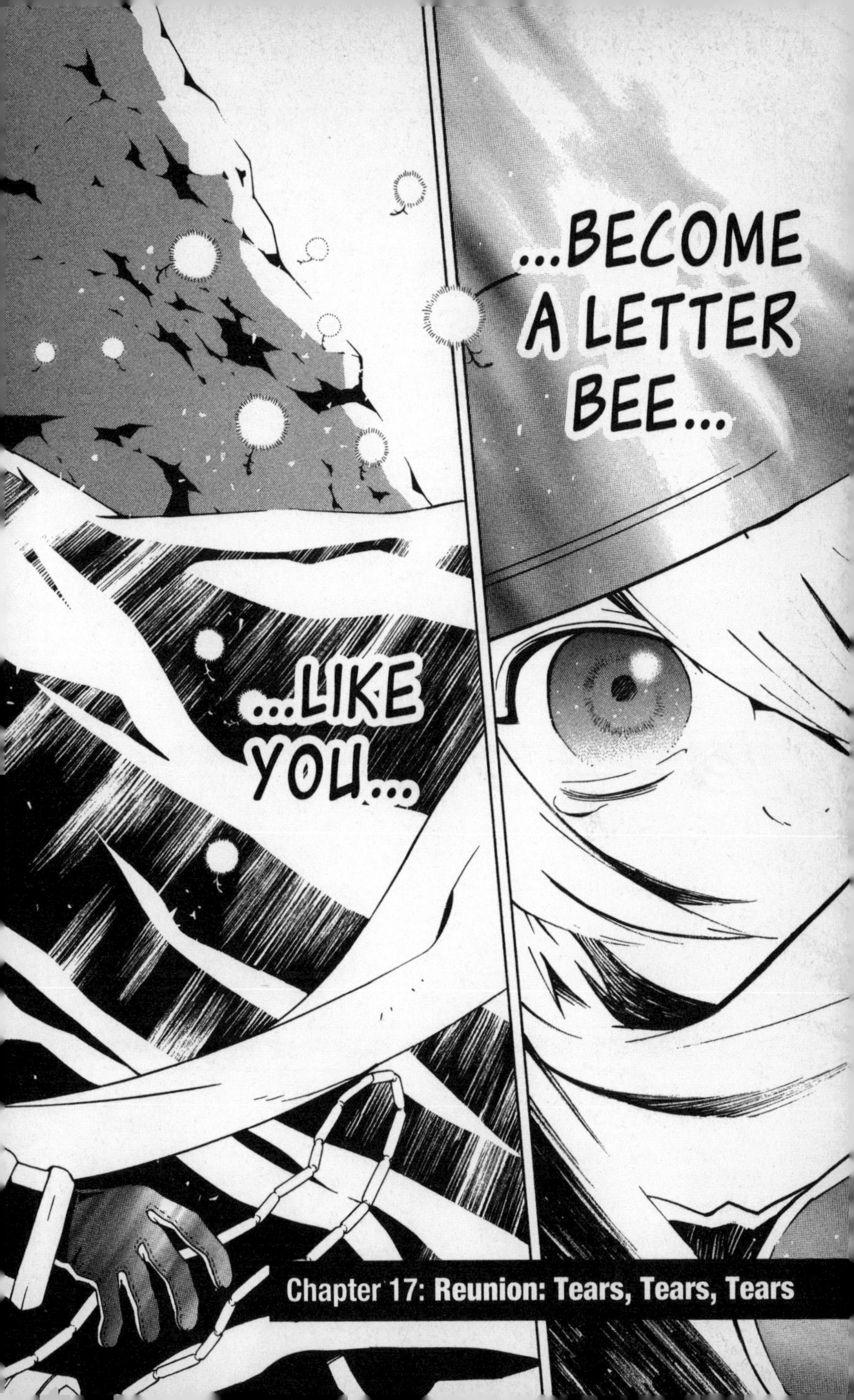
...BECOME A LETTER BEE...
...LIKE YOU...

Chapter 17: Reunion: Tears, Tears, Tears

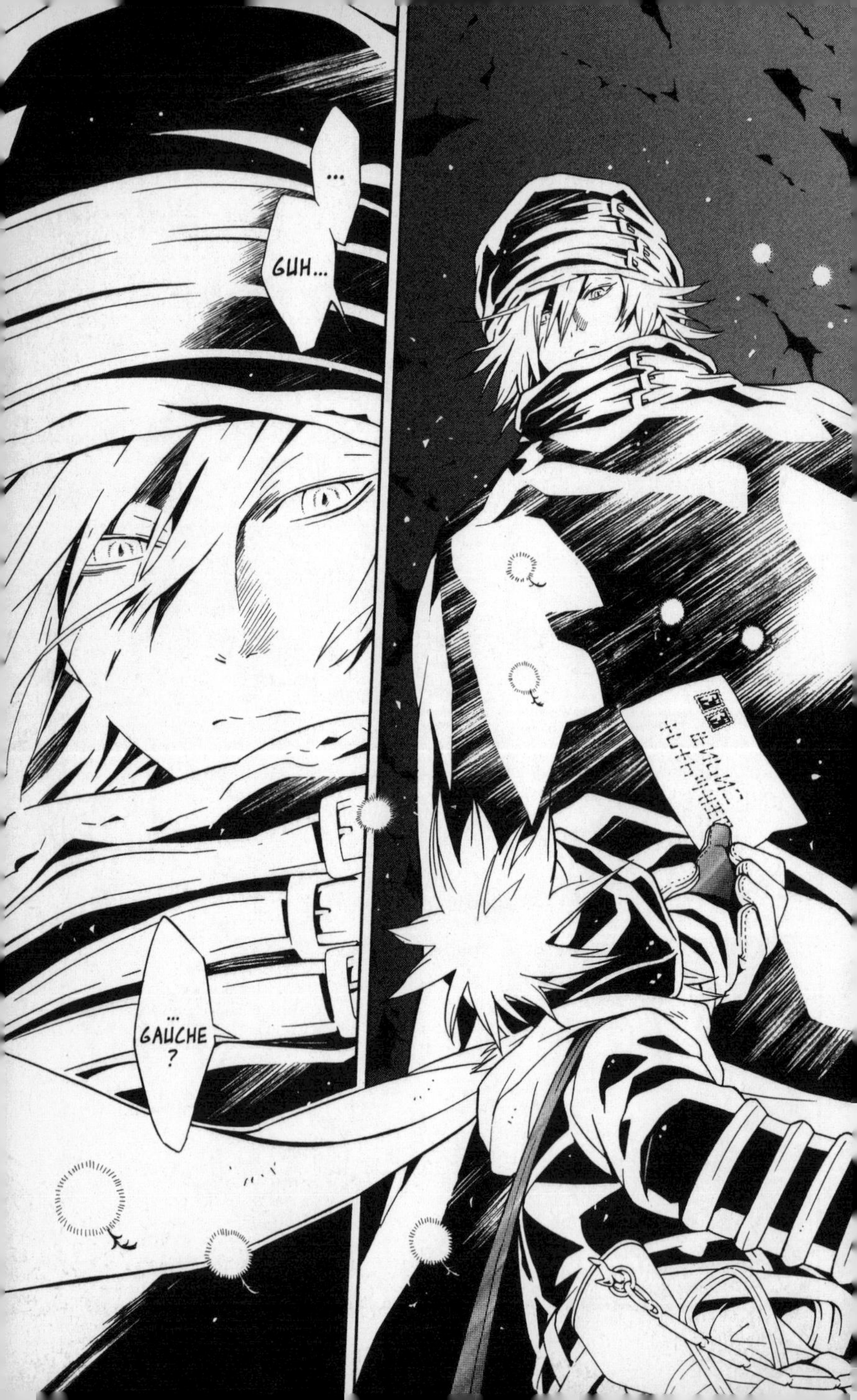
...
GUH...
... GAUCHE ?

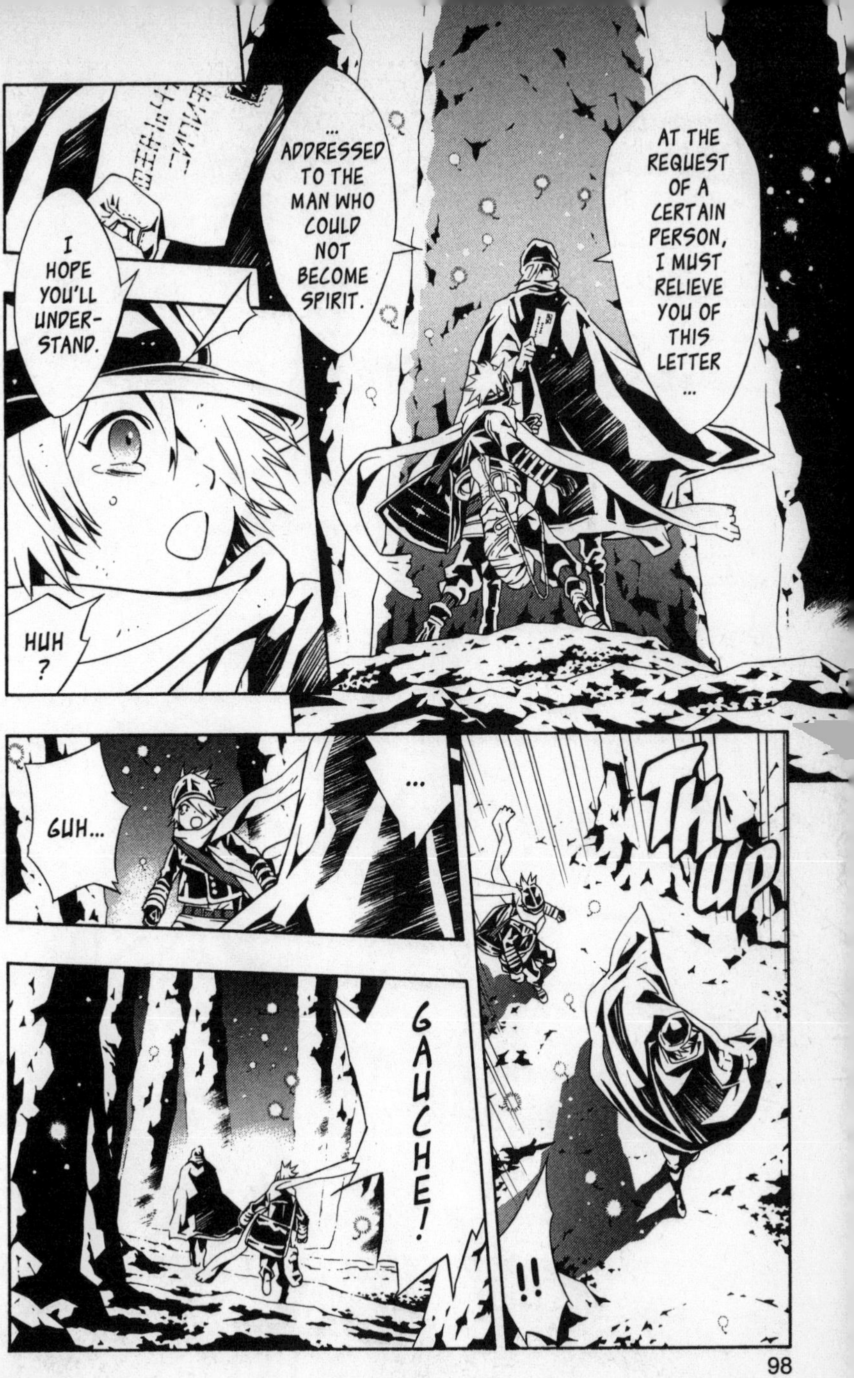
AT THE REQUEST OF A CERTAIN PERSON, I MUST RELIEVE YOU OF THIS LETTER ...
... ADDRESSED TO THE MAN WHO COULD NOT BECOME SPIRIT.
I HOPE YOU'LL UNDER-STAND.
HUH ?
THUP
!!
GUH...
...
GAUCHE!

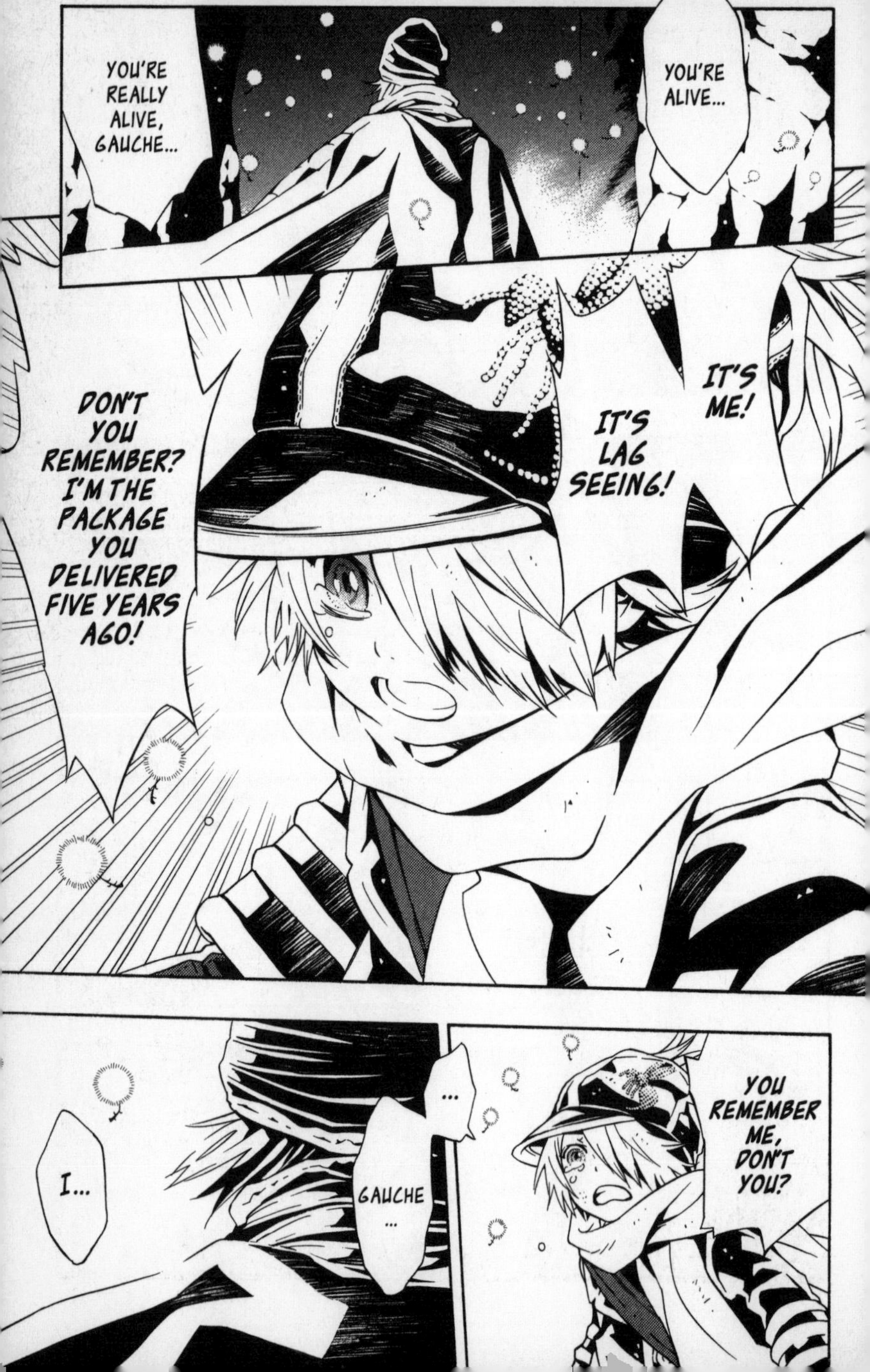
YOU'RE ALIVE...
YOU'RE REALLY ALIVE, GAUCHE...
IT'S ME!
IT'S LAG SEEING!
DON'T YOU REMEMBER? I'M THE PACKAGE YOU DELIVERED FIVE YEARS AGO!
YOU REMEMBER ME, DON'T YOU?
...
GAUCHE ...
I...

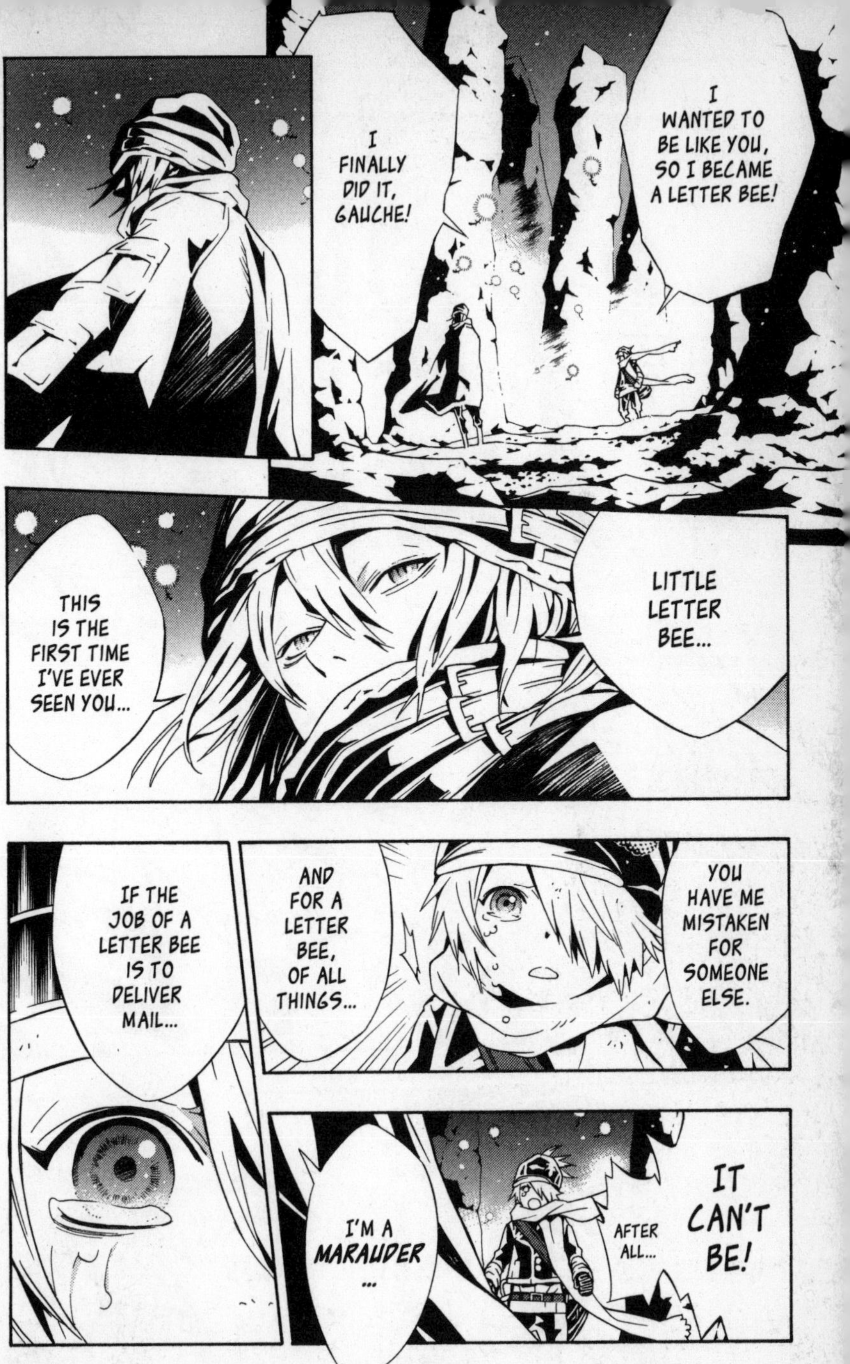
I WANTED TO BE LIKE YOU, SO I BECAME A LETTER BEE!
I FINALLY DID IT, GAUCHE!
LITTLE LETTER BEE...
THIS IS THE FIRST TIME I'VE EVER SEEN YOU...
YOU HAVE ME MISTAKEN FOR SOMEONE ELSE.
AND FOR A LETTER BEE, OF ALL THINGS...
IF THE JOB OF A LETTER BEE IS TO DELIVER MAIL...
IT CAN'T BE!
AFTER ALL...
I'M A *MARAUDER* ...

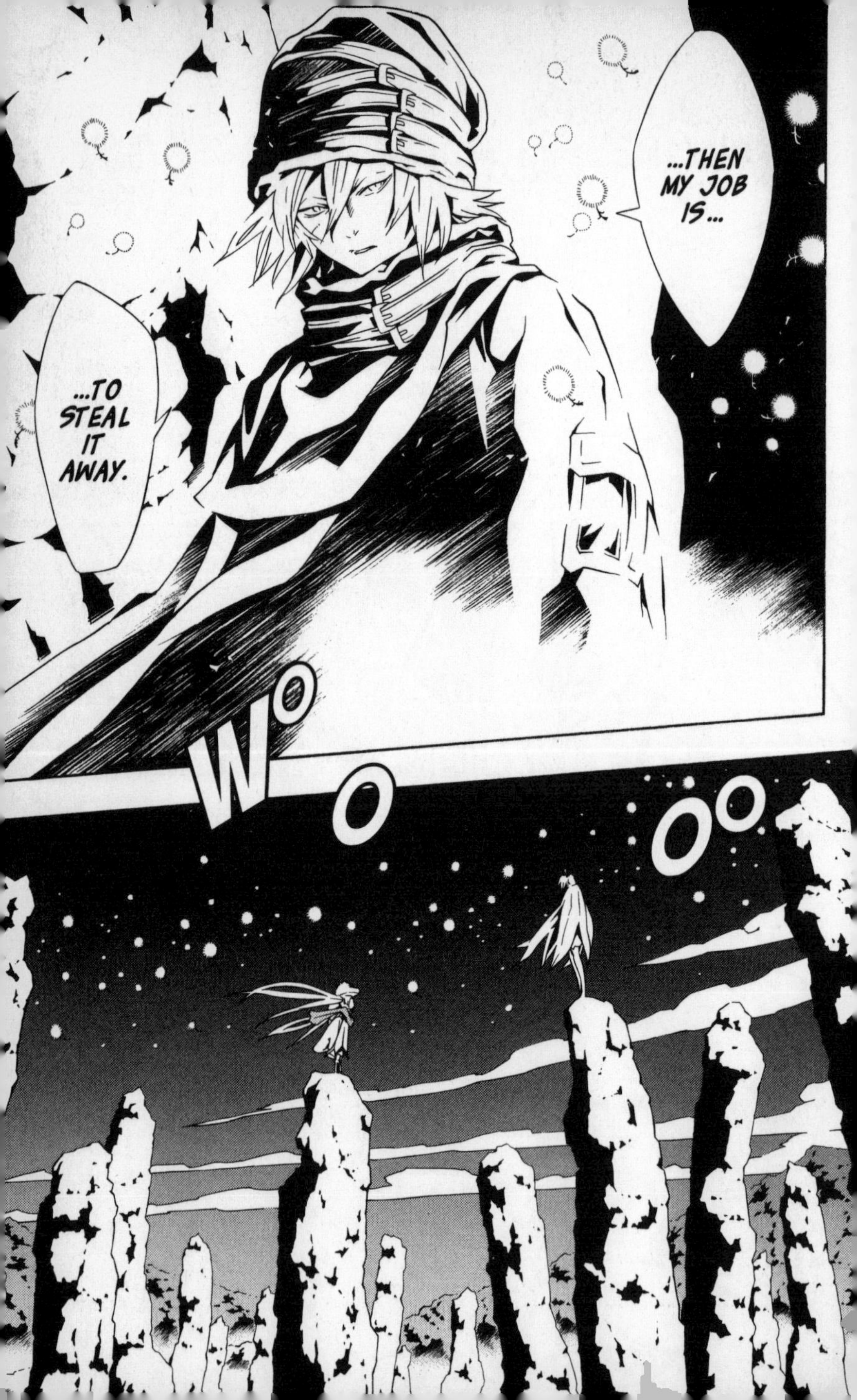
...THEN MY JOB IS...
...TO STEAL IT AWAY.
WOOOO

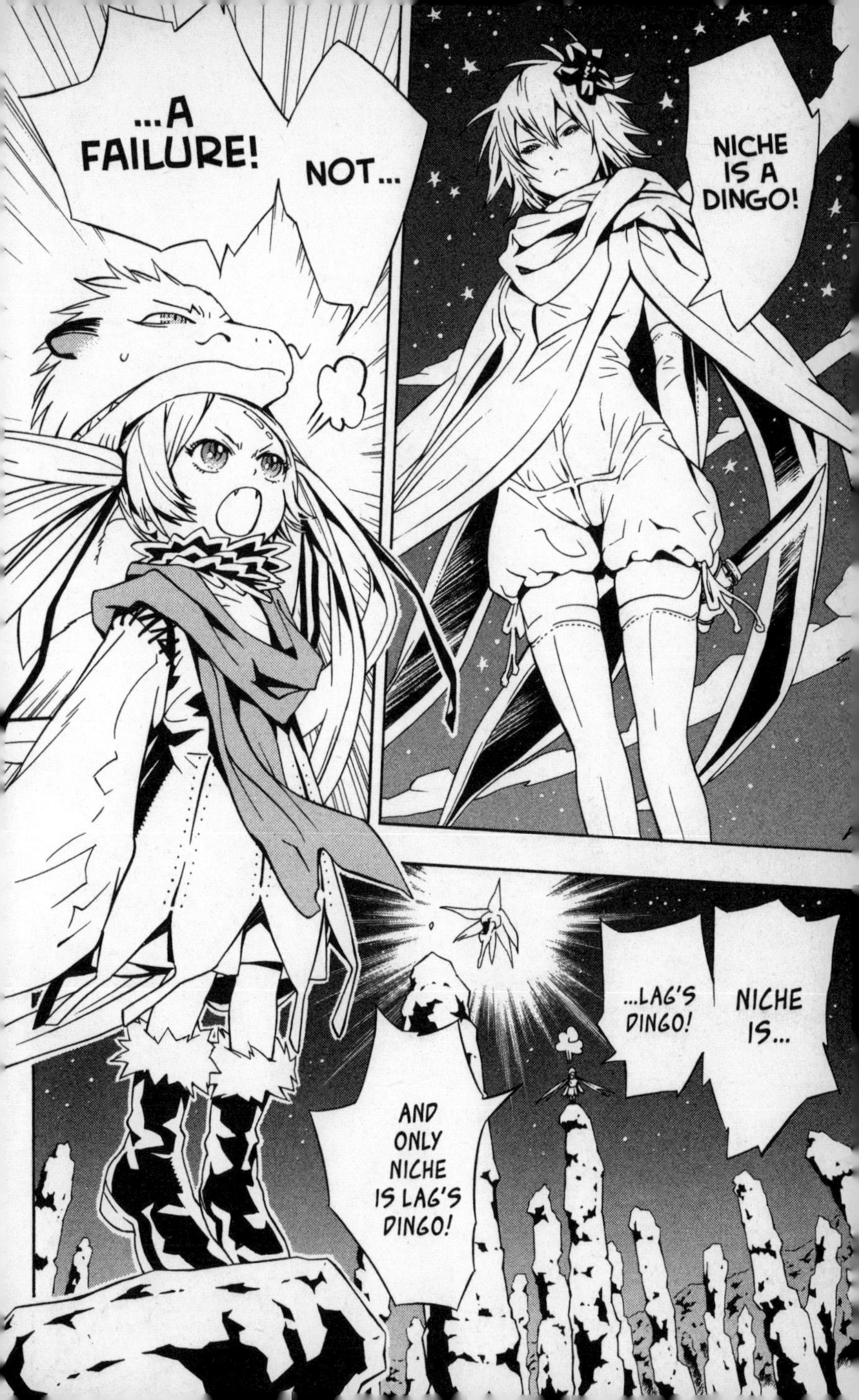
NICHE IS A DINGO!
NOT...
...A FAILURE!
NICHE IS...
...LAG'S DINGO!
AND ONLY NICHE IS LAG'S DINGO!

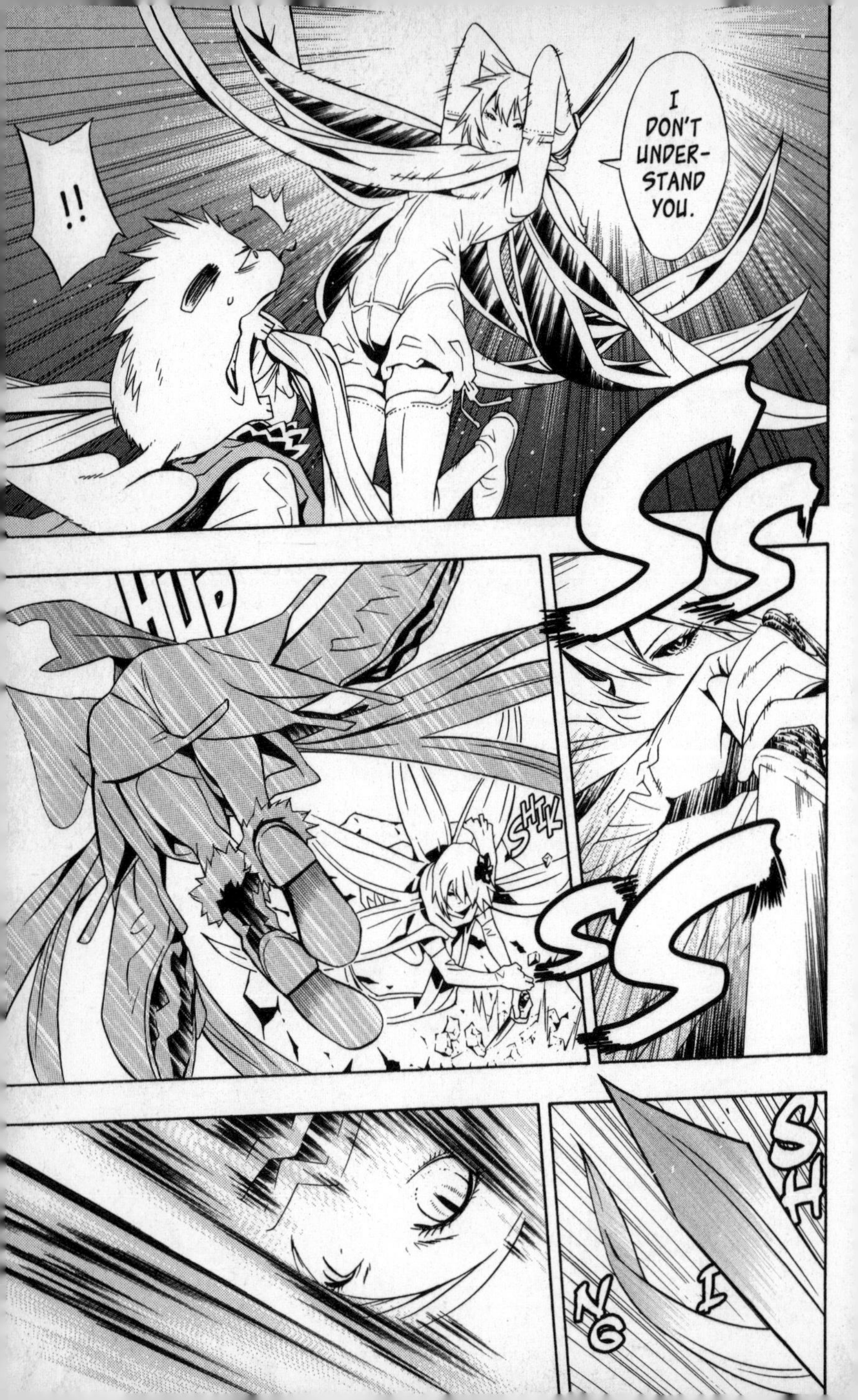
I DON'T UNDERSTAND YOU.
!!
SS
SHIK
HUP
SS
SHIING

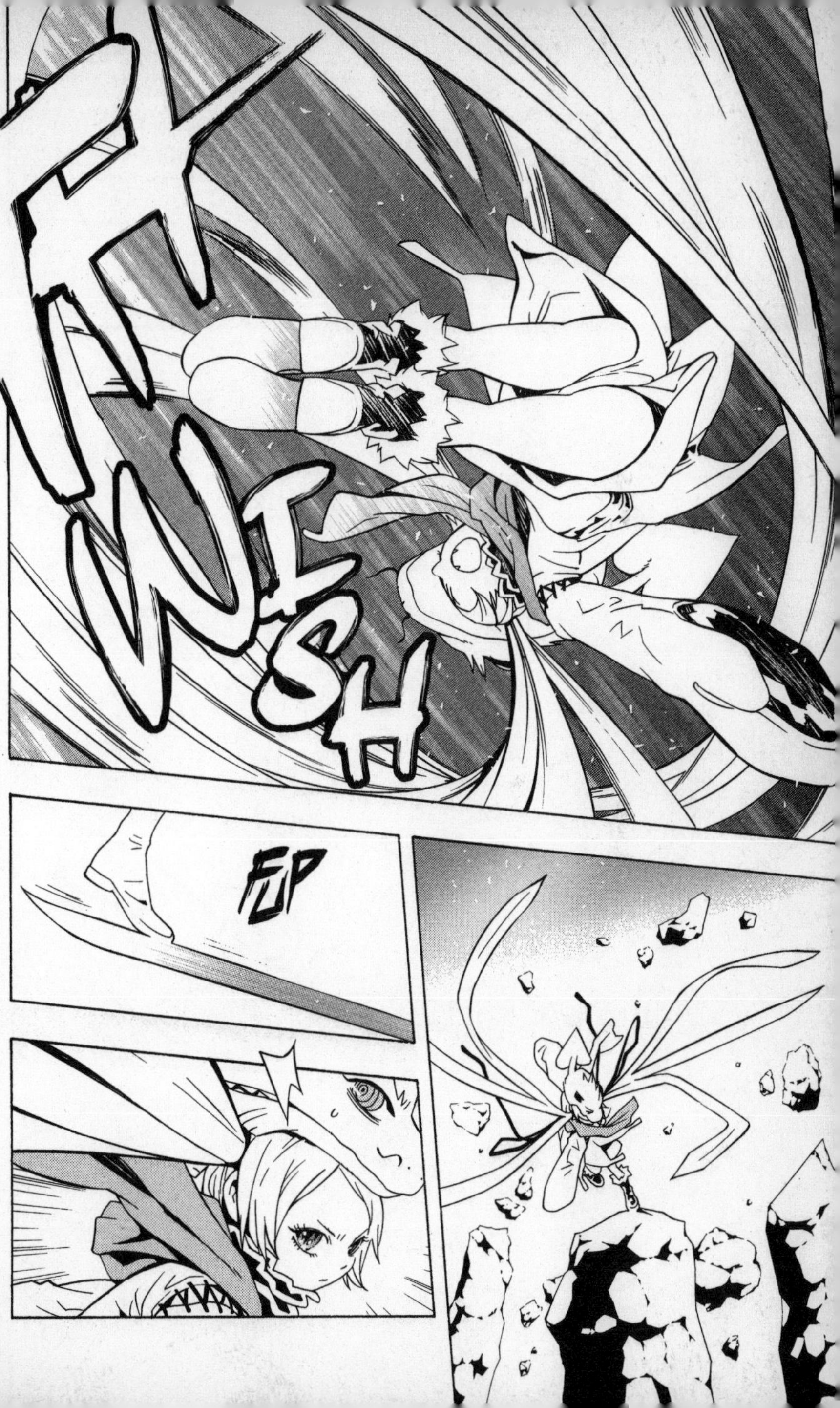
SWISH
FUP

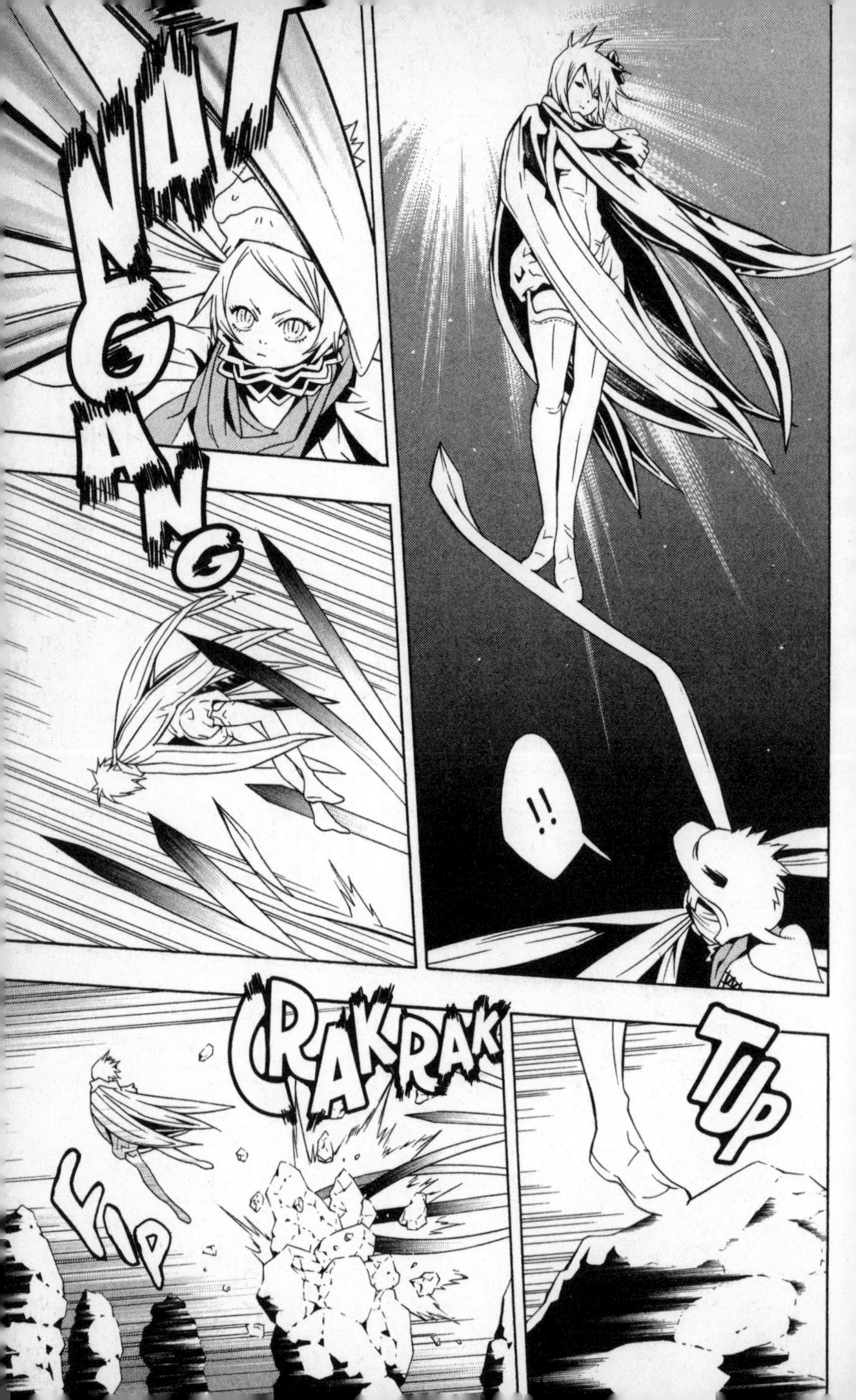
!!
WHANG
TUP
CRAKRAK
HOP

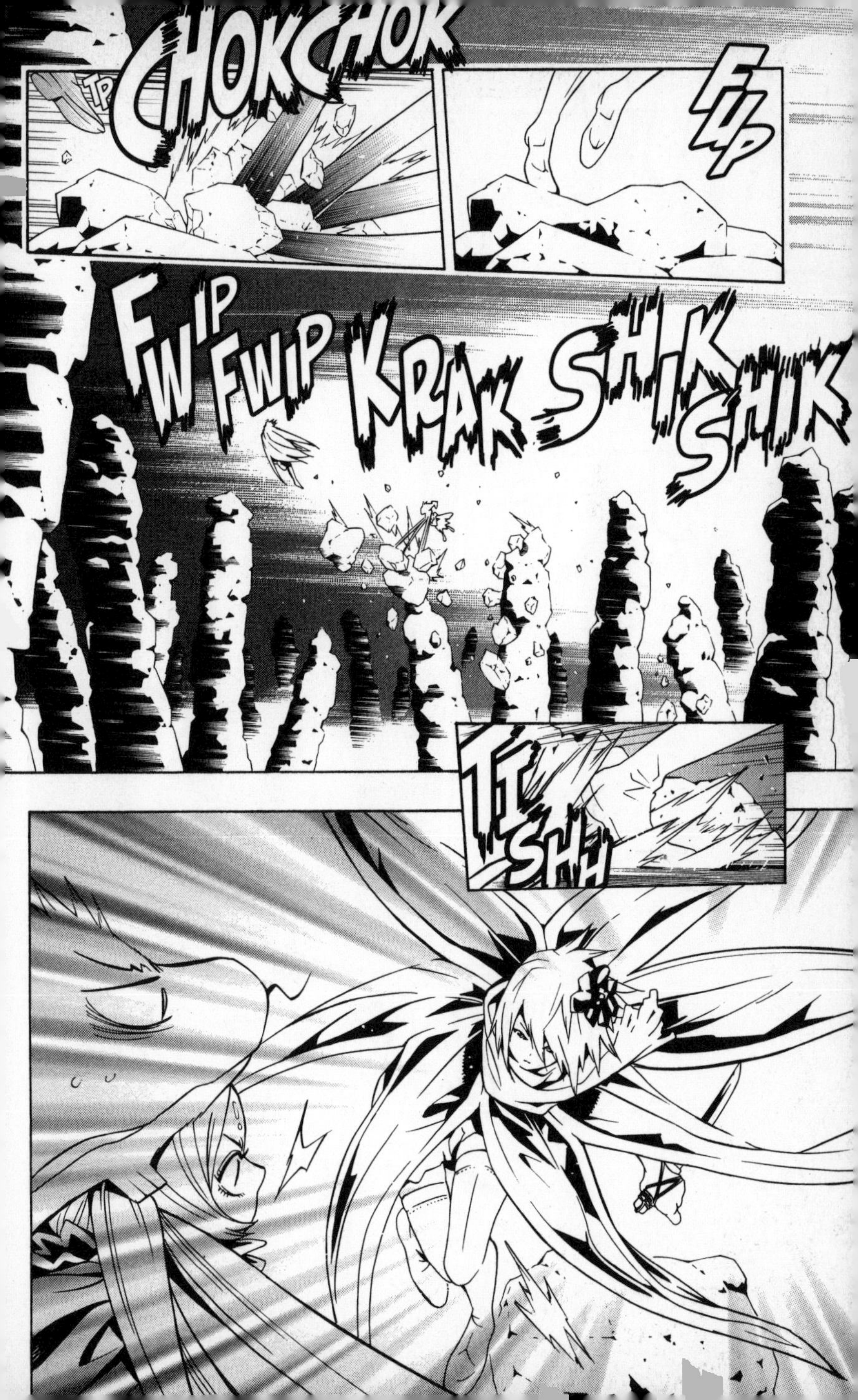

FLIP
CHOKCHOK
TP
SHIK SHIK
SHIK
KRAK
FWIP FWIP
TI
SHH

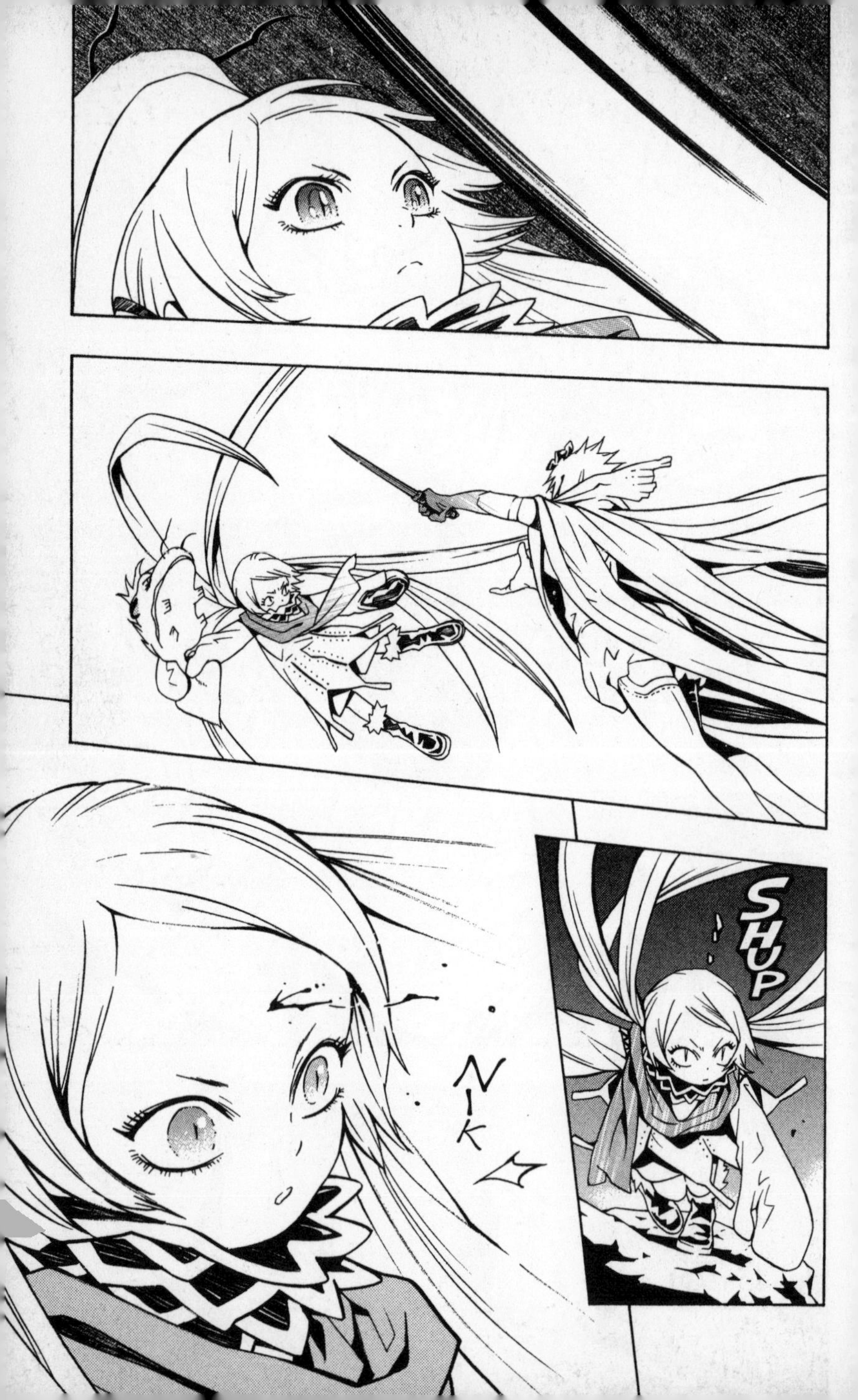
SHUP
NIK

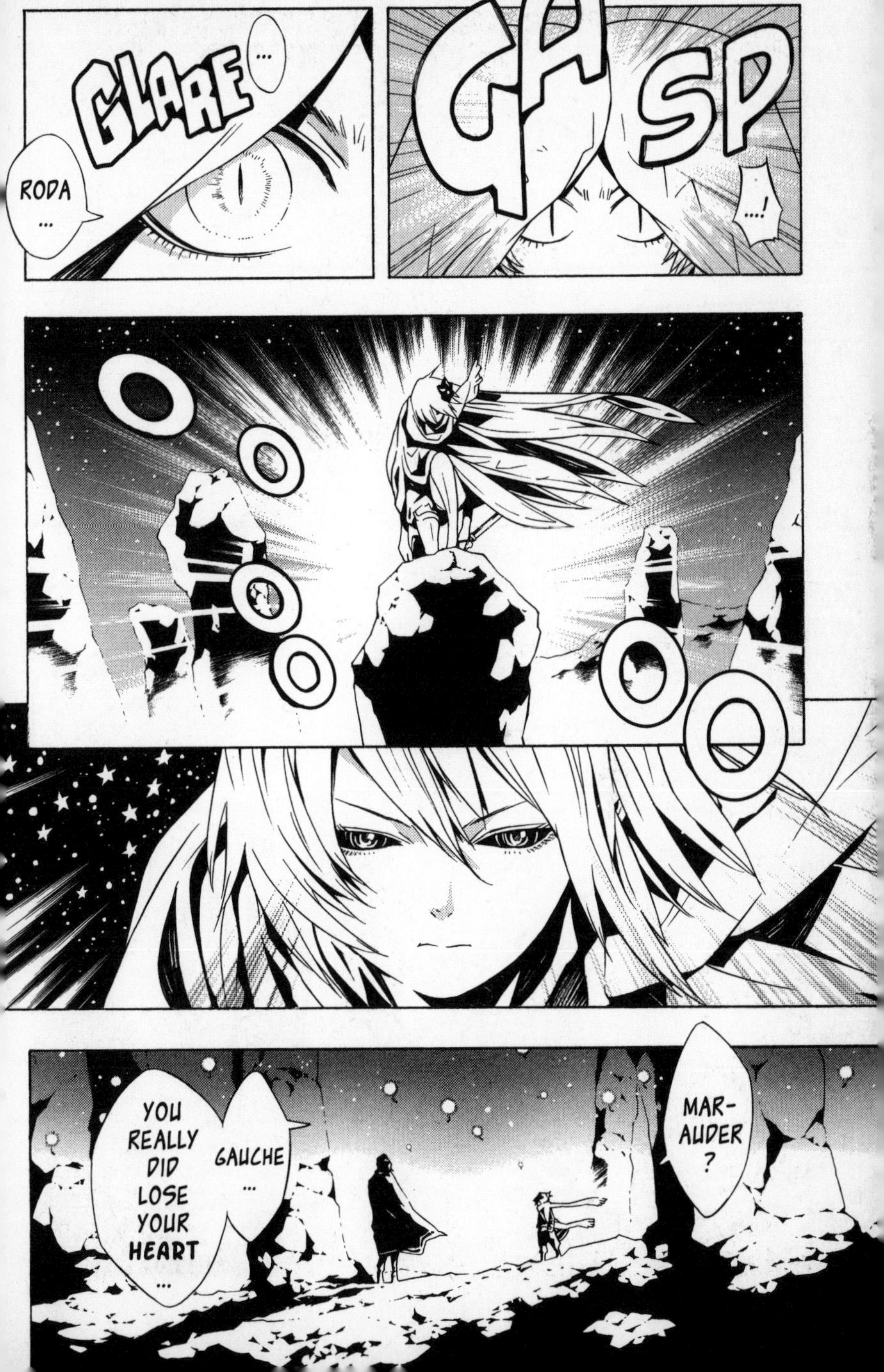
GASP
...!
...
GLARE
RODA ...
OOOOOO
MAR-AUDER?
GAUCHE ...
YOU REALLY DID LOSE YOUR HEART ...

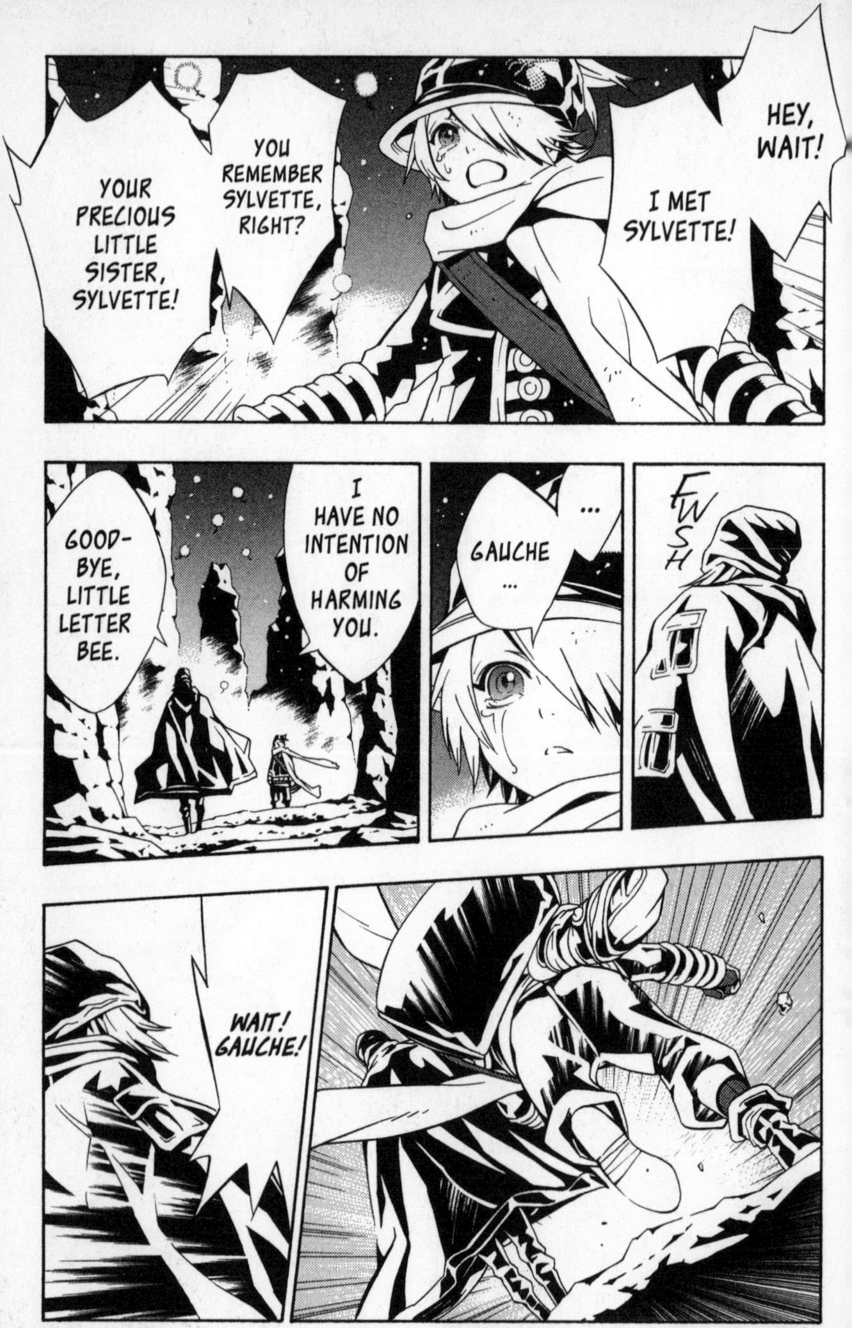
HEY, WAIT!
I MET SYLVETTE!
YOU REMEMBER SYLVETTE, RIGHT?
YOUR PRECIOUS LITTLE SISTER, SYLVETTE!
FWSH
... GAUCHE ...
I HAVE NO INTENTION OF HARMING YOU.
GOOD-BYE, LITTLE LETTER BEE.
WAIT! GAUCHE!

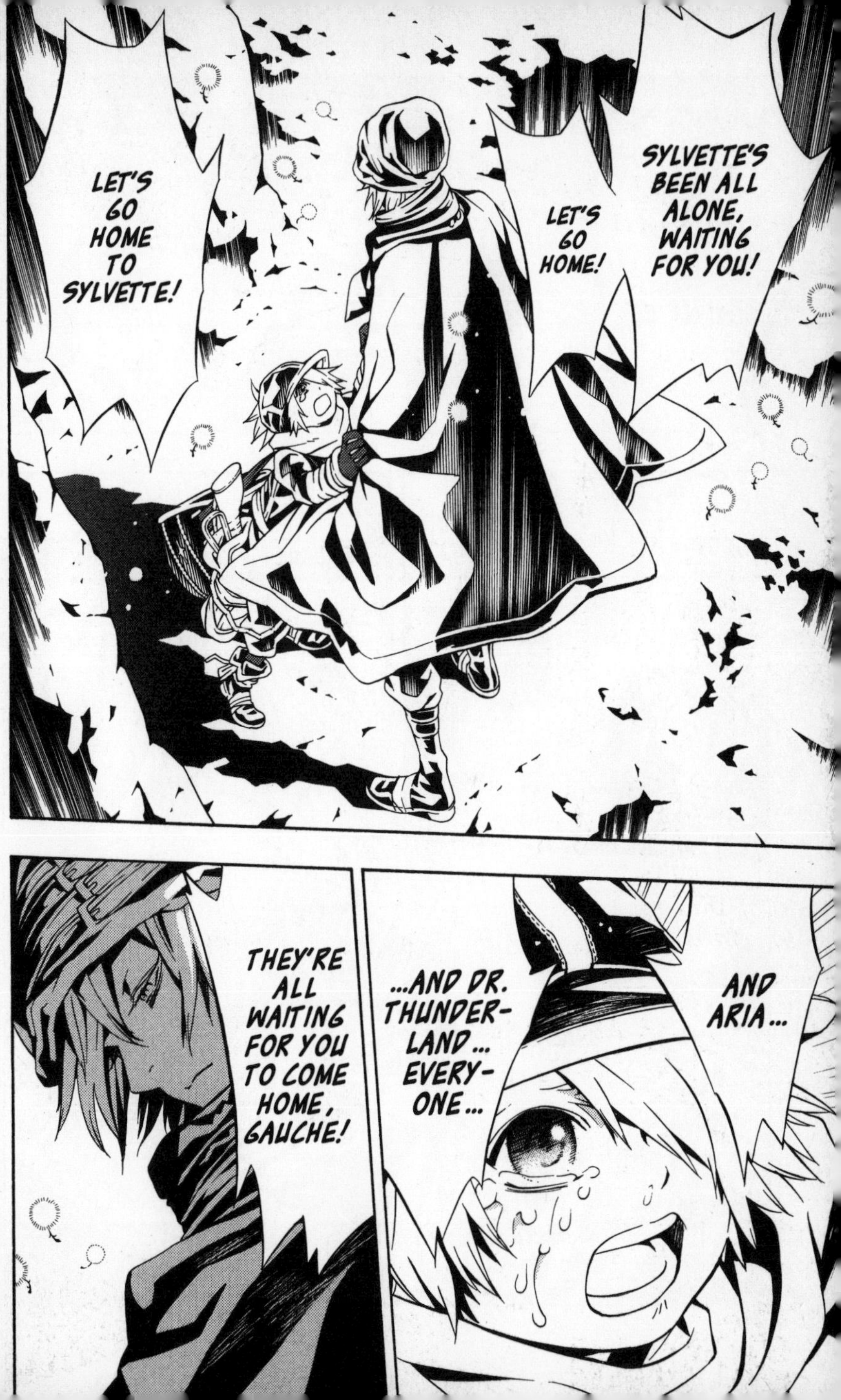
SYLVETTE'S BEEN ALL ALONE, WAITING FOR YOU!
LET'S GO HOME!
LET'S GO HOME TO SYLVETTE!
AND ARIA...
...AND DR. THUNDER-LAND... EVERY-ONE...
THEY'RE ALL WAITING FOR YOU TO COME HOME, GAUCHE!

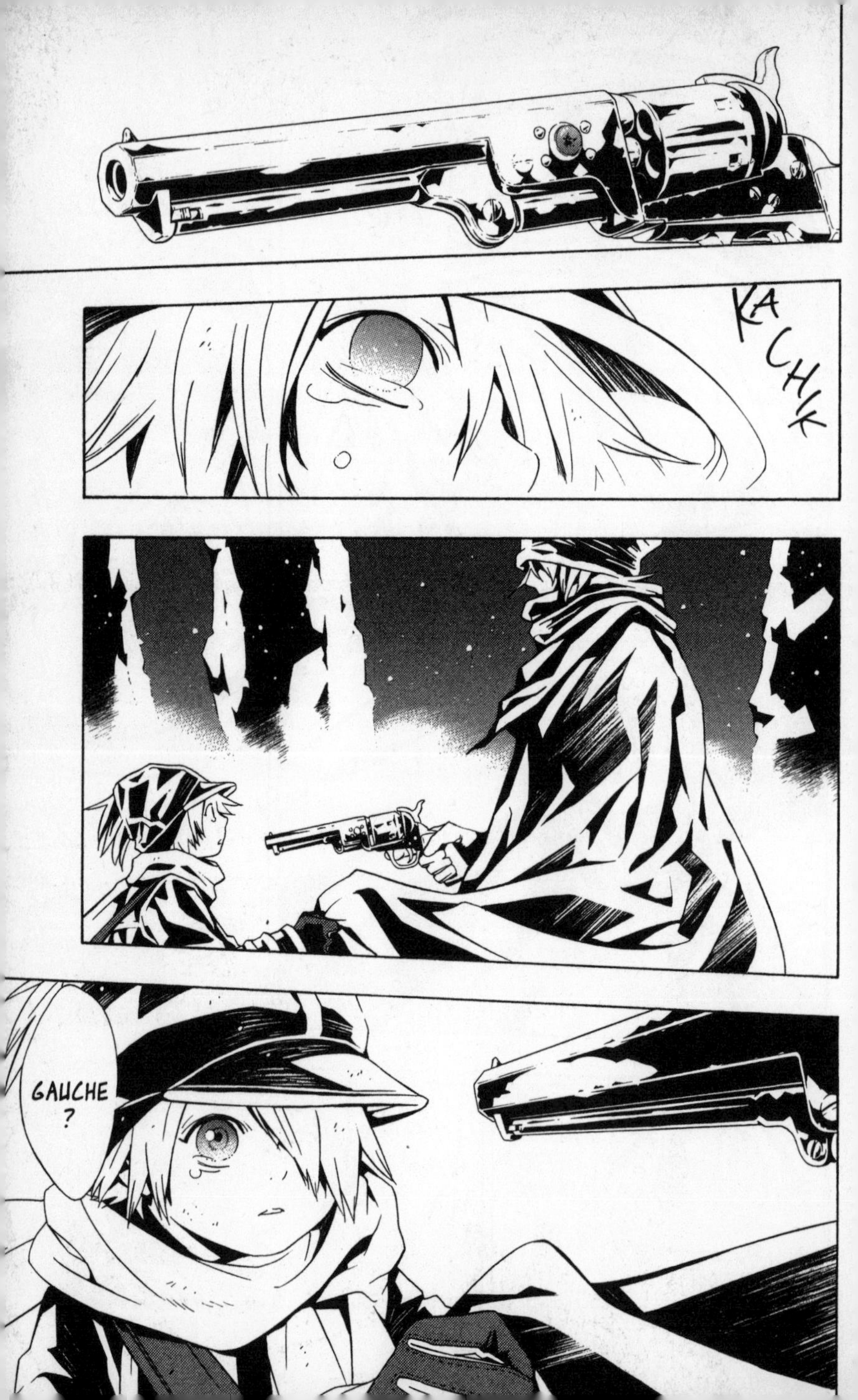
KA CHIK
GAUCHE ?

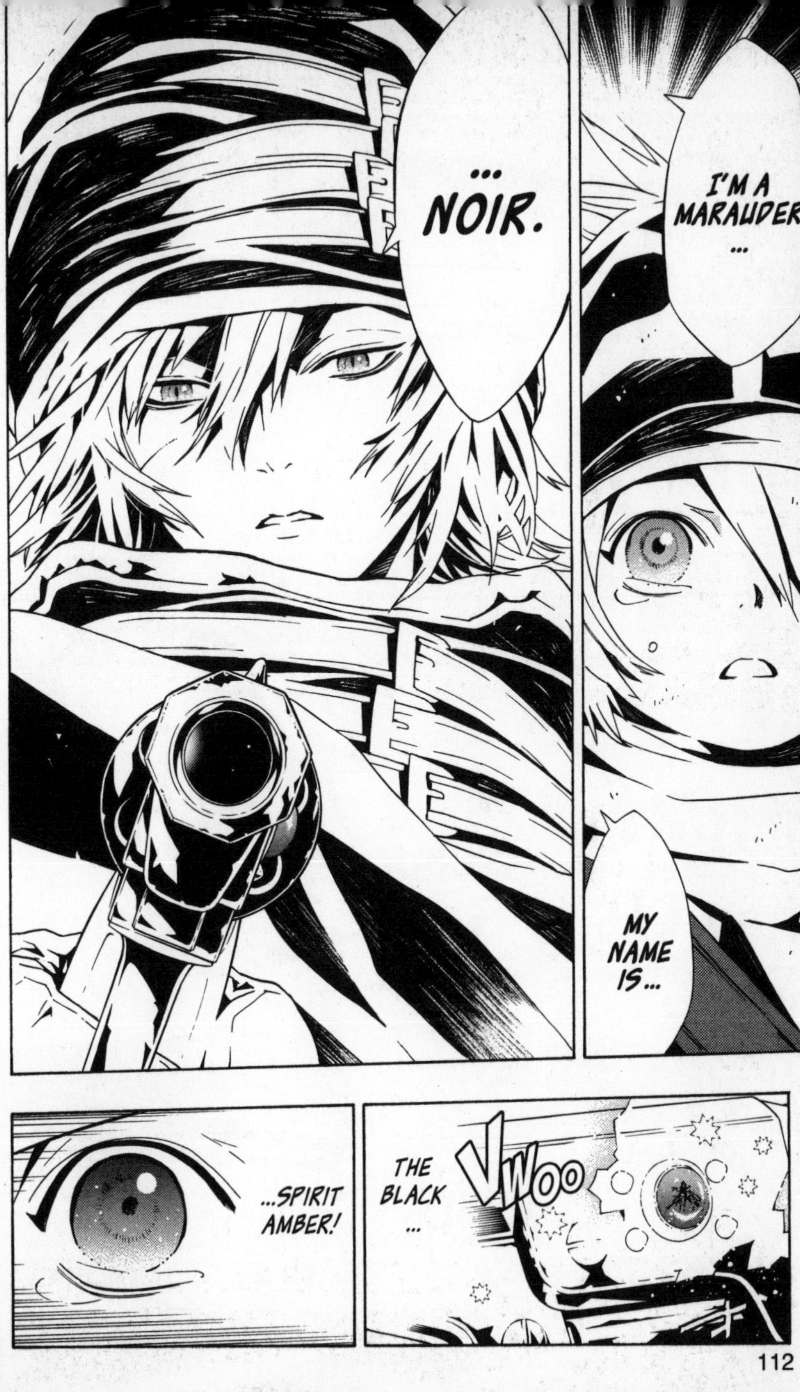
I'M A MARAUDER ...
MY NAME IS...
...NOIR.
THE BLACK ...
VWOO
...SPIRIT AMBER!

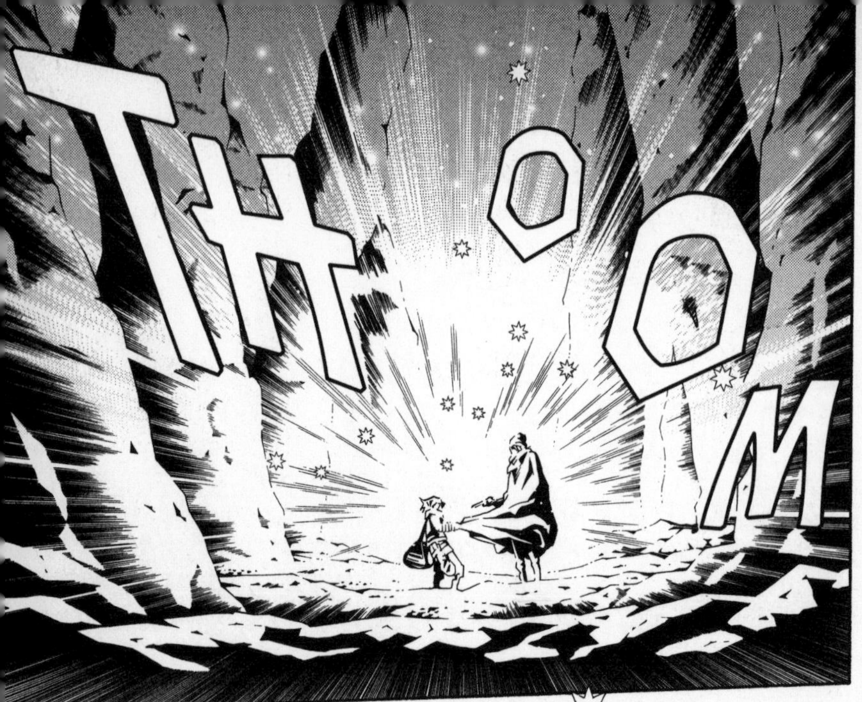
THOOM
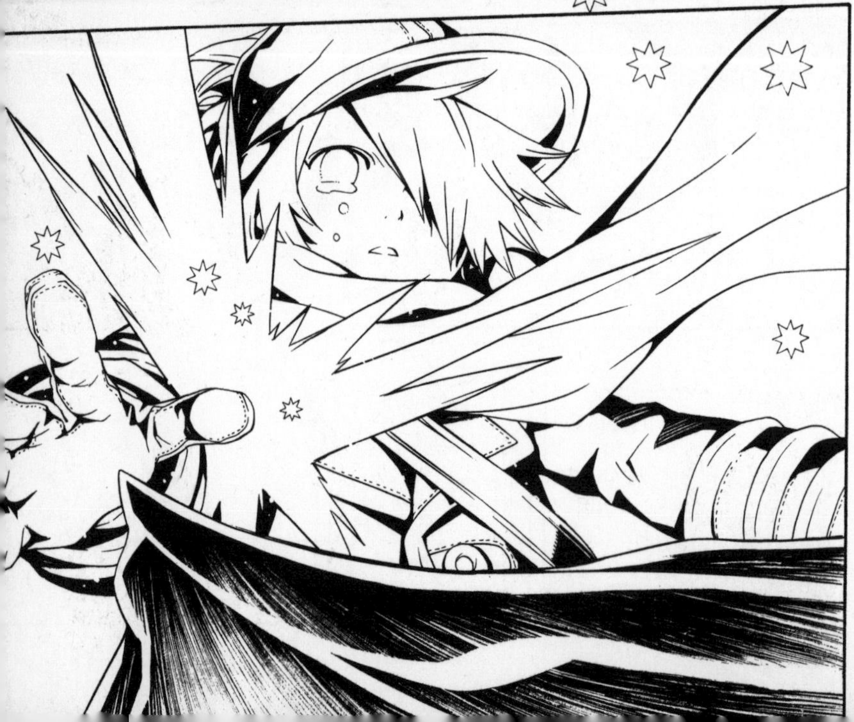

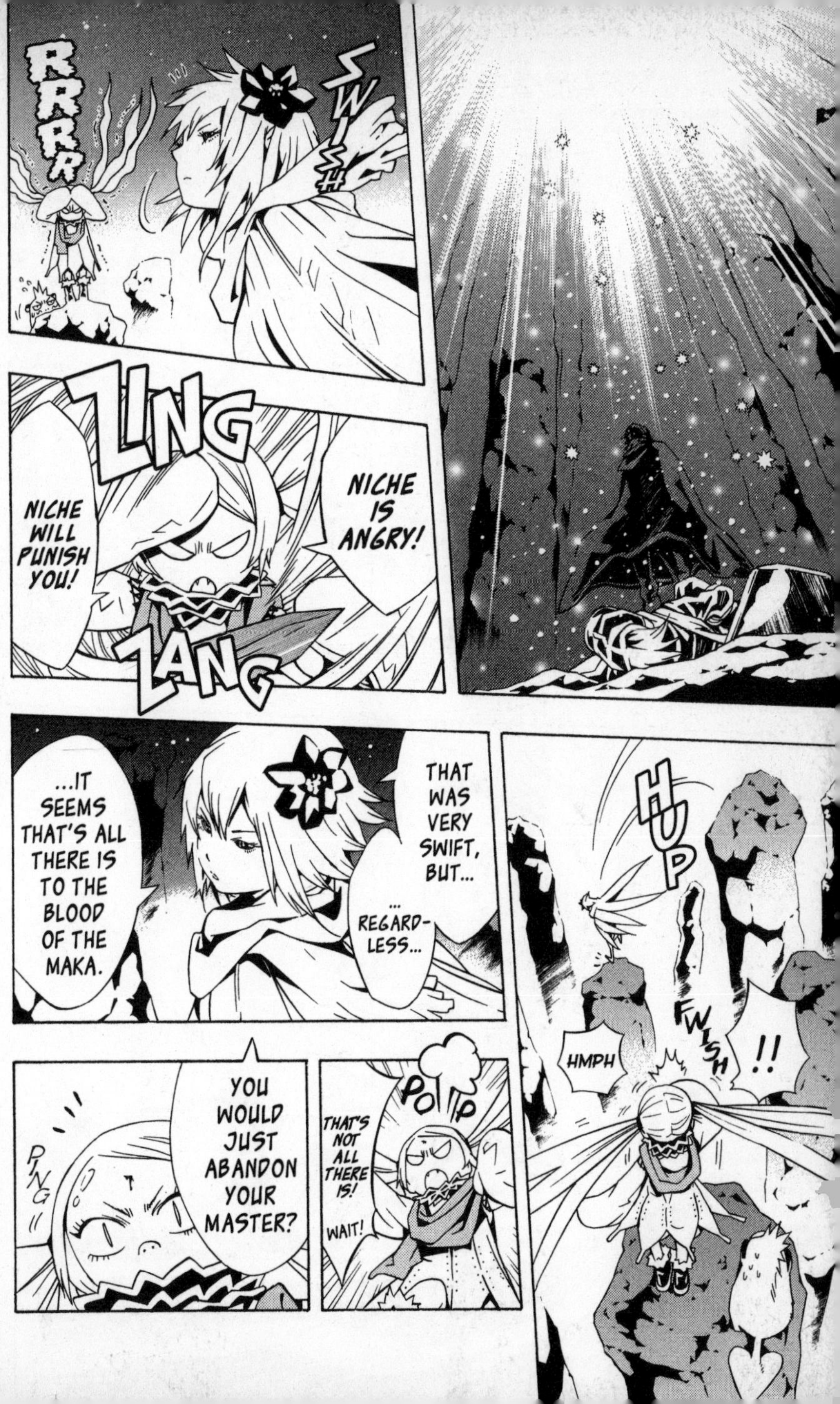
RRRRR
SWISH
ZING
NICHE IS ANGRY!
NICHE WILL PUNISH YOU!
ZANG
HUP
HMPH
FWISH
!!
THAT WAS VERY SWIFT, BUT...
...REGARDLESS...
...IT SEEMS THAT'S ALL THERE IS TO THE BLOOD OF THE MAKA.
POP
THAT'S NOT ALL THERE IS!
WAIT!
YOU WOULD JUST ABANDON YOUR MASTER?
PING

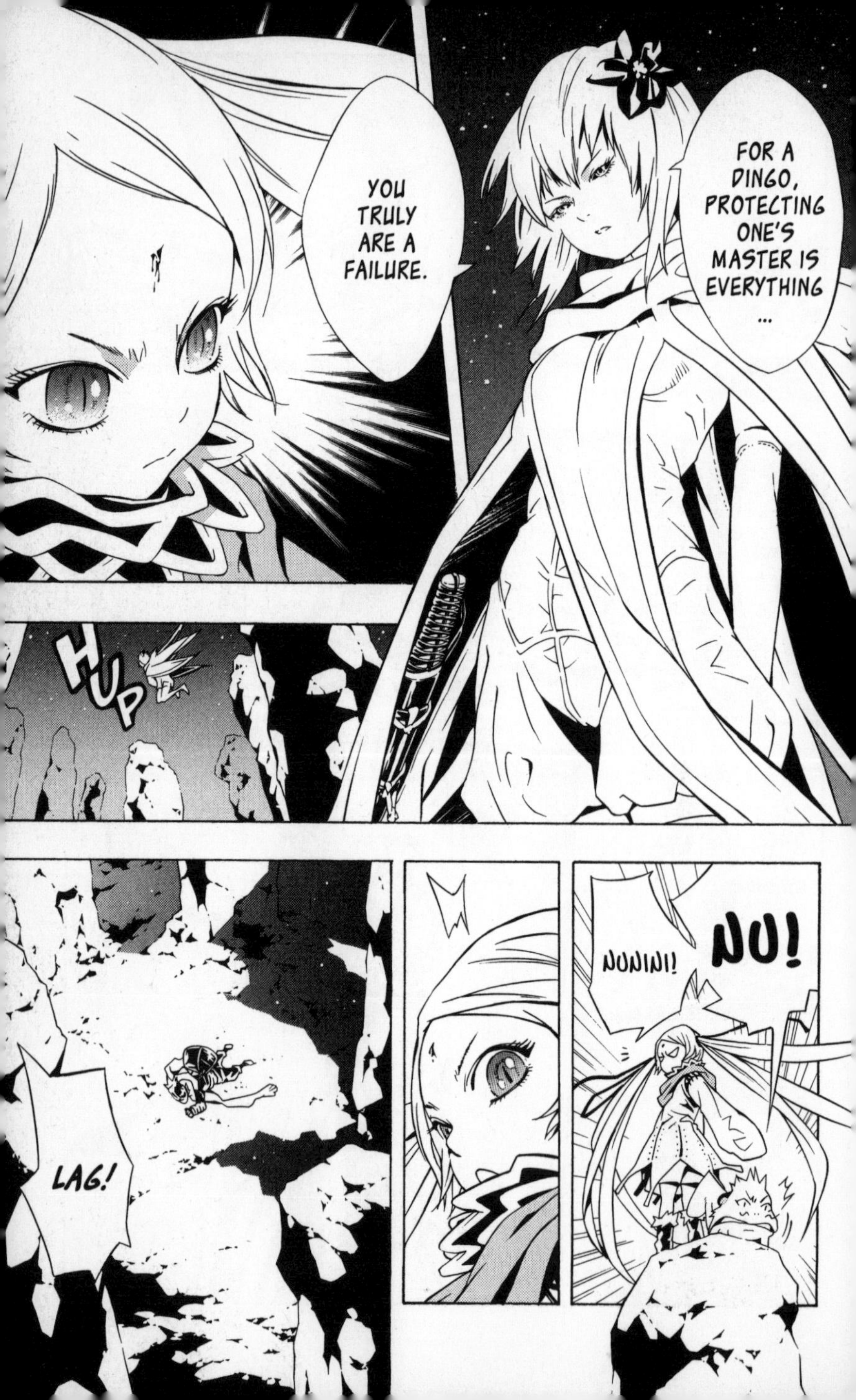
FOR A DINGO, PROTECTING ONE'S MASTER IS EVERYTHING ...
YOU TRULY ARE A FAILURE.
HUP
NU!
NUNINI!
LAG!

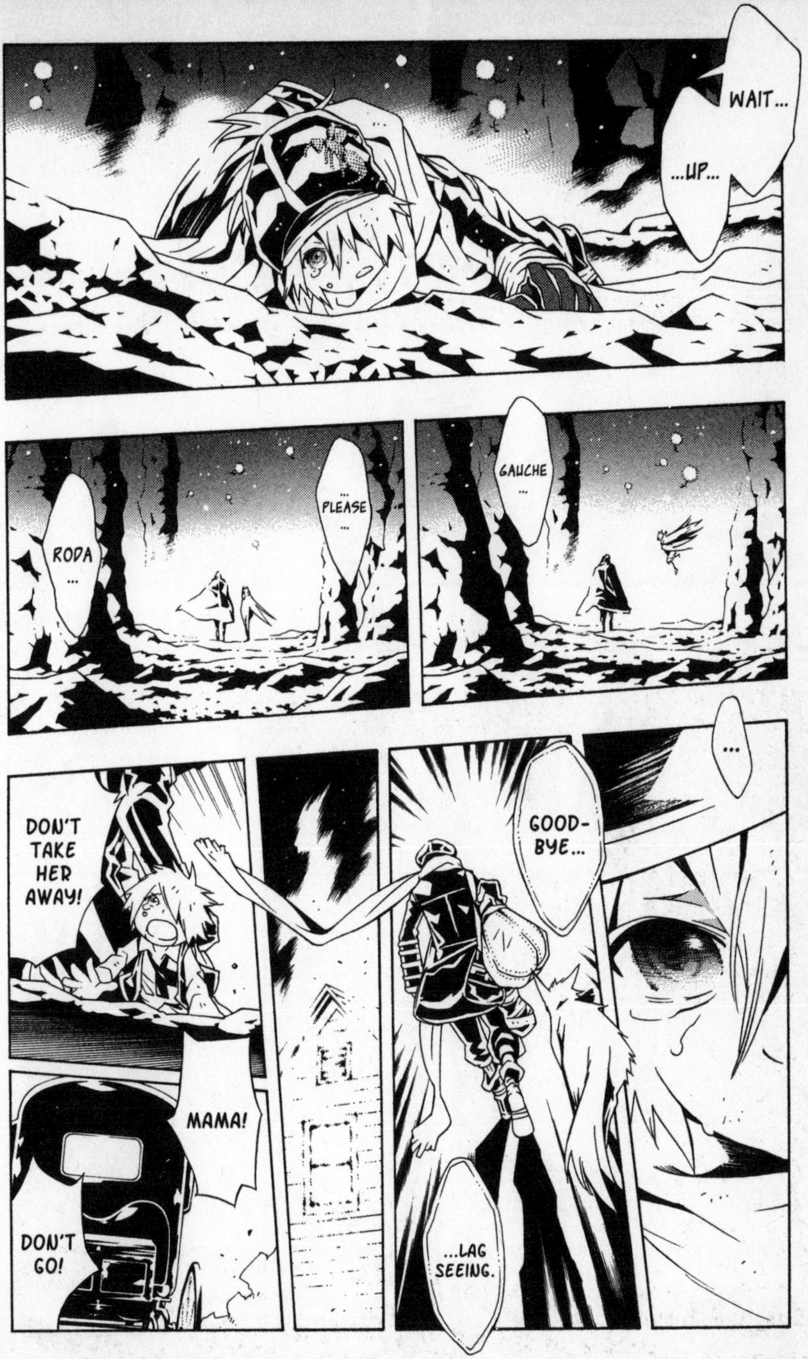
WAIT...
...UP...
GAUCHE ...
... PLEASE ...
RODA ...
...
GOOD-BYE...
...LAG SEEING.
DON'T TAKE HER AWAY!
MAMA!
DON'T GO!

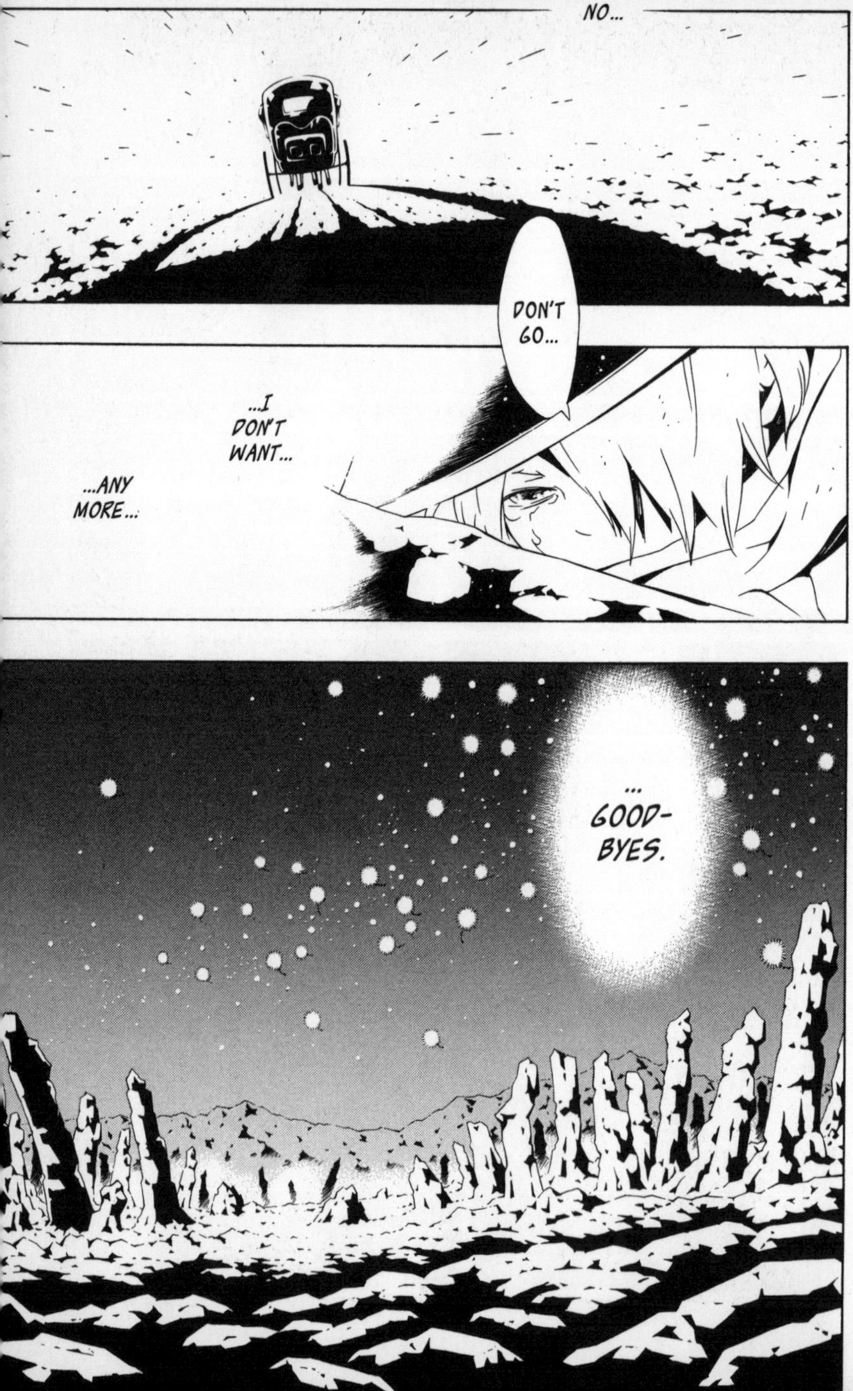
NO...
DON'T GO...
...I DON'T WANT...
...ANY MORE...
... GOOD-BYES.

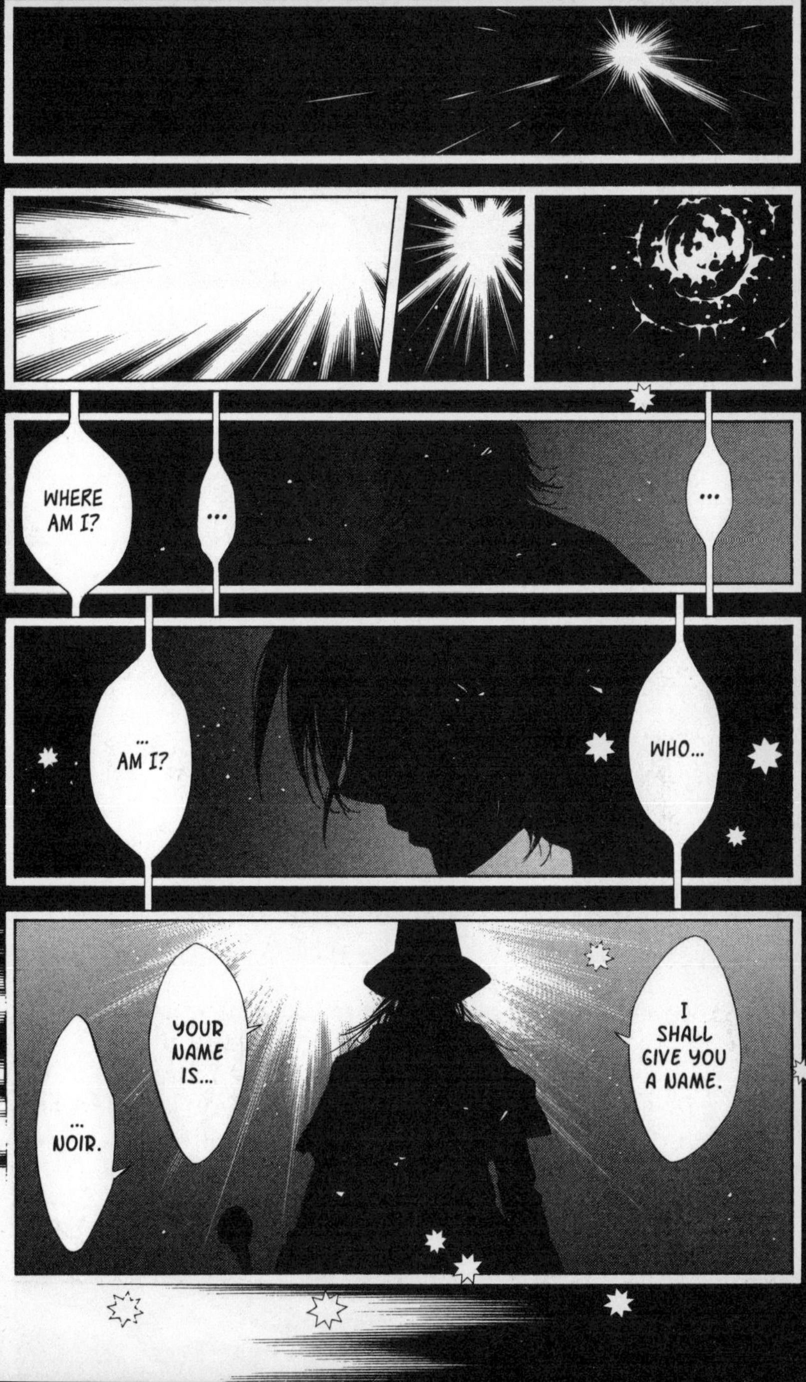
...
...
WHERE AM I?
WHO...
... AM I?
I SHALL GIVE YOU A NAME.
YOUR NAME IS...
... NOIR.

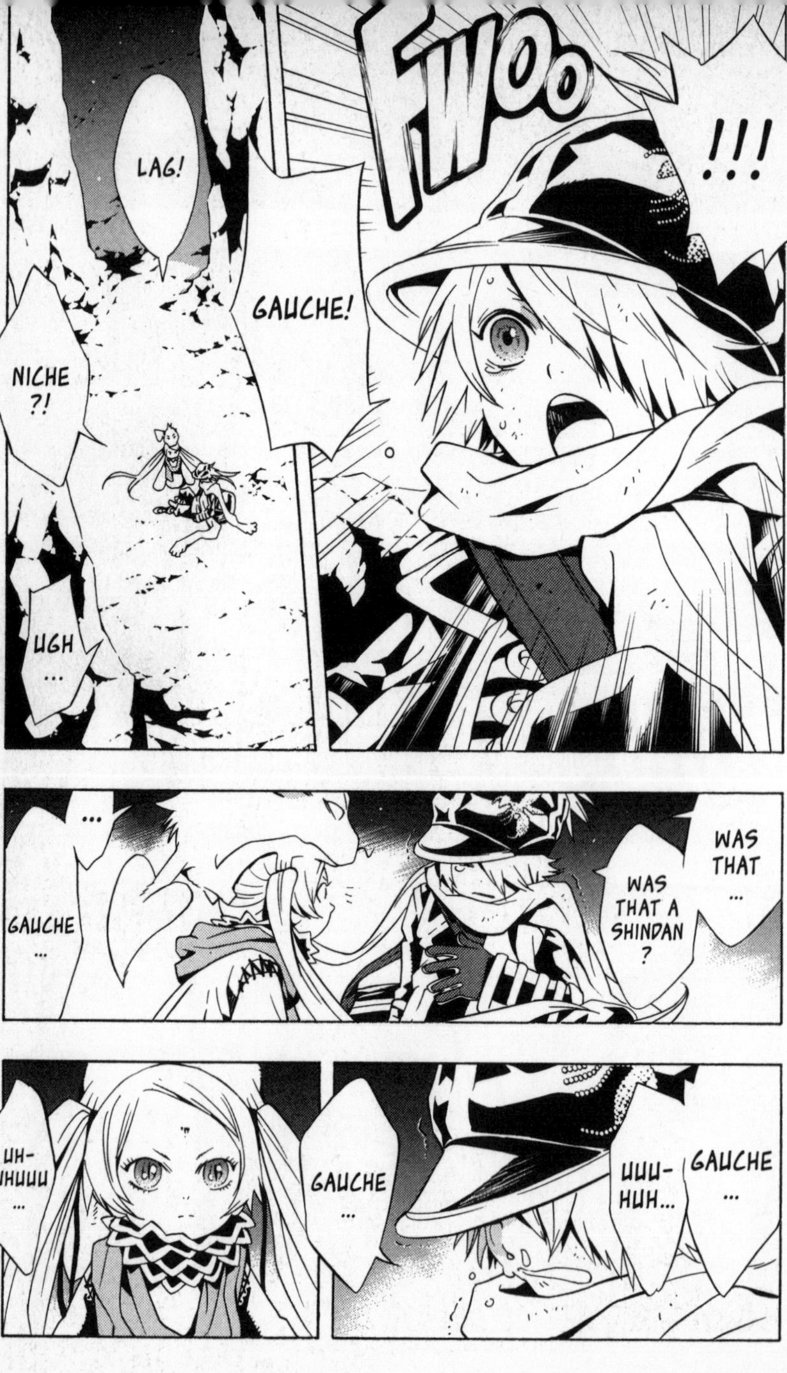
FWOO
!!!
GAUCHE!
LAG!
NICHE ?!
UGH ...
WAS THAT ...
WAS THAT A SHINDAN ?
...
GAUCHE ...
GAUCHE ...
UUU-HUH...
GAUCHE ...
UH-WHUUU ...

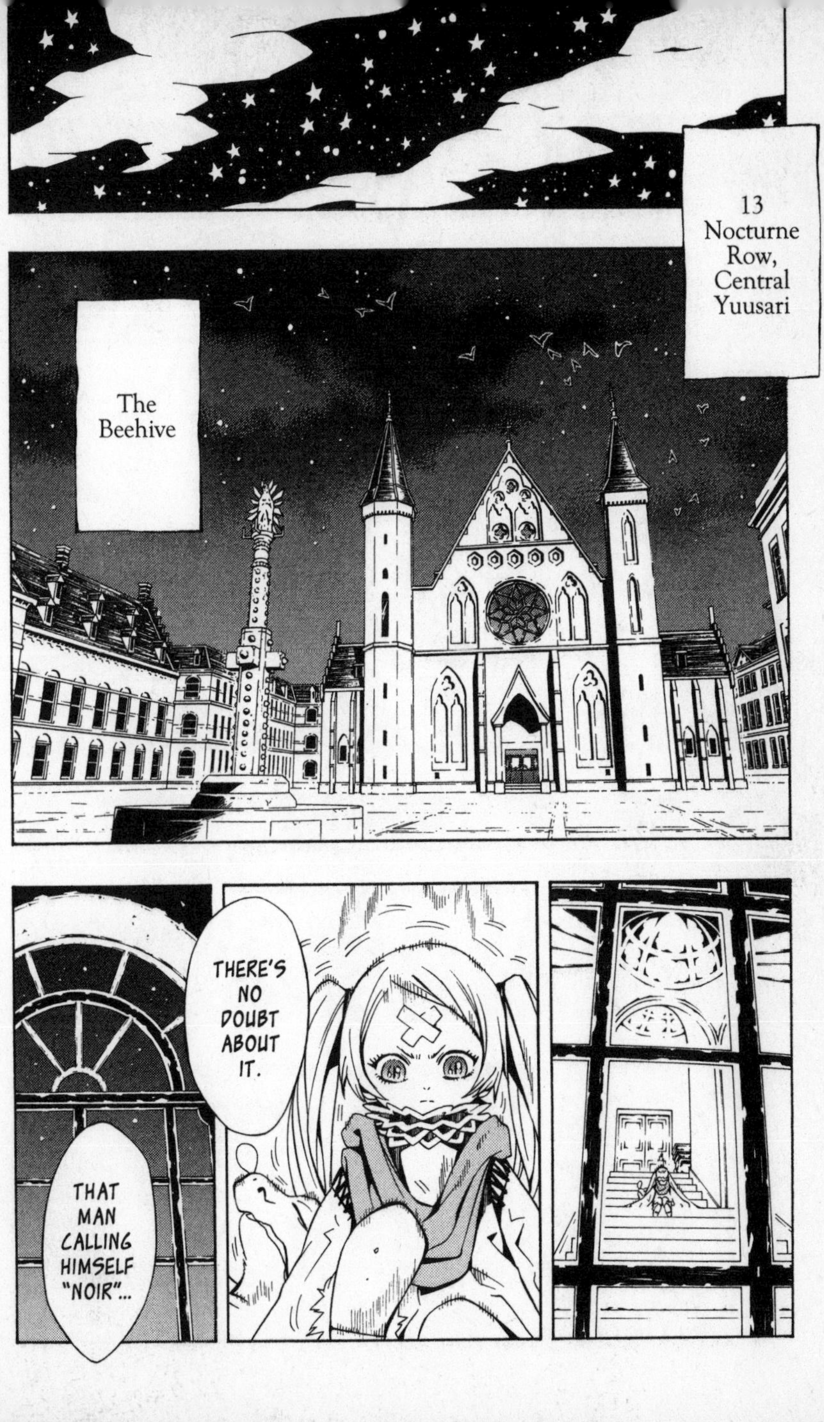
13 Nocturne Row, Central Yuusari
The Beehive
THERE'S NO DOUBT ABOUT IT.
THAT MAN CALLING HIMSELF "NOIR"...

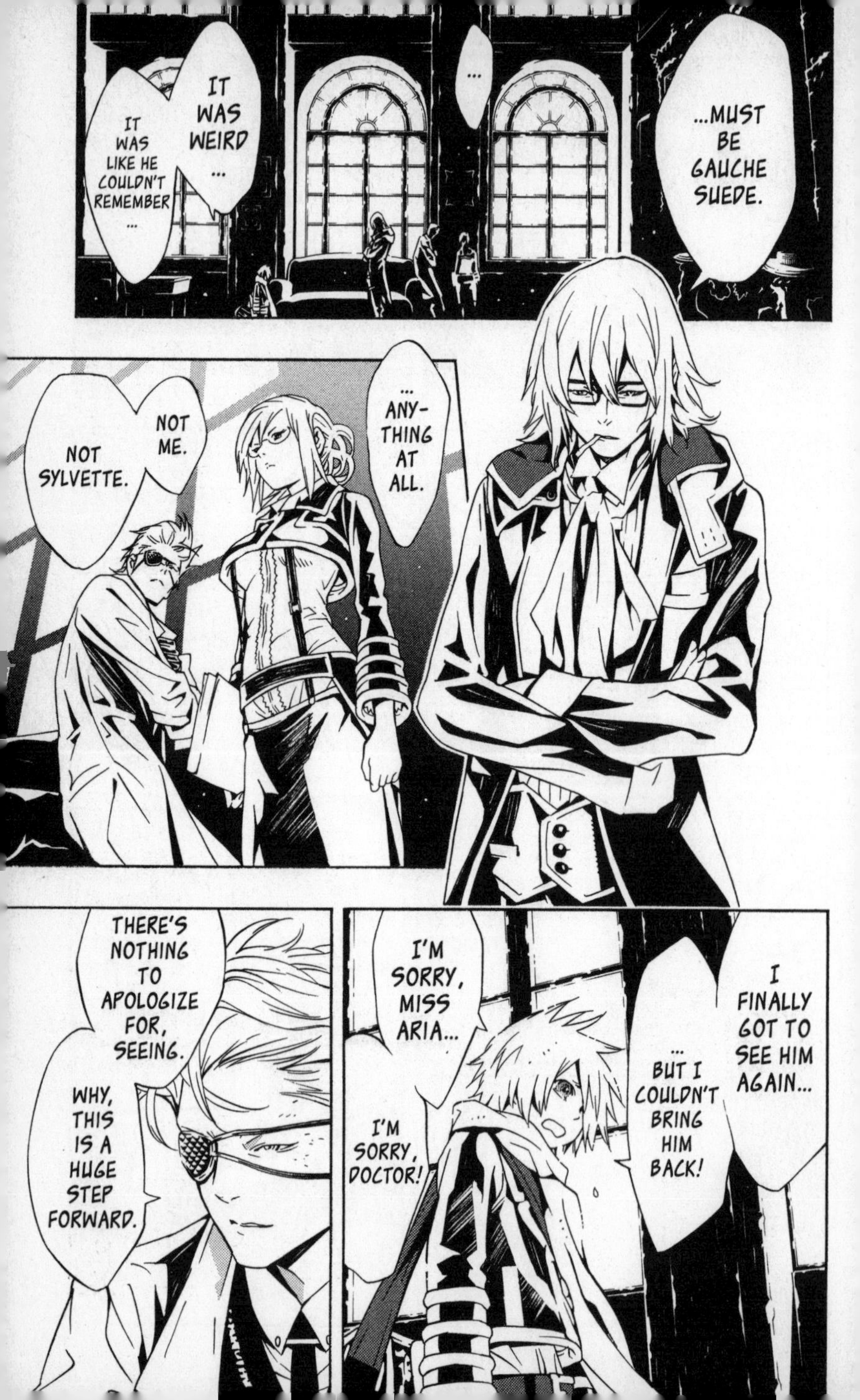
...MUST BE GAUCHE SUEDE.
...
IT WAS WEIRD...
IT WAS LIKE HE COULDN'T REMEMBER...
... ANYTHING AT ALL.
NOT ME.
NOT SYLVETTE.
I FINALLY GOT TO SEE HIM AGAIN...
... BUT I COULDN'T BRING HIM BACK!
I'M SORRY, MISS ARIA...
I'M SORRY, DOCTOR!
THERE'S NOTHING TO APOLOGIZE FOR, SEEING.
WHY, THIS IS A HUGE STEP FORWARD.

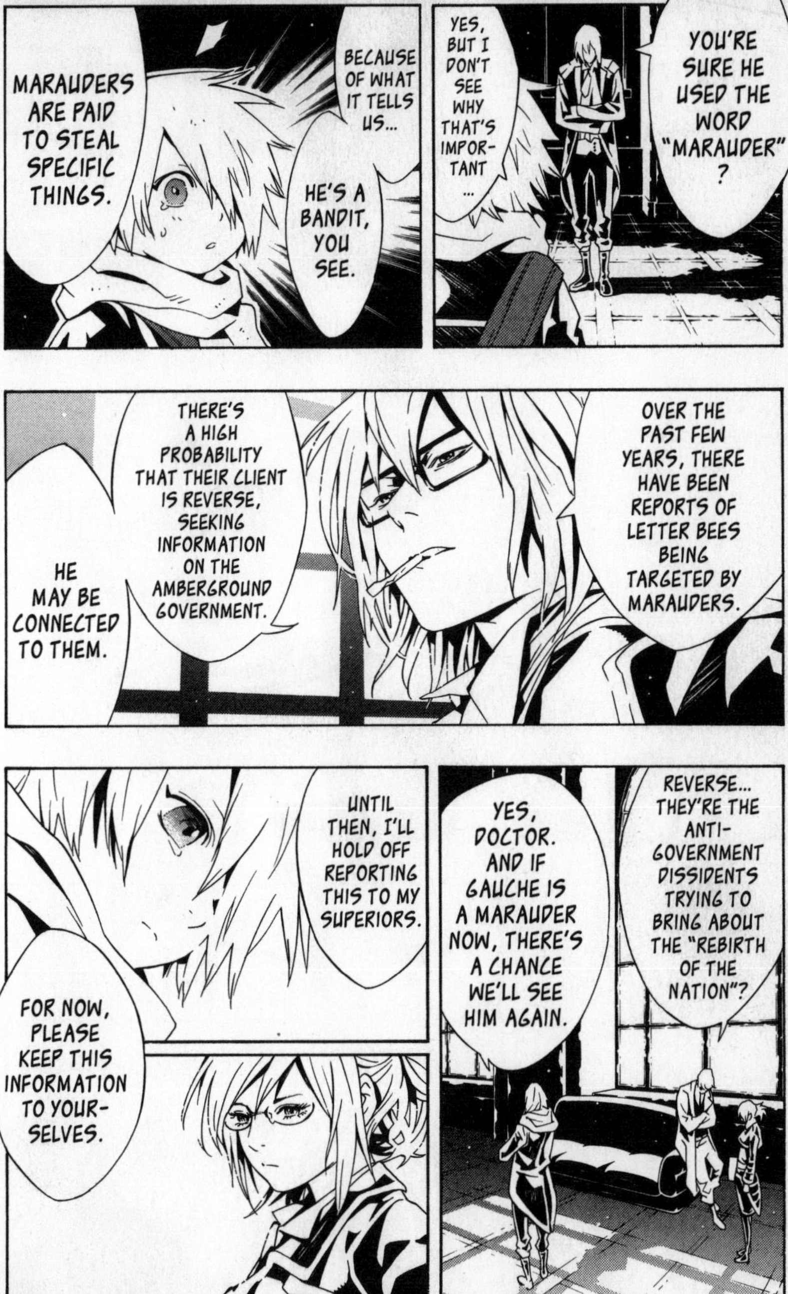
YOU'RE SURE HE USED THE WORD "MARAUDER"?
YES, BUT I DON'T SEE WHY THAT'S IMPORTANT...
BECAUSE OF WHAT IT TELLS US...
HE'S A BANDIT, YOU SEE.
MARAUDERS ARE PAID TO STEAL SPECIFIC THINGS.
OVER THE PAST FEW YEARS, THERE HAVE BEEN REPORTS OF LETTER BEES BEING TARGETED BY MARAUDERS.
THERE'S A HIGH PROBABILITY THAT THEIR CLIENT IS REVERSE, SEEKING INFORMATION ON THE AMBERGROUND GOVERNMENT.
HE MAY BE CONNECTED TO THEM.
REVERSE... THEY'RE THE ANTI-GOVERNMENT DISSIDENTS TRYING TO BRING ABOUT THE "REBIRTH OF THE NATION"?
YES, DOCTOR. AND IF GAUCHE IS A MARAUDER NOW, THERE'S A CHANCE WE'LL SEE HIM AGAIN.
UNTIL THEN, I'LL HOLD OFF REPORTING THIS TO MY SUPERIORS.
FOR NOW, PLEASE KEEP THIS INFORMATION TO YOURSELVES.

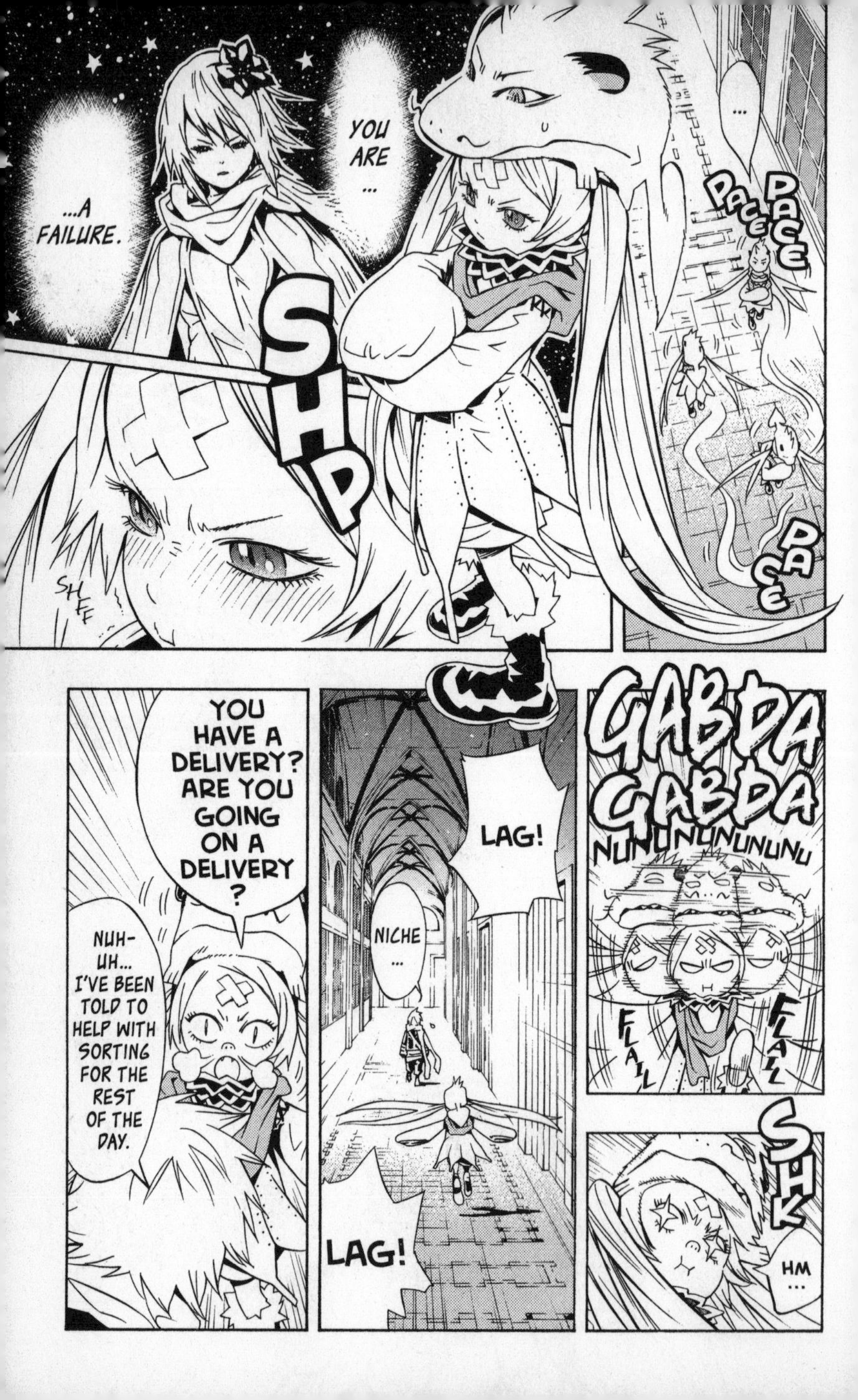
...
PACE PACE
PACE
YOU ARE ...
...A FAILURE.
SHP
SHFF
GABBA GABBA
NUNUNUNUNUNU
FLAIL FLAIL
SHK
HM ...
LAG!
NICHE ...
LAG!
YOU HAVE A DELIVERY? ARE YOU GOING ON A DELIVERY?
NUH-UH... I'VE BEEN TOLD TO HELP WITH SORTING FOR THE REST OF THE DAY.

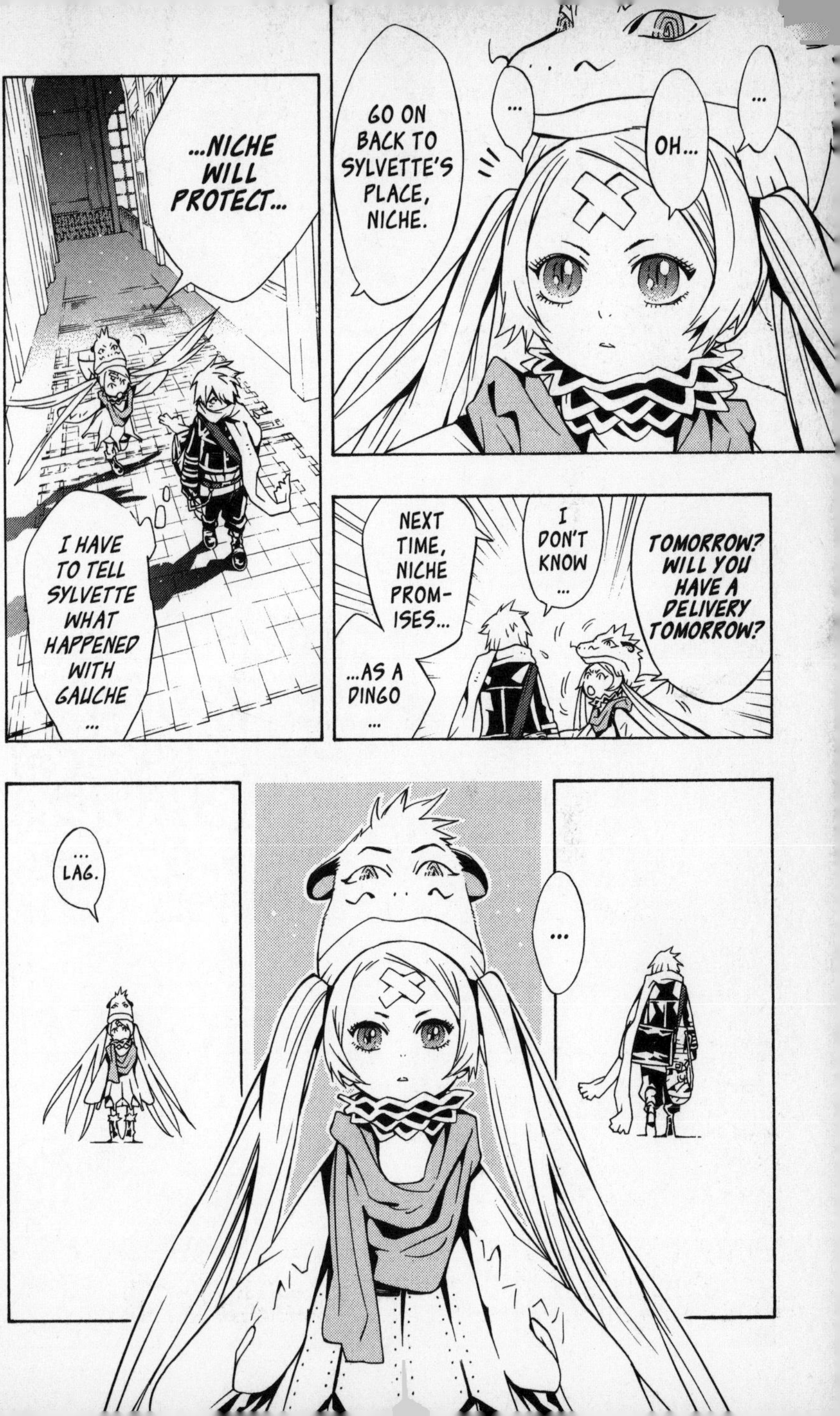
GO ON BACK TO SYLVETTE'S PLACE, NICHE.
...
OH...
...
TOMORROW? WILL YOU HAVE A DELIVERY TOMORROW?
I DON'T KNOW ...
NEXT TIME, NICHE PROMISES...
...AS A DINGO ...
...NICHE WILL PROTECT...
I HAVE TO TELL SYLVETTE WHAT HAPPENED WITH GAUCHE ...
...
... LAG.

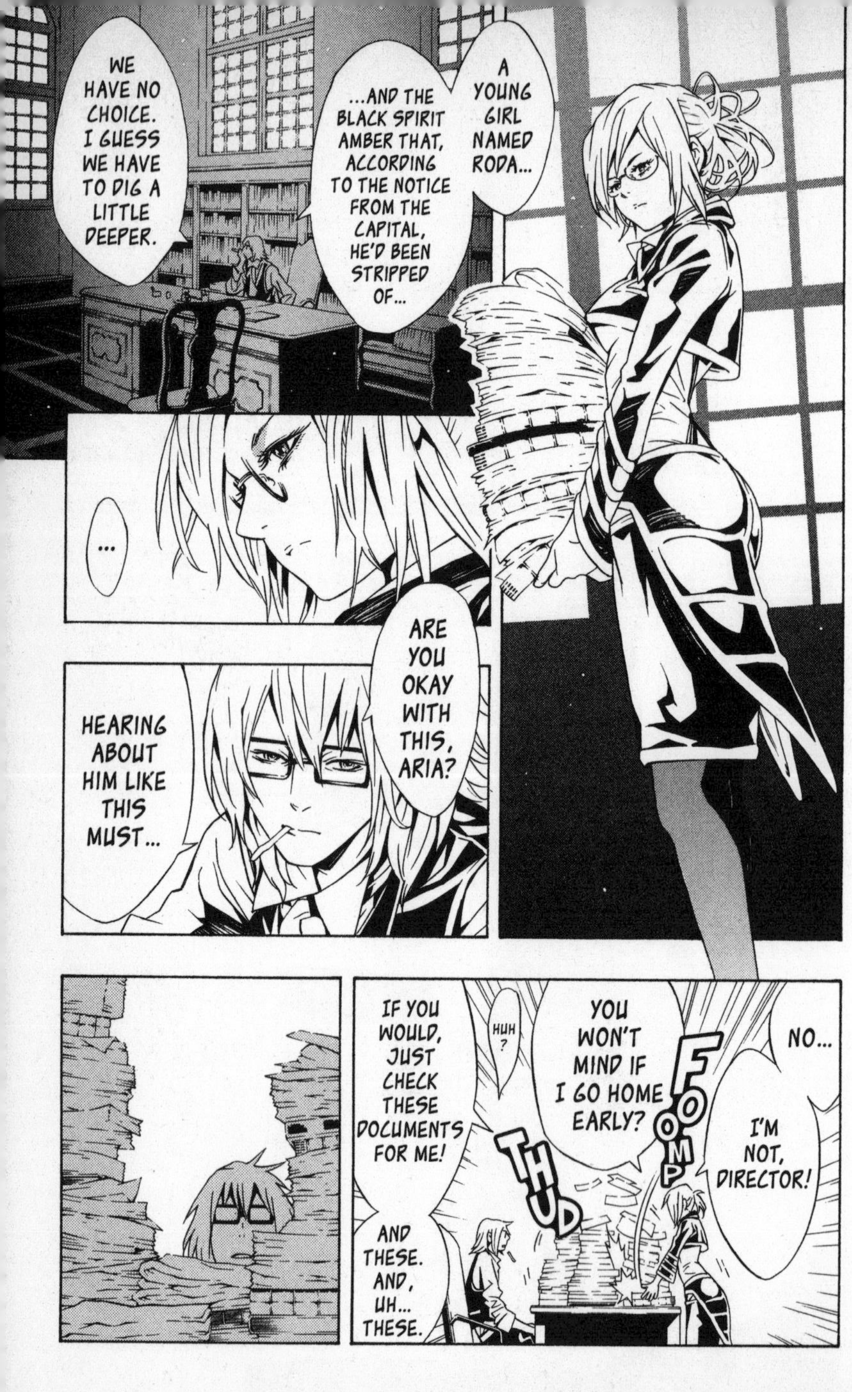
A YOUNG GIRL NAMED RODA...
...AND THE BLACK SPIRIT AMBER THAT, ACCORDING TO THE NOTICE FROM THE CAPITAL, HE'D BEEN STRIPPED OF...
WE HAVE NO CHOICE. I GUESS WE HAVE TO DIG A LITTLE DEEPER.
...
ARE YOU OKAY WITH THIS, ARIA?
HEARING ABOUT HIM LIKE THIS MUST...
NO...
I'M NOT, DIRECTOR!
FOOMP
YOU WON'T MIND IF I GO HOME EARLY?
THUD
HUH?
IF YOU WOULD, JUST CHECK THESE DOCUMENTS FOR ME!
AND THESE. AND, UH... THESE.

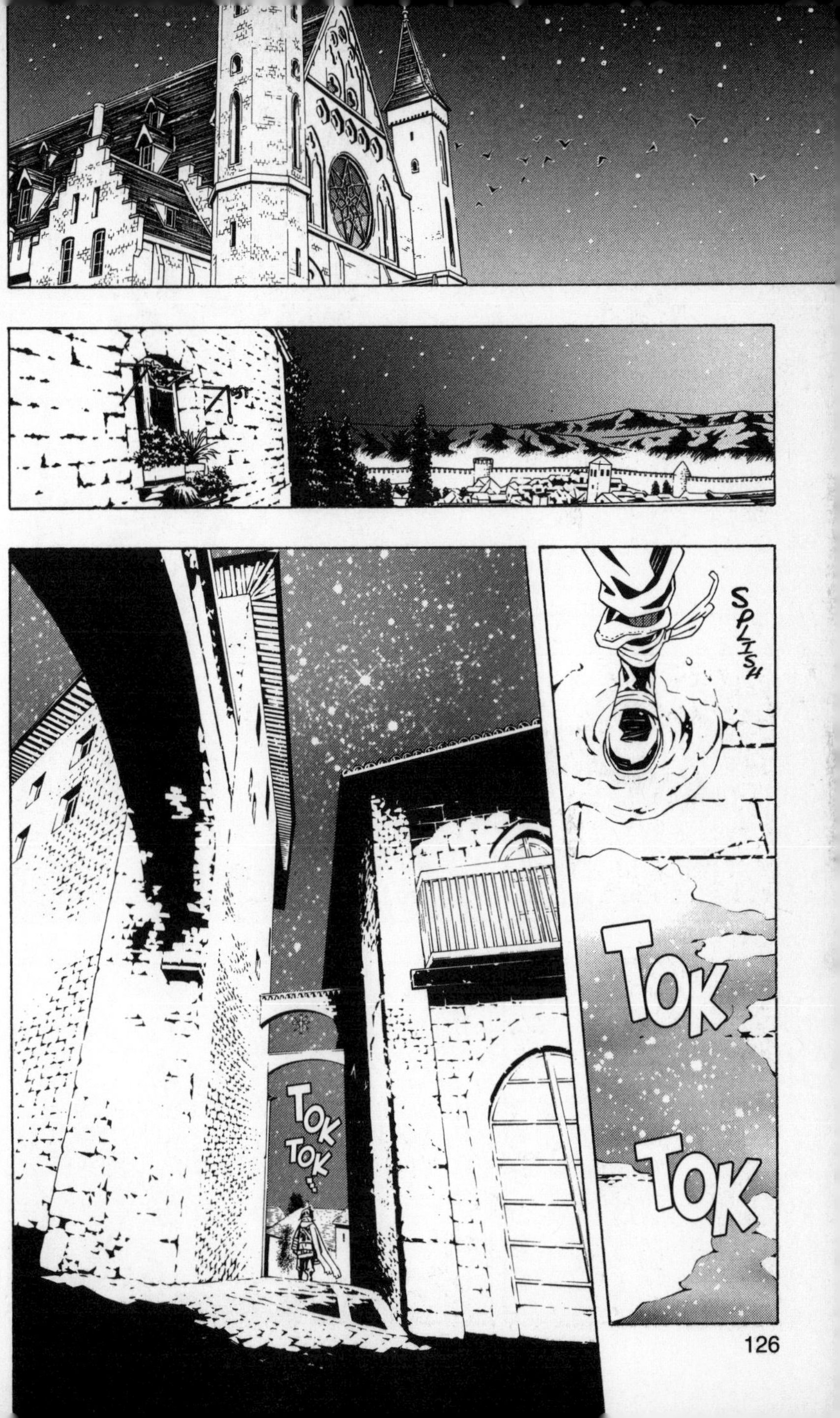
SPLISH
TOK
TOK
TOK TOK...

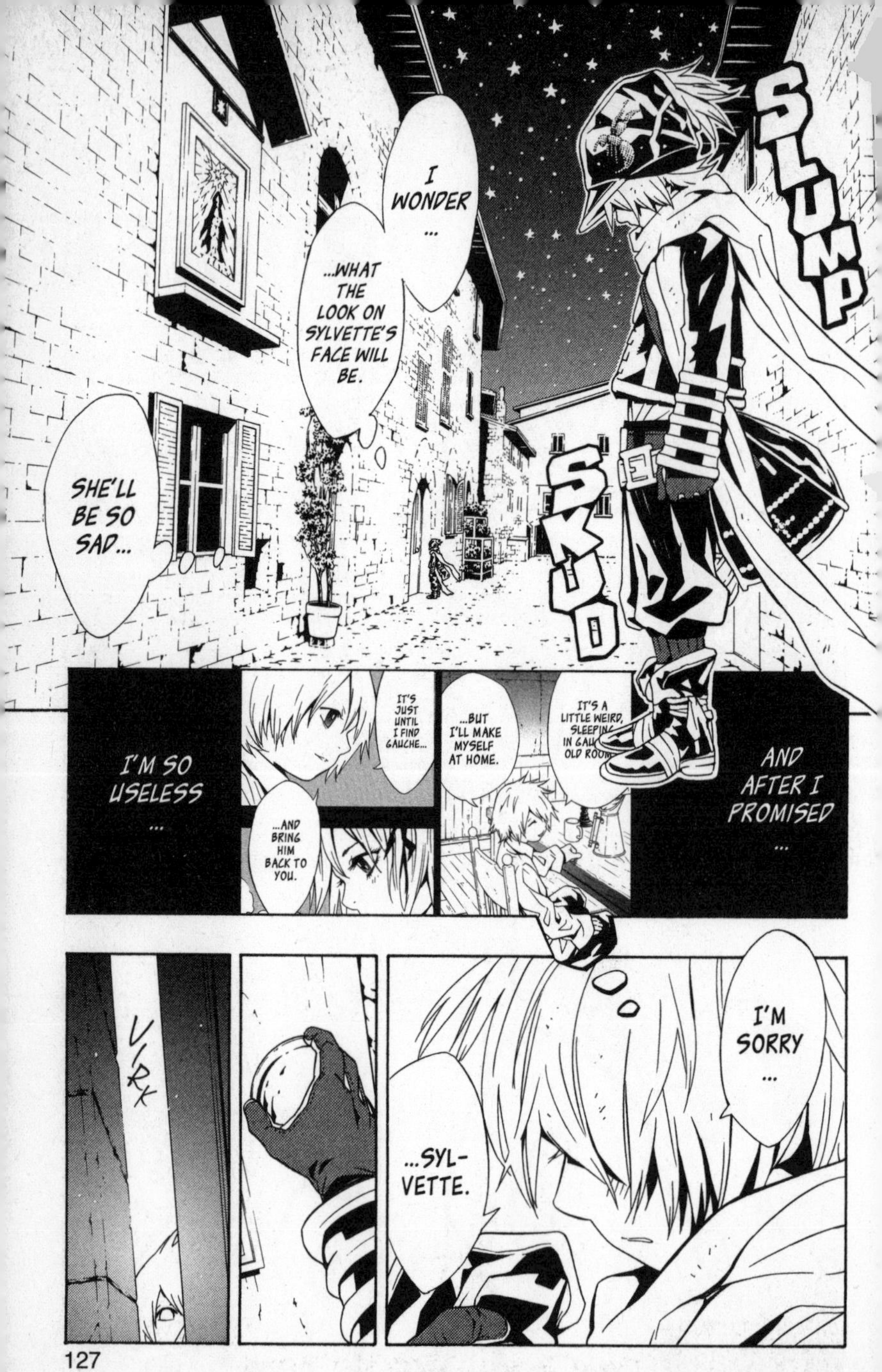
SLUMP
I WONDER ...
...WHAT THE LOOK ON SYLVETTE'S FACE WILL BE.
SKUD
SHE'LL BE SO SAD...
AND AFTER I PROMISED ...
IT'S A LITTLE WEIRD, SLEEPIN
...BUT I'LL MAKE MYSELF AT HOME.
IT'S JUST UNTIL I FIND GAUCHE...
...AND BRING HIM BACK TO YOU.
I'M SO USELESS ...
I'M SORRY ...
...SYL-VETTE.
VIRK

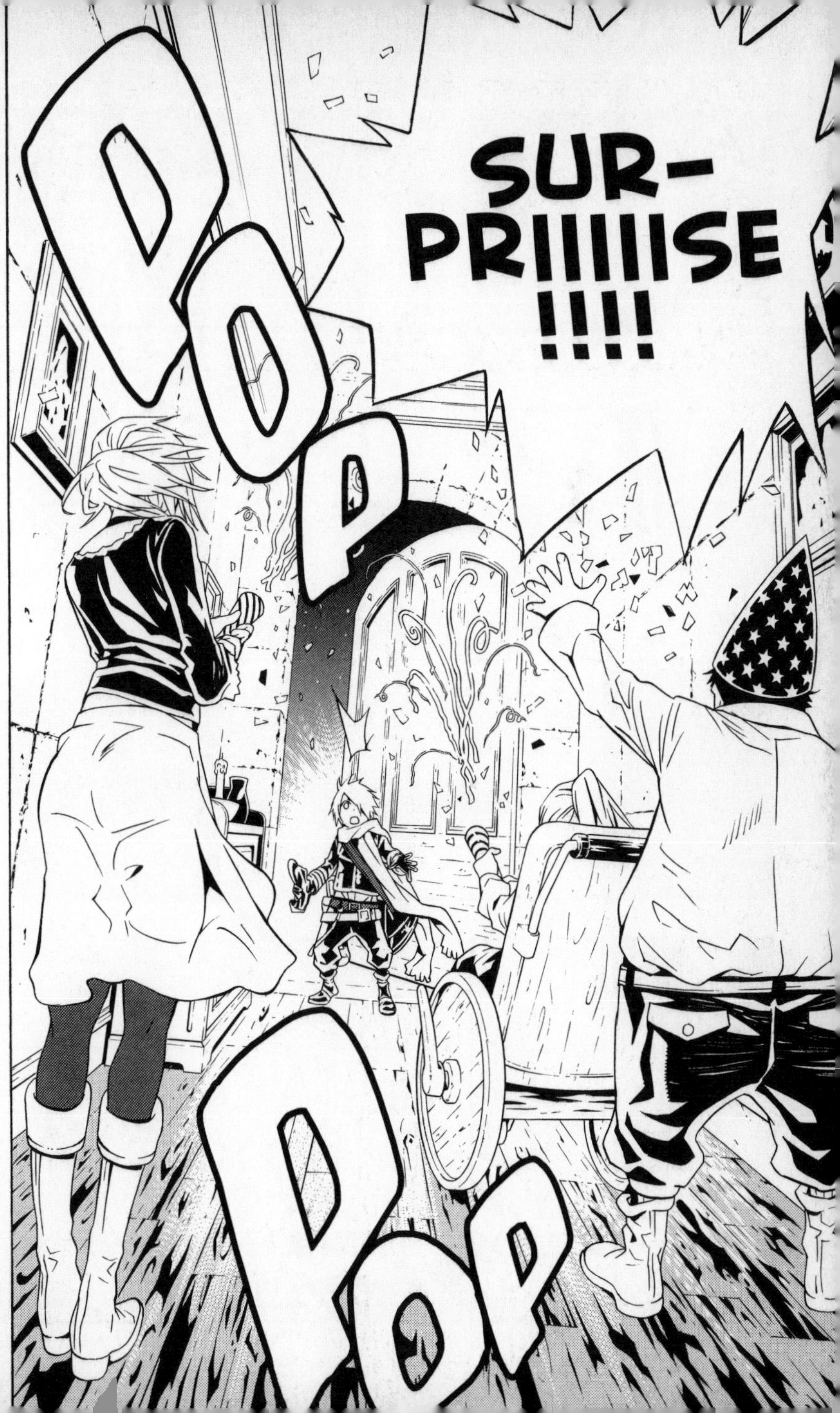
POP
SUR-
PRIIIIISE
!!!!
POP

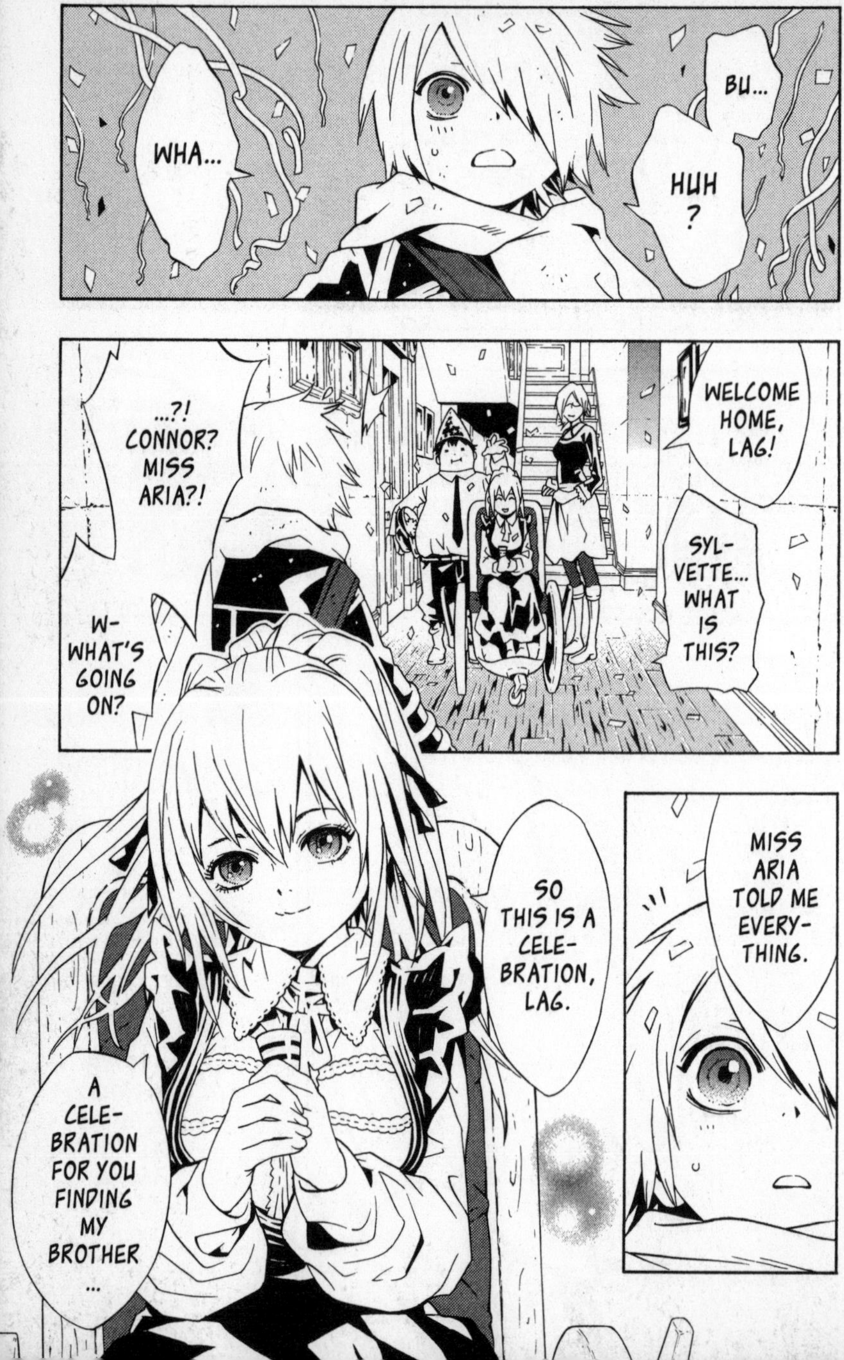
BU...
HUH?
WHA...
WELCOME HOME, LAG!
SYLVETTE... WHAT IS THIS?
...?! CONNOR? MISS ARIA?!
W-WHAT'S GOING ON?
MISS ARIA TOLD ME EVERYTHING.
SO THIS IS A CELEBRATION, LAG.
A CELEBRATION FOR YOU FINDING MY BROTHER...

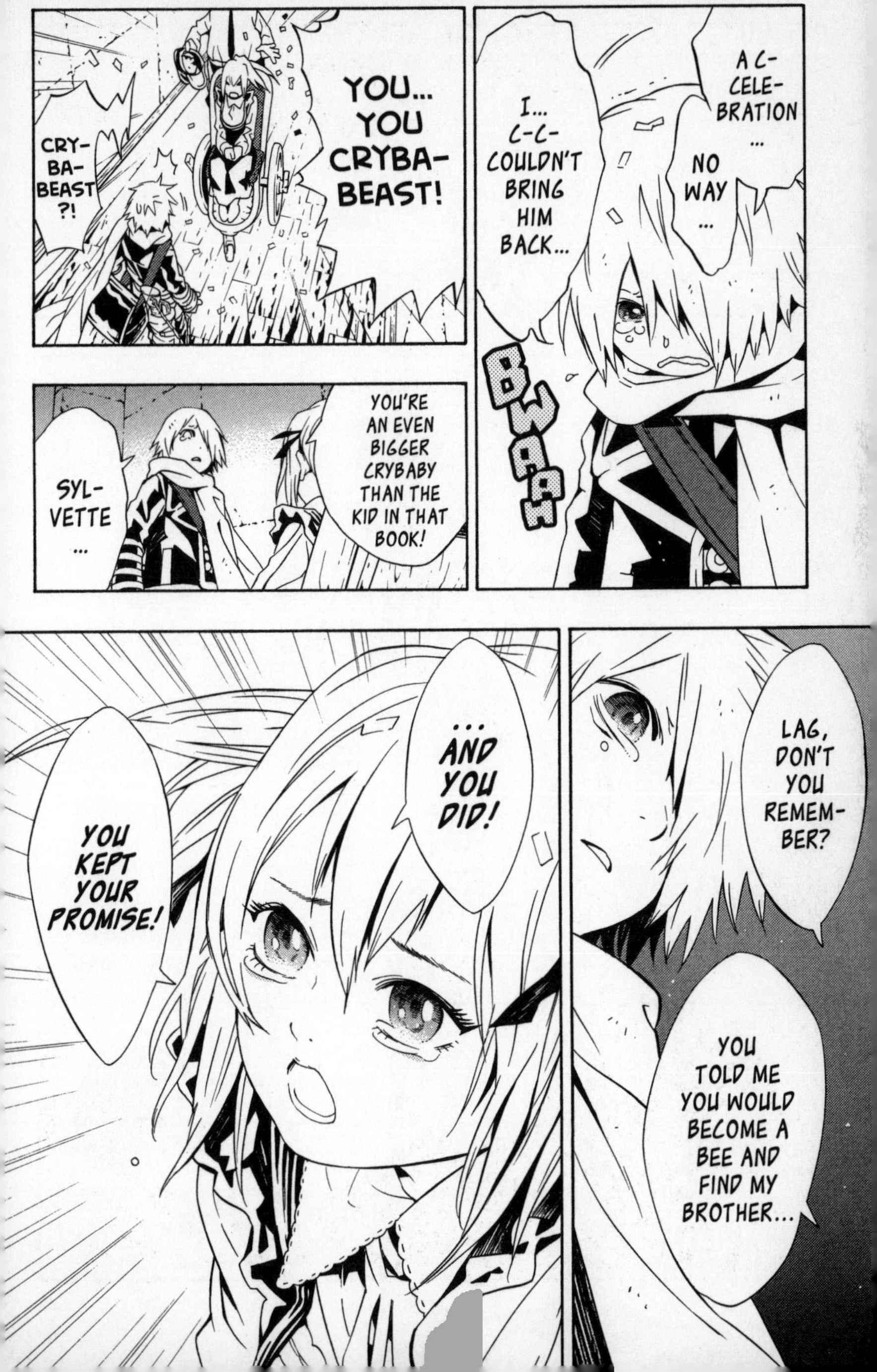
A C-CELEBRATION ...
NO WAY ...
I... C-C-COULDN'T BRING HIM BACK...
BWAAH
YOU... YOU CRYBA-BEAST!
CRYBA-BEAST?!
YOU'RE AN EVEN BIGGER CRYBABY THAN THE KID IN THAT BOOK!
SYLVETTE ...
LAG, DON'T YOU REMEMBER?
YOU TOLD ME YOU WOULD BECOME A BEE AND FIND MY BROTHER...
... AND YOU DID!
YOU KEPT YOUR PROMISE!

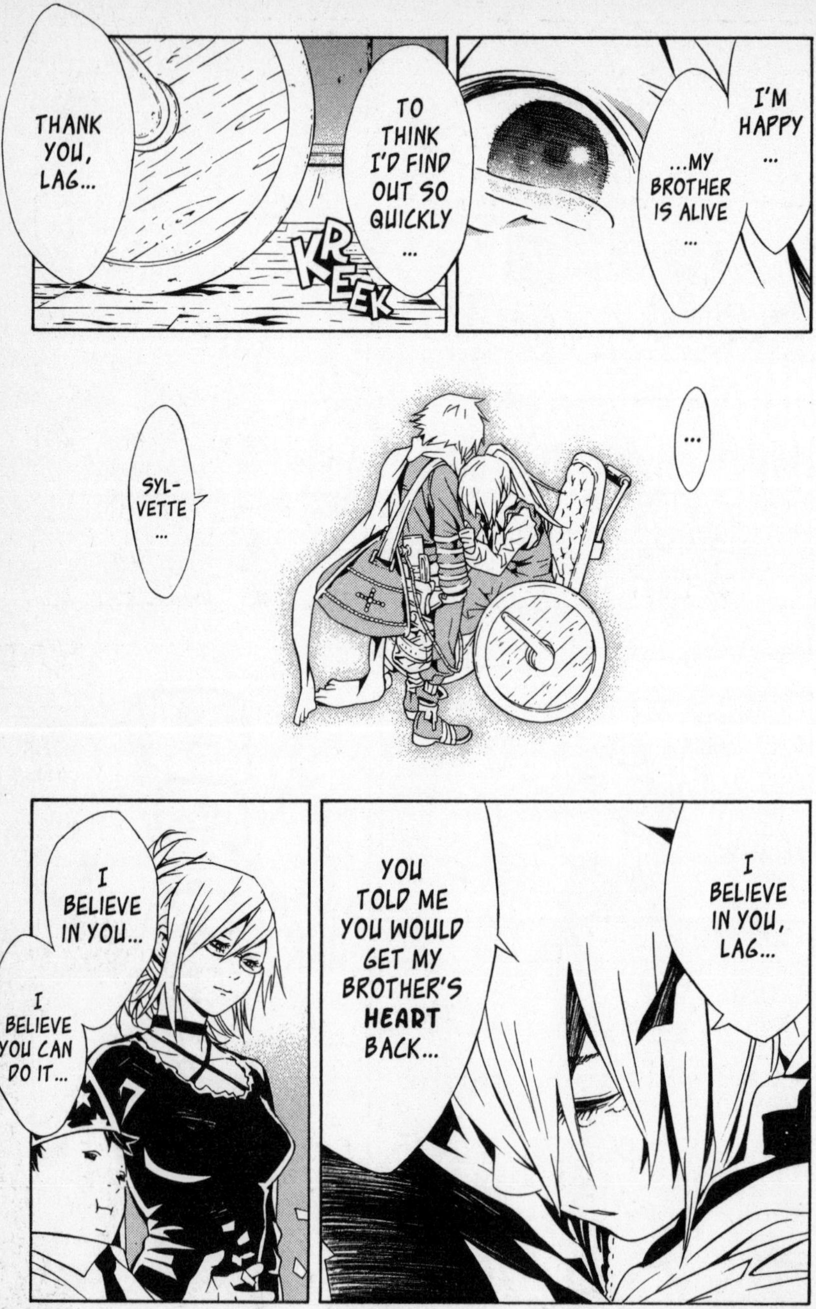
I'M HAPPY ...
...MY BROTHER IS ALIVE ...
TO THINK I'D FIND OUT SO QUICKLY ...
KREEEK
THANK YOU, LAG...
...
SYL-VETTE ...
I BELIEVE IN YOU, LAG...
YOU TOLD ME YOU WOULD GET MY BROTHER'S HEART BACK...
I BELIEVE IN YOU...
I BELIEVE YOU CAN DO IT...

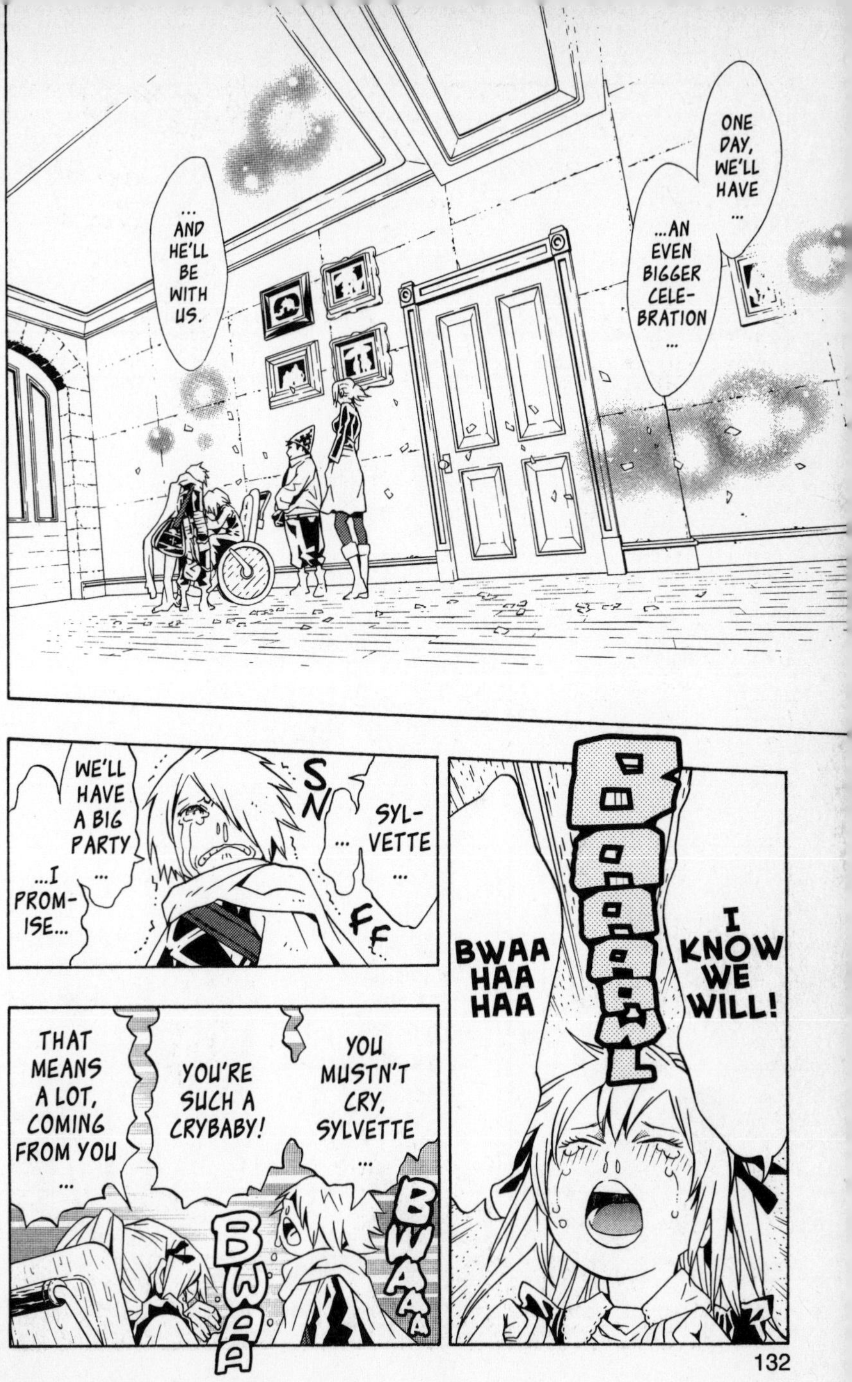
ONE DAY, WE'LL HAVE ...
...AN EVEN BIGGER CELEBRATION ...
... AND HE'LL BE WITH US.
I KNOW WE WILL!
BAAAAWL
BWAA HAA HAA
SYLVETTE ...
SNIFF
WE'LL HAVE A BIG PARTY ...
...I PROMISE...
YOU MUSTN'T CRY, SYLVETTE ...
YOU'RE SUCH A CRYBABY!
THAT MEANS A LOT, COMING FROM YOU ...
BWAAAA
BWAA

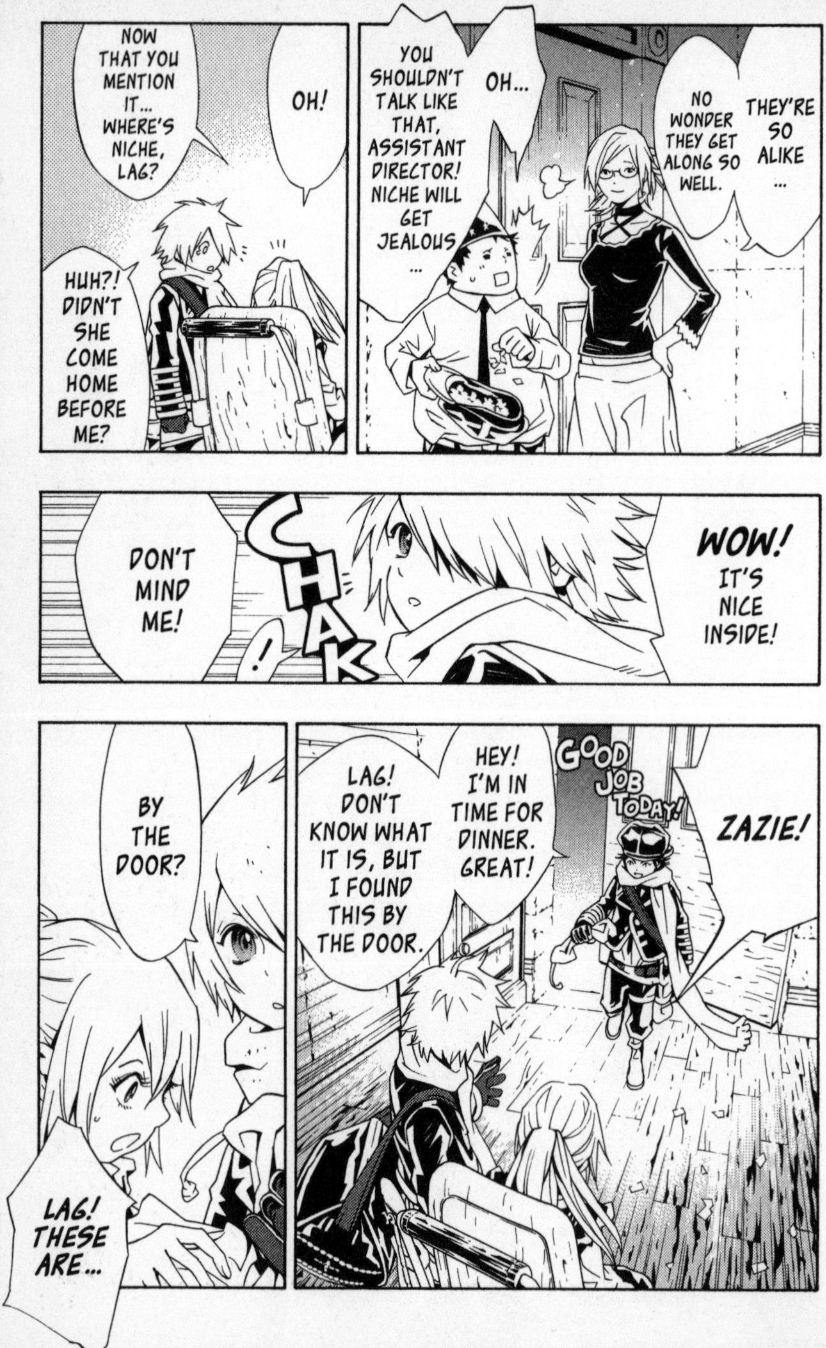
THEY'RE SO ALIKE ...
NO WONDER THEY GET ALONG SO WELL.
OH...
YOU SHOULDN'T TALK LIKE THAT, ASSISTANT DIRECTOR! NICHE WILL GET JEALOUS ...
NOW THAT YOU MENTION IT... WHERE'S NICHE, LAG?
OH!
HUH?! DIDN'T SHE COME HOME BEFORE ME?
WOW! IT'S NICE INSIDE!
CHAK
!
DON'T MIND ME!
ZAZIE!
GOOD JOB TODAY!
HEY! I'M IN TIME FOR DINNER. GREAT!
LAG! DON'T KNOW WHAT IT IS, BUT I FOUND THIS BY THE DOOR.
BY THE DOOR?
LAG! THESE ARE...

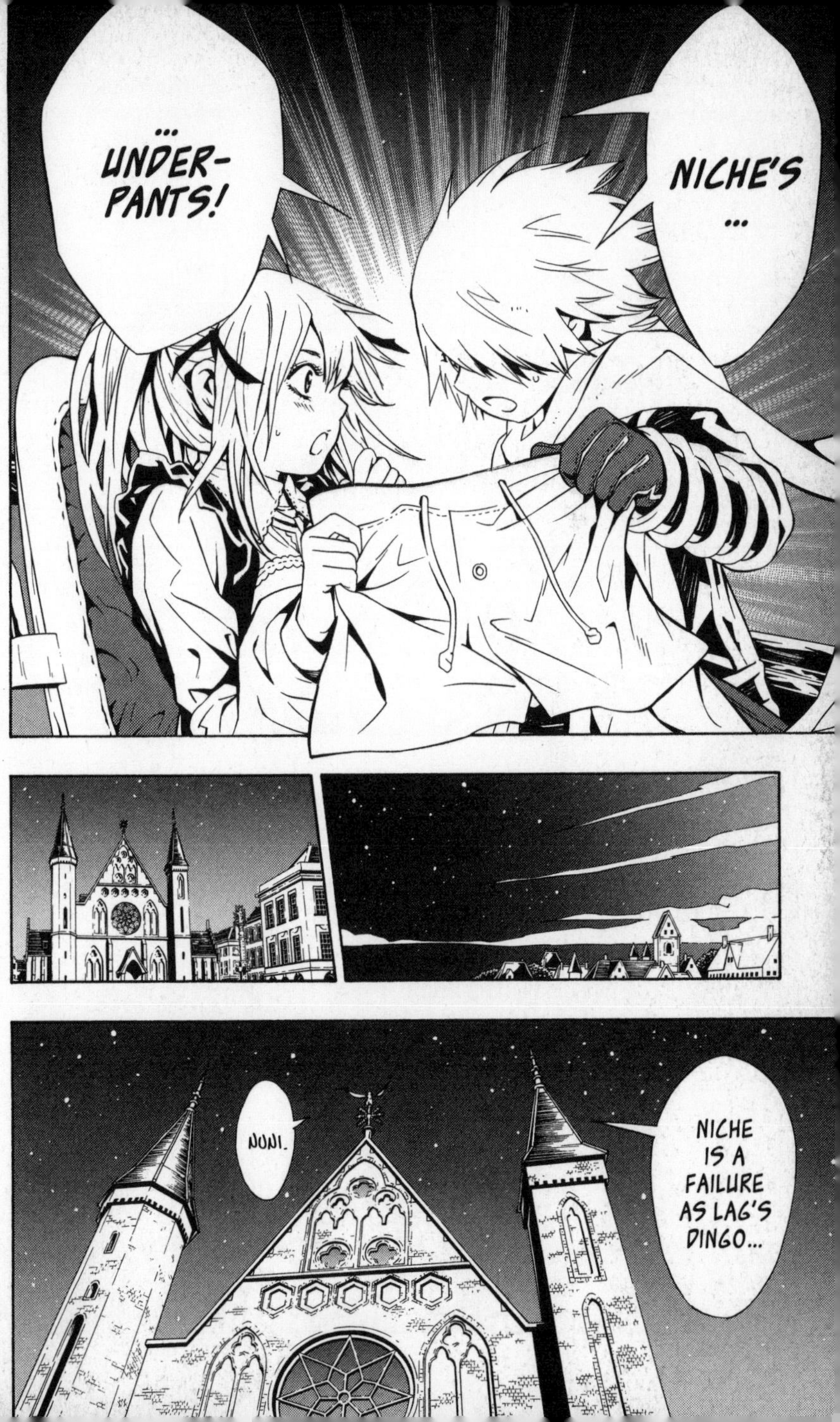
NICHE'S ...
... UNDER-PANTS!
NICHE IS A FAILURE AS LAG'S DINGO...
NUNI.

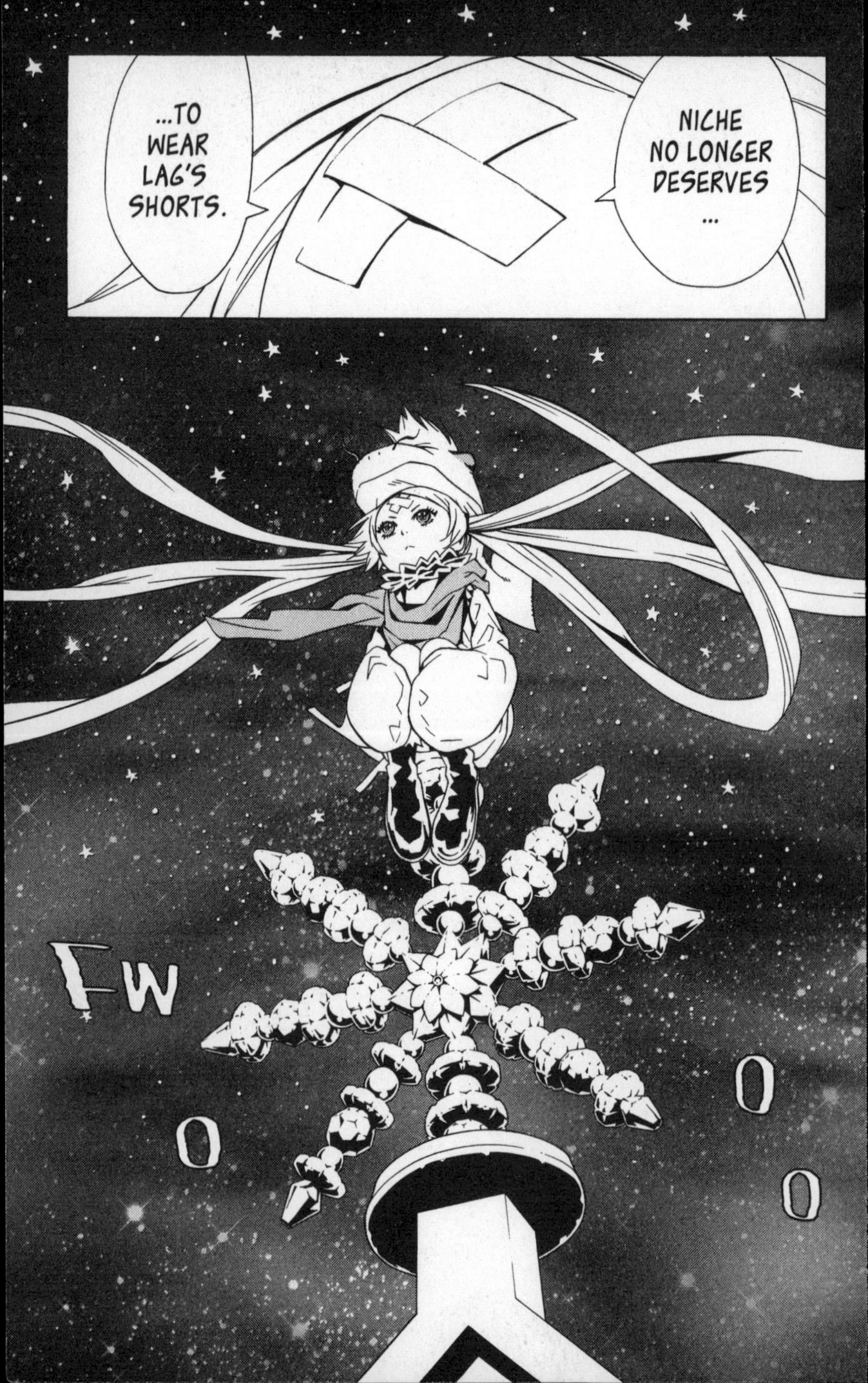
NICHE NO LONGER DESERVES ...
...TO WEAR LAG'S SHORTS.
FW O O O O

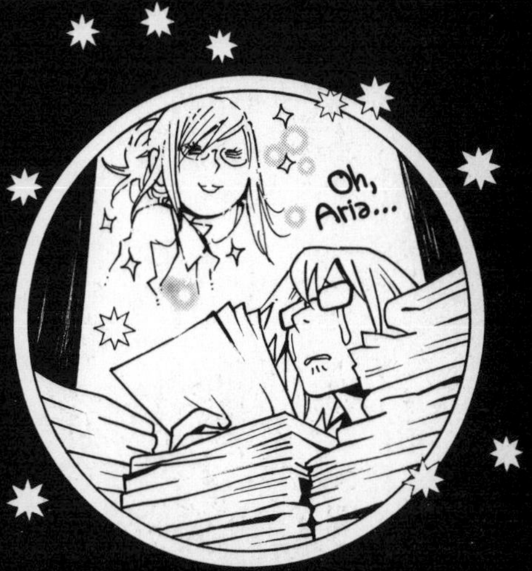
Oh, Aria...

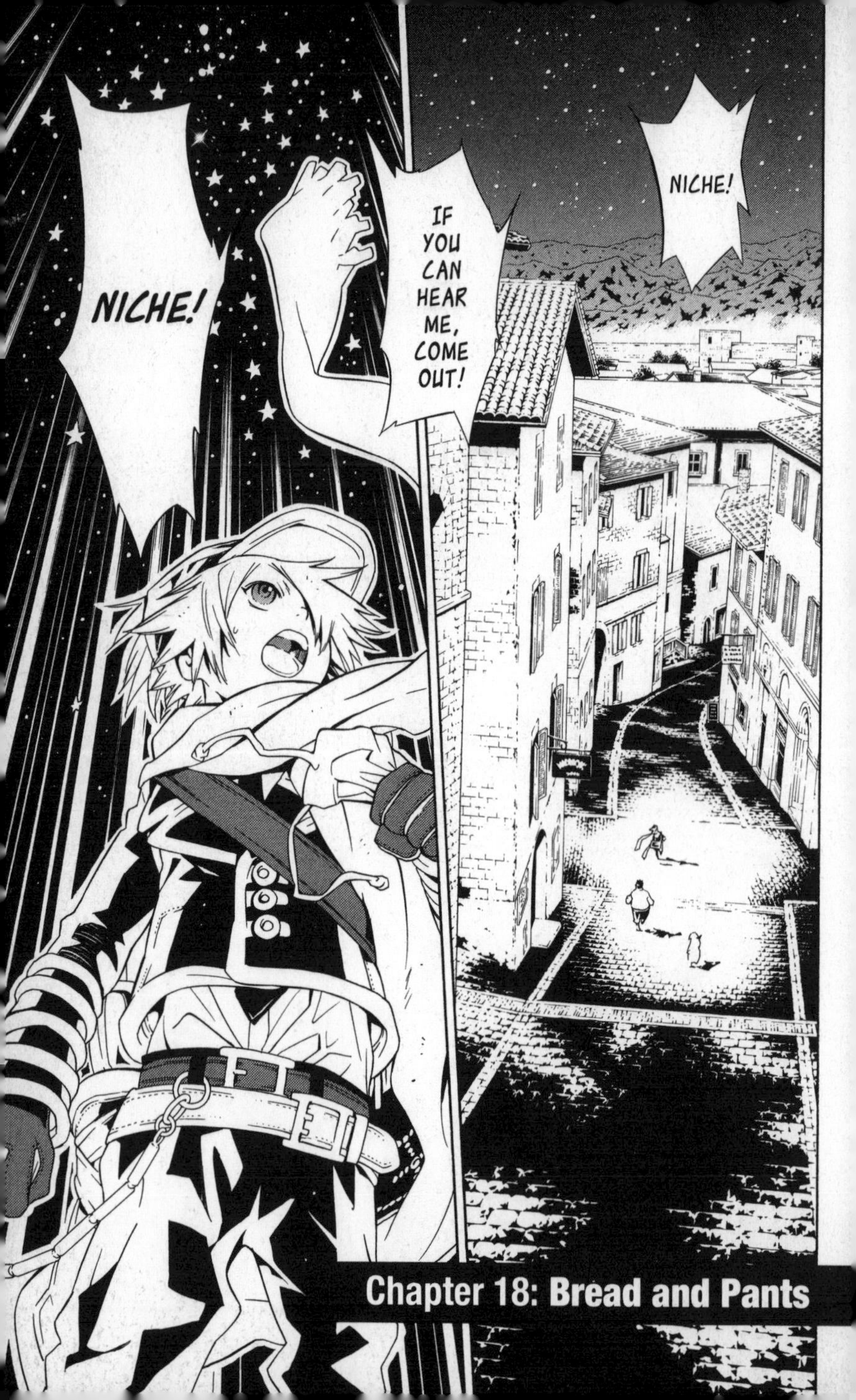
NICHE!
IF YOU CAN HEAR ME, COME OUT!
NICHE!

Chapter 18: Bread and Pants

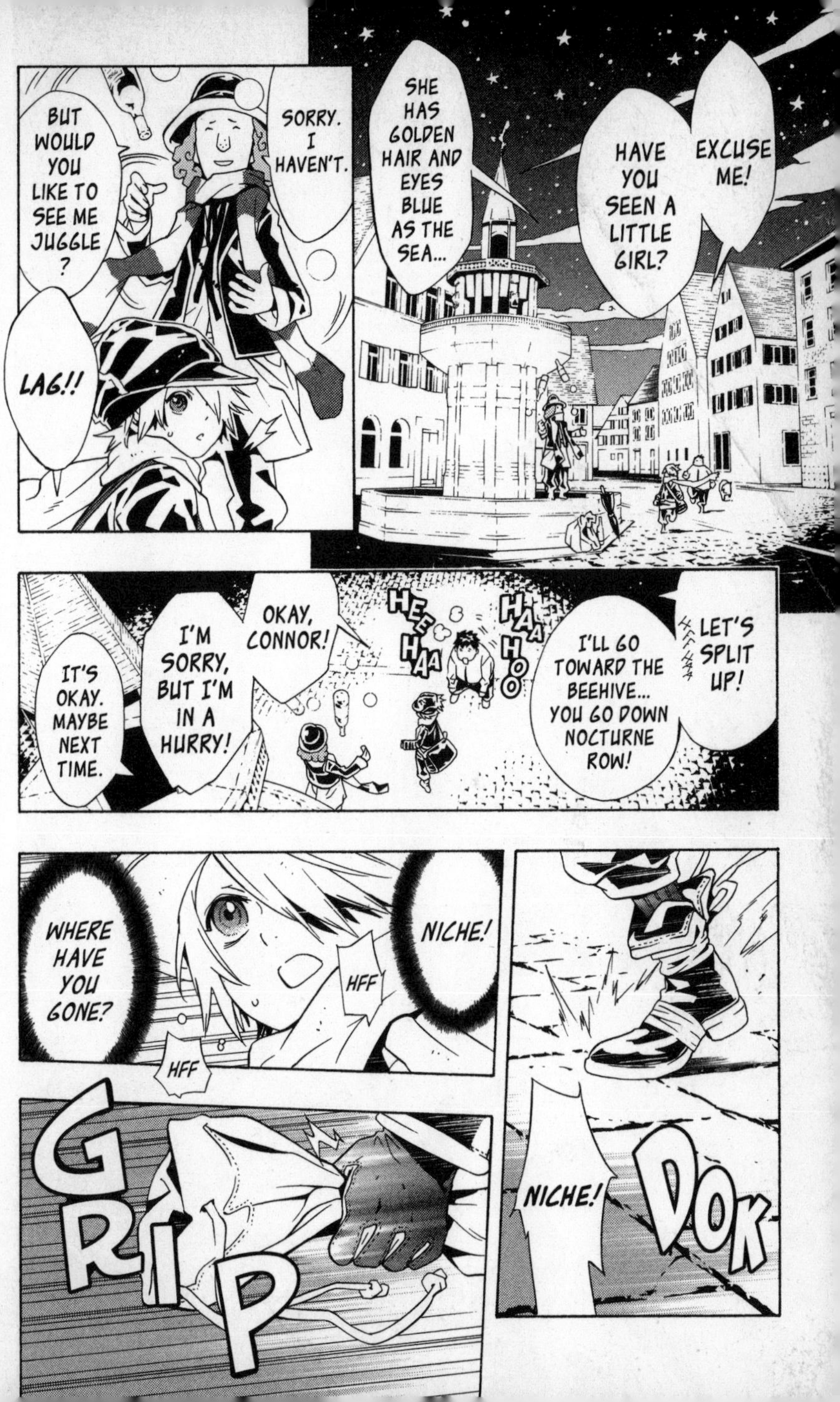
EXCUSE ME!
HAVE YOU SEEN A LITTLE GIRL?
SHE HAS GOLDEN HAIR AND EYES BLUE AS THE SEA...
SORRY. I HAVEN'T.
BUT WOULD YOU LIKE TO SEE ME JUGGLE?
LAG!!
LET'S SPLIT UP!
I'LL GO TOWARD THE BEEHIVE... YOU GO DOWN NOCTURNE ROW!
HAA HOO
HEE HAA
OKAY, CONNOR!
I'M SORRY, BUT I'M IN A HURRY!
IT'S OKAY. MAYBE NEXT TIME.
DOK
NICHE!
NICHE!
HFF
WHERE HAVE YOU GONE?
HFF
GRIP

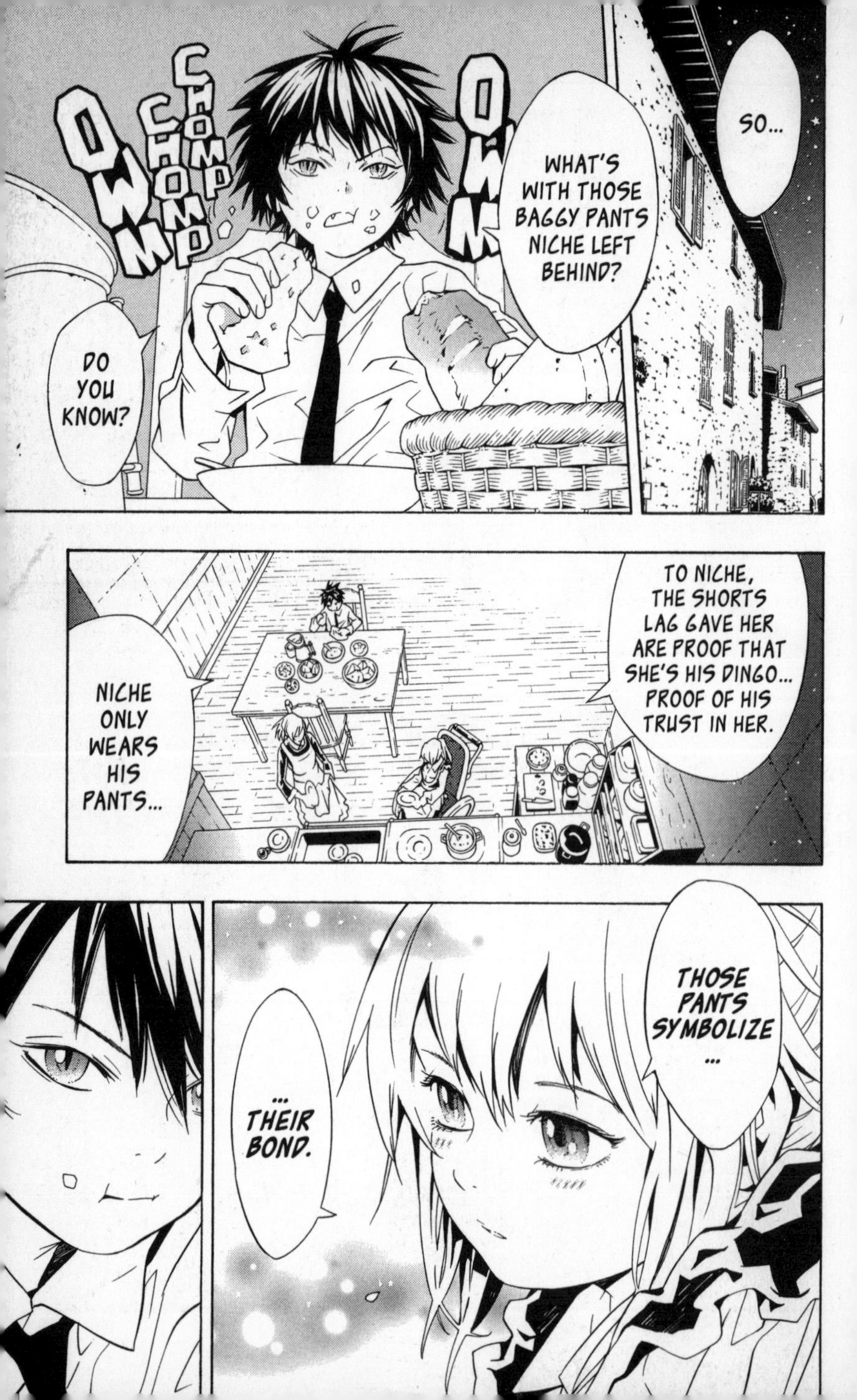
SO...
WHAT'S WITH THOSE BAGGY PANTS NICHE LEFT BEHIND?
DO YOU KNOW?
TO NICHE, THE SHORTS LAG GAVE HER ARE PROOF THAT SHE'S HIS DINGO... PROOF OF HIS TRUST IN HER.
NICHE ONLY WEARS HIS PANTS...
THOSE PANTS SYMBOLIZE ...
... THEIR BOND.

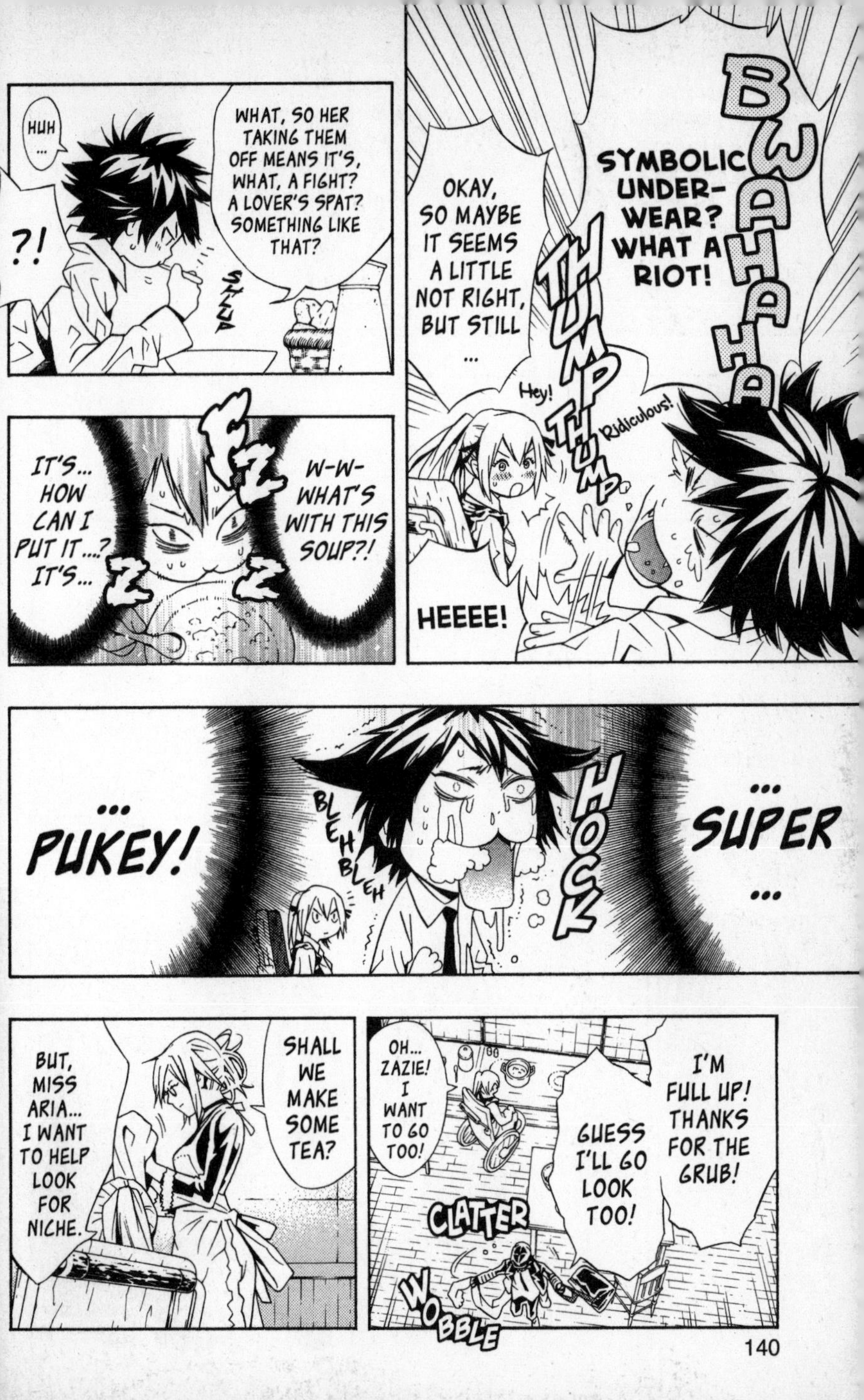
BWAHAHAHA
SYMBOLIC UNDER-WEAR? WHAT A RIOT!
OKAY, SO MAYBE IT SEEMS A LITTLE NOT RIGHT, BUT STILL ...
THUMP THUMP
Ridiculous!
Hey!
HEEEE!
WHAT, SO HER TAKING THEM OFF MEANS IT'S, WHAT, A FIGHT? A LOVER'S SPAT? SOMETHING LIKE THAT?
SHLUP
HUH ...
?!
W-W-WHAT'S WITH THIS SOUP?!
IT'S... HOW CAN I PUT IT...? IT'S...
... SUPER ...
HOCK
BLEH BLEH
... PUKEY!
I'M FULL UP! THANKS FOR THE GRUB!
GUESS I'LL GO LOOK TOO!
OH... ZAZIE! I WANT TO GO TOO!
CLATTER
WOBBLE
SHALL WE MAKE SOME TEA?
BUT, MISS ARIA... I WANT TO HELP LOOK FOR NICHE.

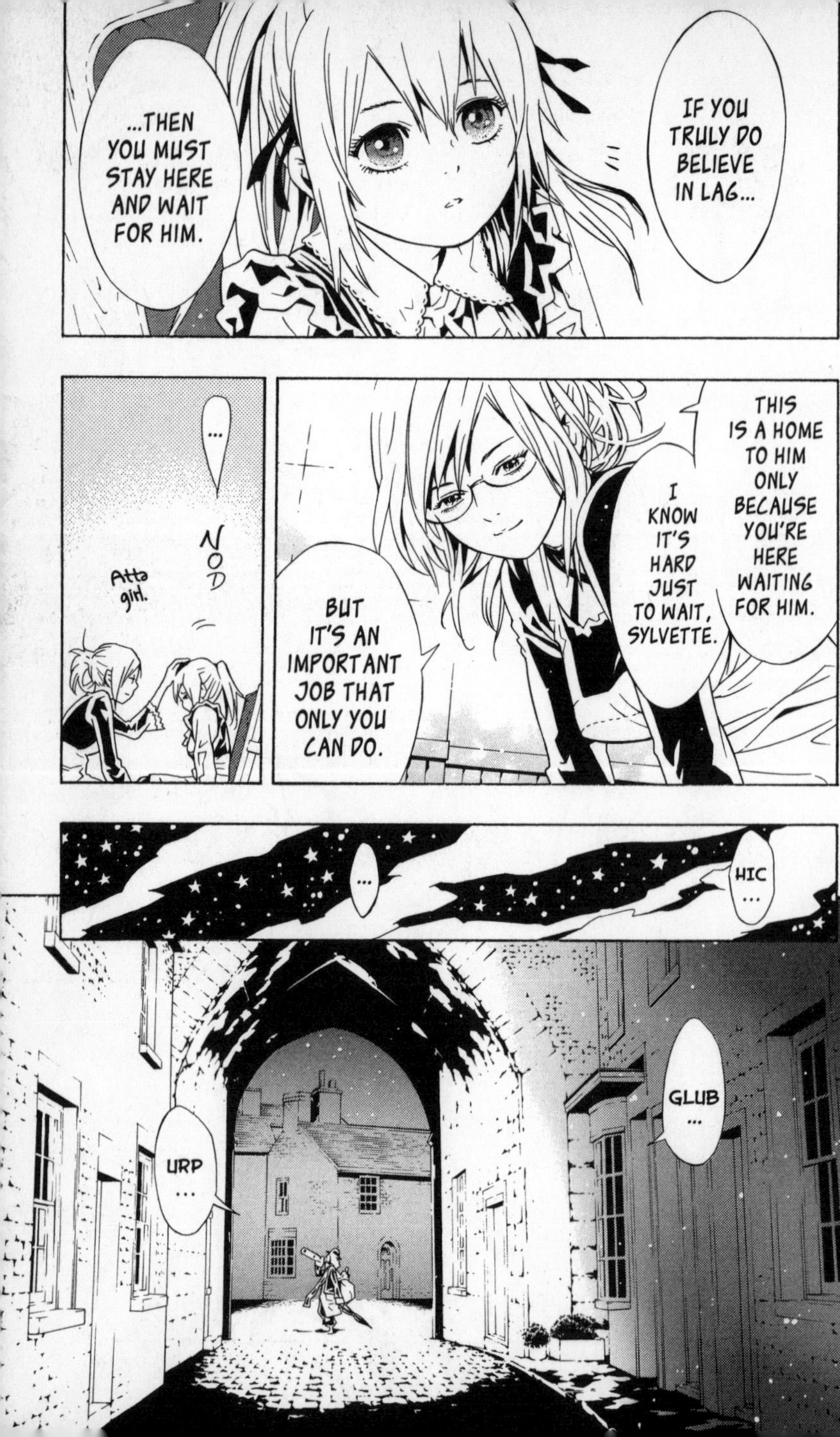
IF YOU TRULY DO BELIEVE IN LAG...
...THEN YOU MUST STAY HERE AND WAIT FOR HIM.
THIS IS A HOME TO HIM ONLY BECAUSE YOU'RE HERE WAITING FOR HIM.
I KNOW IT'S HARD JUST TO WAIT, SYLVETTE.
BUT IT'S AN IMPORTANT JOB THAT ONLY YOU CAN DO.
...
NOD
Atta girl.
HIC...
...
GLUB...
URP...

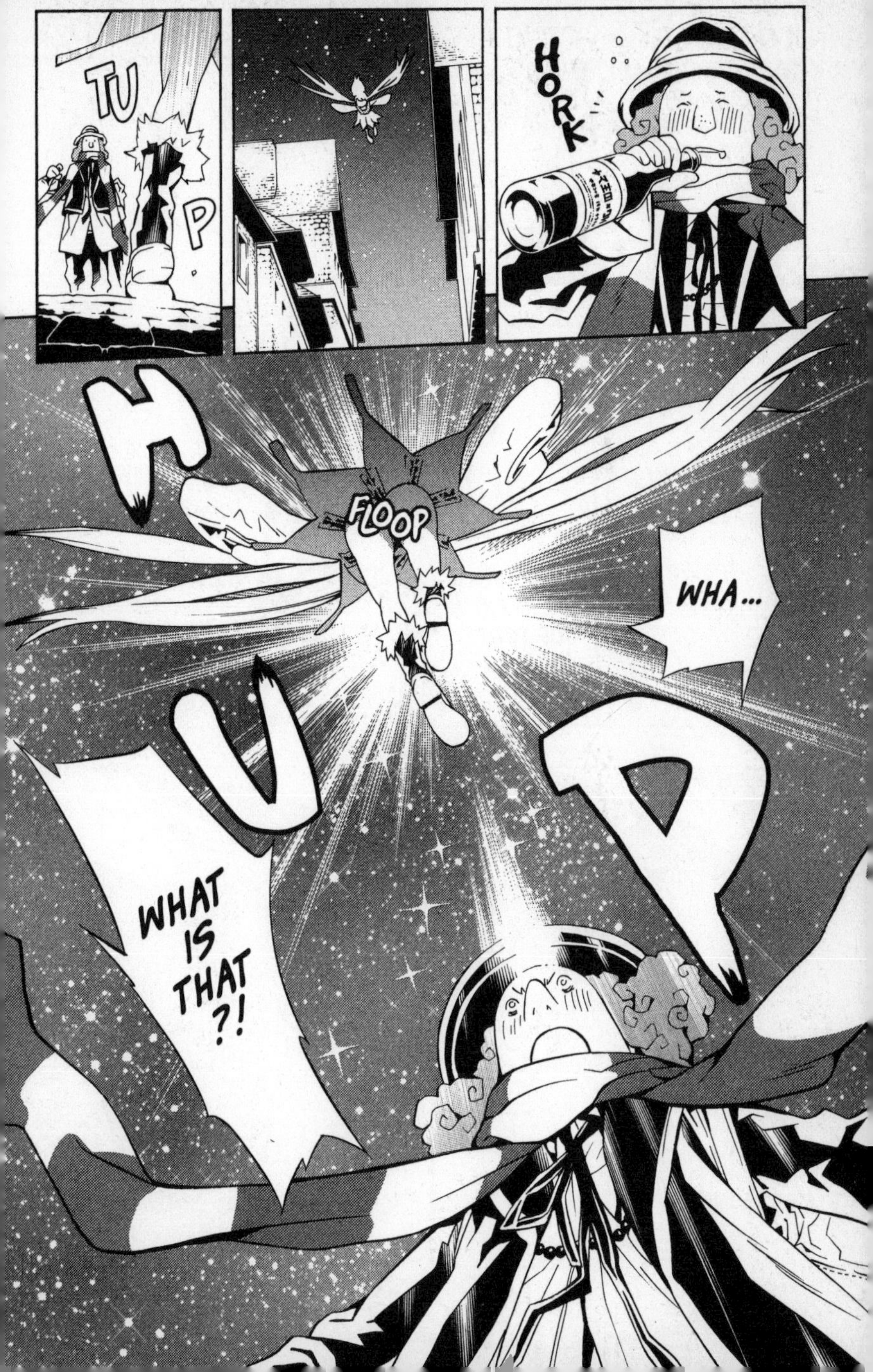
HORK
TUP
HUP
FLOOP
WHA...
WHAT IS THAT?!

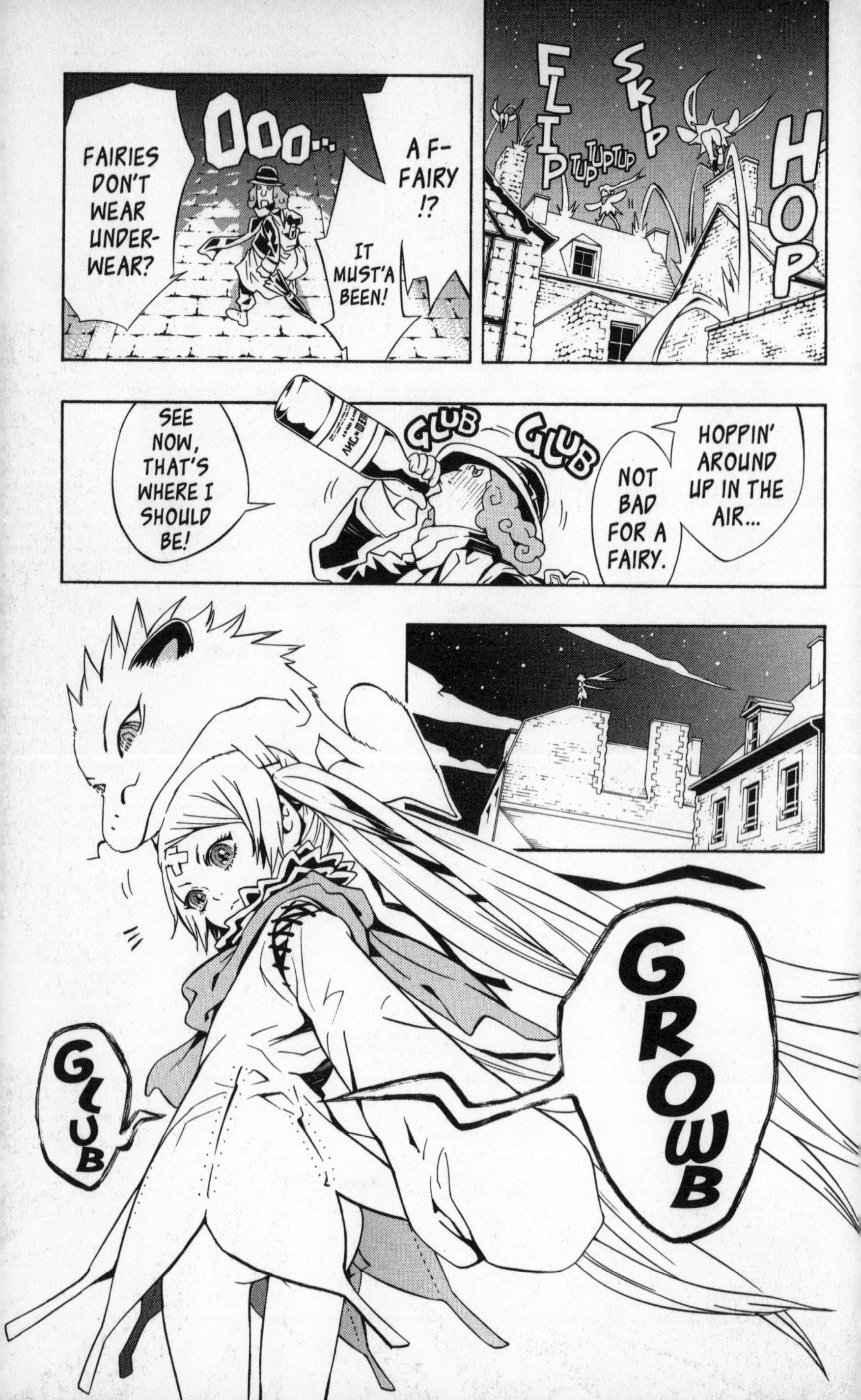
HOP
SKIP
FLIP
TUP TUP TUP TUP
A F-FAIRY!?
IT MUST'A BEEN!
OOO...
FAIRIES DON'T WEAR UNDER-WEAR?
HOPPIN' AROUND UP IN THE AIR...
NOT BAD FOR A FAIRY.
GLUB
GLUB
SEE NOW, THAT'S WHERE I SHOULD BE!
GROWB
GLUB

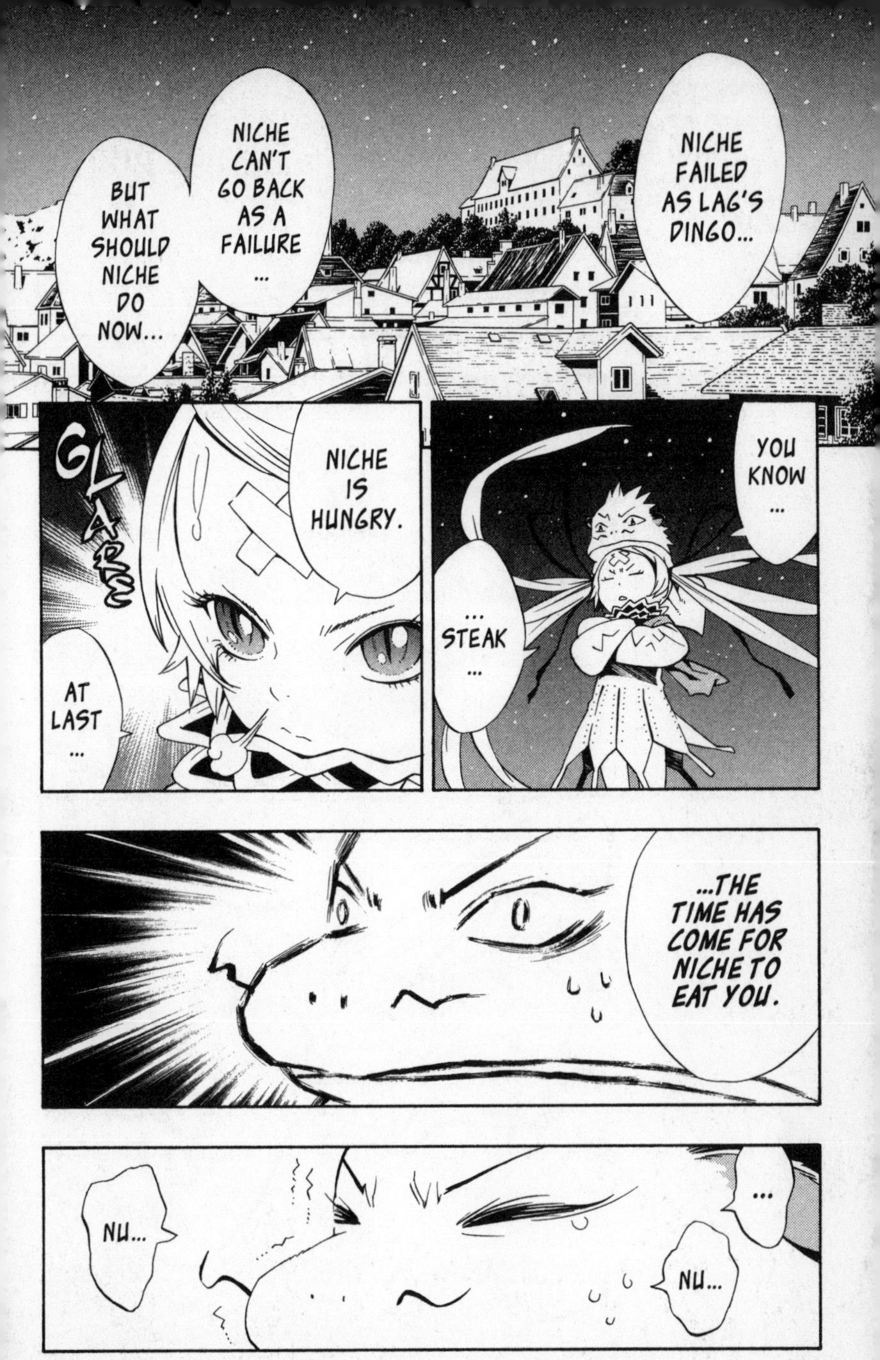
NICHE FAILED AS LAG'S DINGO...
NICHE CAN'T GO BACK AS A FAILURE ...
BUT WHAT SHOULD NICHE DO NOW...
YOU KNOW ...
... STEAK ...
NICHE IS HUNGRY.
GLARE
AT LAST ...
...THE TIME HAS COME FOR NICHE TO EAT YOU.
...
NU...
NU...

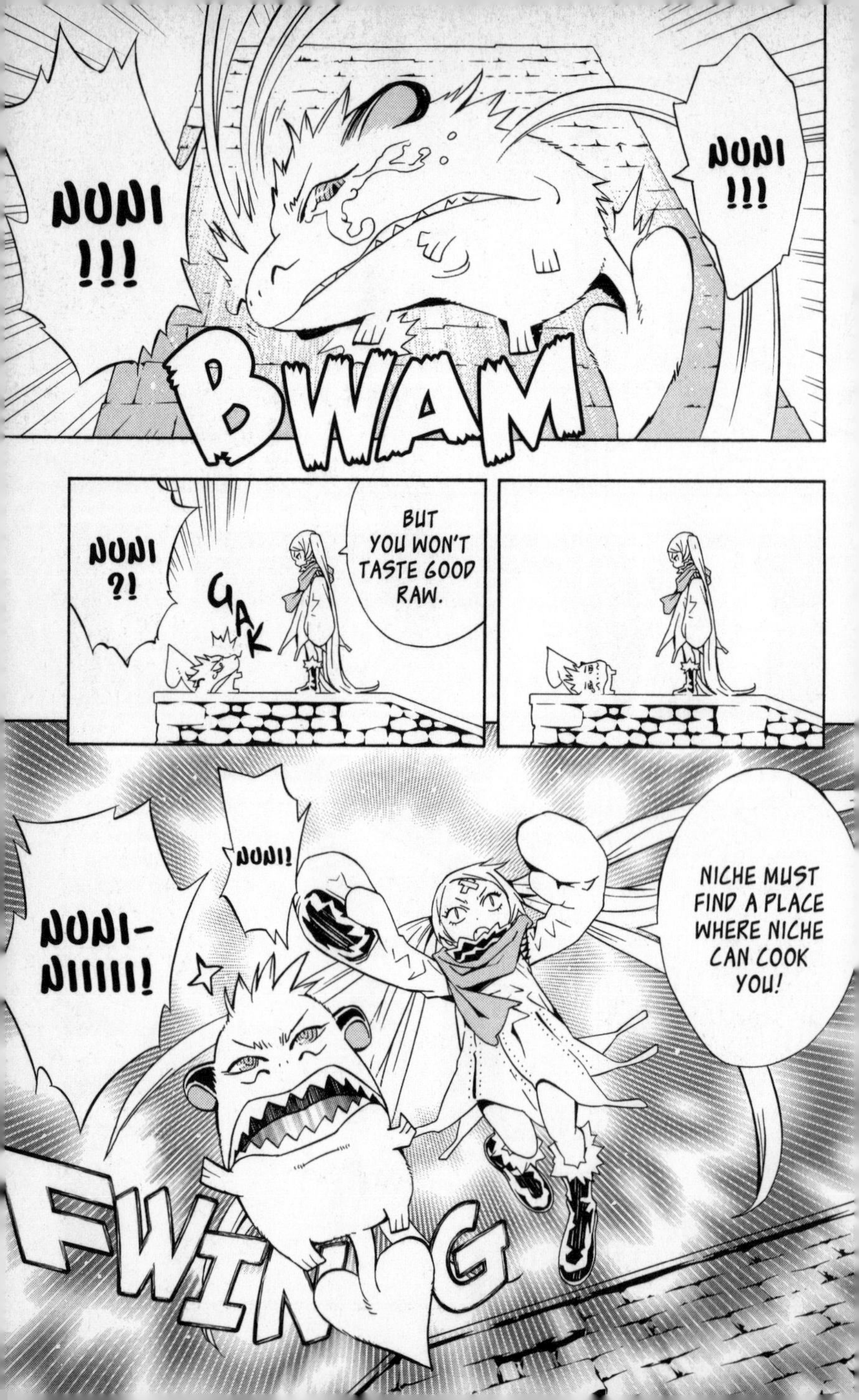
NUNI !!!
NUNI !!!
BWAM
BUT YOU WON'T TASTE GOOD RAW.
NUNI ?!
GAK
NICHE MUST FIND A PLACE WHERE NICHE CAN COOK YOU!
NUNI!
NUNI-NIIIIII!
FWING

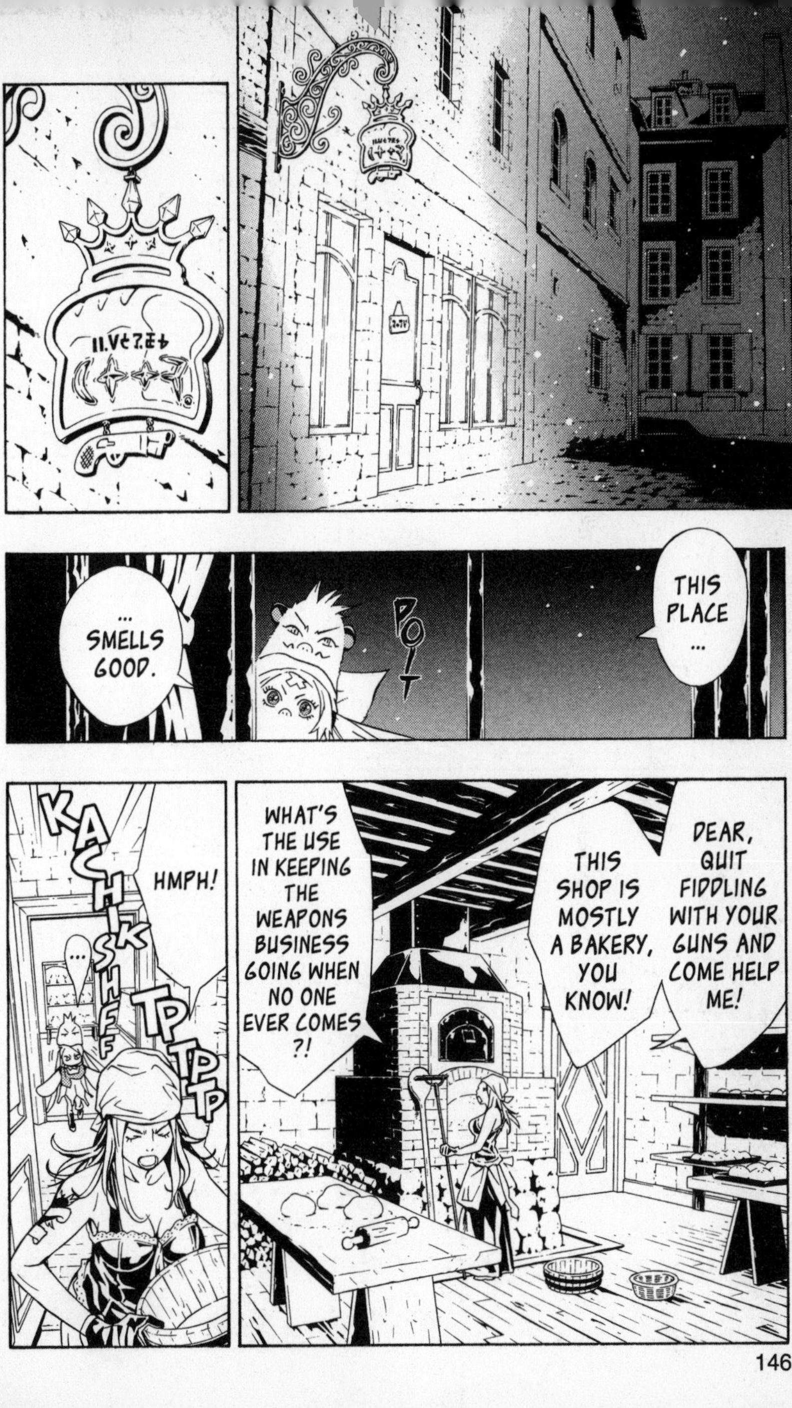
THIS PLACE ...
POIT
... SMELLS GOOD.
DEAR, QUIT FIDDLING WITH YOUR GUNS AND COME HELP ME!
THIS SHOP IS MOSTLY A BAKERY, YOU KNOW!
WHAT'S THE USE IN KEEPING THE WEAPONS BUSINESS GOING WHEN NO ONE EVER COMES ?!
HMPH!
KACHIK
SHFF
TP TP TP
...

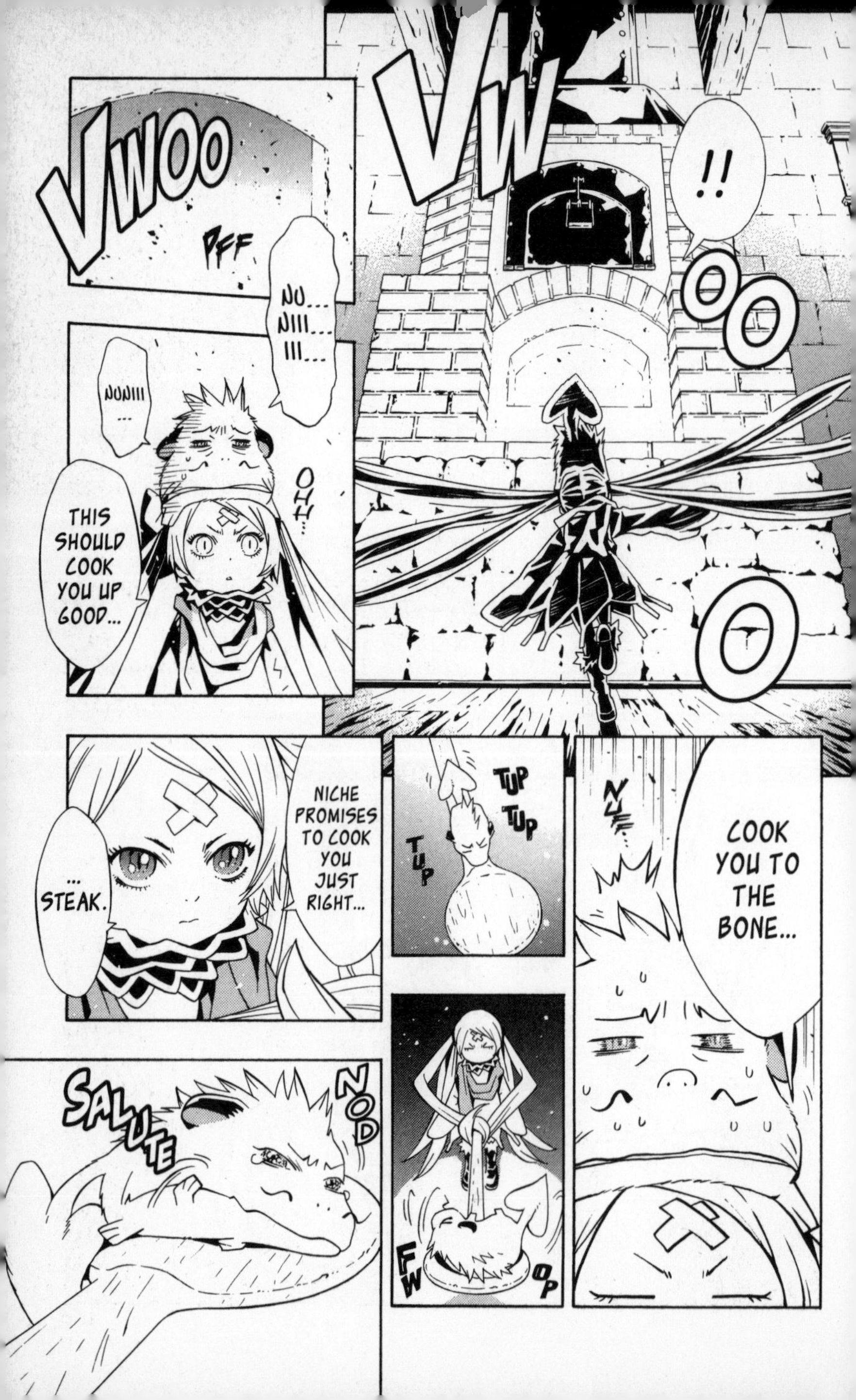
VW
!!
OO
O
VWOO
PFF
NU... NIII... III...
NUNIII ...
OHH...
THIS SHOULD COOK YOU UP GOOD...
NUF...
COOK YOU TO THE BONE...
TUP
TUP
TUP
NICHE PROMISES TO COOK YOU JUST RIGHT...
... STEAK.
FWOOP
NOD
SALUTE

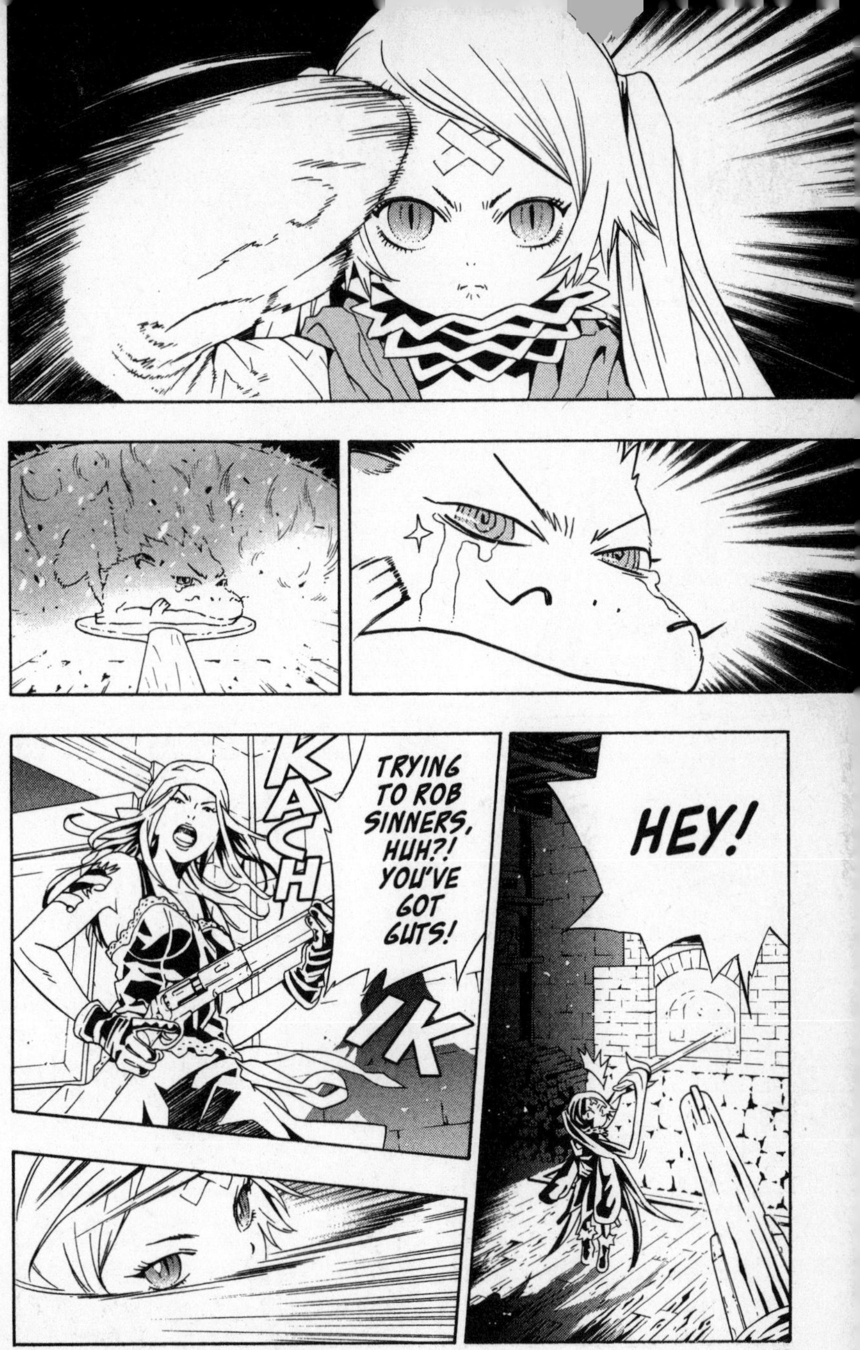
HEY!
TRYING TO ROB SINNERS, HUH?! YOU'VE GOT GUTS!
KACH
IK

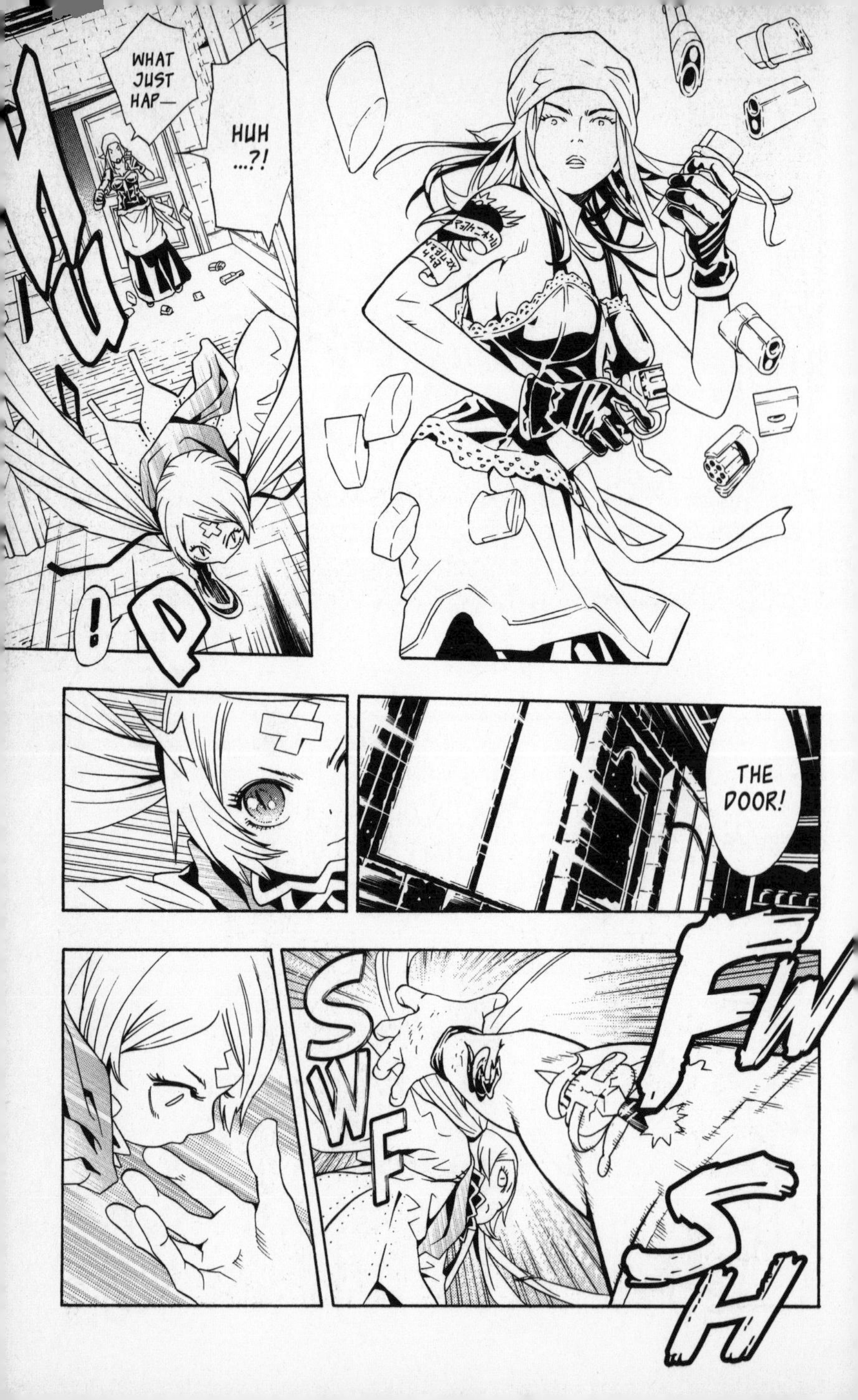
WHAT JUST HAP—
HUH ...?!
THE DOOR!
FWSH
SWF

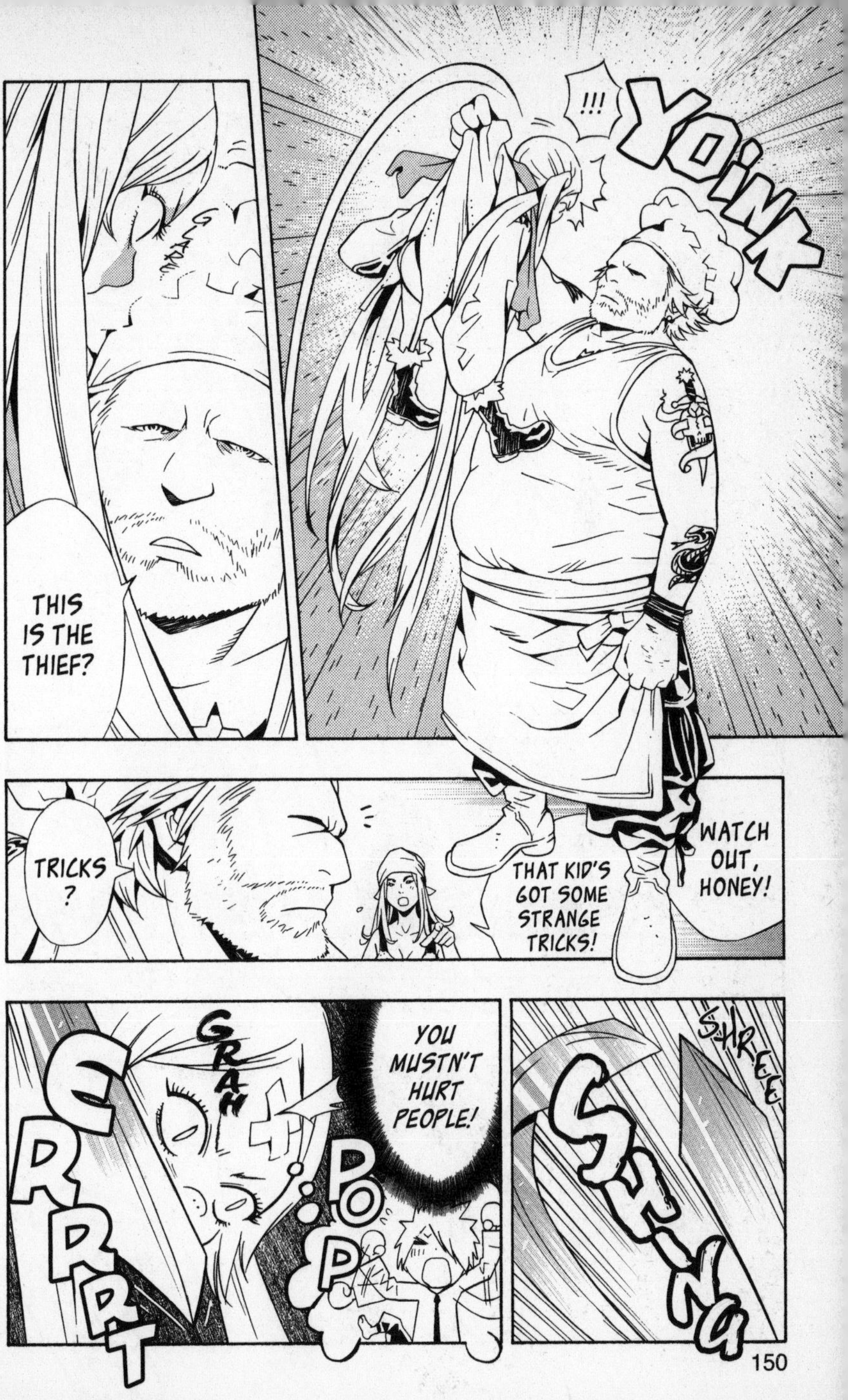
!!!
YOINK
GLARE
THIS IS THE THIEF?
WATCH OUT, HONEY!
THAT KID'S GOT SOME STRANGE TRICKS!
TRICKS?
SHREEE
SHING
YOU MUSTN'T HURT PEOPLE!
POP
GRAH
ERRRRT

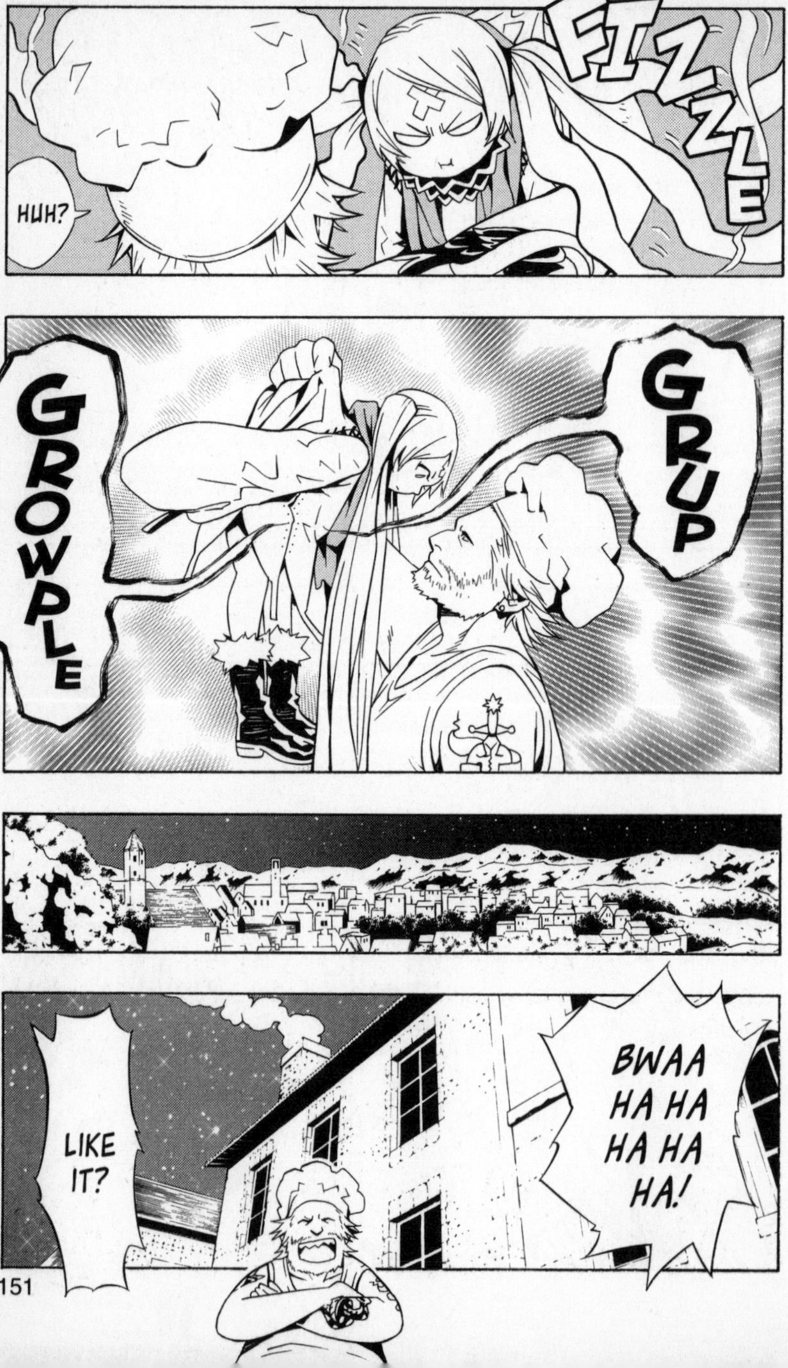
FIZZLE
HUH?
GRUP
GROWPLE
BWAA HA HA HA HA HA!
LIKE IT?

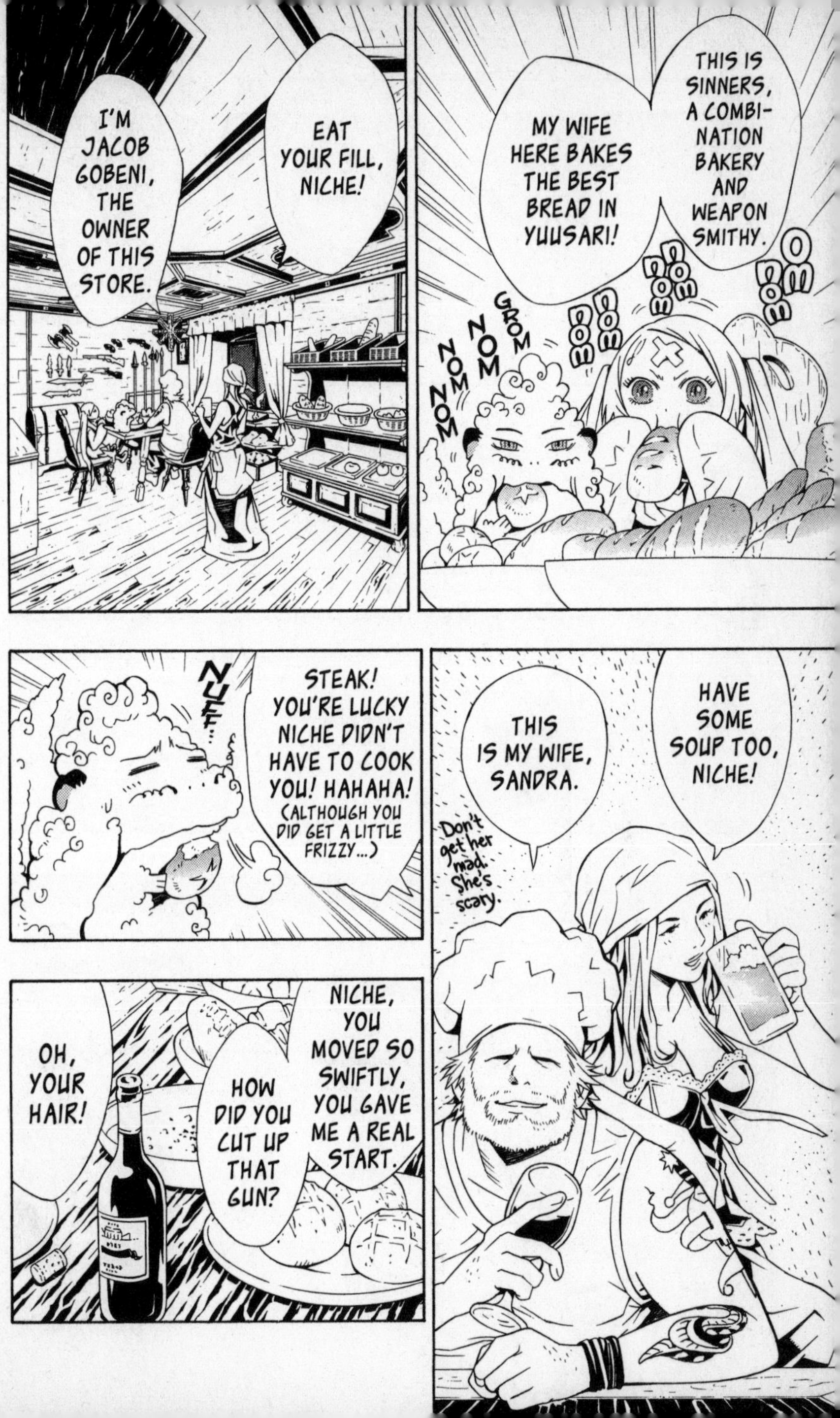
THIS IS SINNERS, A COMBINATION BAKERY AND WEAPON SMITHY.
MY WIFE HERE BAKES THE BEST BREAD IN YUUSARI!
GROM
NOM NOM NOM
EAT YOUR FILL, NICHE!
I'M JACOB GOBENI, THE OWNER OF THIS STORE.
HAVE SOME SOUP TOO, NICHE!
THIS IS MY WIFE, SANDRA.
Don't get her mad. She's scary.
STEAK! YOU'RE LUCKY NICHE DIDN'T HAVE TO COOK YOU! HAHAHA!
(ALTHOUGH YOU DID GET A LITTLE FRIZZY...)
NUFF...
NICHE, YOU MOVED SO SWIFTLY, YOU GAVE ME A REAL START.
HOW DID YOU CUT UP THAT GUN?
OH, YOUR HAIR!

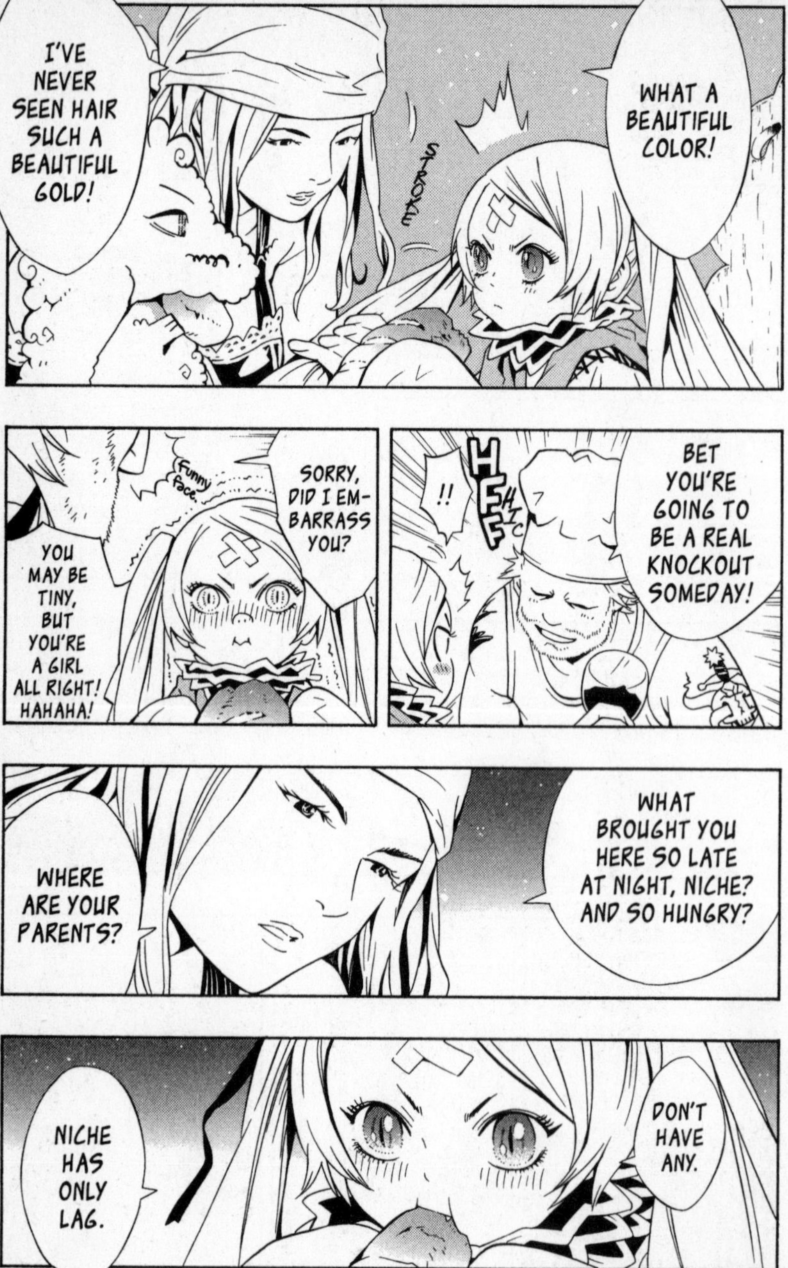
WHAT A BEAUTIFUL COLOR!
STROKE
I'VE NEVER SEEN HAIR SUCH A BEAUTIFUL GOLD!
BET YOU'RE GOING TO BE A REAL KNOCKOUT SOMEDAY!
HFF
HIC
!!
SORRY, DID I EM-BARRASS YOU?
Funny face.
YOU MAY BE TINY, BUT YOU'RE A GIRL ALL RIGHT! HAHAHA!
WHAT BROUGHT YOU HERE SO LATE AT NIGHT, NICHE? AND SO HUNGRY?
WHERE ARE YOUR PARENTS?
DON'T HAVE ANY.
NICHE HAS ONLY LAG.

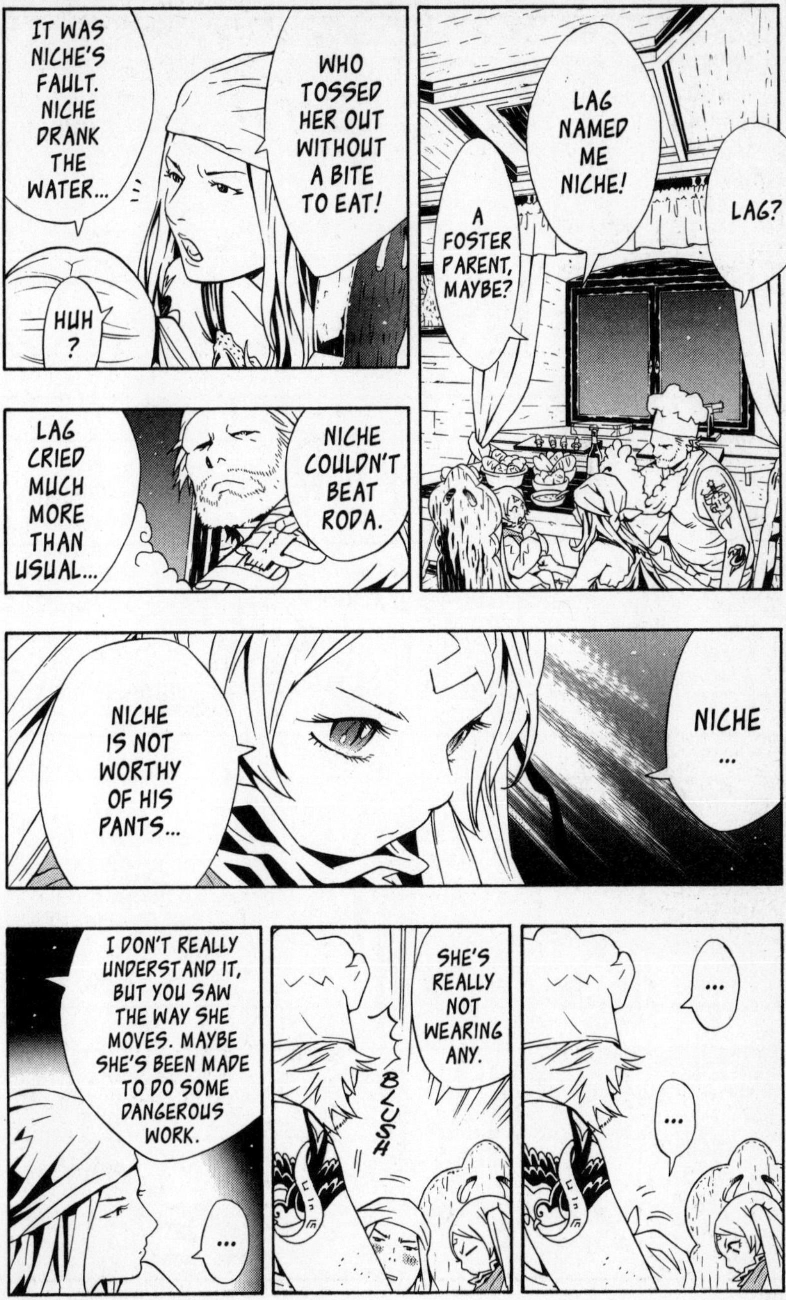
LAG?
LAG NAMED ME NICHE!
A FOSTER PARENT, MAYBE?
WHO TOSSED HER OUT WITHOUT A BITE TO EAT!
IT WAS NICHE'S FAULT. NICHE DRANK THE WATER...
HUH?
NICHE COULDN'T BEAT RODA.
LAG CRIED MUCH MORE THAN USUAL...
NICHE ...
NICHE IS NOT WORTHY OF HIS PANTS...
...
...
SHE'S REALLY NOT WEARING ANY.
BLUSH
I DON'T REALLY UNDERSTAND IT, BUT YOU SAW THE WAY SHE MOVES. MAYBE SHE'S BEEN MADE TO DO SOME DANGEROUS WORK.
...

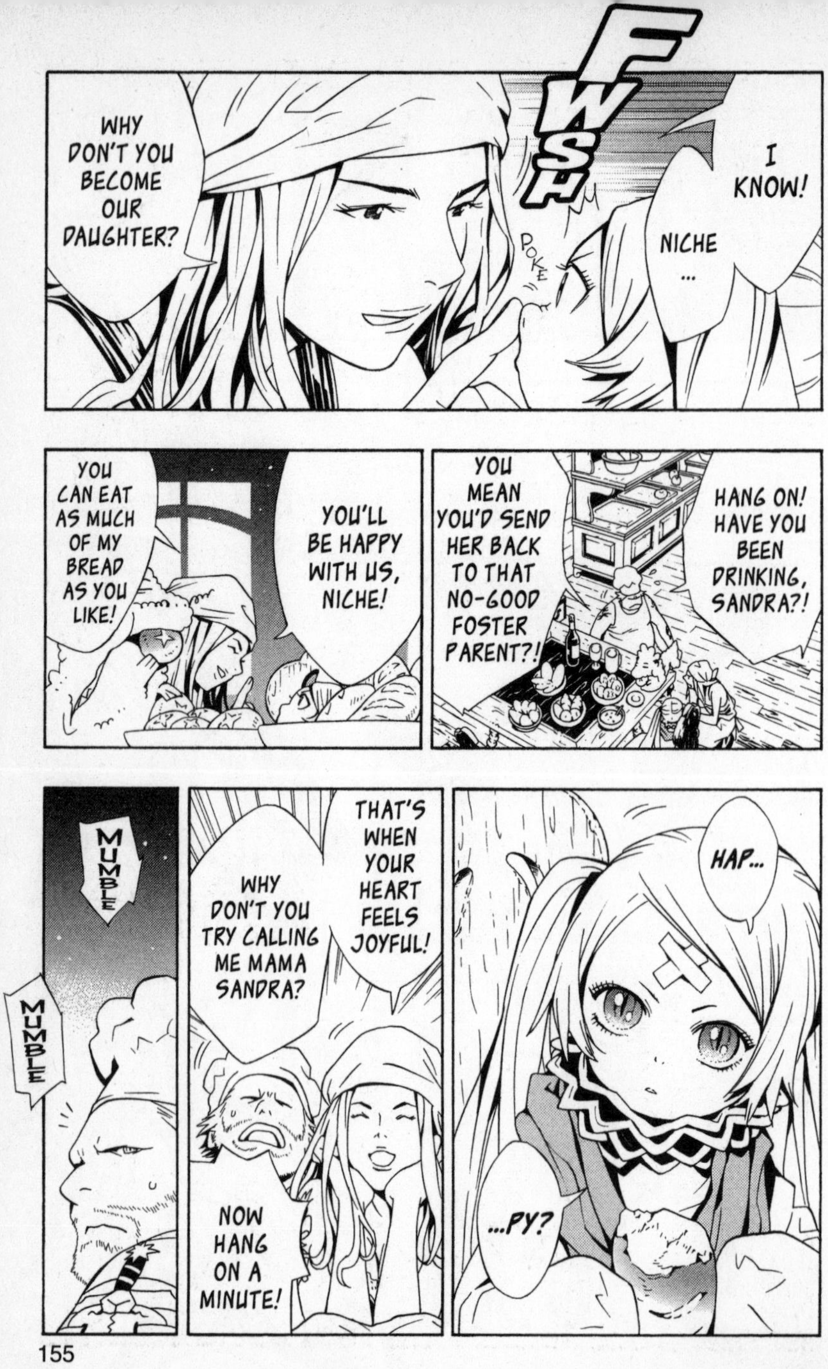
FWSH
I KNOW!
NICHE ...
POKE
WHY DON'T YOU BECOME OUR DAUGHTER?
HANG ON! HAVE YOU BEEN DRINKING, SANDRA?!
YOU MEAN YOU'D SEND HER BACK TO THAT NO-GOOD FOSTER PARENT?!
YOU'LL BE HAPPY WITH US, NICHE!
YOU CAN EAT AS MUCH OF MY BREAD AS YOU LIKE!
HAP...
...PY?
THAT'S WHEN YOUR HEART FEELS JOYFUL!
WHY DON'T YOU TRY CALLING ME MAMA SANDRA?
NOW HANG ON A MINUTE!
MUMBLE
MUMBLE

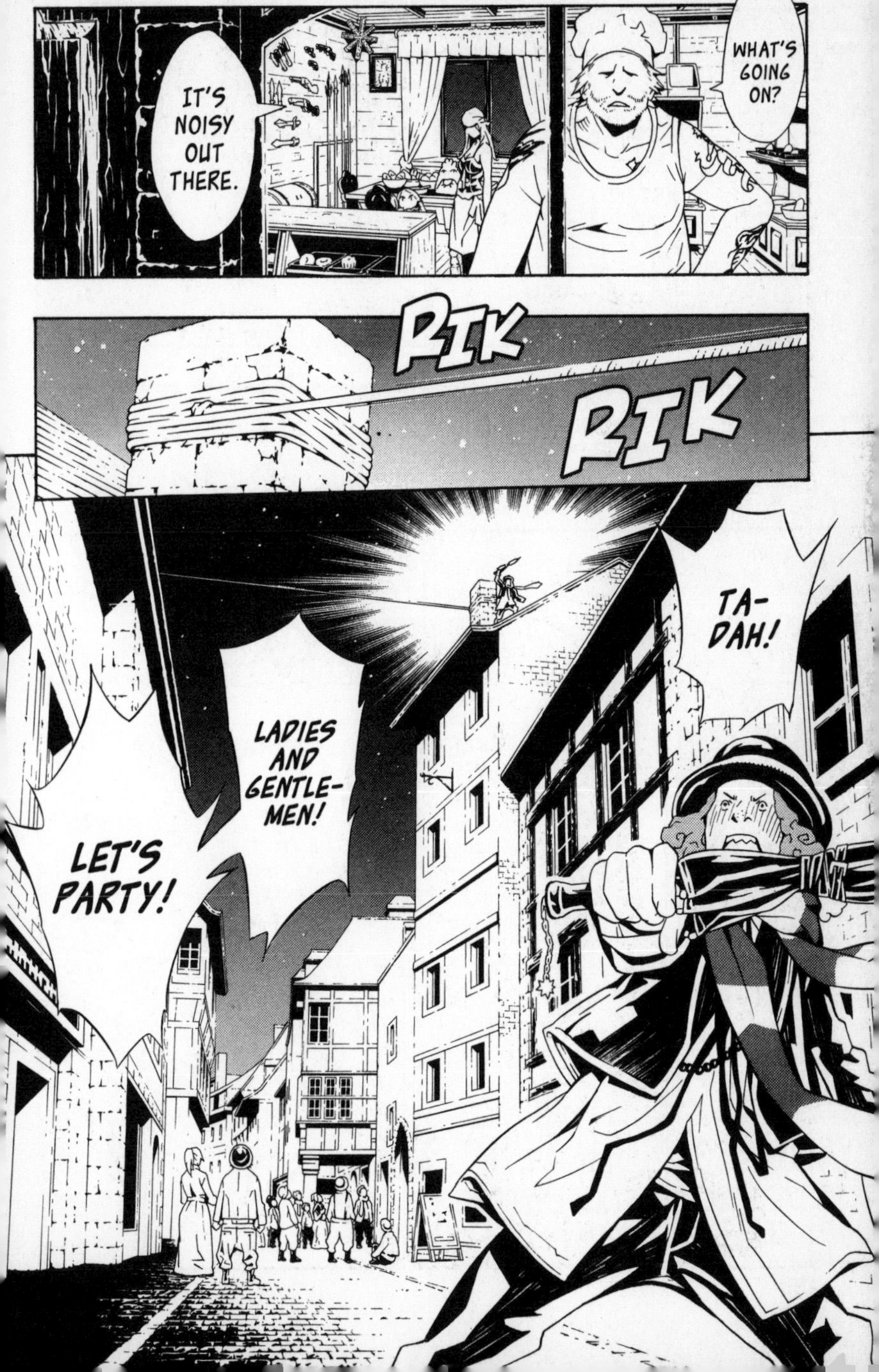
WHAT'S GOING ON?
IT'S NOISY OUT THERE.
RIK
RIK
TA-DAH!
LADIES AND GENTLE-MEN!
LET'S PARTY!

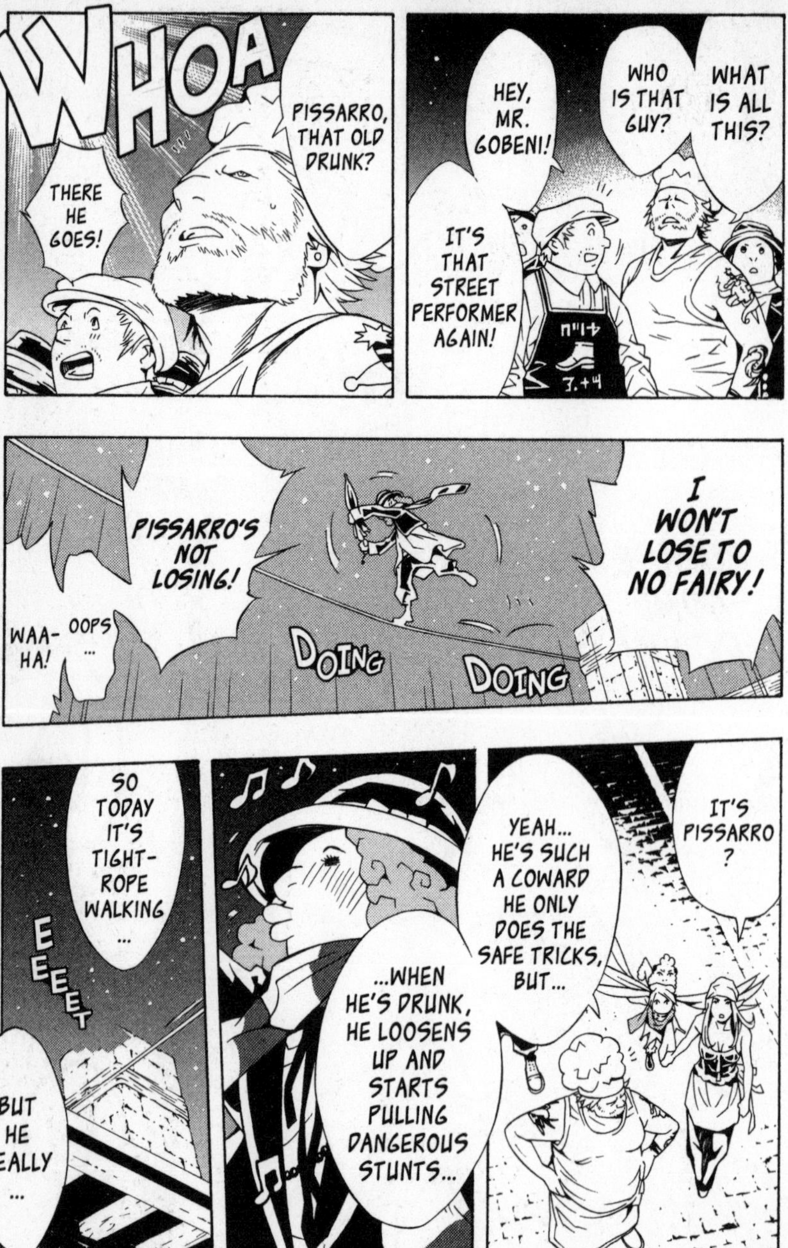
WHAT IS ALL THIS?
WHO IS THAT GUY?
HEY, MR. GOBENI!
IT'S THAT STREET PERFORMER AGAIN!
WHOA
PISSARRO, THAT OLD DRUNK?
THERE HE GOES!
I WON'T LOSE TO NO FAIRY!
PISSARRO'S NOT LOSING!
DOING
DOING
OOPS...
WAA-HA!
IT'S PISSARRO?
YEAH... HE'S SUCH A COWARD HE ONLY DOES THE SAFE TRICKS, BUT...
...WHEN HE'S DRUNK, HE LOOSENS UP AND STARTS PULLING DANGEROUS STUNTS...
SO TODAY IT'S TIGHT-ROPE WALKING...
EEEEET
BUT HE REALLY...

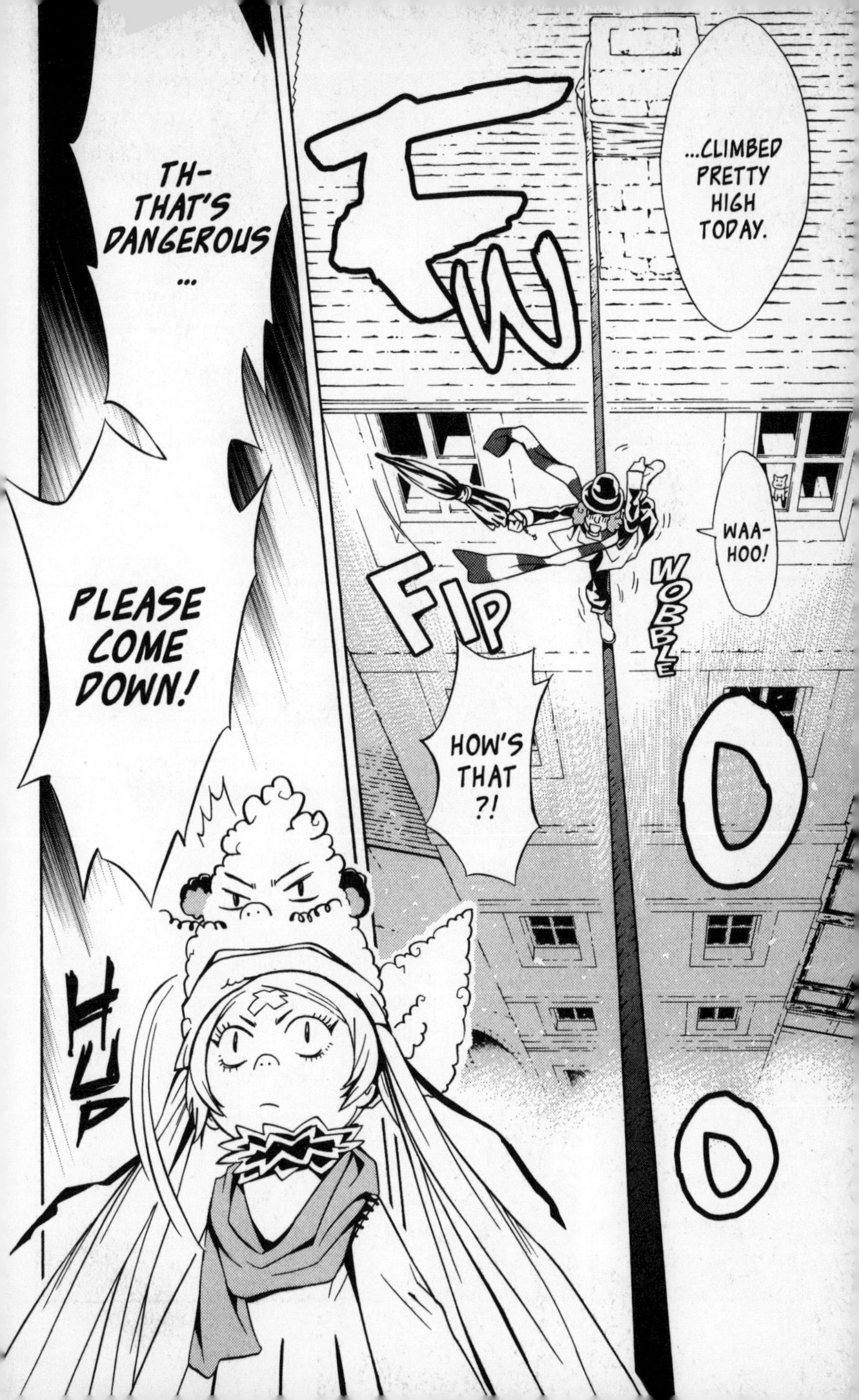

...CLIMBED PRETTY HIGH TODAY.
FW
WAA-HOO!
WOBBLE
FIP
HOW'S THAT?!
TH-THAT'S DANGEROUS...
PLEASE COME DOWN!
HUP

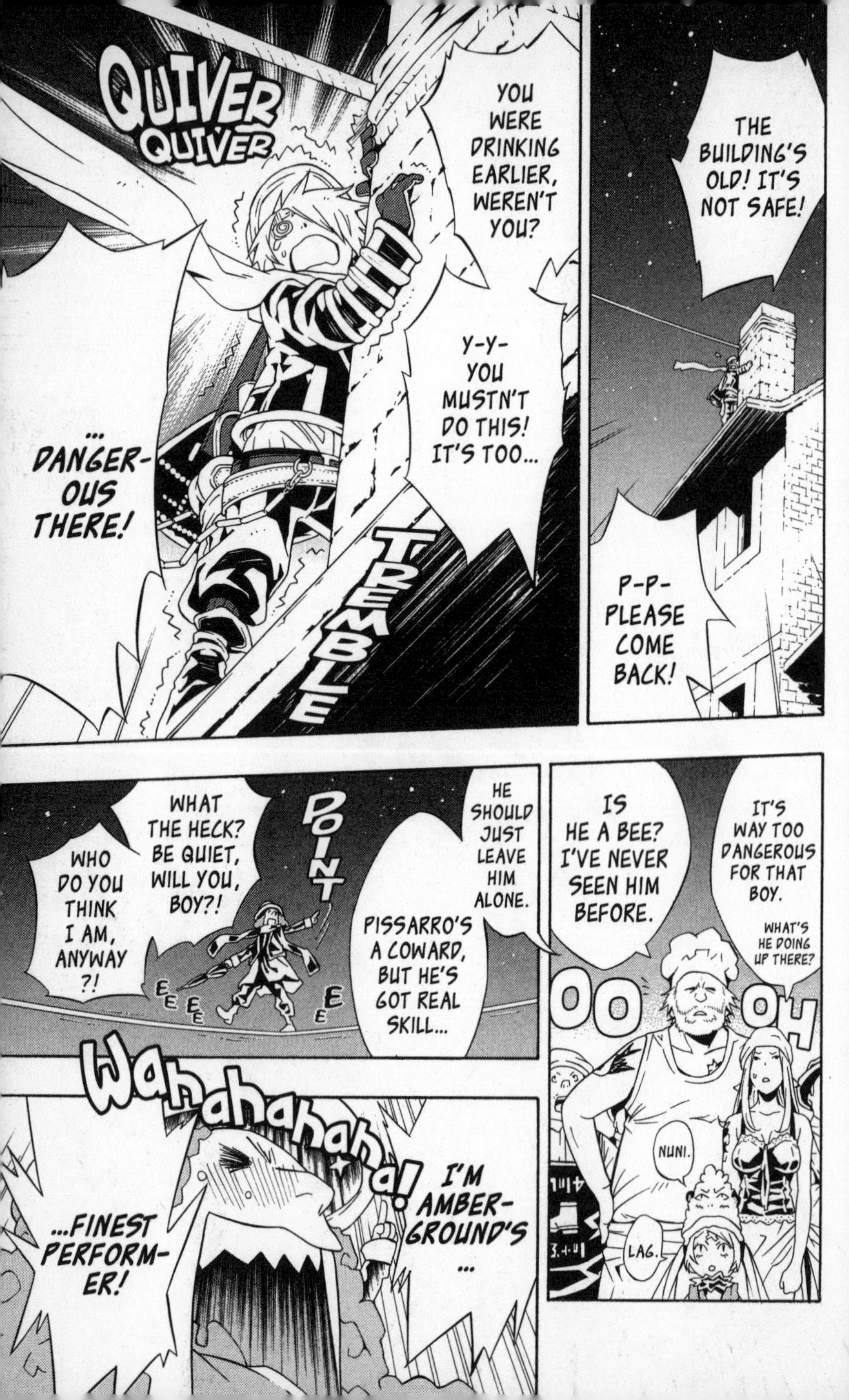
THE BUILDING'S OLD! IT'S NOT SAFE!
P-P-PLEASE COME BACK!
YOU WERE DRINKING EARLIER, WEREN'T YOU?
QUIVER QUIVER
Y-Y-YOU MUSTN'T DO THIS! IT'S TOO...
TREMBLE
...DANGER-OUS THERE!
IT'S WAY TOO DANGEROUS FOR THAT BOY.
WHAT'S HE DOING UP THERE?
IS HE A BEE? I'VE NEVER SEEN HIM BEFORE.
OOOH
NUNI.
LAG.
HE SHOULD JUST LEAVE HIM ALONE.
PISSARRO'S A COWARD, BUT HE'S GOT REAL SKILL...
POINT
WHAT THE HECK? BE QUIET, WILL YOU, BOY?!
WHO DO YOU THINK I AM, ANYWAY?!
EEEEEE
Wahahahaha!
I'M AMBER-GROUND'S ...
...FINEST PERFORM-ER!

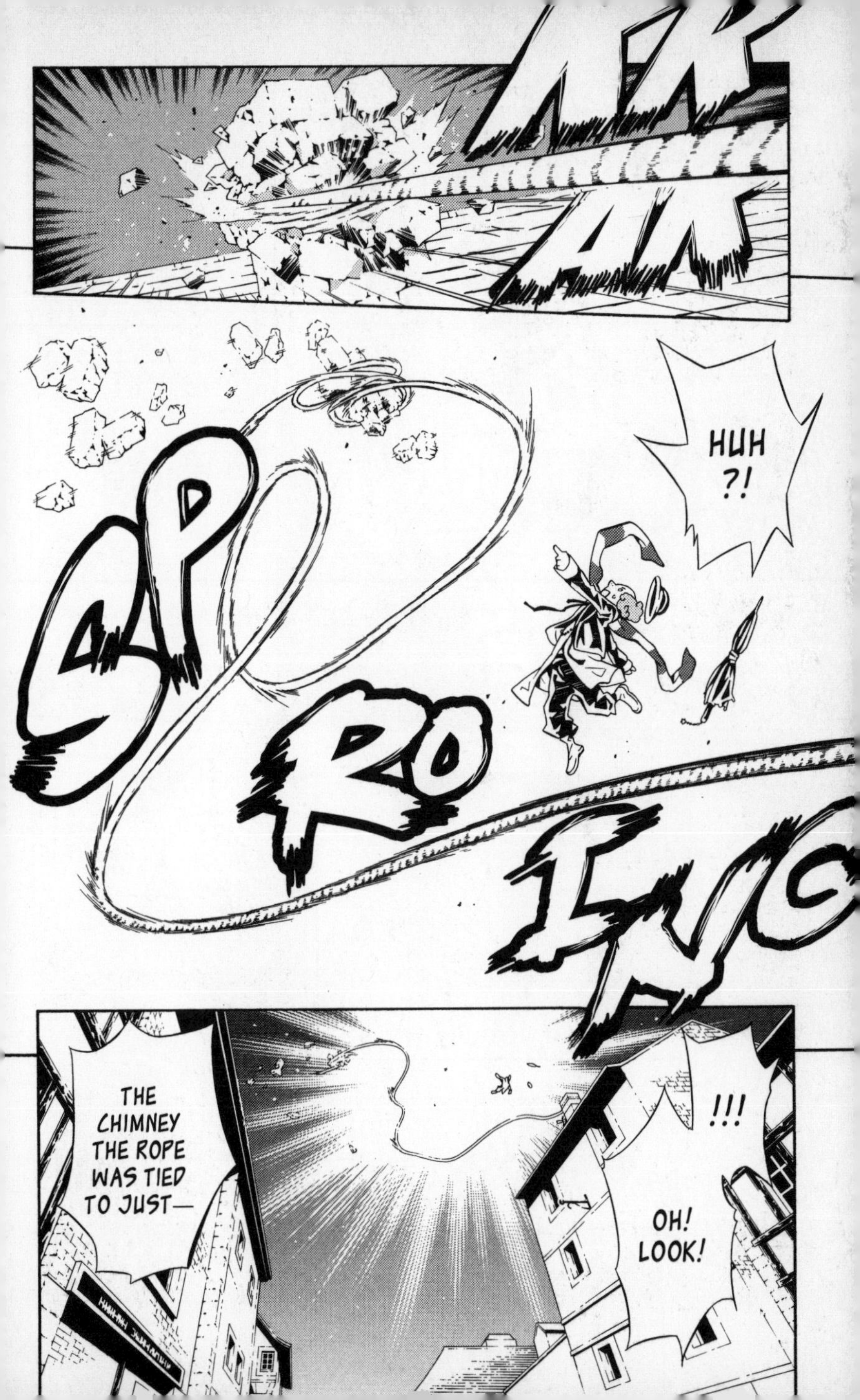
HUH ?!
!!!
THE CHIMNEY THE ROPE WAS TIED TO JUST—
OH! LOOK!

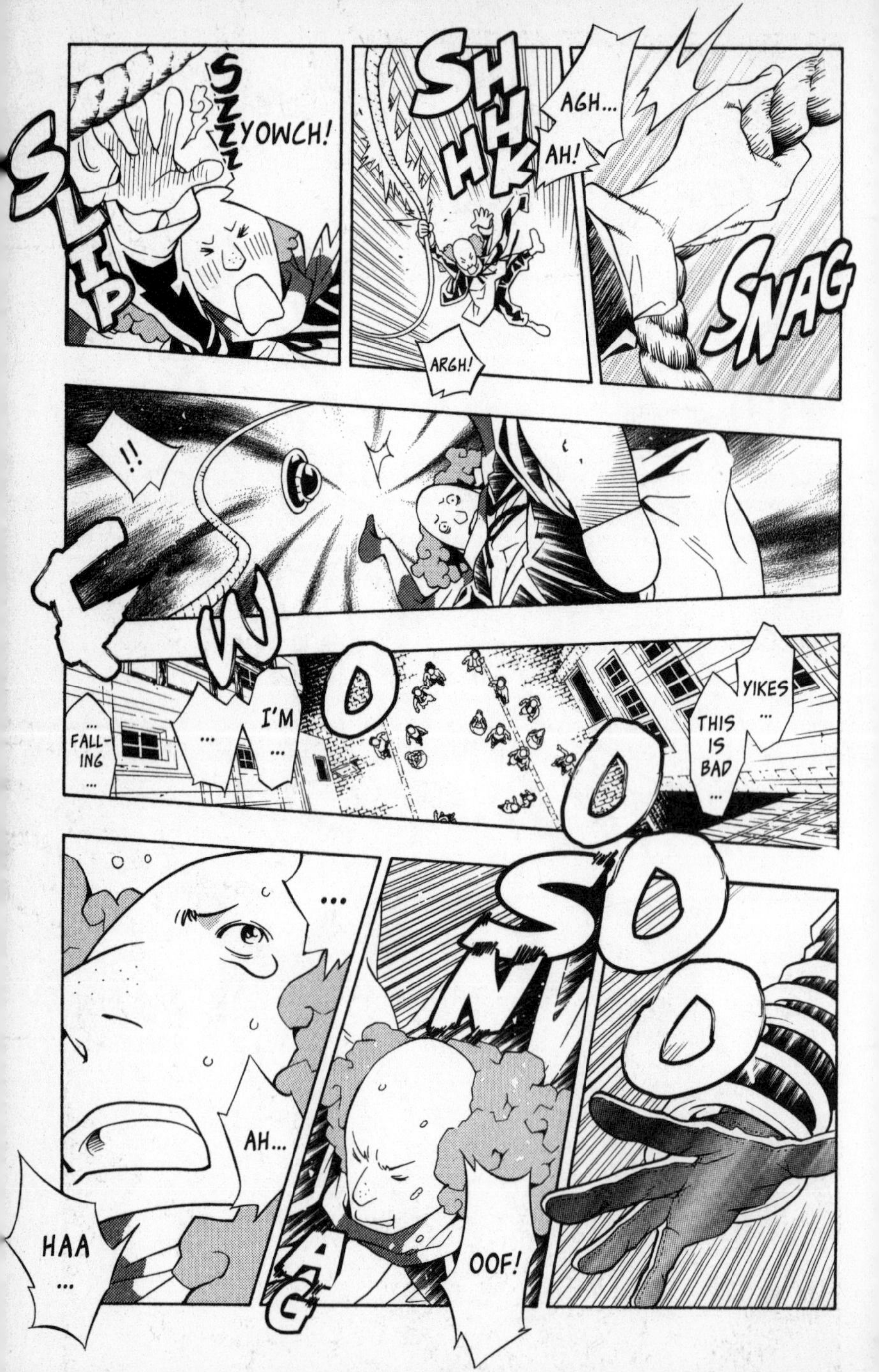
AGH...
AH!
SNAG
SHHHK
ARGH!
SZZZ
YOWCH!
SLIP
!!
TWOOSOO
YIKES...
THIS IS BAD...
I'M...
...
...FALLING...
NAG
OOF!
...
AH...
HAA...

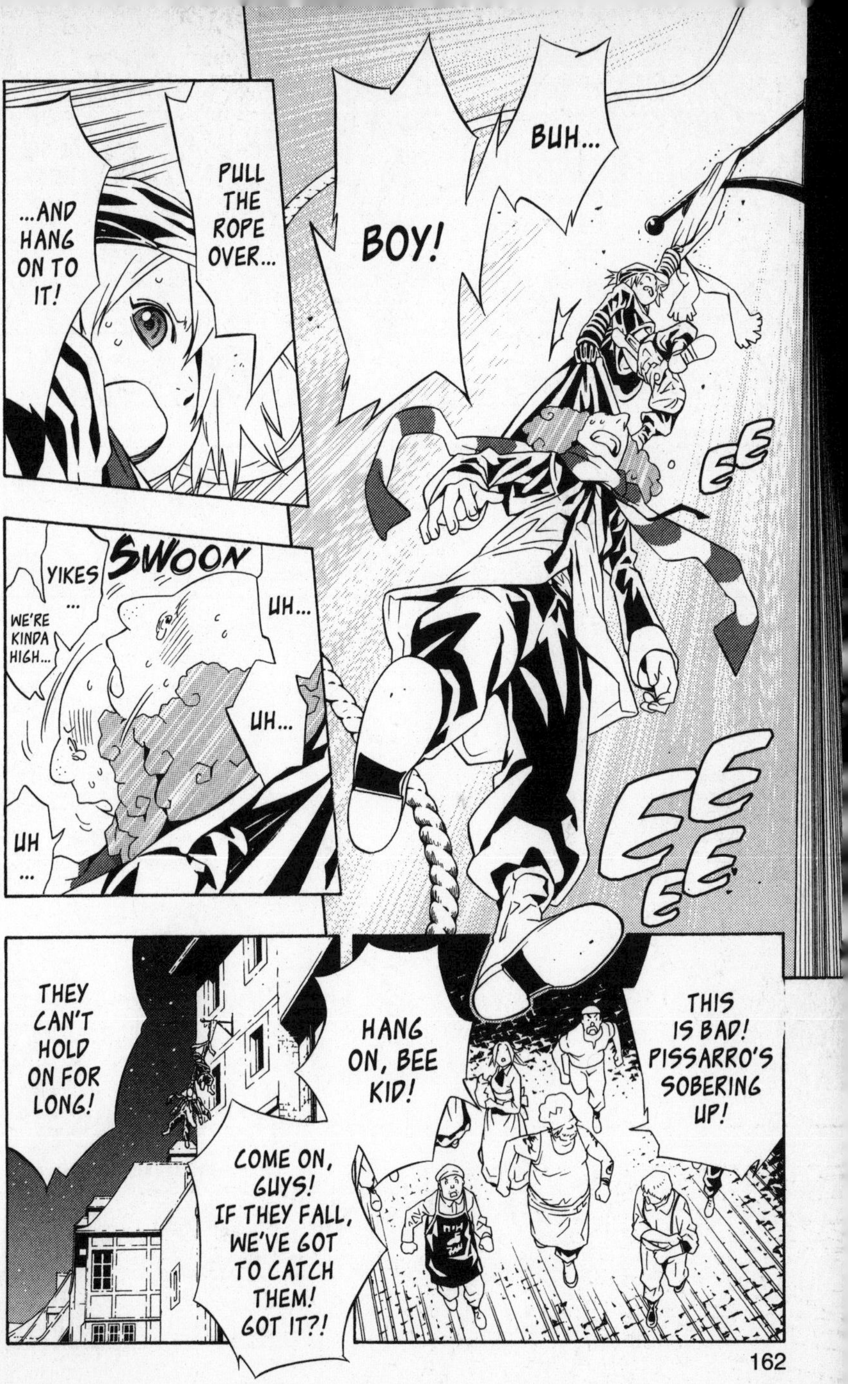
BUH...
BOY!
EE
EEEE
PULL THE ROPE OVER...
...AND HANG ON TO IT!
UH...
SWOON
YIKES...
WE'RE KINDA HIGH...
UH...
UH...
THIS IS BAD! PISSARRO'S SOBERING UP!
HANG ON, BEE KID!
COME ON, GUYS! IF THEY FALL, WE'VE GOT TO CATCH THEM! GOT IT?!
THEY CAN'T HOLD ON FOR LONG!

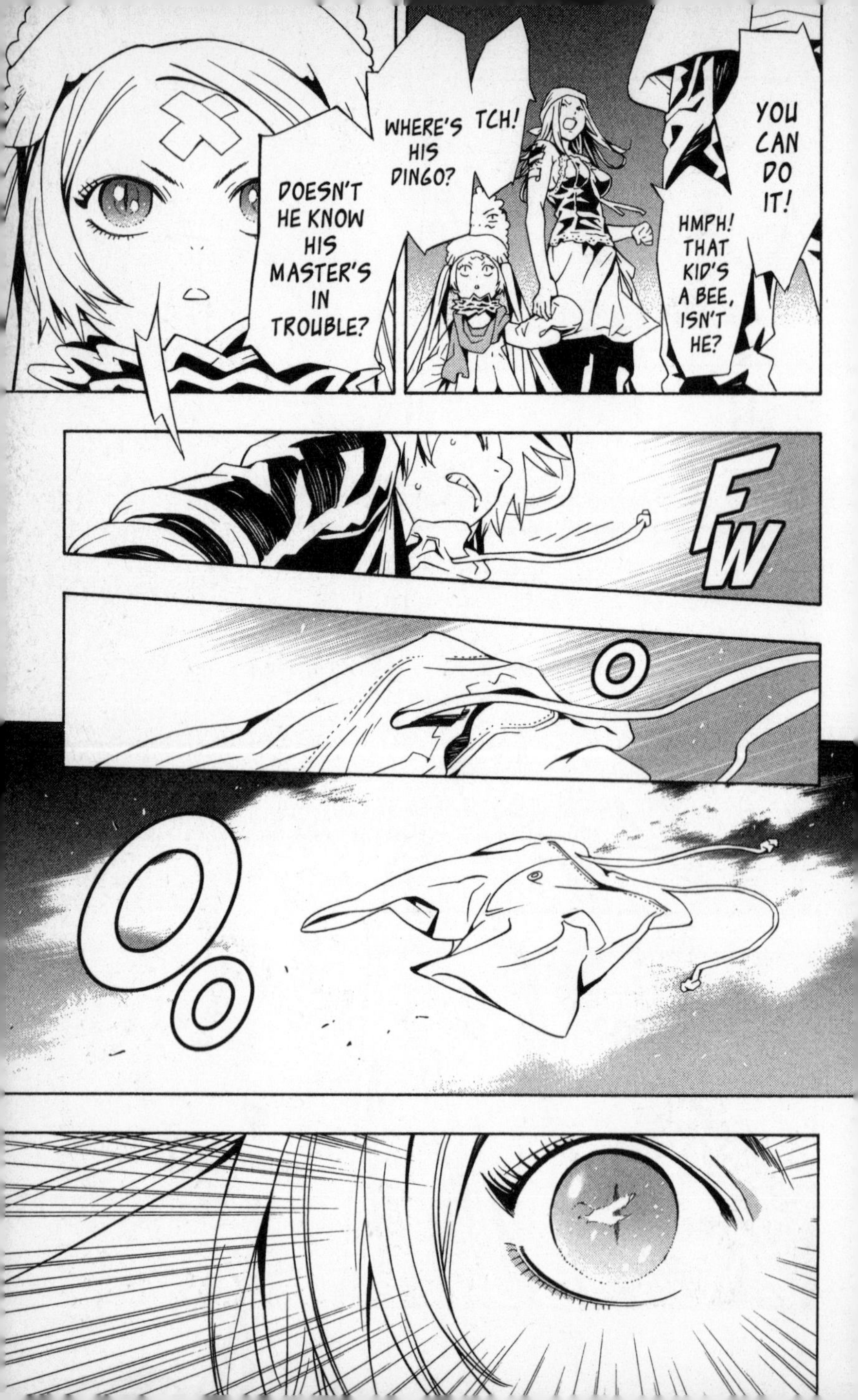
YOU CAN DO IT!
HMPH! THAT KID'S A BEE, ISN'T HE?
TCH!
WHERE'S HIS DINGO?
DOESN'T HE KNOW HIS MASTER'S IN TROUBLE?
FW

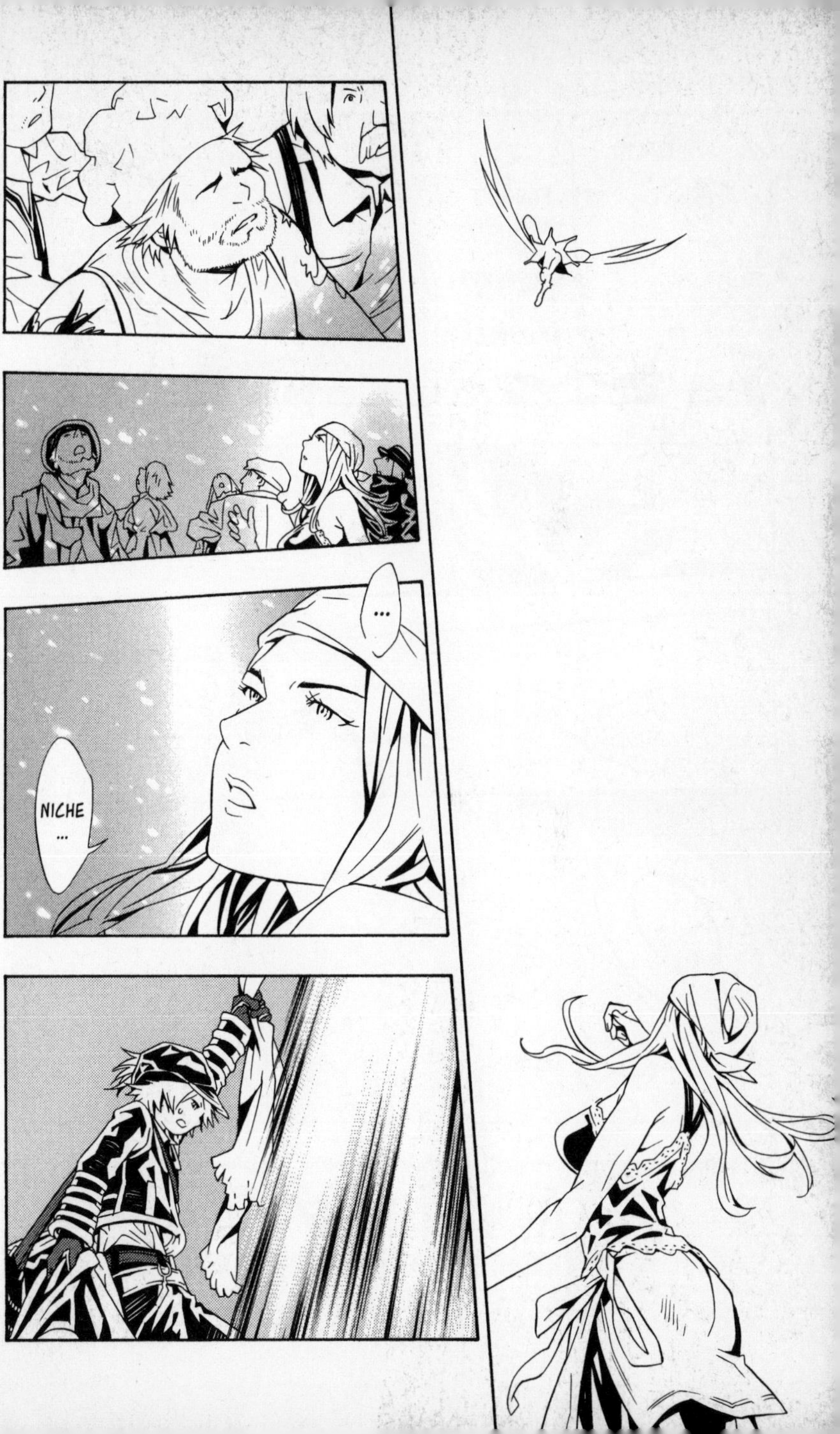
...
NICHE ...

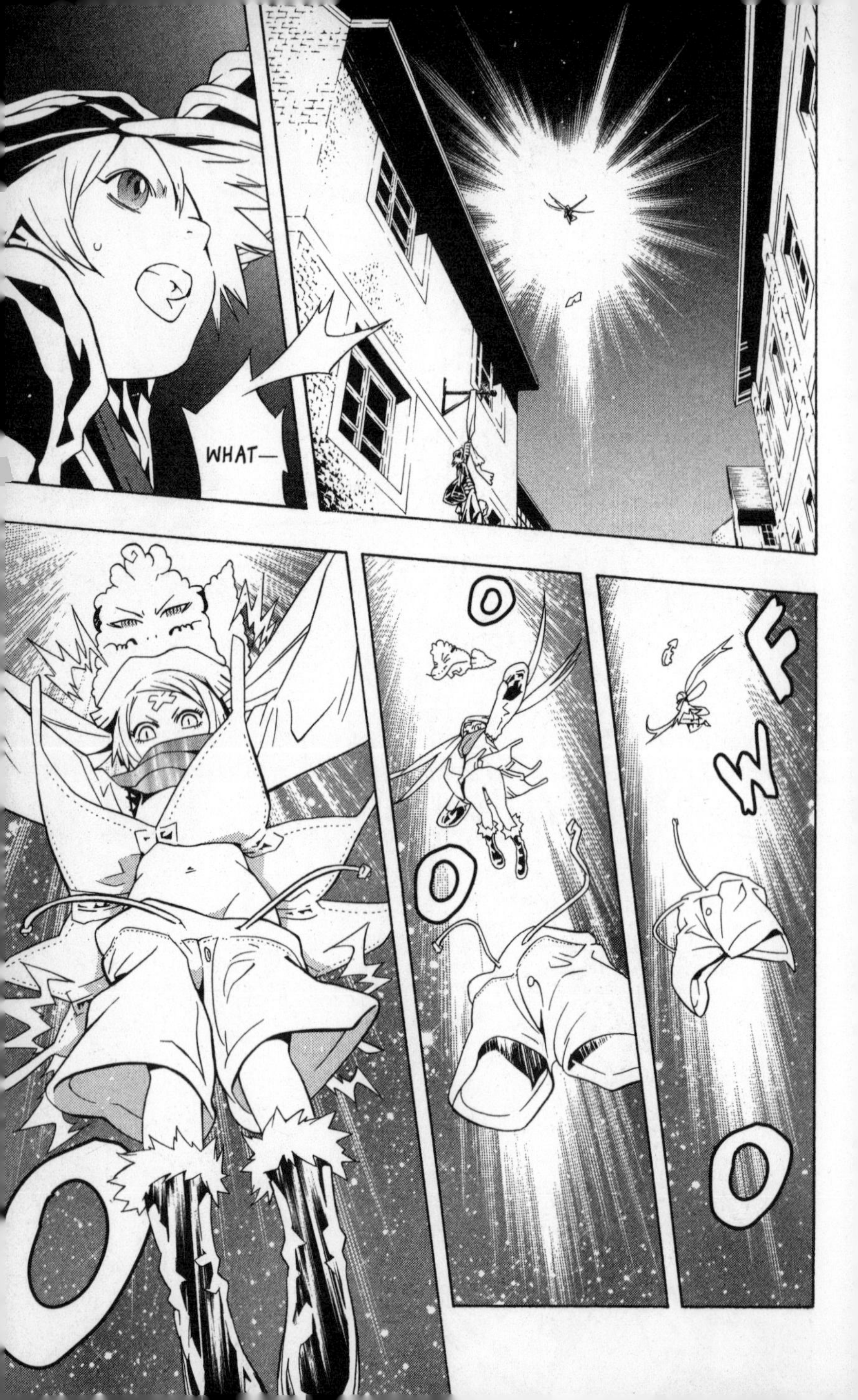
WHAT—
FWOOOO

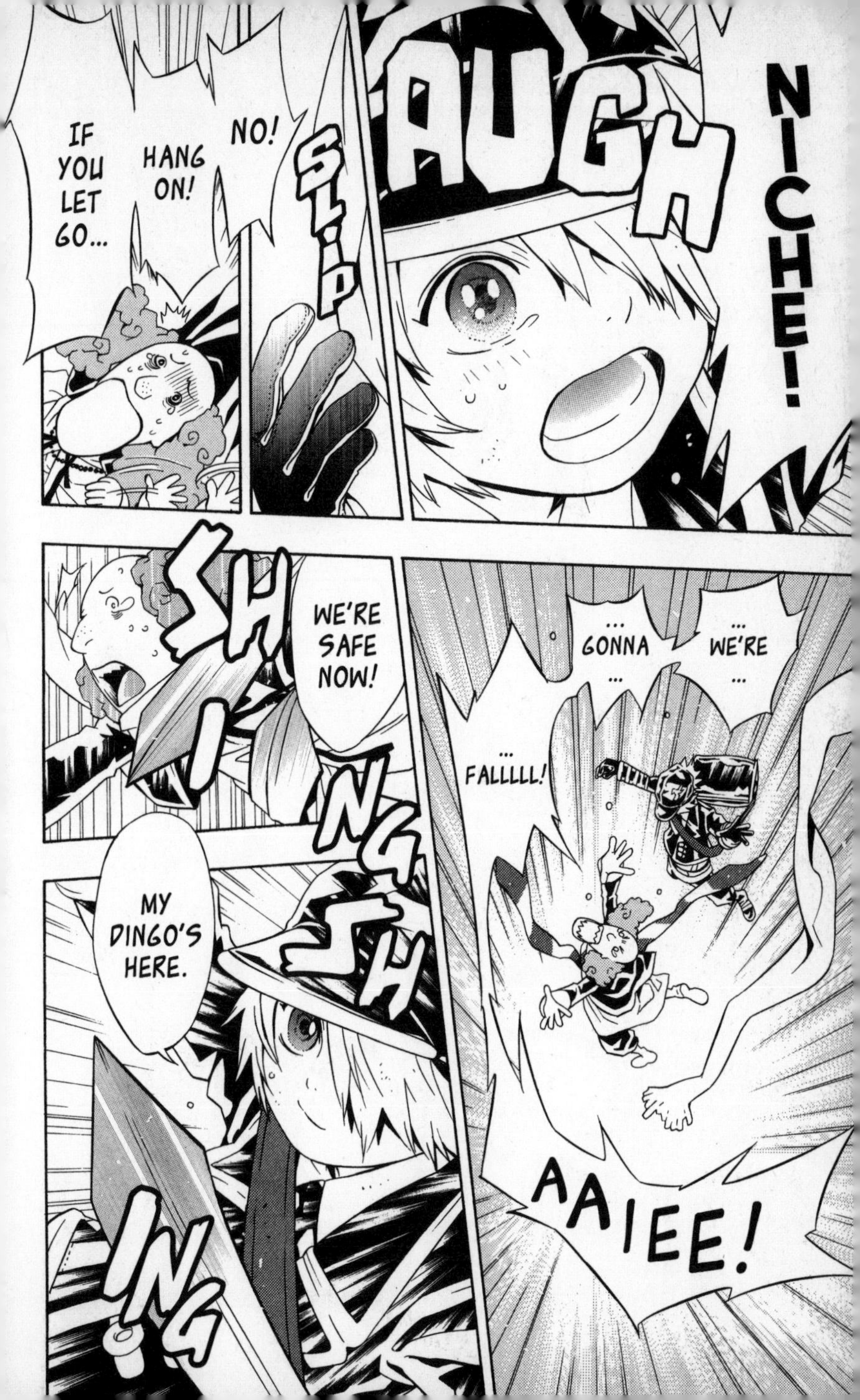
NICHE!
AUGH
SLIP
NO!
HANG ON!
IF YOU LET GO...
... WE'RE ...
... GONNA ...
... FALLLLL!
AAIEE!
SHING
WE'RE SAFE NOW!
MY DINGO'S HERE.
SHING

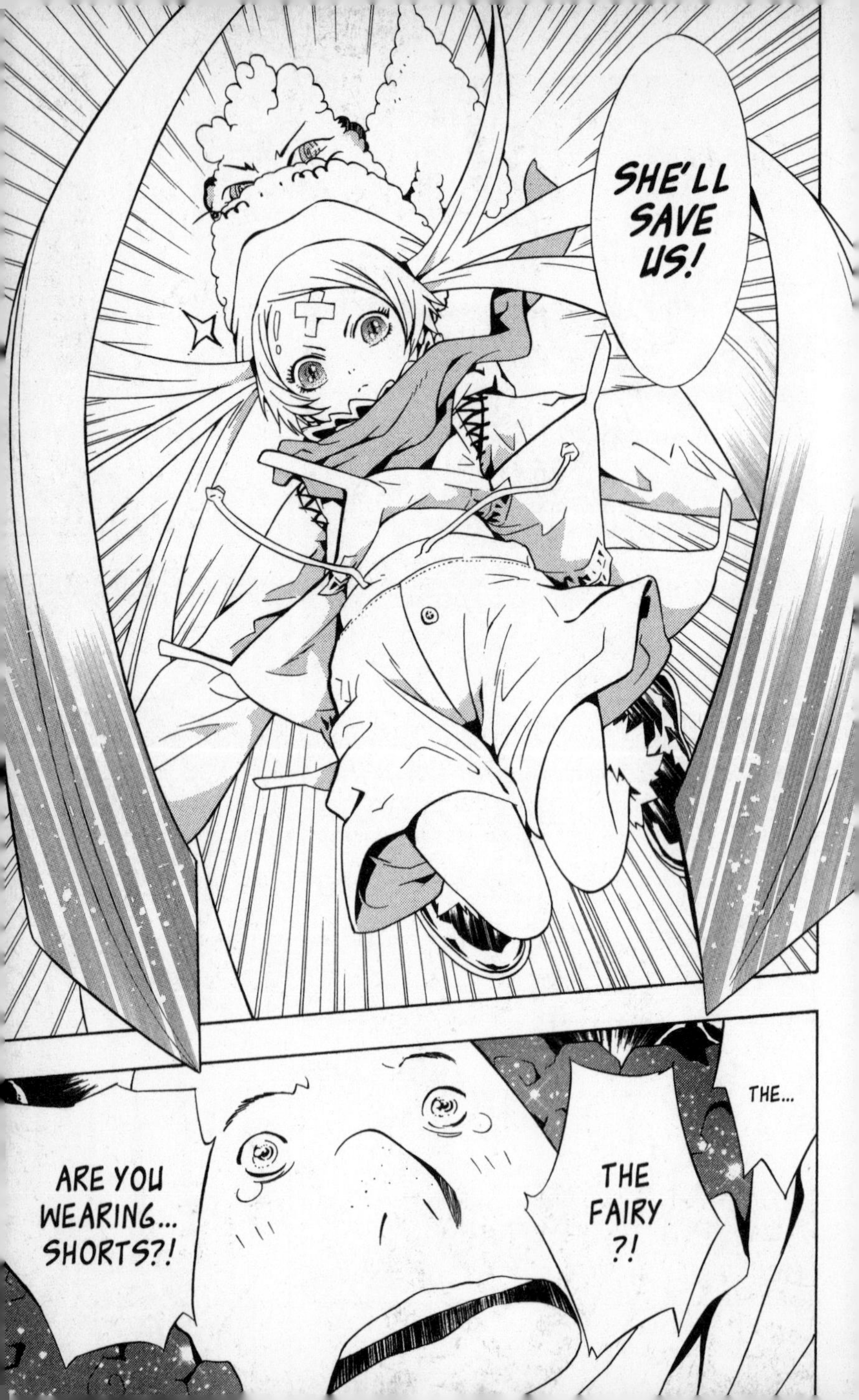
SHE'LL SAVE US!
THE...
THE FAIRY ?!
ARE YOU WEARING... SHORTS?!

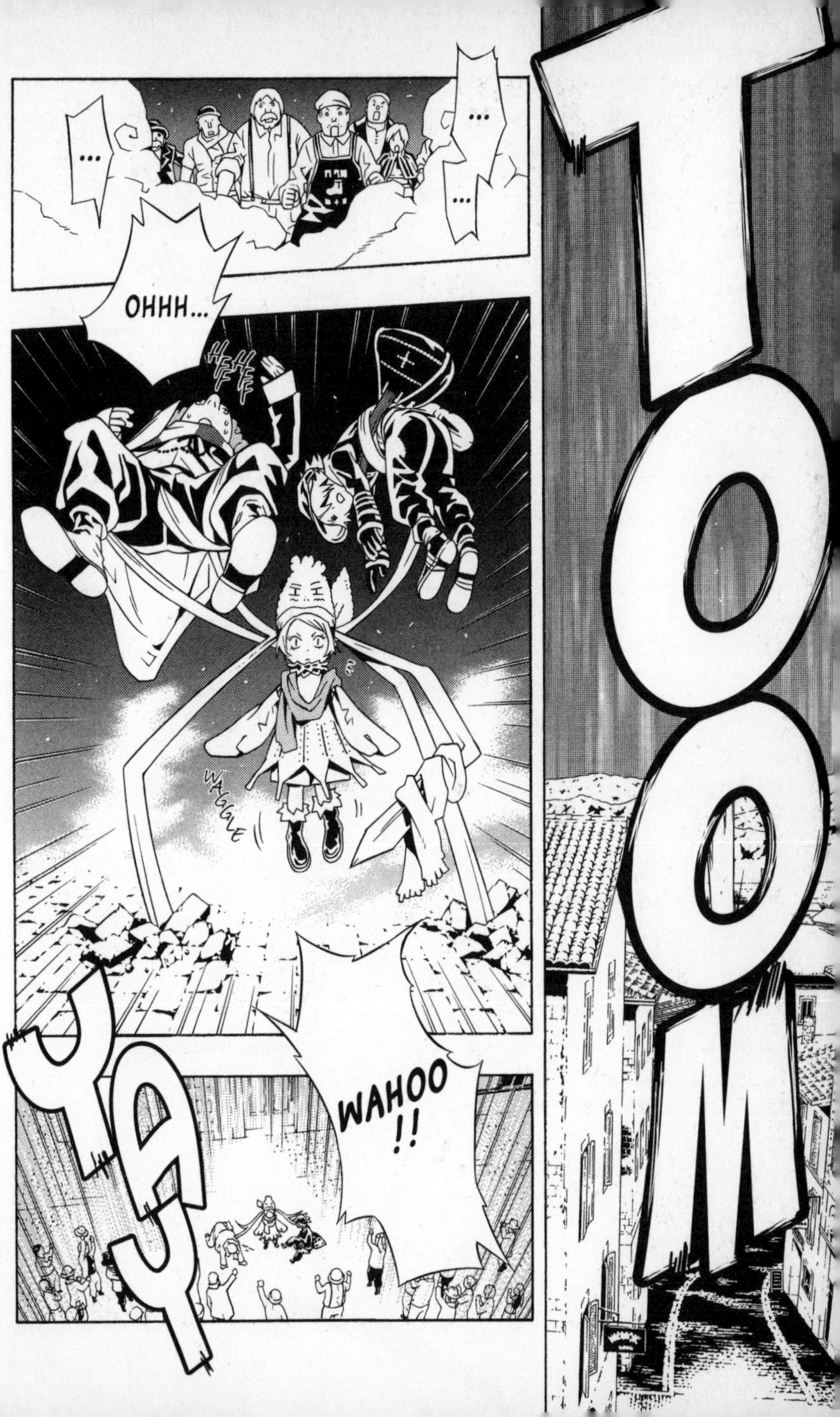
TOOM
...
...
...
OHHH...
WAGGLE
WAHOO !!
YAY

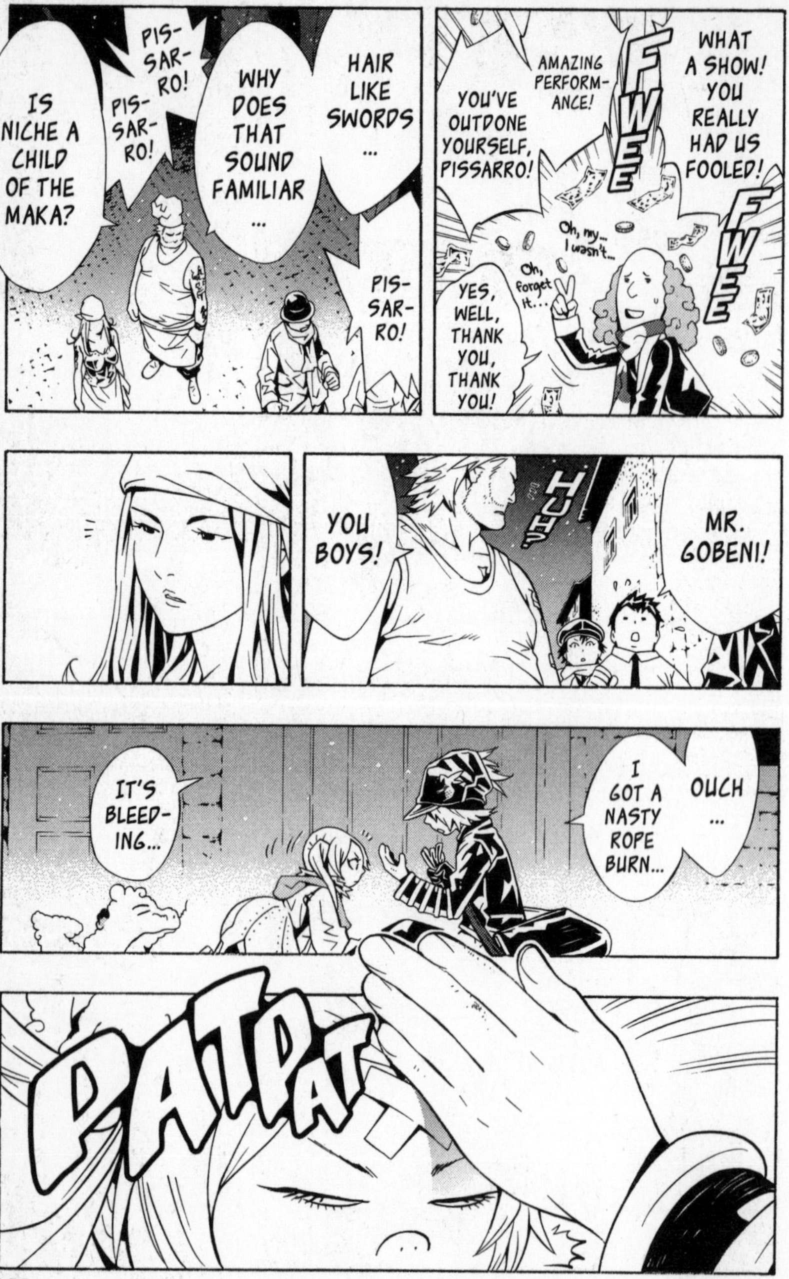

WHAT A SHOW! YOU REALLY HAD US FOOLED!
FWEE
FWEE
AMAZING PERFORMANCE!
YOU'VE OUTDONE YOURSELF, PISSARRO!
Oh, my... I wasn't...
Oh, forget it...
YES, WELL, THANK YOU, THANK YOU!
HAIR LIKE SWORDS...
PIS-SAR-RO!
WHY DOES THAT SOUND FAMILIAR...
PIS-SAR-RO!
PIS-SAR-RO!
IS NICHE A CHILD OF THE MAKA?
MR. GOBENI!
HUH?
YOU BOYS!
OUCH...
I GOT A NASTY ROPE BURN...
IT'S BLEEDING...
PAT PAT

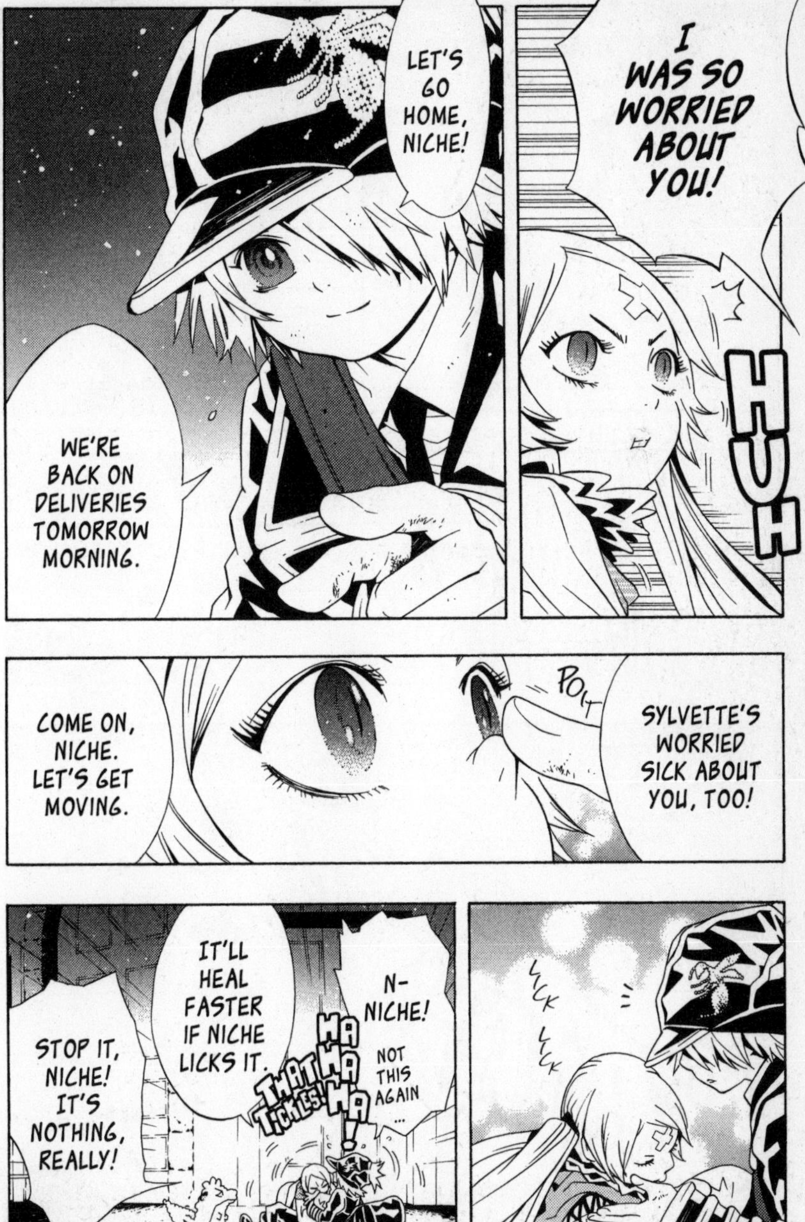
I WAS SO WORRIED ABOUT YOU!
HUH
LET'S GO HOME, NICHE!
WE'RE BACK ON DELIVERIES TOMORROW MORNING.
SYLVETTE'S WORRIED SICK ABOUT YOU, TOO!
POK
COME ON, NICHE. LET'S GET MOVING.
LICK LICK
N-NICHE!
NOT THIS AGAIN...
HA HA HA!
THAT TICKLES!
IT'LL HEAL FASTER IF NICHE LICKS IT.
STOP IT, NICHE! IT'S NOTHING, REALLY!

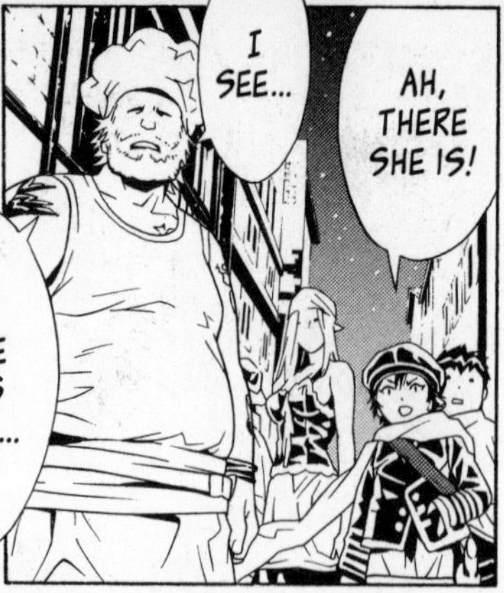
AH, THERE SHE IS!
I SEE...
SO NICHE IS HIS DINGO...
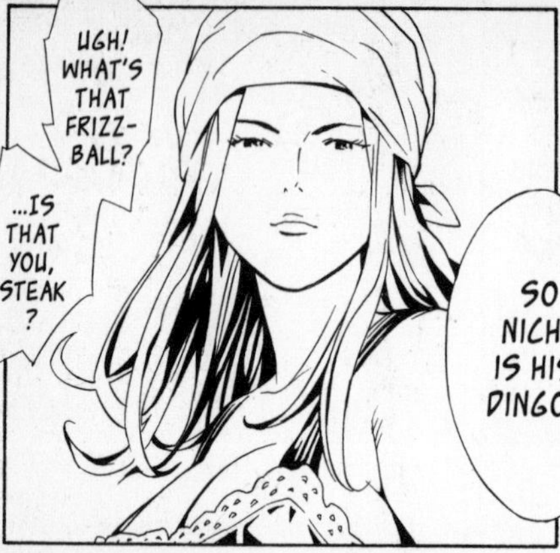
UGH! WHAT'S THAT FRIZZ-BALL?
...IS THAT YOU, STEAK?
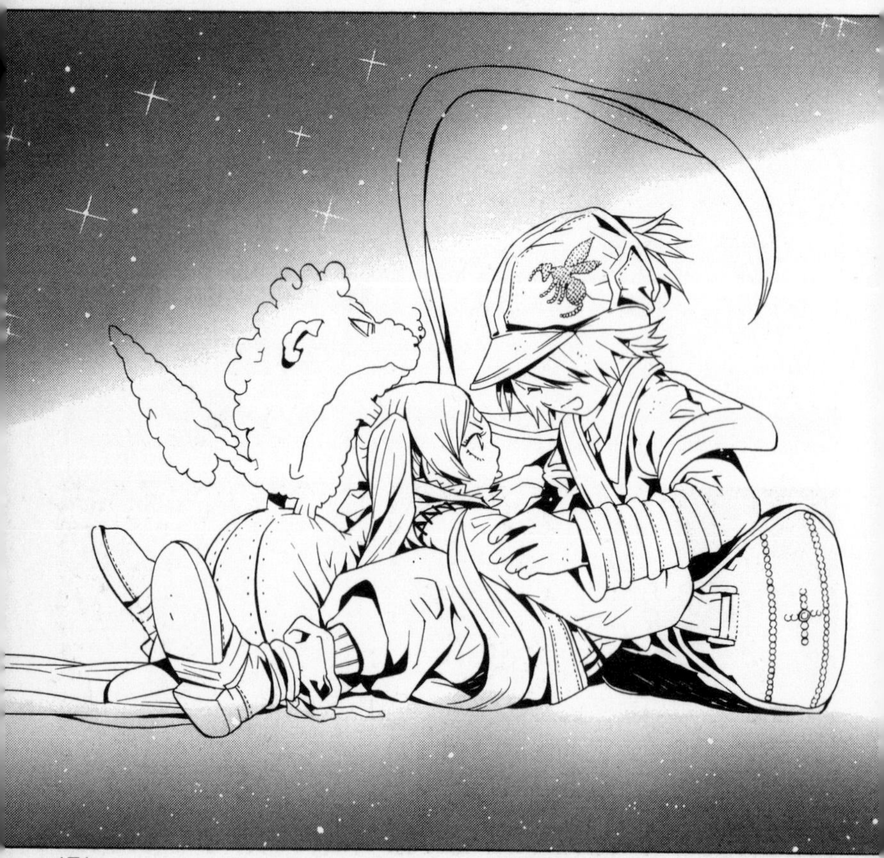

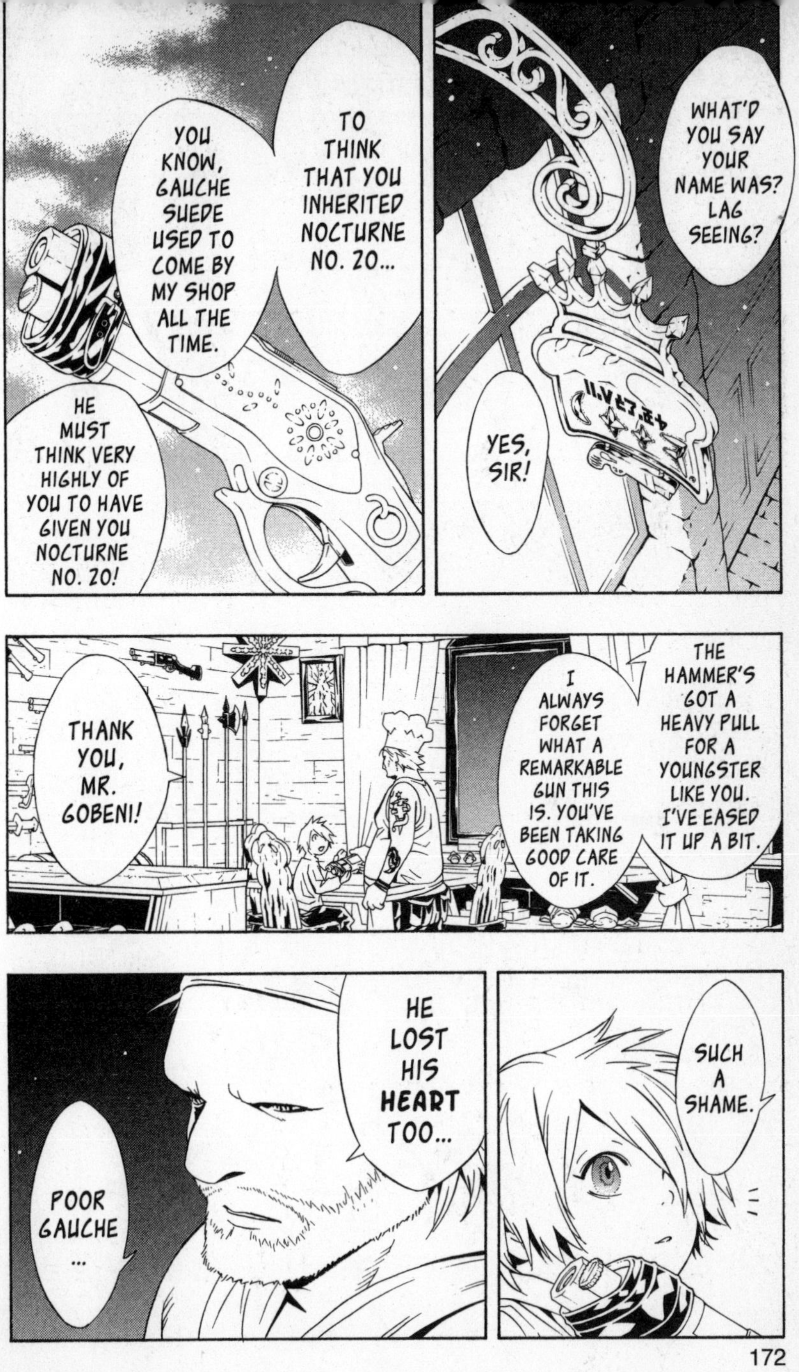
WHAT'D YOU SAY YOUR NAME WAS? LAG SEEING?
YES, SIR!
TO THINK THAT YOU INHERITED NOCTURNE NO. 20...
YOU KNOW, GAUCHE SUEDE USED TO COME BY MY SHOP ALL THE TIME.
HE MUST THINK VERY HIGHLY OF YOU TO HAVE GIVEN YOU NOCTURNE NO. 20!
THE HAMMER'S GOT A HEAVY PULL FOR A YOUNGSTER LIKE YOU. I'VE EASED IT UP A BIT.
I ALWAYS FORGET WHAT A REMARKABLE GUN THIS IS. YOU'VE BEEN TAKING GOOD CARE OF IT.
THANK YOU, MR. GOBENI!
SUCH A SHAME.
HE LOST HIS **HEART** TOO...
POOR GAUCHE ...

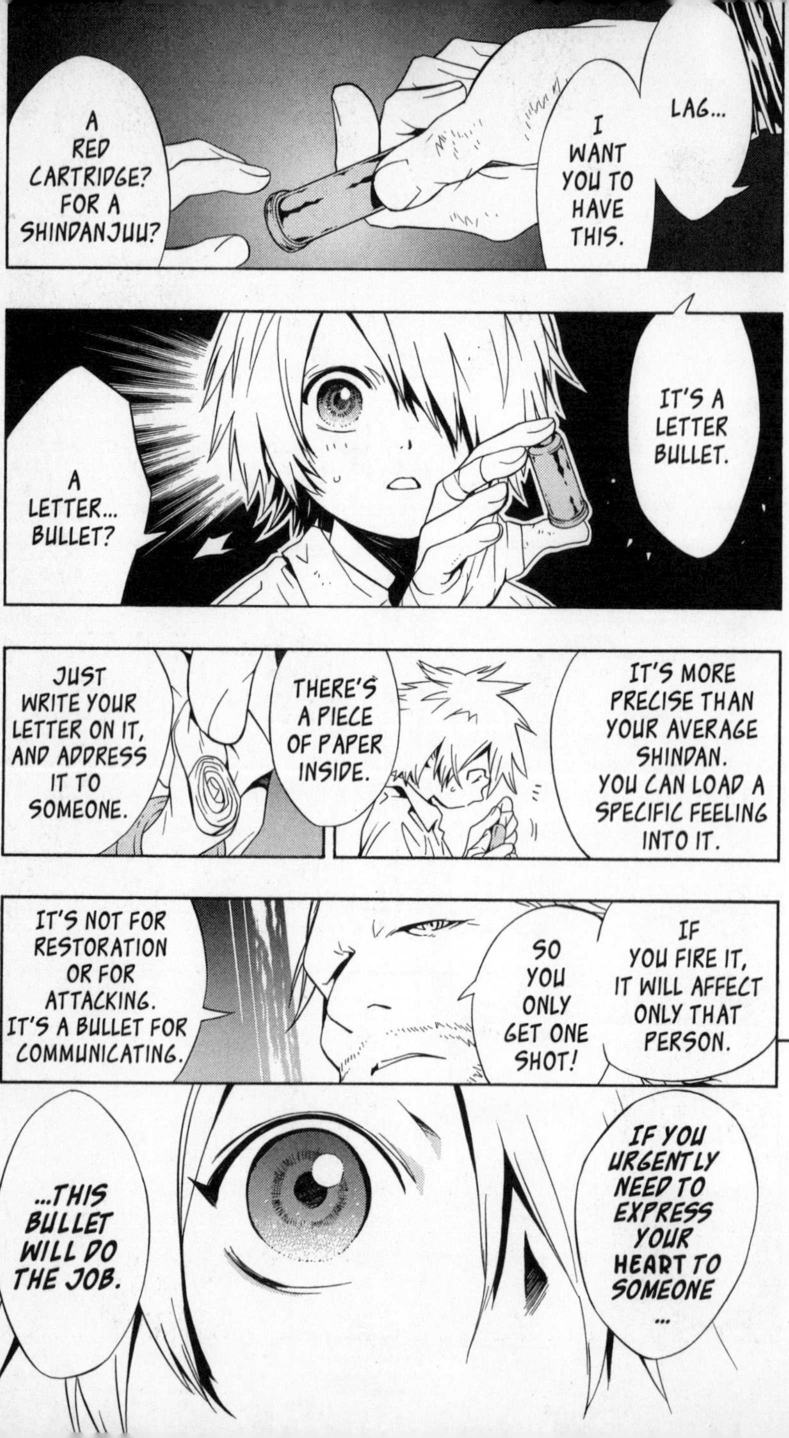
LAG...
I WANT YOU TO HAVE THIS.
A RED CARTRIDGE? FOR A SHINDANJUU?
IT'S A LETTER BULLET.
A LETTER... BULLET?
IT'S MORE PRECISE THAN YOUR AVERAGE SHINDAN. YOU CAN LOAD A SPECIFIC FEELING INTO IT.
THERE'S A PIECE OF PAPER INSIDE.
JUST WRITE YOUR LETTER ON IT, AND ADDRESS IT TO SOMEONE.
IF YOU FIRE IT, IT WILL AFFECT ONLY THAT PERSON.
SO YOU ONLY GET ONE SHOT!
IT'S NOT FOR RESTORATION OR FOR ATTACKING. IT'S A BULLET FOR COMMUNICATING.
IF YOU URGENTLY NEED TO EXPRESS YOUR HEART TO SOMEONE ...
...THIS BULLET WILL DO THE JOB.

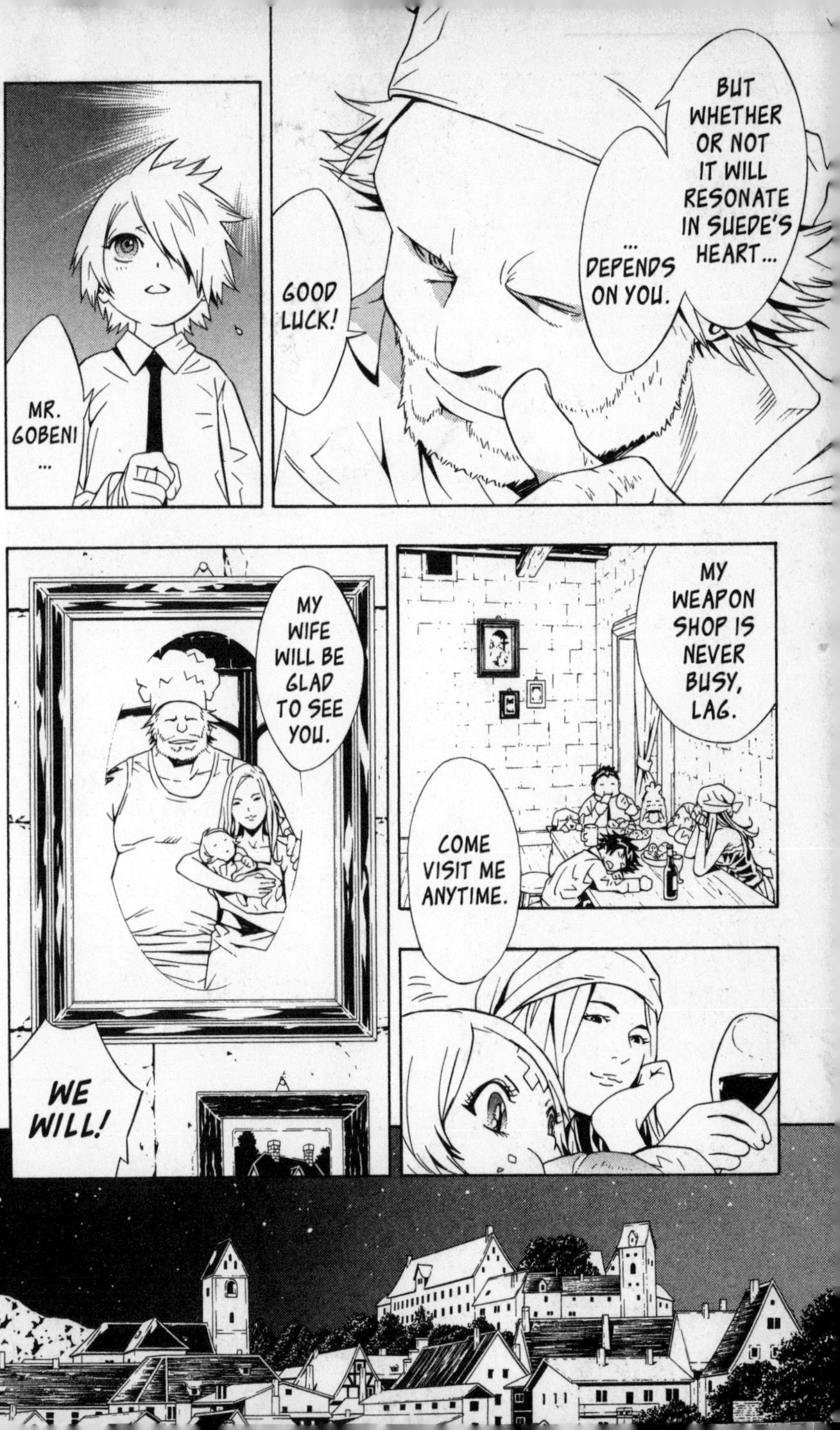
BUT WHETHER OR NOT IT WILL RESONATE IN SUEDE'S HEART...
...DEPENDS ON YOU.
GOOD LUCK!
MR. GOBENI ...
MY WEAPON SHOP IS NEVER BUSY, LAG.
COME VISIT ME ANYTIME.
MY WIFE WILL BE GLAD TO SEE YOU.
WE WILL!

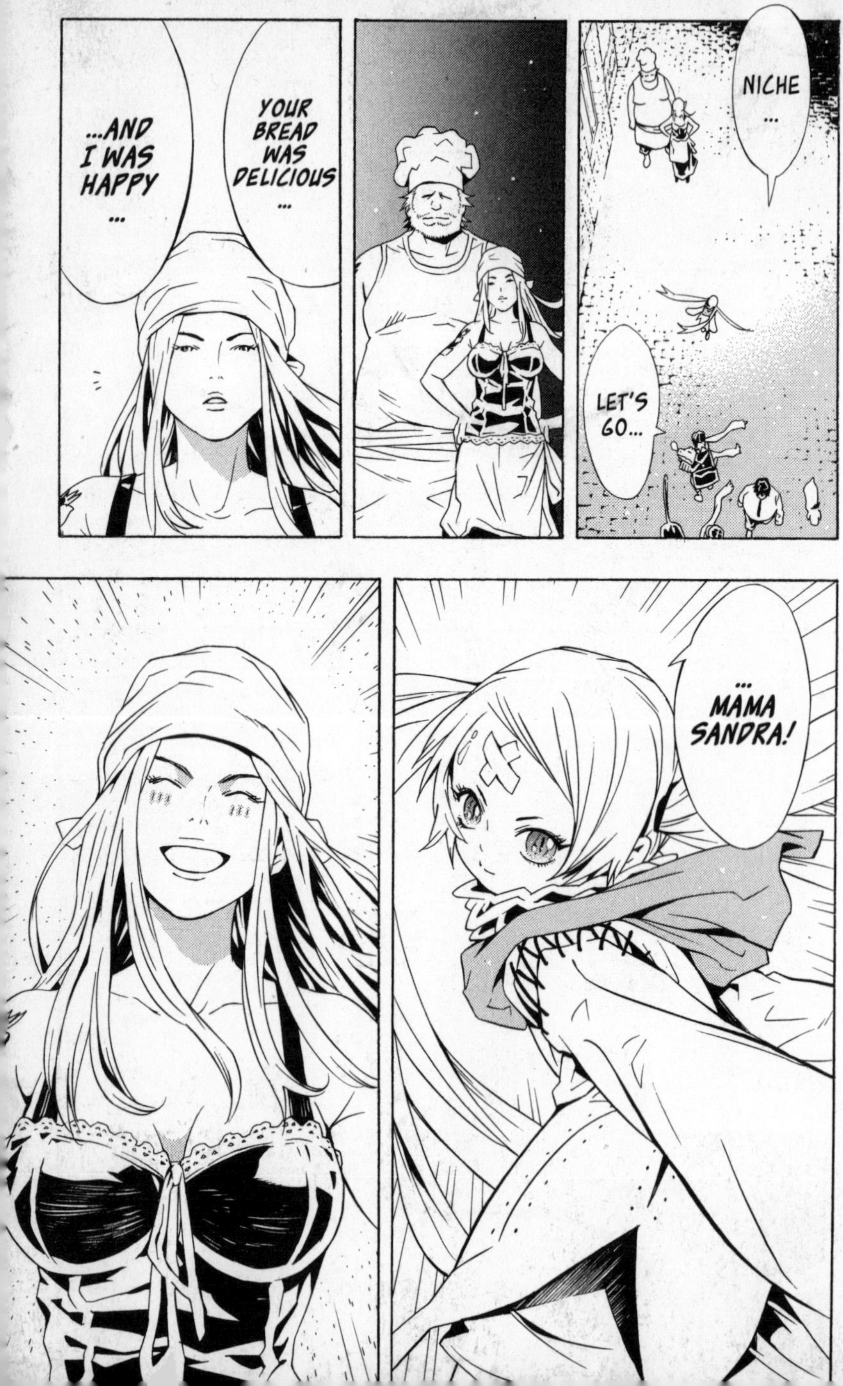
NICHE ...
LET'S GO...
YOUR BREAD WAS DELICIOUS ...
...AND I WAS HAPPY ...
... MÄMA SANDRA!

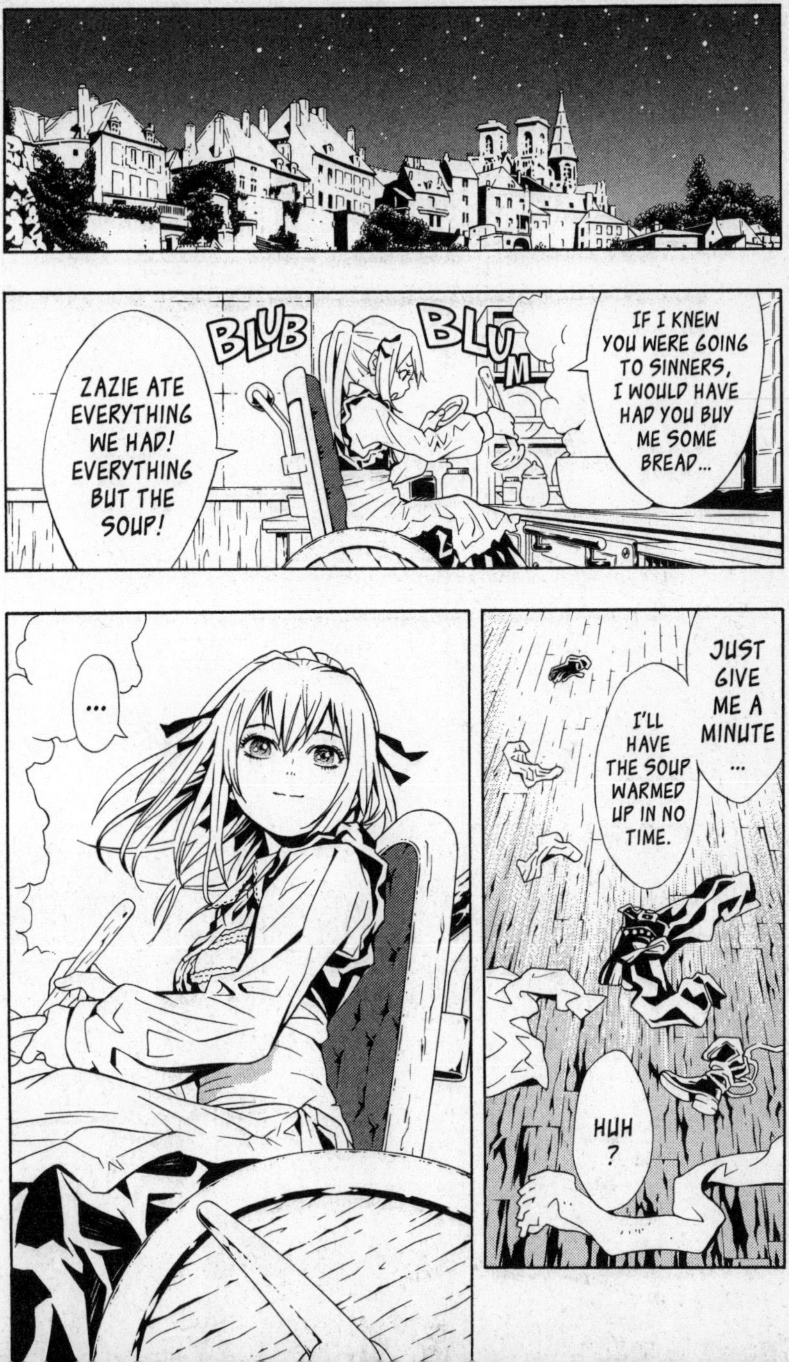
IF I KNEW YOU WERE GOING TO SINNERS, I WOULD HAVE HAD YOU BUY ME SOME BREAD...
BLUM
BLUB
ZAZIE ATE EVERYTHING WE HAD! EVERYTHING BUT THE SOUP!
JUST GIVE ME A MINUTE...
I'LL HAVE THE SOUP WARMED UP IN NO TIME.
HUH?
...

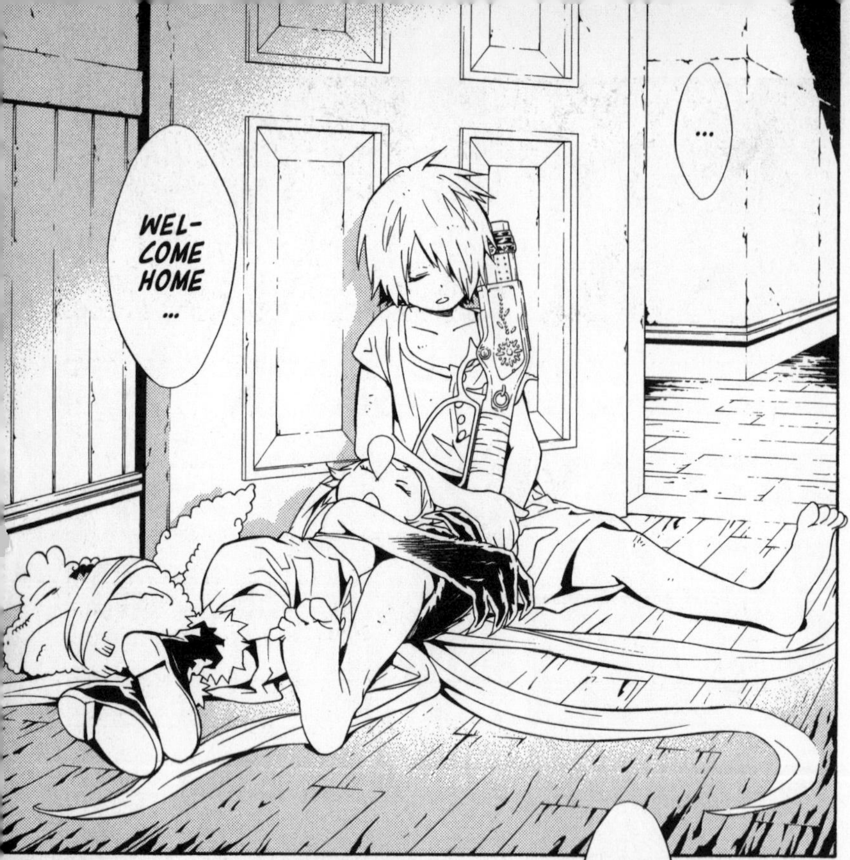
...
WEL-COME HOME ...
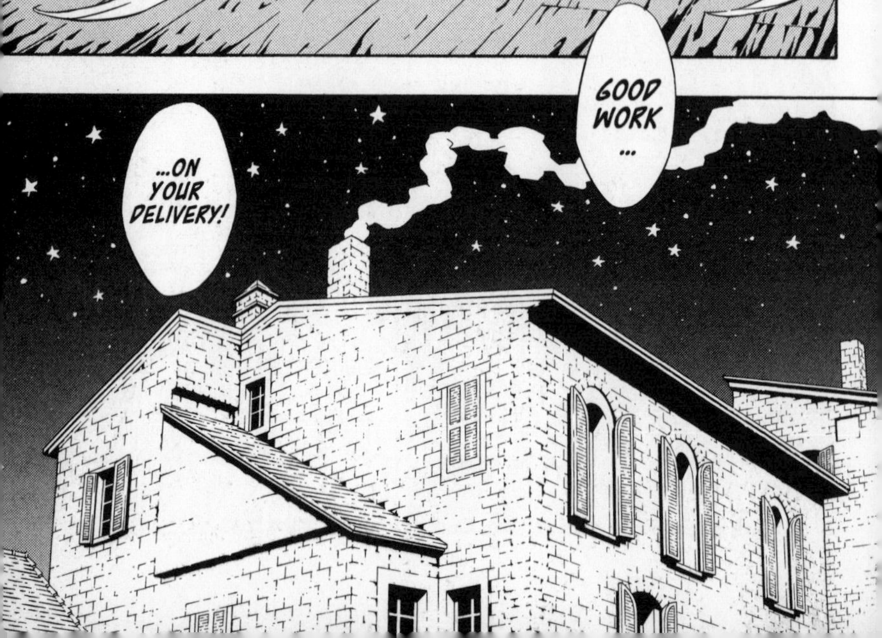
GOOD WORK ...
...ON YOUR DELIVERY!

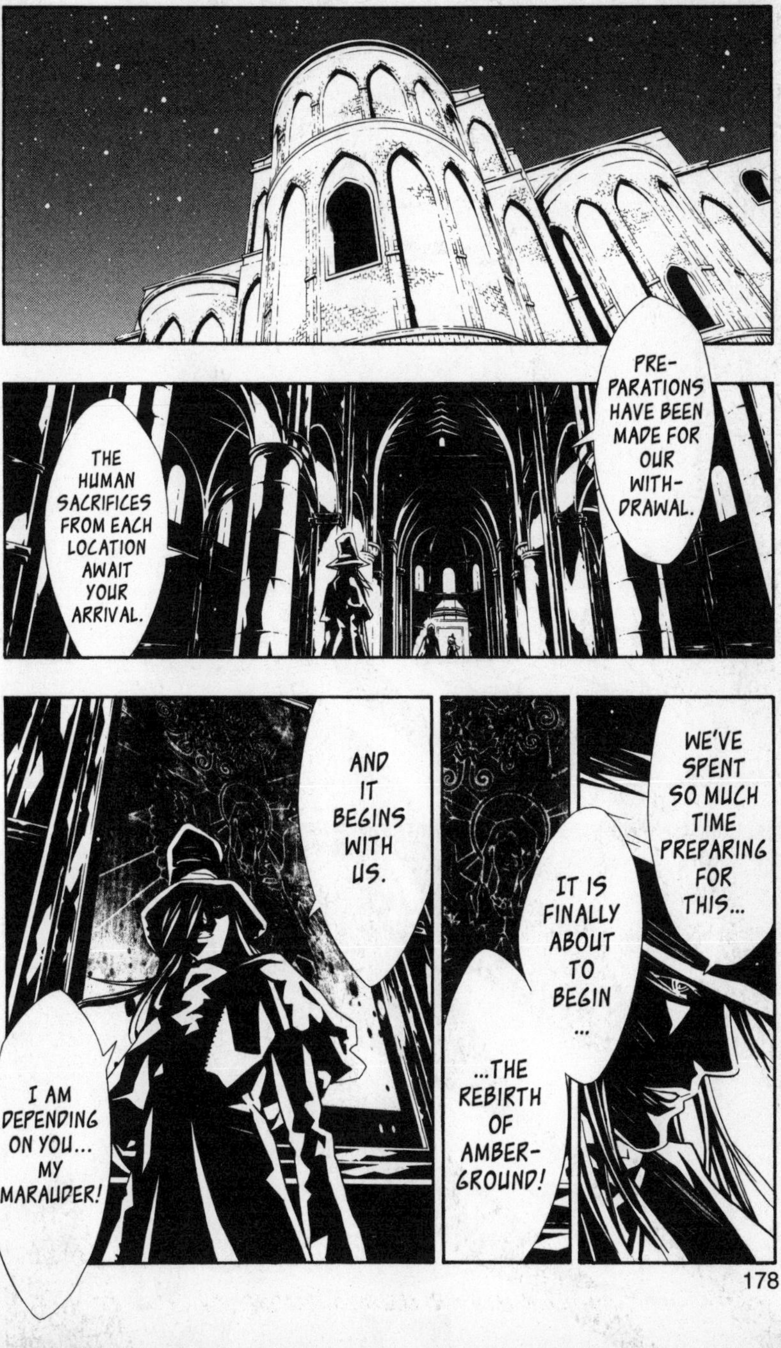
PRE-PARATIONS HAVE BEEN MADE FOR OUR WITH-DRAWAL.
THE HUMAN SACRIFICES FROM EACH LOCATION AWAIT YOUR ARRIVAL.
WE'VE SPENT SO MUCH TIME PREPARING FOR THIS...
IT IS FINALLY ABOUT TO BEGIN ...
...THE REBIRTH OF AMBER-GROUND!
AND IT BEGINS WITH US.
I AM DEPENDING ON YOU... MY MARAUDER!

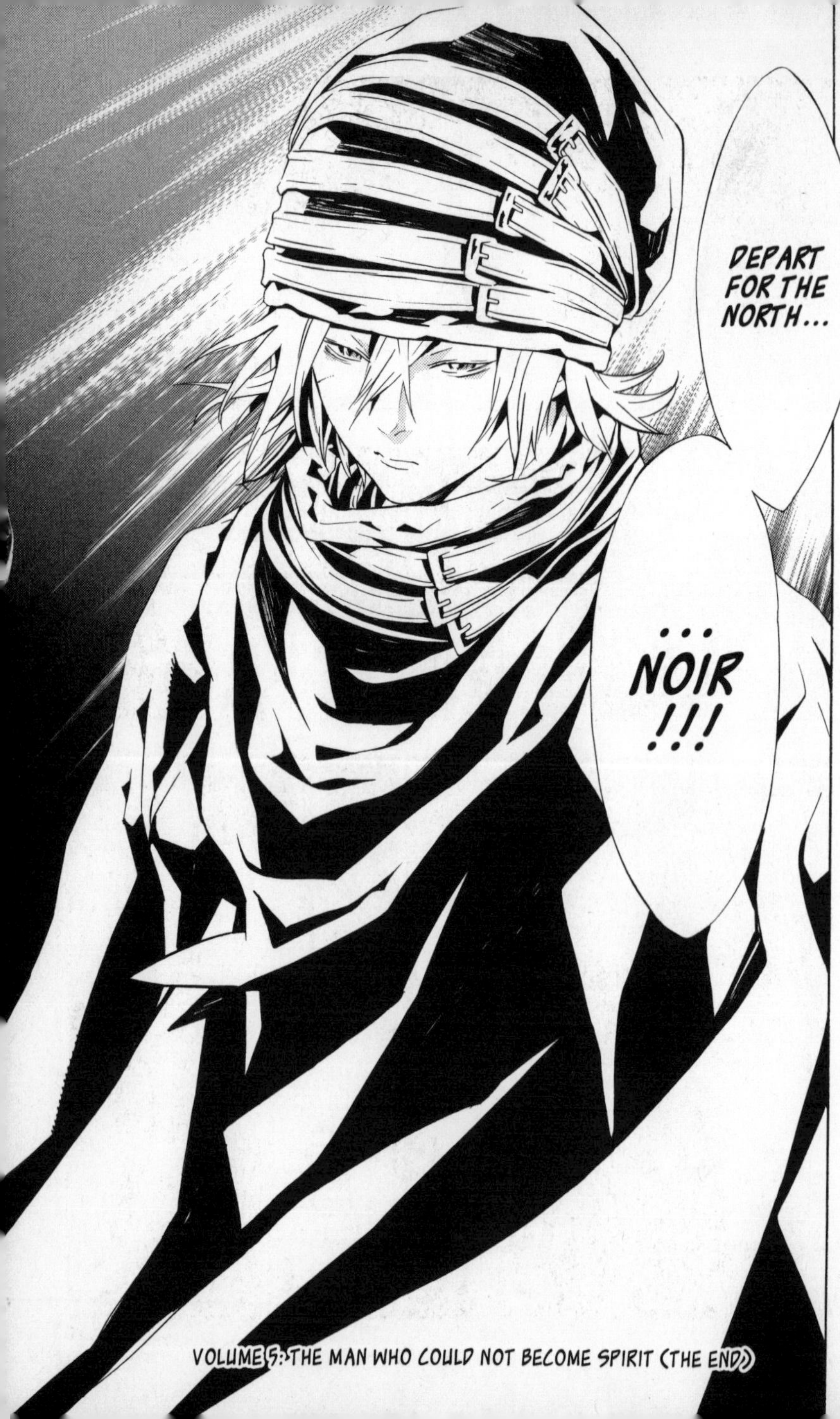
DEPART FOR THE NORTH...
...NOIR !!!
VOLUME 5: THE MAN WHO COULD NOT BECOME SPIRIT (THE END)

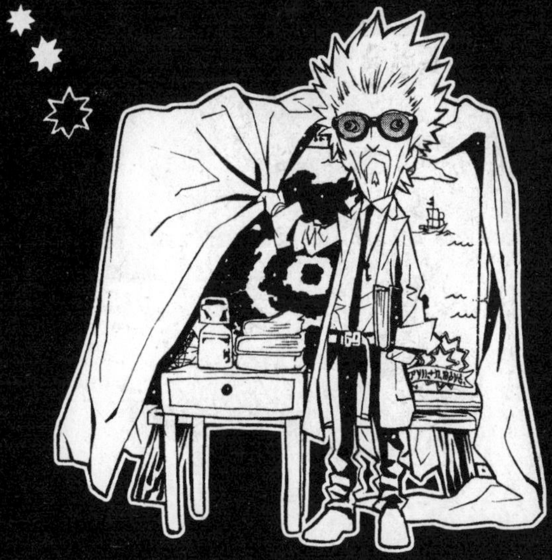

Dr. Thunderland's Reference Desk

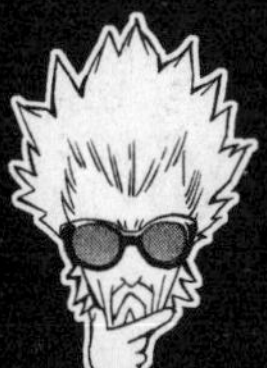

I am Dr. Thunderland.

Blast it all! Once again, I have not appeared in another volume! I could have sworn I was the Man Who Could Not Become Spirit. I didn't even get on the cover! I'm very disappointed! Weeping, even! I've been waiting for five volumes! When does the waiting end?

I work at the Yuusari Beehive, as you well know, and I spend my days waiting for my chance in the spotlight. Oh, and also doing SCIENCE.

Science will help keep me calm while I wonder why I HAVEN'T APPEARED IN THIS MANGA YET!

Sigh... Maybe I'll just quit this life and go start a farm somewhere.

It would mean giving up show business, I know, but my heart can't take much more of this disappointment!

Goodbye, Central Yuusari! Oh, what times we've had!

■ TRAVELING SIDESHOW

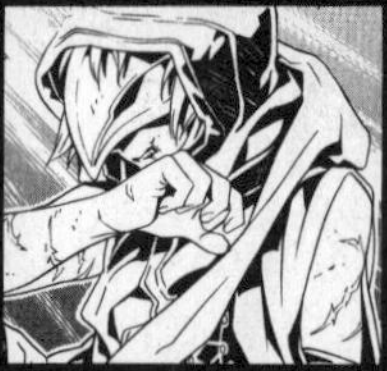

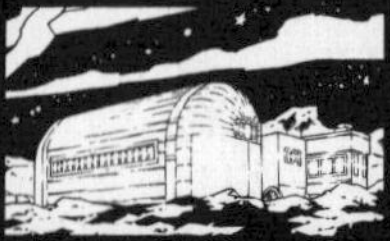

In this world, especially in this district, sideshows are a very popular and valuable source of entertainment. Some sideshows consist of unusual beasts, acrobats, and even art. Each promoter has his own peculiarities, making the shows quite entertaining. Of course, there are a lot of shady shows, like the one Hunt and Sarah were with. Niche and Steak may have come from a similar sideshow, in fact! But Niche has never exactly been "trainable," so she was probably sold from show to show. You're lucky you met up with Lag, weren't you, Niche? What power does Lag have that he could train her so swiftly? If I had done that she'd have had my head. Slash...

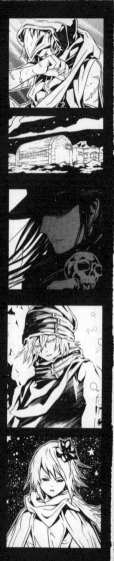

■ THE *REAL* MAN WHO COULD NOT BECOME SPIRIT

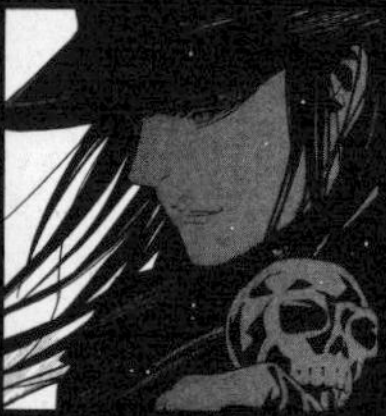

Boy, there is a real one... He's a member of the dissident organization Reverse. In fact, he seems to hold a position of some power with them. Considering that he *is* real, is Sarah's story about the government's artificial Spirit Amber plan real too? And what if I had a hand in it too? In the next volume, I do some sort of strange surgery on him. This could mean trouble...

■ MARAUDER

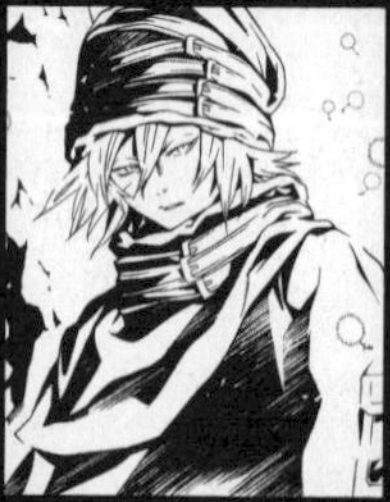

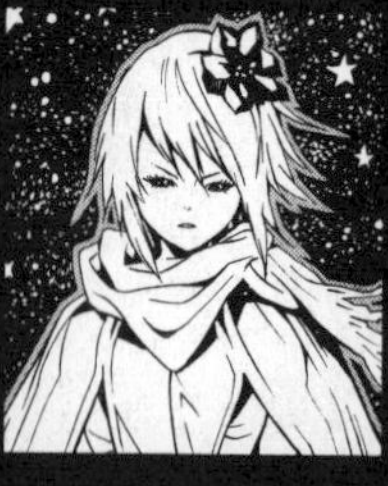

Marauders are a dangerous bunch who are hired to plunder. Theirs is an underground business that only those very confident in their abilities dare undertake. To think that Gauche is one... Poor Lag cried even more than he usually does (based on an unofficial survey here at the Beehive). Noir, as he is now known, works with Reverse and the Man Who Could Not Become Spirit. He seems to be plotting something. He has the black Spirit Amber and can still fire Shindan. Judging from the Shindan that he shot into Lag, he seems to have lost his memory of his former life. What's more, his dingo, Roda, has turned into a pretty, dark-eyed girl. What in the world is going on? Is that the same Roda as before?

Hm... Things have gotten quite puzzling, it seems. Perhaps I should go to Reverse, destroy them, and rescue Gauche myself! I'll be an action hero, like Steven Seagal! And I will have a majestic ponytail. Yes, this sounds like a plan. Maybe I should forget about that farm and start working out a little bit to prepare...

■ THE CRYBABEAST AUTHOR:
MUSHUNOKOUJI SANEYATSU

This very moving children's book enjoyed enormous sales for a while in Yuusari. It follows the life of a crybaby orphan whose facial hair grows into a beard so impressive he is called the Beard King. It's the heartbreaking story of a boy and his beard. Everyone in Yuusari wept when they read it. Even I cried a little. I tried to grow my beard out, but it looked weird. Read it with someone who loves beards.

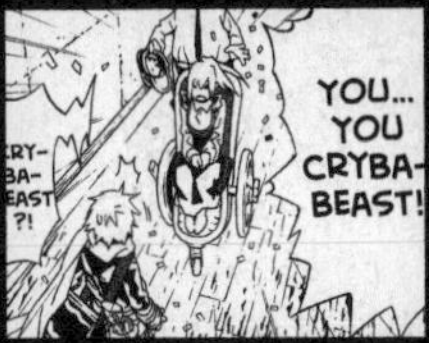
YOU... YOU CRYBA-BEAST!
RY-BA-EAST ?!

■ WEAPONS AND BAKE SHOP SINNERS

This shop on Nocturne Row belongs to Mr. and Mrs. Gobeni. This is the second time they have appeared in both the story and here—I'm jealous. Why do they get special treatment? Hmph! As usual, the weapons don't seem to be selling at all, but their breads are almost legendary for their deliciousness. This is all because of Sandra, of course. It seems this couple once lost a child, but perhaps they have overcome that loss by pouring themselves into their work. When he hears that Gauche has lost his *heart*, Gobeni says, "So he lost his *heart* too..." Sinners has been a government-accredited seller of Shindanjuu for generations. Perhaps he has seen other Bees go down Gauche's path over the years.

Ever since this day, Niche has become a fan of Mama Sandra's bread and can often be seen munching away at a loaf.

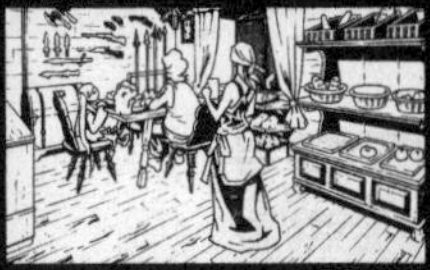

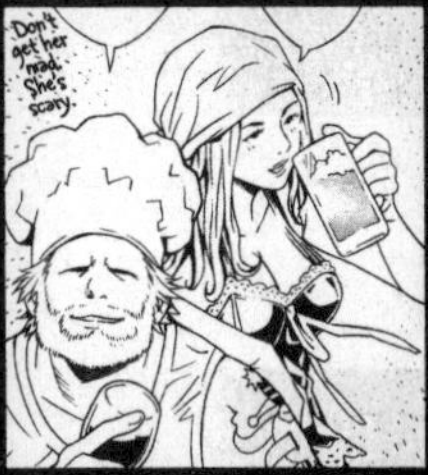
Don't get her mad. She's scary.

■ LETTER BULLET

The bullet that Lag receives from Mr. Gobeni...or rather, a cartridge. The shell is painted red and made so that a letter can be tucked into it. It is basically no different from a Shindan, since a fragment of *heart* is tucked inside it. However, by writing a letter and putting it into the cartridge, a highly specific *heart* can be fired. But that means that it has an effect only upon the person to whom the letter was written. That's understandable. I mean, if it wasn't written for you, it wouldn't have much impact, would it? Lag, think long and hard about what you write in that letter to Gauche.

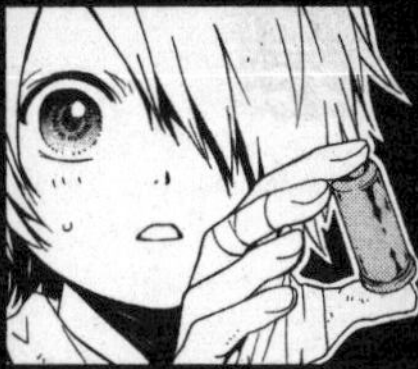

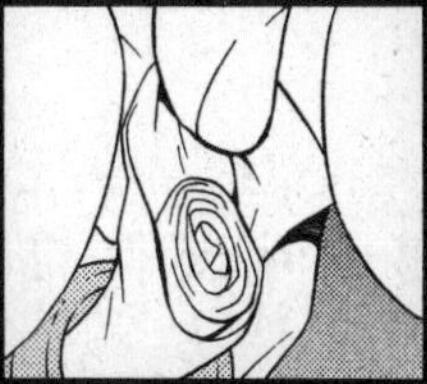

Route Map

Finally, I am including a map indicating the route followed in this volume, created by the gentle souls at Lonely Goatherd Map Station of Central Yuusari.

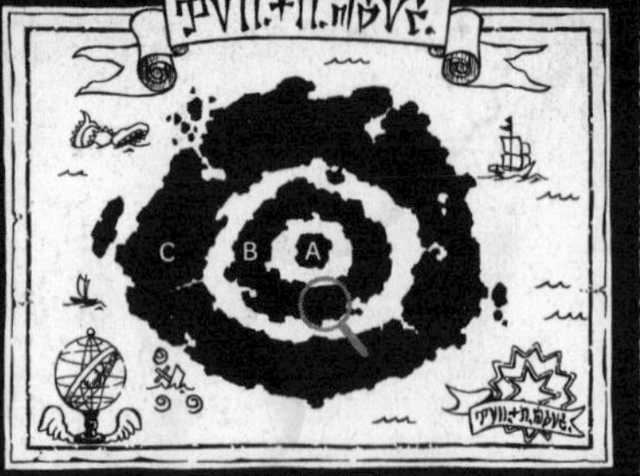
C
B
A

A: Akatsuki B: Yuusari C: Yodaka

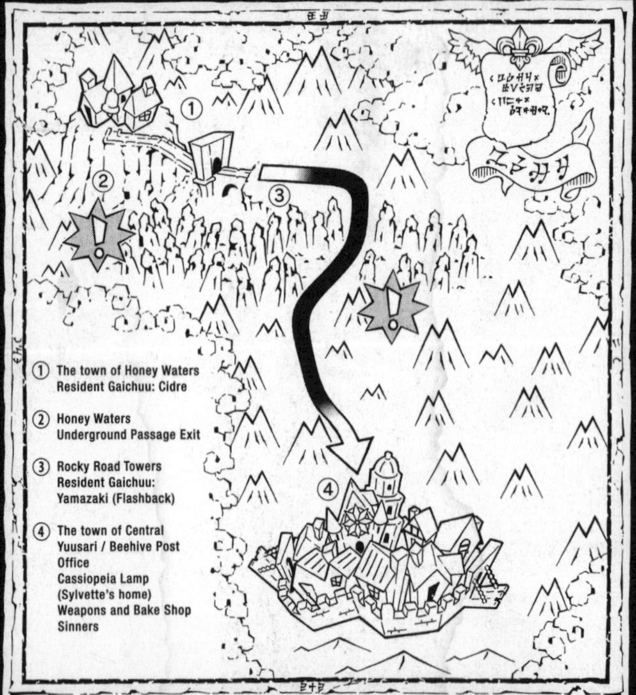
①
②
③
④
① The town of Honey Waters
Resident Gaichuu: Cidre
② Honey Waters
Underground Passage Exit
③ Rocky Road Towers
Resident Gaichuu:
Yamazaki (Flashback)
④ The town of Central
Yuusari / Beehive Post
Office
Cassiopeia Lamp
(Sylvette's home)
Weapons and Bake Shop
Sinners

How was this lesson? Well, forget it. In the next volume, there won't be a lesson! There will be REVENGE! Dr. Thunderland's revenge! I will destroy Reverse! In person! You will be astounded. And wait until you see my anime!

P9-DNM-217

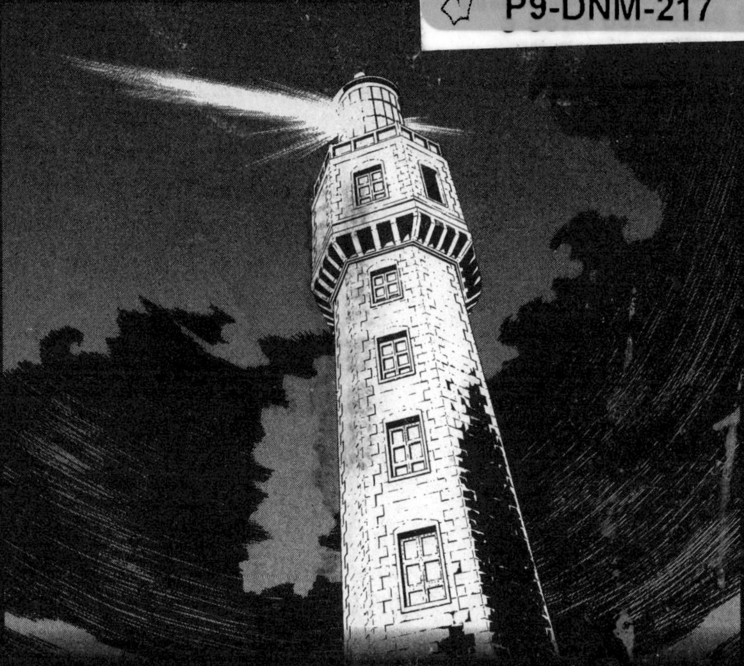

In the next volume...

The Lighthouse in the Wasteland

While trying to compose the perfect letter to Gauche, Lag continues his duties as a Letter Bee, learning more about the people of Amberground and their hearts. In a desolate lighthouse, Lag plays a role in the broken heart of a lonely old man. Then, Director Largo Lloyd sends Lag on a journey through the northern reaches of Yodaka, to the mysterious town of Blue Notes Blues, hot on the trail of Noir and the anti-government organization Reverse!

Available August 2011!

CH